experimental
Psychology in Industry

Edited by D. H. Holding

Penguin Modern Psychology Readings

General Editor
B. M. Foss

Advisory Board
P. C. Dodwell
Marie Jahoda
S. G. Lee
W. M. O'Neil
R. L. Reid
Roger Russell
P. E. Vernon
George Westby

WITHDRAWN

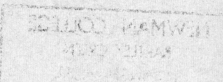

Experimental Psychology in Industry

Selected Readings

Edited by D. H. Holding

Penguin Books

Penguin Books Ltd, Harmondsworth,
Middlesex, England
Penguin Books Inc., 7110 Ambassador Road,
Baltimore, Md 21207, U.S.A.
Penguin Books Australia Ltd, Ringwood,
Victoria, Australia

First published 1969
This selection copyright © D. H. Holding, 1969
Introduction and notes copyright © D. H. Holding, 1969

Made and Printed in Great Britain by
Richard Clay (The Chaucer Press), Ltd.,
Bungay, Suffolk
Set in Monotype Times

Contents

Introduction

A modern society consists of men and machines. This volume is concerned with the ways in which they interact as system components, and thus with the bearing of experimental psychology upon technology. The readings are about the traditional topics of perception, attention, learning, remembering and responding, in relation to electronics, textiles, computers and glassware. What they represent is the application of experimental laboratory methods to research in industrial psychology.

The selection is chosen from experiments on the behaviour of men as operators, controllers and monitors of their instruments, vehicles and equipment. Man–machine relationships, human performance and efficiency are now well established as subjects for research, with many active proponents. Unfortunately, there are a number of different labels for this group of activities. The term 'human engineering' is now less used, although many workers retain the designation of 'engineering psychologist'. The area is represented by a 'human factors' society in the United States and by the 'ergonomics' society in Great Britain. Of course, it is not suggested that all these terms are identical in meaning; for example, ergonomics includes in addition the activities of anatomists and physiologists, engineers and physical education workers. The term used quite early for the area represented in this volume was 'applied experimental psychology' and, although this has little impact, it is rather accurate.

The applied, industrial form of experimental psychology stands in a particularly direct relation to the parent discipline. It is often possible to use findings from laboratory studies in direct application and it is equally possible to draw conclusions from industrial studies which have immediate relevance for general theory. Any experiment requires the choice of some task or materials and these may often with advantage be real rather than artificially constructed. It is as valid to look for the incidental learning of telephone dial layouts as to examine incidental learning in nonsense syllables; and it is as useful to investigate the gap judgements of bus drivers as the weight judgements of students. Of course, in many *ad hoc* investigations it happens that too many factors are left uncontrolled for it to be possible to draw firm conclusions of universal validity, but there is a sizeable body of cogent findings which have general relevance. The present selection stresses this relevance, concentrating upon those studies which have theoretical implications in addition to practical value.

It is no accident that most of the papers selected are recent. The reason is that this kind of work is largely a post-war development. Both world wars have in different ways provided a considerable stimulus to research in industrial psychology. In the first, the urgency of producing munitions led to studies of industrial fatigue and hours of work, and to research on the related problems of environmental conditions like heat, lighting, vibration and noise. With the Second World War, independently of the growing background of personnel work concerned with vocational selection, adjustment and social organization, a new field of study emerged. Small margins of error are permitted by the high speed aircraft, radar, tanks and missiles of a technological war, with the result that attention was urgently directed to the characteristics of human operating performance and to the alignment of equipment design with those characteristics. Experimental psychologists began to examine new topics, from target tracking and display-control relationships to human vigilance.

The initial work on man–machine systems was therefore military in origin and application. However, the same kinds of problem at the interface arise in industrial systems, and research on these problems is growing in scope. Despite the fact that many issues are common to both industry and the armed forces, this selection of readings largely omits the military and aerospace work in order to lay emphasis upon the industrial contribution.

A further emphasis in the selection is upon those aspects of human performance which are likely to increase in importance as a result of current trends towards *automation*. The traditional industrial skills are likely to be widely modified or supplanted with the advent of automatic methods of machine control, continuous flow production techniques and the use of computers for calculation, decision making and control. What will be required is a more flexible range of skills in which perceptual and intellectual components predominate. These issues are discussed in Reading 1.

Part One, which introduces the groundwork of equipment design for human use, ranges from the discussion of basic ideas to detailed practical recommendations in one area of application. Following upon the consideration of equipment design must come the problems of servicing the equipment. Clearly, increasing mechanization and automation increases the demands upon maintenance and fault-finding skills. This is an area of applied problem-solving in which a good deal more research is needed. However, Part Two illustrates the kinds of procedure in use, with some representative findings.

Automatic equipment requires monitoring, and the quality control of its products often involves human inspection. The duties of the process controller, the radar watch-keeper and the industrial inspector are all basically perceptual, and require long periods of concentrated attention. These different tasks therefore share certain common characteristics which are discussed in Part Three. The next group of papers, Part Four, is less homogeneous. The intention here is to sample the range of studies dealing with the skills demanded by advanced technology. These vary from problems of operating at speed to decision making and memorizing tasks.

New skills require training. In any case, insufficient attention was given in the past to the training of traditional skills. These are areas in which interest is growing rapidly and in which the applied psychology of learning has a great deal to offer. Part Five assembles representative examples of the contribution which the psychology of training can make. The need for re-training is one of the common problems of the older worker, and one which will affect an increasing proportion of the population as the age distribution in industry changes. The effects of ageing upon human performance, together with the consequent difficulties of older workers, are discussed in Part Six.

Finally, in Part Seven a typical problem of environmental stress is examined. It is impossible in the available space to give adequate representation to the interacting effects of heat and lack of sleep with noise, or to cover the more specialized topics of vibration, anoxia or air pollution. However, the subject of noise

11

is not only of theoretical interest but one in which considerable progress has been made. The solution adopted is therefore to restrict this section to papers on the problem of noise, omitting other examples of stress.

The volume as a whole covers a broad range of human performance and contains papers at varying levels of difficulty. Some of the work assumes a fairly advanced background knowledge, as the intention is primarily to meet the needs of psychology students. However, since the sampling is wide and the collection provides an account of many practical contributions, the book should be useful also to those who are directly concerned with industrial efficiency.

Part One Human Engineering

These are papers on designing equipment for human use. The approach is one of evaluating engineering design by measuring human performance on the equipment, thus making for greater efficiency by 'fitting the machine to the man'. This contrasts with the traditional policy of considering engineering requirements in isolation, consequently hoping to match men to machines by selection, training or chance.

   Reading 1 by Welford provides an introduction to the subject, putting it in the context of the development of automation. In the excerpt chosen, he discusses changes in the types of skill demanded by modern methods and the principles of design of instruments and controls for ease of operation. The brief history of the subject shows several theoretical developments, which Taylor (Reading 2) attempts to evaluate. He suggests that the most significant ideas have been the limited adaptability of men, man–machine systems, the matching of human input and output, and the use of engineering models. Reading 3 by Loveless takes up the problem of input–output matching, reviewing the evidence on the spatial relationships between instrument displays and controls. Finally, McFarland (Reading 4) provides a review of human engineering applied to the practical problem of traffic safety.

1 A. T. Welford

Ergonomics of Automation

Excerpt from A. T. Welford, Ergonomics of automation, *Problems of Progress in Industry*, no. 8, H.M.S.O., 1960, pp. 6–32.

The Scope of Automation

The developments now known as automation have grown out of the piecemeal mechanization that has been gradually producing a 'new industrial revolution' over many years. In the present context three main types may be distinguished.

1. The replacement of manufacturing methods in which each product is dealt with separately, or in a batch, by some form of continuous-flow process

The most clear-cut examples of these processes are in the chemical and petroleum industries. The same principles are, however, widespread and apply, for example, to transfer machining in engineering works, where a product is automatically passed from one stage in manufacture to another.

If carried to their logical limits these developments would result in completely automatic factories where all stages of manufacture could be accomplished with no human intervention. Such a state of affairs has not yet been realized. The processes commonly included under the heading of 'automation' are carried out by machinery which although automatic in operation still leaves the human controller a substantial part to play. In many cases the process has to be controlled by the direct action of an operator. In others, automatic devices exercise routine control, but leave the operator the tasks of monitoring the process and of overriding the automatic controls in case of emergency. These processes thus link closely with certain other remote-control operations such as railway signalling and the control of planes at airports.

2. *The automatic machining of engineering products by means of electronically controlled machine tools*

The tool is controlled, via an electronic control unit, by a magnetic tape or a punched tape or card. The operator has to monitor the machine but no longer has the task of accurately determining the individual machining operations. Whereas the first type of automation applies only to large-scale manufacture, this second type can apply throughout the range right down to 'one-off' jobs.

3. *The use of high-speed computers in offices*

These enable various routine accounting operations, such as those for payrolls, to be done with less labour and greater accuracy. They also, by virtue of the large amount of detailed calculation they achieve in a short time, can provide management with a wider range of technical and business information and so enable it to exercise much closer control over stocks, production programmes and the disposition of transport facilities and other resources.

From the human point of view, work with all these types of automatic equipment falls into three classes:

(a) Setting out the processes: the order of operations in a continuous-flow process must be determined; the sequence of actions by a tape-fed machine tool must be worked out and punched on the control tape; the computers used in office work need 'programming'.
(b) Operating the processes and machines, and monitoring their working.
(c) Keeping the equipment in running order and repair.

The first of these three classes of work has, unfortunately, not yet been systematically studied to any appreciable extent. The main emphasis in this booklet will therefore be on operators and maintenance engineers, and among these, present knowledge makes it inevitable that the main stress should be on those dealing with large-scale continuous-flow equipment rather than with electronically controlled machine tools or high-speed computers. (See Plates 1–4, central inset.)

Traditional Industrial Skills

The customary industrial definition of 'skilled work' is that for which an apprenticeship training is required, as opposed to 'unskilled work' which needs no training beyond that which common experience of life can provide. Semi-skilled work is regarded as falling between these two in that it requires a period of training or experience on the job shorter than a full apprenticeship. It has indeed been suggested that the period of training or experience needed can give an indication of the 'level' of any semi-skilled job.

Few people are entirely satisfied with this type of definition. It is often argued that the grading of a job is more a matter of its history or of the bargaining power of a craft union than of current job requirements. The fundamental objection to such a definition is, however, that skill results from knowledge and *expertise* which are gained by *experience*, rather than from mere exposure to training. If this fact is accepted, it must be obvious that many jobs are highly skilled even though they are not approached through a formal apprenticeship. In order to assess skill in this more fundamental sense, it is necessary to consider not only length of training, but also the various ways in which performance can display an expert quality.

Broadly speaking a man who is skilled, either in the traditional or in the wider sense, possesses two important abilities:

(a) He has a knowledge of the products of his craft, or of the objects of his trade, and of the materials he handles, so that his work is not carried out by 'rule of thumb' but with insight into what is being done and why. This insight lends flexibility to his approach and means that he can do a wider variety of jobs than one who is not skilled.
(b) He has at his command a range of procedures or 'strategies' which give his performance a similar flexibility under changing conditions of work, and enable him to order and co-ordinate his efforts in a wider range of conditions than a man who is not skilled.

He has also one or more of three further abilities:

(c) Fine, detailed control of action in using tools, especially hand tools, for both the graded application of force and the rhythm and timing of actions.

(d) Fine judgement of sensory qualities such as colour, sound or texture. The quality judged varies from one job to another and the ability acquired is usually specific to the job concerned.

(e) The ability to imagine and understand 'in the abstract' processes and events that are not directly observable. This is especially required in the case of electricians.

Changes of Demand for Skill among Operatives

The most obvious change in demand upon operatives resulting from automation is the shift from manual to a more 'intellectual' type of skill; as a speaker once felicitously put it 'the machine operator is becoming a *mental craftsman*'. The change makes work both easier and more difficult. Replacement of handtools which require finely graded hand movements, can bring substantial easing of work as these movements are often some of the most difficult features of traditional skills, requiring constant practice if a high level of performance is to be maintained – the rustiness of a tennis player at the beginning of a season, or of a concert pianist out of practice, has its industrial counterparts.

At the same time, however, replacement of hand tools by machines may substantially increase the *mental load* upon the operator because it complicates the relationship between what he sees and the actions he takes. With hand tools, this relationship is simple and direct, depending upon 'rules' of co-ordination between eye and hand learnt early in life. With machine tools, however, there is an element of 'arbitrariness' in the sense that the actions of levers, handwheels and other controls bear only indirect or symbolic relationships to their effects.

All these tendencies are carried further in remote-control systems than they are in more conventional mechanization. With remote control there is usually less effort involved in moving around to keep check on machinery and still less requirement of finely graded muscular action, but the operator is no longer able to observe the process directly, having instead to rely on the symbolic indications of meters or other signalling devices.

The difficulty resulting from increase of mental load upon the operative can, unless care is taken, far outweigh any easing of the task in terms of physical effort or fine muscular control. Whether or not it does so depends upon a number of detailed points in the design of the machinery concerned and the extent to which automation is carried. For example, *remote* control of operations without *automatic* control is liable to make the operator's mental load so great that his job is far more difficult than almost any in a conventional factory. Where, however, fully automatic control is installed, the operator's mental load is likely to be very substantially lightened.

Although automation may lessen the need for traditional skill, the need remains for some expertise or skill in the wider sense. This is shown by the effects that come from the knowledge possessed by a man who has controlled the same plant for a long time. His understanding is often incomplete and may not be wholly accurate, and his performance may not have acquired flexibility beyond that needed for the particular machines he uses. He is, nevertheless, skilled in the sense that he possesses a 'mental picture' of his machine and its working, which enables him to get more from it and to be 'kinder' to it than a less experienced man. This type of skill has been aptly termed 'control skill'.

In one sense it can, of course, be said that automation does not in any of its forms dispense with the need for skills of the traditional types, but merely shifts the need for them back from operatives to those who construct and maintain the automation plant. While this is undoubtedly true, there is a clear gain from automation in that human skill is no longer used repetitively for the manufacture of each individual article, but is reserved for those operations of control and construction in which the adaptability of human beings can be used to full advantage. Viewed in these terms automation appears not as an abolisher but as a conserver of skill.

Skill Required of Maintenance Staff

Much of the maintenance work on automatic machinery is that for which a trained fitter is required. Whether the full training of an apprenticeship is needed or whether some shorter course of instruction will suffice depends partly upon the factory organization and partly upon the construction of the machinery concerned. For example, rigid standardization of replacement parts simplifies maintenance and reduces, although it does not entirely remove, the need for fully trained fitters.

The maintenance of electronic equipment presents an additional problem since the fully competent electrical or electronic tradesman requires an intellectual capacity attained by relatively few people. The type of ability required appears to be similar to that needed for performing so-called 'intelligence' tests, and it is noteworthy that studies of Naval personnel during the war found that electrical artificers attained intelligence test scores higher on average than those of any other class of rating. They were a little higher than those of R.N. executive officers and Fleet Air Arm observers and pilots, and were exceeded only by those of R.N. engineer officers. It seems clear that any large scale expansion of the need for electronic maintenance tradesmen with the qualifications now customary would cause a serious drain on intellectual manpower. This fact seems to have been tacitly recognized in the attempts now being made to simplify electronic maintenance so that it can be carried out by less gifted people.

Personal Qualities

In many operations certain personal qualities broadly indicated by the terms 'stability' and 'sense of responsibility' need to be taken into account when assessing the grade and status of employees. These are just as important as skill, although probably not subject to much improvement with training. In many of the more advanced forms of mechanization and process control the operator can be thought of as exercising the function of a supervisor and as requiring the attitudes and personal qualities appropriate to that grade, although his supervision is of machines rather than of men.

These personal qualities and the stability of employment needed if 'specific control skill' is to be developed, mean that the status of operators is likely to rise as automatic equipment becomes established.

The Net Effect of These Changes

It is a well-nigh impossible task to forecast any over-all effect of automation on employment and redundancy over the next few years, but the indications are that it is likely to be much less than is sometimes believed and feared. Automatic methods are applicable only to a limited range of manufacturing and office procedures. All work involving personal attention must remain largely unaffected, and even in highly mechanized factories human operatives are likely to continue for a long time to be the most economic means of carrying out many assembly and inspection operations. Indeed, the need for men and women to inspect products may substantially rise since automatic processes often cut down the amount of inspection that can be done by an operator in the course of actual production.

Furthermore, even where new machinery effects a substantial saving of operators for a given output, the increase of maintenance and servicing work can often absorb many who would otherwise be redundant, and the tendency for output to rise and the fact that the automatic methods open up possibilities of manufacture not present with older methods, are likely to increase available jobs still more. There seems no justification, therefore, for the fear that the introduction of automatic methods will cause widespread unemployment. Indeed the reverse seems more likely.

Design for Ease of Operation

When assessing the demands of work involving heavy physical effort it is appropriate to think of man as a heat engine converting calories from food into muscle power. Mechanization, however, makes this analogy of little importance and stresses instead the fact that man is a *communication channel* taking in information through his senses and using it as a basis for guiding action.

21

The actual sense organs and the members with which action is taken are seldom the links in this chain which set limits to his performance: the limitations lie rather in the brain 'mechanisms' involved in perception, in relating perception to action and in the shaping and ordering of movements. It is, therefore, convenient to consider firstly the *presentation of information* to the operator; secondly the *design of machine controls*; and thirdly the effects upon ease of operation of different relationships between the information presented and the responding action required, or as they are termed *relationships between display and control*.

1. Presentation of information

One of the most thoroughly worked areas in this field is the optimum design of scales. Some of the recommendations from this work are obvious, others less so. The main ones are:

(a) The length of the scale and thus, ultimately, the size of the instrument, must be related to the distance at which the scale is to be viewed.

(b) Some scale shapes are easier to read than others; for example, circular dials have been found easier than linear scales, and among the latter horizontal have been found easier than vertical.

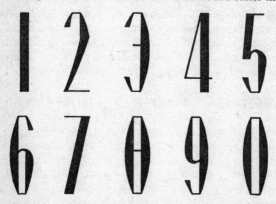

Figure 1 A set of figures in current use on a car speedometer. Designed to be of striking and decorative appearance, they have poor legibility. Note, for example, the possibility of confusion between 8 and 0, and between 6 and 5

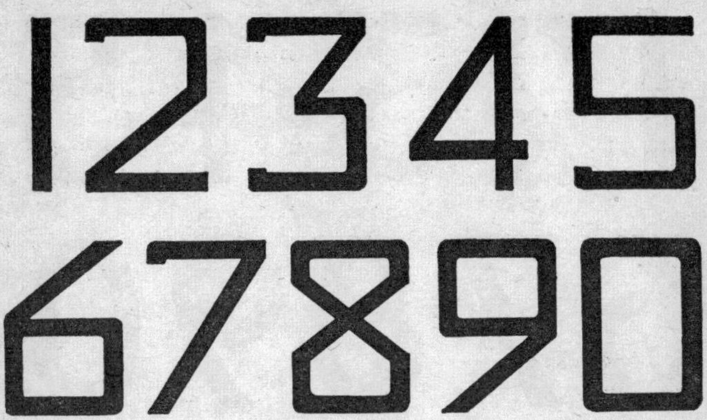

Figure 2 These figures were designed to be clearly legible and easily distinguishable from each other. They have the disadvantage that they look somewhat unattractive

(c) If speed of reading is not a consideration, scales are read more accurately when individual scale marks are placed for each unit. Quick check readings, however, are made more accurately if fewer marks are provided and the reader interpolates between them. Interpolation can usually be made accurately into five parts. Thus when a scale is to be read to an accuracy of 1 per cent, only twenty scale marks should be provided.

(d) The numbering should be in ones, twos, fives, or in multiples or submultiples of these by ten or 100, rather than in threes, fours or other intervals.

(e) The scale division marks should not be enclosed between parallel lines.

(f) The area swept by the pointer of an instrument should be clear of marks, such as the maker's name, or the statement of what the instrument shows, such as 'current consumption' or 'air pressure', or the designation of units, such as 'milliamps' or 'lb per sq. in'.

(g) The pointer should reach the scale division marks and, while it should be thick enough to be seen against the instrument face, it should be thin enough where it reaches the scale to enable a precise reading to be made.

1234567890

Figure 3 Legibility and easy discrimination are combined with good appearance on these figures. They have been constructed taking both form and width of stroke into account

(h) The pointer should normally move clockwise on a circular dial or to the right or up on a linear scale to indicate increase.

(i) Figures should be oriented in such a way that they are read upright and, other considerations being equal, positioned so that they are not covered by the pointer. The main exception to this occurs with circular scales where placing of the figures inside the scale marks and allowing the pointer to move over them enables a larger scale to be provided for a given diameter of instrument face.

(j) Too low an angle of viewing may cause errors of reading.

(k) Moving scales may, in certain circumstances, be more accurately read than moving pointers, although they are slower to use for check readings. When extreme accuracy is required, counters are recommended instead of scales.

Optimum values have also been ascertained for the sizes of numbers and letters, for the relation of height to width, for the relation of stroke width to size and for the spacing between individual digits and letters.

Few meters and other devices incorporating scales which are in use today conform to these recommendations. Several manufacturers are, however, altering their designs in the light of recommendations such as these. Others are as yet unwilling to adopt designs which they believe may not be acceptable to customers. Responsibility for changing designs should not be placed upon manufacturers alone but must also rest upon users.

Figure 4 Positioning of instrument dials. Instruments should be positioned so that their faces are perpendicular to the line of sight and at or a little below eye level

Scales are, of course, only one way of displaying information and any comprehensive survey should also cover other signalling devices both visual and auditory. Less systematic work has been done on these, but taking the results together with what is known generally about perception, a number of points seem clear enough. (See Plates 5 and 6, central inset.)

Adequacy of signal. Signals must obviously be of a sufficient strength and size to be received clearly by the sense organs concerned. Such tasks as the discrimination of fine detail are profoundly affected by lighting, glare, vibration and the contrast of figures or other indicators with their background. Poor conditions in any of these may not lead to a total breakdown of performance but they are likely to make it slow and thus cause trouble in times of stress or emergency.

It goes without saying that signals requiring different actions should be clearly distinguishable from one another, but the implications of this are not quite as obvious as they might seem. Sensitivity is normally greater *to differences between stimuli* than to their absolute magnitudes. Thus while most people are extremely sentitive to change in the pitch of a note, few have the ability to recognize 'absolute pitch'. In the same way, it is easier to perceive a change of intensity in a light or sound than it is to judge brightness or loudness in the absence of change. When, for example, brake lights of a car are combined with rear lights it is not easy to decide whether they are on unless the actual moment of braking is observed. The difficulty would be removed if the brake lights flashed continuously while the brake was acting or if they were in a different position, and perhaps of a different colour, from the rear lights. The number of intensities or pitches that can be *confidently* distinguished in an absolute way is probably very small and it seems best to avoid signals which depend on this type of discrimination.

Colours are more easily discriminated than intensities. The number of spectral hues absolutely identifiable by a person with normal colour vision is put at between six and eleven by different authors, ease of identification depending somewhat on how far the colours can be given names.

Colours may, however, be less reliably distinguished than signals showing numbers, letters or other symbols. The main reason is, presumably, that the operator has to remember what the colours mean, but the numbers, letters or other symbols, can be chosen to convey their meaning directly. Colour is perhaps most useful for enabling several light signals to be grouped together and separated from other groups.

Codes and meaning. The fact that an operator has to learn and remember what signals mean has other important implications beyond the one just noted. He may not be conscious of having to remember the meaning, but even when he is thoroughly experienced occasional lapses of memory may occur and lead to momentary confusion. Some codes, such as the association of red with danger, are so well known that they seem 'natural', although they are really arbitrary and have had to be learnt. A few researches have shown that some codes are easier to follow than others and that 'appropriateness' of symbols to the meaning they have to convey is a field needing further study. Although there is room for more research in this field, three points can be made from what is already known.

(a) Signal sources, such as instruments, should be clearly labelled with their functions.

(b) Pictorial or semi-pictorial representation may in some cases be worth while even if more difficult to arrange, from an engineering point of view, than a simple but arbitrary code of signals such as coloured lights or pointer readings on dials.

(c) Any one *set* of signals should, if possible, be logically connected according to a single principle so that only one 'rule' has to be learnt in order to understand the whole set.

Complexity and selection. All perception is selective; some objects are observed while others are neglected. A large part of this selection is determined by the interests of the observer and the task he has on hand. However, some portions of a display tend to secure more attention than others, and certain stimuli such as bright lights, strong colours or loud, high-pitched sounds tend to attract attention away from the task in hand and thus to impair performance. There is considerable scope for designing visual displays so as to 'lead the eye naturally' to the points at which the required information is to be obtained and to avoid striking but irrelevant and, therefore, confusing, objects in the field of vision. For example, a heavy instrument bezel in polished black or chromium may distract attention from the pointer, or a maker's name plate in a prominent position may constitute a distraction on a display panel. Confusing conditions cannot always be avoided in a display and may not be noticed during normal working by an operator who is familiar with the machinery or plant concerned. However, the selectivity he is called upon to exercise imposes a load upon his perceptual powers, and the greater the load the more likely he is to make errors, especially in times of stress.

Confusing conditions of this kind are likely to occur where large amounts of data have to be presented together in a display comprising many instruments, for instance the large banks of dials in aircraft and many process control rooms. There are, however, ways in which the danger of confusion can be reduced. One example is the marking of permitted ranges of variation on the dials of instruments, so that the operator can identify deviations beyond these ranges without having to carry in mind the extent of the permitted zone. Another, which applies especially to large banks of indicators, is the alignment of scales so that the pointers, when reading correctly, are all in approximately the same direction, and thus deviant readings stand out from the general pattern.

The spacing of different indicators can also be important. The rapid scanning of multi-indicator displays is obviously easier when the individual items are close together than if they are widely separated. It is, however, often difficult to pick out an individual item from a large block and where this has to be done it is desirable to divide the block into groups. The best arrangement is to place together indicators which are functionally related

Figure 5 Marking the permissible range of variation on the instrument dial relieves the operator of the need to remember it and thus reduces the mental load and the possibility of error

and separate them by a short distance from others. Groups of more than about seven items may be further subdivided on an arbitrary basis. (See Plate 7, central inset.)

Series of signals arriving at intervals over a period of time. Ideally, signals and responding actions should keep in step with one another. This requirement has two facets. Firstly, the signals for a series of actions will often best be given one at a time so that those for one action are not liable to be confused with those for another. Secondly, signals should, for maximum accuracy and ease of reading, give their information 'all at once' and not require the piecing together of data over a period of time.

Any requirement for integration of data means that information must be temporarily 'stored' in some form of short-term memory. 'Storage' of this kind appears to be of limited capacity and gives rise to a number of difficulties due to information being lost. This problem will be discussed in more detail later.

Visual v. sound indicators. Most indicators are either visual or auditory and there are certain fairly obvious differences between the types of data they convey best. Auditory signals have the advantage of being able to attract attention from any direction, but are ill-adapted to conveying precise information unless by speech. Much more information can be rapidly conveyed by vision, but only, of course, if the subject is looking in the appropriate direction. A combined auditory and visual system, often suitable where large displays have to be monitored, is an auditory warning of the imminent need for action combined with a simple visual signal, such as a light, indicating which part of the display is involved. The operator can then rapidly identify the instrument giving the detailed information which requires his attention.

The need for appropriate information. If equipment is to be well designed for use, it is necessary to consider what information the operator needs in order to do his work both accurately and with confidence. Broadly speaking, he must have data of two types. Firstly, he needs unambiguous indications of what is happening in the process he is controlling or monitoring, and of the effects of his actions upon it, and secondly, he should have *positive*

29

(a)

(b)

Figure 6 (a) It takes the operator the same time to check the four dials on the left as it does to check the thirty-two dials on the right. The difference is due to the fact that the scales of the right-hand bank are aligned so that when reading correctly the pointers are all in the same direction

(b) The slight spacing between groups makes it easier to identify a particular dial in the bank on the left than in that on the right

indications that his apparatus is working properly and that the process is proceeding correctly. It is not enough for correct working to be signified by absence of any warning signal, because the operator may be seriously misled if the warning signal should fail and, even if it does not, the possibility of its doing so may destroy his confidence and thus impair his efficiency.

The information an operator requires in order to get the best out of his machine is often more than the designer has considered necessary, and operators tend to supplement the information given on the display panel by making use of 'unplanned' indications such as the sound of the machine running. The information an operator uses may be more than is logically necessary, but is probably required because the strictly logical approach would be beyond his intellectual powers. With this extra information operators can often obtain a performance from their machines beyond that envisaged by the designer even though they may have a very imperfect idea of how the machines work.

2. Design of machine controls

Factors in the design of controls fall into two main groups. Firstly, there are anatomical considerations of body size, ranges of movement and the application of muscular force. Secondly, there are several problems which have essentially to do with the perception required to grade movements accurately and to operate the correct controls in the right sequence when performing complex tasks.

Anatomical considerations. Body measurements such as sitting height and length of limbs are important data for the design of vehicles and of many machine tools. Neglect of such data may make a machine well-nigh impossible to use, or at least so uncomfortable that the operator cannot concentrate his full attention on the job. The body measurements should not only be those which can be taken on a human being at rest or from the jointed models sometimes used by designers, but must take account of body movements.

A considerable number of studies have been made to determine the optimum measurements of work spaces, the forces which can be exerted by limbs in different positions and the ranges of

31

adjustment necessary so as to cater not only for the averages but also for the ranges of body dimensions found in various populations.

Other studies have been made to determine the optimum sizes of handwheels, cranks and other manual controls requiring considerable force. Ease of operating these types of control appears to depend on the relationships between the extent and force of the muscular movements required and the speed at which graded, co-ordinated action can be carried out. Thus, although less force is required to turn a large diameter crank than a small one, the greater extent of movement needed to turn the large crank may result in a slower speed of rotation.

The co-ordination of movement seems to be of special importance in relation to 'handedness'. The dominant hand has been found to be superior as a controlling member only where 'timing' or the serial organization of muscular activity is required. With coarser control movements there seems to be little difference between the hands. Differences between the two feet in the accuracy of control also appear to be small. (See Plate 8.)

Perceptual factors. An important feature of design for ease of use is that the state of the controls should be readily seen. Some designs are obviously better than others in this respect. Thus an 'up–down' switch indicates more clearly than a 'push–pull' switch whether it is on, and among rotary switches a 'pointer' knob is better than a circular one; switches of the 'rocker-dolly' and double-acting push-button types, give *no* indication of whether or not they are on.

Similar considerations apply to the 'feel' of controls. The sensory receptors in the muscles, tendons and joints, which enable the appreciation of limb movements give only poor indications of the absolute positions of limbs. Because of this, controls of the joystick type are often difficult to use if the stick moves freely. *Change* of limb position is perceived better, but the best sensory indications come from the application of *force*.

Joystick and lever controls are thus easier to use when they require pressure, and when the degree of deflection from zero position is related to the pressure applied. There is, indeed, evidence that more rapid and accurate control is achieved where the stick or lever hardly moves at all and practically the whole controlling effect is produced by pressure. Part of this is doubtless due to the control being self-centering. How much pressure is desirable depends upon the balance between two conflicting factors. On the one hand, pressure which requires muscular tension, and cannot be exerted simply by the weight of a limb resting on a lever or pedal, will tend to be fatiguing. On the other hand, very light pressures may not be sufficient to produce a clear 'feel'.

Identifying different controls. A number of studies have aimed at specifying designs to facilitate the rapid selection of the correct one from among a number of controls.

For knobs which have to be selected by 'feel', experiments have shown that differences of shape are more readily distinguished than differences of size; they have also suggested sets of shapes that are unlikely to be confused with one another.

More important as regards automation equipment are the problems arising when several controls have to be used in sequence. As in the perception of displays, the operator's task is greatly eased if he can apply a uniform rule of procedure by which to select the right control at each point in the sequence instead of having to 'think' about each controlling action separately. The best rule is not always intuitively obvious, and depends upon how much the sequence of actions varies on different occasions. Where controls are always used in the same order it is easier to have them arranged so that the operator has to work first one and then the next along a row. Where the order is not always the same the operator will need to rely to a greater extent on his 'mental picture' of the process he is controlling and of the ways it is affected by control actions. In this case it may be better to arrange the controls in such a way as to emphasize their function, and indicate the way their functions are related to one another.

The kind of rule required will also depend upon how the operator conceives the task. To take a simple example, when starting up a plant he may have to switch on some circuits and switch off others used during 'standing' conditions. The question is, should all the switches move in the same direction to start the plant so that he can follow a single rule of action to start up and shut down? Alternatively, should all the switches move down for 'on' and up for 'off' (or vice versa) so that they consistently indicate the state of the circuits concerned? If the operator needs to conceive the process in detail, the first type of rule may conflict with his 'mental picture' and the second type would be preferred. The first type, however, is less likely to lead to confusion and mistakes should an emergency shut-down be required.

Research on the design of controls has in the past brought a number of surprises, and the principles to be followed are not yet fully understood. This does not mean that nothing can be done immediately to improve designs, but that careful thought needs to be given to individual cases and should be supplemented wherever possible with experiments on prototypes or 'mock-ups'.

2 F. V. Taylor

Four Basic Ideas in Engineering Psychology

F. V. Taylor, 'Four basic ideas in engineering psychology', *American Psychologist*, vol. 15 (1960), pp. 643–9.

The Human has Limitations

Engineering psychology began with the intellectual discovery that the human was not a perfectly adaptable organism. Of course, no one had ever formally asserted that the man was perfectly adaptable, but up until a few years ago the applied psychologist acted as if the human's flexibility were sufficient to make possible all important adjustments between man and his environment. We now know that this is not so. All of us are aware of how, during the Second World War, the approach of designing the task to fit the operator was added to the more traditional psychological procedures of selecting and training operators to fit their jobs. This was necessitated by the variety and complexity of military equipment. Machinery had finally outrun the man's ability to adapt. And the recognition of this fact was the first important insight in the development of engineering psychology.

Since, then, many other ideas have emerged in the course of trying to fit tasks, tools and equipments to the man. Although it is certainly difficult to judge the significance of events and ideas which are historically too close to one's eyes, as are all things in engineering psychology, three further ideas seem to me to be sufficiently important to allow them to be placed on a par with the first as effecting major changes in the direction of the engineering psychologist's thought and action. It is the purpose of this article to identify these basic ideas and to discuss their implications for the science of psychology.

The Concept of the Man–Machine System

Although it is hard to discern any historical sequence in a sample of time as short as that spanning the existence of engineering psychology, one important concept certainly entered the discipline soon after it began to have substance. This was the notion of the man–machine system. The term 'system' had long been in general use in the other sciences to refer to any configuration of elements in which the behavioral properties of the whole are functions of both the nature of the elements and of the manner in which they are combined. Thus, it had long been common to speak of planetary systems or nervous systems or digestive systems. There were economic systems also and political systems. Engineering, too, had its weapon systems and control systems. And it was probably through the extension of the latter that the notion of the man–machine system came into being.

Whatever its origin, the concept made very obvious the fact that one could not hope to design the mechanical portions of a system of which the man was a working part without a knowledge of the characteristics of the human component. Furthermore, psychologists soon found that their subject became acceptable to the engineer when it was tied in to the engineer's way of thinking, through the use of the man–machine system paradigm. One suspects that even today a part of the appeal of the system approach to the psychologist is its demonstrated sales value to those customers who are not used to thinking of psychologists as experts in hardware design. Anyway, the standard man–machine system diagram makes an excellent cover sketch for human engineering advertising brochures!

But, seriously, the system concept has affected psychology in at least two important ways.

1. Dependent variables

Man–machine systems are created for two different purposes. One class of systems is constructed to affect the condition of the human component in that system in some favorable way. Examples are the pilot in his pressure suit, the soldier in his gas mask, the hospital patient in his iron lung, the Harvard student in his teaching machine and the Yale student in the Sterling

Library. In all these cases, the purpose of inserting the non-human elements into the system is to improve in some way the well-being of efficiency of the man within the system. With such internally referenced systems, the dependent variable of importance is some indication of the human's state or condition. Thus, the things measured are familiar psychological variables.

However, this is not so with the other type of man–machine system. The purpose of the system in this case is to alter the environment or to change relationships between the system and other entities external to it. The workman with his crowbar or with his bulldozer are examples of this kind of externally referenced system. So also are the pilot and his plane, air traffic control centers, and human-operated gunnery and missile control systems, to name but a few. With these systems, the dependent variable of greatest interest is a measure of the performance of the total system. In reference to the bulldozer, it might be the amount of earth moved in an eight-hour day, or with a missile control system, the hit probability against a variety of targets. In any case, the measure reflects the combined performance of all the components in the system, and not just that of the human element.

The introduction into psychology of a dependent variable which so clearly confounds human behavior with the contribution of the mechanical and electronic portions of the system has not universally been hailed with enthusiasm. As if life were not already sufficiently difficult for the psychologist without making it even more trying by introducing contaminated performance measures! However, the manifest unwieldiness of these measures is actually a virtue. The experience gained in working with dependent variables which are so demonstrably system measures, rather than human measures, is alerting psychologists to the fact that in many instances they have been working with system performance all along without recognizing it. In some so-called human skills, for example, the man is actually a component in a man–machine system, and it is the performance of the total system and not that of the man alone which the psychologist records and theorizes about. To recognize this is to avoid drawing faulty inferences about human behavior (Taylor and Birmingham, 1959).

2. Independent variables

Engineering psychology has introduced many new independent variables which some call task variables and others call engineering variables. They consist of such things as display mode, control mode, input frequency, system order, aided tracking time constant and display or control configuration. Much of the effort of the engineering psychologist has gone into work with these variables; in fact he has been so preoccupied with them that he has tended to neglect the more conventional psychological variables.

The system concept provides an excellent antidote to this scientific parochialism. A glance at any man–machine system flow chart makes it instantly apparent that the performance of the total system reflects (a) the human's level of ability and the extent of his training as well as (b) the nature and performance characteristics of the mechanical or electronic system elements. This insight immediately suggests two things. First, it impels those psychologists who are working in industry or elsewhere to take a unified human factors approach and to combine procedures of operator selection and training with those of designing the equipment to fit the man. Secondly, it makes it appear extremely unlikely that these different human factors approaches are, in fact, separate; it suggests that, since the human and the machine components are all cooperating within a single system, there will often be strong interactions between psychological and engineering variables. In part, it is the job of the engineering psychologist to look into these interrelationships and to exploit them whenever possible.

Although there have been relatively few studies in the past which have probed these interactions, one finding which has obtained repeated corroboration is that proper attention to engineering variables reduces the dependence of system performance upon selection and training. A clear demonstration of this is provided by data graphed in Figure 1 (Birmingham, Kahn and Taylor, 1954). Figure 1(a) shows the learning curves of six subjects attempting to control through a complex dynamic system something like that of a submarine. It is apparent that most subjects are learning, although wide individual differences appear.

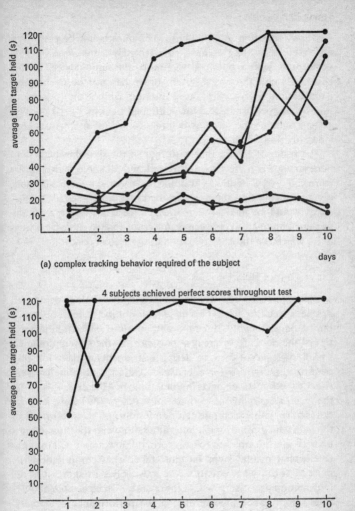

(a) complex tracking behavior required of the subject

4 subjects achieved perfect scores throughout test

(b) simple tracking behavior required of the subject

Figure 1 System performance as affected by individual differences and practice. Actually, the data plotted in the lower graph were obtained while the subjects were simultaneously carrying out three additional simple tracking tasks

Certainly selection and training techniques could be employed effectively with this system. Figure 1(b) shows the same subjects performing with a modified version of the same device. In this case, although the basic system order has not been changed, equalization loops have been inserted within the system to improve its performance. Now, although the task of the over-all system remains the same as before, the task of the man is considerably simplified.

The result of this is, that with four of the six subjects, system performance is perfect from the start and all subjects eventually learn the task. Essentially, training has become unnecessary and, except for rejecting the one very bad operator, selection procedures would be ineffective. Clearly, here is an example of the powerful interaction between engineering and psychological variables which is a direct implication of the system concept.

Input–Output Relationships

Much of the early research in engineering psychology dealt with problems relating to getting information into the man or out of him. Unquestionably, the input and output transduction properties of the man are of great importance for the system designer. The knowledge of how to design instrument displays for easy reading and controls for effective operation is absolutely essential for the human engineering practitioner. However, this is but the beginning. In many, perhaps most design situations, it is not the facility with which one can pump information into or out of the man which counts most but, rather, it is what the human must do with this information to transform it into action upon the controls: what mental steps he must take, what computations he must perform, what equations he must solve. In short, it is the information processing task of the operator which is often of overriding importance in determining the performance of a man–machine system. And to a very considerable extent this task is defined not by the human's input nor by his output but, instead, by the relationships that prevail between the input and the output. The recognition of the importance of these relationships I regard as a third significant insight in engineering psychology.

This interest in the operator's task as defined by stimulus–

response relationships has manifested itself in a number of research projects which, superficially, might be considered as quite unrelated. Among the first and clearest demonstrations of the importance of this factor are the classic experiments of Fitts and his associates (Fitts and Deininger, 1954; Fitts and Seeger, 1953) on stimulus–response compatibility. Using signal light displays and stylus controls, they demonstrated that speed and accuracy of operator performance increased as the informational dimensions of the display were made more and more isomorphic with those of the control. The interpretation given these findings was that the greater the display-control compatibility, the fewer became the subject's data processing steps and, hence, the shorter the processing time and the fewer the opportunities for error. These results and conclusions were corroborated in subsequent studies done by other investigators (Garvey and Knowles, 1954).

Closely related to stimulus–response compatibility are the population stereotypes uncovered by numerous investigators (Fitts, 1951). These expected or preferred directional dependencies between the movement of a display indication and the associated control, undoubtedly affect performance accuracy and, in doing so, again attest to the importance of stimulus–response relationships.

Perhaps nowhere in engineering psychology has the nature of the subject's task proved to be more important than in research with continuous control systems. One effective way to alter what the human has to do in such devices is to change his input–output relationships by varying the dynamics of the system from, say, position control to velocity or acceleration control, or to use engineering parlance, from a zero-order to a first- or second-order system. Another way is to hold the order of the system constant and to change the amount of aiding or quickening within the system. Either way, the human's task is very much modified.

The significance of system dynamics as an experimental variable was not always understood. Before the advent of engineering psychology and the recognition of the importance of the operator's task for the performance of the system, the great majority of tracking studies were carried out with position control devices of one kind or another. The reason for this is quite obvious: a zero-order system is the easiest to construct and seems to be the most 'natural' of all following systems. It is the one we use when stirring a cup of coffee or pointing at a blackboard.

However, by confining his attention only to position control – by failing to recognize that system dynamics constitute a powerful set of variables – the pre-human-engineering psychologist was prevented from achieving certain important insights. Quite obviously, for example, he had no way to discover what we now know to be true, namely, that systems of different dynamics respond differently to operator stress (Garvey and Taylor, 1959). Again, as long as only position control tracking was ever tested, a pursuit display was always found to be superior to a compensatory display. However, when system dynamics were allowed to vary, compensatory tracking was found to be superior to pursuit with a first-order system at low input frequencies (Chernikoff and Taylor, 1957).

But by all odds the most serious effect of failing to recognize system dynamics as a relevant dimension was that, until recently, psychologists were blind to the tremendous improvements which could be achieved in system performance by altering the dynamics. So long as the practice of human engineering is confined to the manipulation of display, control or equipment configuration variables, a 50 per cent improvement is highly satisfactory, whereas a 100 per cent improvement is a cause for celebration. In contrast, if a 200 per cent change in accuracy does not result from an alteration in the dynamics of a man–machine control system, something is known to be wrong. One system was even made to perform between five and six times better through an adjustment of mechanism dynamics to complement the man (Sweeney, Bailey and Dowd, 1957). Certainly, such an achievement constitutes a very dramatic affirmation of the importance of the human's input–output relationships in determining the performance of systems composed of men and machines.

Use of Engineering Models

Inherent in the system approach is the idea of an interchangeability of system tasks as performed by men or by mechanical or electronic components. Also, there is an implication in the system concept that inadequate performance on the part of one component can be countered or compensated through the proper choice or design of other components. But these suggestions can be fully exploited only when the behavioral properties of all system elements, whether they be electronic, mechanical or human are reduced to the same system-relevant terms. Then, and only then, can one employ anything resembling a strict logic in the analysis and synthesis of man–machine systems. The recognition of this fact and the decision to attempt to employ engineering constructs to describe the performance of the human as well as of all other system components, I regard as a fourth idea of major significance for engineering psychology.

Although both information theory and servo theory have contributed fruitful models to engineering psychology, the servo approach has been the more effective in guiding the system designer. To illustrate how this latter approach has been used, let us follow in outline the process of designing special information handling networks to improve the performance of a piloted aircraft.

1. The first step is to consider the engineering capacities and limitations of the pilot. For example, it is important to know the human's bandwidth in order to avoid demanding too much of the man. Also the human's precision in carrying out operational transformations such as integration, differentiation, analog addition must be evaluated. In this case, it is not only important to estimate 'baseline' precisions but also the way these precisions change in response to such variables as task complexity, fatigue, stress, etc. The human's 'gain' and the extent to which it can be altered must be looked into and the 'noise' properties of man must be fully considered.

2. Once these and other system-relevant characteristics of the pilot have been examined – and this examination must be largely based upon inference, for very little has been done in the way of quantitative experimentation along this line – the next step is to consider the mathematics of the pilot's task. Figure 2 shows the pilot in a loop where the dynamics consist of two cascaded integrators. These dynamics are something like those of an airplane. The pilot looks at displays (D) and responds by applying force to his controls (C) in the effort to take out wind gusts which constitute the input.

Controlling through two integrators is difficult. Due to the physics of the situation, there is a tendency for such a second-order system to oscillate or hunt from side to side. To stop this oscillation, the pilot actually has to carry out the mathematical processes shown; that is, he has to supply an amplification, two differentiations and two analog additions. The box labeled T represents his reaction time.

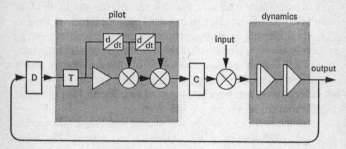

Figure 2 The pilot and his aircraft, considered mathematically

Of course, the pilot does not think of his task in this mathematical way. He knows that he has to estimate turning rate and acceleration and use these estimates to anticipate what the plane is doing. But he does not think of these processes as single and double differentiation and analog addition. Yet, this is precisely what they are, for were they not the plane would not long continue to fly the desired course.

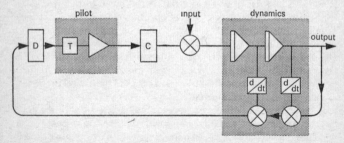

Figure 3 Quickening of the aircraft control loop

3. Having looked at the pilot's engineering properties and having determined the mathematical requirements of the system, the final step is to design the electronics and mechanics so that when all the components, human and nonhuman, perform their function properly, system requirements will be met.

One such design is shown in Figure 3. This is an oversimplified picture of quickening (Birmingham and Taylor, 1954). Although quickening accomplishes several different things, two effects are easily noted. First of all, the differentiations and analog additions are effectively shifted from the pilot into the dynamics. In this way, accurate and relatively noise-free computing circuits are substituted for the low precision, analog mathematics of the pilot. Second, in shifting the bulk of the computation onto the electronic equipment, the pilot is left free to devote all of his bandwidth and other resources to the simple job of amplification which remains.

Here, then, is an example of how one goes about employing an engineering model to help in the design of a man–machine system. That the approach is very effective is suggested by the fact that quickening theory has been used or is being used today in the design of theodolites, radar gunfire control systems, missile control devices, aircraft instruments, drone landing systems, and submarine diving displays. Taking full account of man's system-relevant properties has made for improvements in performance of control systems by as much as a factor of ten (Rund, Birmingham, Tipton and Garvey, 1957). Thus, viewing the human operator in terms of engineering models is certainly having an important effect upon human engineering technology. Furthermore, as has been suggested elsewhere (Taylor, 1957), it is also influencing our science through broadening our subject matter and our construct language.

Epilog

My vote for the four most significant ideas in engineering psychology has now been cast. In summary, these ideas relate to: the limited flexibility of the man, the concept of the man–machine system, the importance of human input–output relationships and the use of engineering models to describe the behavior of the human elements within a system.

Certainly, I have voted as thoughtfully and as honestly as I could. Yet in all frankness, I am not satisfied. I have a feeling of incompleteness which I am sure some of you share with me. I fear that these important ideas have helped to illuminate only certain aspects of engineering psychology, while other portions of the field still lie in deep shadow. In concluding I will attempt to suggest why this may be so.

With the possible exception of the first significant idea, all of them involve system thinking in one way or another. Actually, the latter three ideas can be viewed as system notions of progressive sophistication, with the simplest being the system concept itself at the level of pure description, the next beginning to specify the role of the human component in terms of input–output relationships, and the third providing more precise and useful mathematical descriptions of system-relevant human behavior. Actually, it can be argued that the recognition of the man as insufficiently adaptable to adjust himself to all machines also implies the idea of the human and the mechanism working together as a system, but this will not be pushed. It is enough to note that at least three of the four insights involve the system view and that, therefore, if any one idea can be said to have achieved supremacy in our field it is that the operator and his machine can profitably be considered as forming a single, integrated complex.

My uneasiness then, restated in these terms, derives from my conviction that system thinking has been far less productive for some areas of human engineering technology and psychological research than for others. For example, it seems to have been of little or no real importance in helping in the design of body armor, gas masks, space suits, vehicular seats, library books, sensory aids and many other physical products made by man for his protection or for the enhancement of his well-being. Of course, all these products must be tailored to the man in one way or another, but such tailoring hardly requires that the man and his product be regarded as two portions of one over-all same thing.

In a similar way, it is hard to show that the system concept *per se* has improved the design of radios, television sets, cook stoves, vacuum cleaners and many other household appliances and aids to daily living. Certainly, the housewife and the washing machine constitute a man– or, rather, woman–machine system, but it is doubtful if the recognition of this fact by the washing machine designer has inspired his designs in any important way. Even in the case of such out-and-out systems as shipboard combat information centers and other types of information processing networks, it is hard to show that the human engineer recommends a different design because he recognizes that he is dealing with man–machine systems rather than with a configuration of machines operated by men.

As a matter of fact, I would now like to suggest that it is only in the case of one type of man–machine complex where the system concept has truly been technologically productive. I refer to the closed-loop control systems. All of these, whether they are in submarines, aircraft or motor skill laboratories, are structured in such a way that the amplitude-time pattern of the input is closely reproduced in the output or at some other point within the system. This is accomplished by feeding back some function of the output into the system input.

It is in the design of man–machine systems of this type where the system approach has demonstrated its greatest effectiveness. On the other hand, for internally referenced systems or for data processing networks such as C.I.C.s, air traffic control centers, or air defense complexes, system thinking has been far less fruitful. It is to be noted that these latter systems are either open loop and contain no feedback or they are characterized by feedback which is discontinuous and more a matter of minutes and hours than of milliseconds. It may be suggested, then, that the presence or absence of a tight feed-back loop is the key to the puzzle as to which of the undertakings of human engineering have benefited most from the system viewpoint.

The reason success has crowned the efforts of those working with continuous feedback systems is that a useful mathematical theory based on automatic systems has been available to the engineering psychologist from the start. Although it is certainly true that servo theory is still undergoing development and that it assumes a component linearity which the human violates in a very fundamental way, it is possible to employ the mathematical logic of servo theory very directly and effectively with man–machine control systems.

Thus, it seems to have happened that when the engineering psychologist needed a model for the man as an element in a tracking or control system, he found one ready-made. But for the other roles which men play in systems, no equally fruitful models have been developed. True, information theory has stimulated considerable research on the human as a straight information transmission device. Yet this has not been too helpful for the engineering psychologist, for the human is generally not required to act in such a simple capacity in man–machine systems. What man does have to do, in addition to controlling, is to collect information, filter it, store it, evaluate it and apply rules to it; in other words, he has to make decisions and to think. And for these processes there are no adequate engineering models because we do not know enough about decision making and thinking to reduce them to mathematical logic.

Someday we will have this knowledge. Whether it will be developed through psychological studies of men deciding and thinking, or as a result of a formal logical analysis of the tasks of complex systems, or through the development and use of heuristic computer programs (Reitman, 1959), cannot now be foretold. However, regardless of how it is come by, such knowledge will provide us with new insights to add to our basic four and new models which, hopefully, will be as fruitful for the design of man–machine decision complexes as the servo model now is for the synthesis of continuous control systems.

References

BIRMINGHAM, H. P., KAHN, A., and TAYLOR, F. V. (1954), A demonstration of the effects of quickening in multiple coordinate control tasks, *USN Res. Lab. Rep.*, no. 4380.

BIRMINGHAM, H. P., and TAYLOR, F. V. (1954), 'A design philosophy for man–machine control systems', *Proc. IRE*, vol. 42, pp. 1748–58.

CHERNIKOFF, R., and TAYLOR, F. V. (1957), 'Effects of course frequency and aided time constant on pursuit and compensatory tracking', *J. exp. Psychol.*, vol. 53, pp. 285–92.

FITTS, P. M. (1951), 'Engineering psychology and equipment design', in S. S. Stevens (ed.), *Handbook of Experimental Psychology*, Wiley.

FITTS, P. M., and DEININGER, R. L. (1954), 'S–R compatibility: correspondence among paired elements within stimulus and response codes', *J. exp. Psychol.*, vol. 48, pp. 483–92.

FITTS, P. M., and SEEGER, C. M. (1953), 'S–R compatibility: spatial characteristics of stimulus and response codes', *J. exp. Psychol.*, vol. 46, pp. 199–210.

GARVEY, W. D., and KNOWLES, W. B. (1954), 'Response time patterns associated with various display-control relationships', *J. exp. Psychol.*, vol. 47, pp. 315–22.

GARVEY, W. D., and TAYLOR, F. V. (1959), 'Interactions among operator variables, system dynamics, and task-induced stress', *J. appl. Psychol.*, vol. 43, pp. 79–85.

REITMAN, W. R. (1959), 'Heuristic programs, computer simulation and higher mental processes', *Behav. Sci.*, vol. 4, pp. 330–35.

RUND, P. A., BIRMINGHAM, H. P., TIPTON, C. L., and GARVEY, W. D. (1957), The utility of quickening techniques in improving tracking performance with a binary display, *USN Res. Lab. Rep.*, no. 5013.

SWEENEY, J. S., BAILEY, A. W., and DOWD, J. F. (1957), Comparative evaluation of three approaches to helicopter instrumentation for hovering flight, *USN Res. Lab. Rep.*, no. 4954.

TAYLOR, F. V. (1957), 'Psychology and the design of machines', *Amer. Psychol.*, vol. 12, pp. 249–58.

TAYLOR, F. V., and BIRMINGHAM, H. P. (1959), 'That confounded system performance measure – A demonstration', *Psychol. Rev.*, vol. 66, pp. 178–82.

3 N. E. Loveless

Direction-of-Motion Stereotypes

N. E. Loveless, 'Direction-of-motion stereotypes: a review', *Ergonomics*, vol. 5 (1962), pp. 357-83.

The effects of directional relationships between controls and displays are examined, with special reference to the influence of experience and of conditions of stress. Methods of investigation are discussed. The literature is reviewed to determine what stereotypes appear to be reasonably well-established, and attention is drawn to a number of deficiencies in current knowledge. Consideration is given to the effects of the operator's orientation, the hand he employs for response, the initial position of the display, and the direction of scale numbering.

1. Introduction

Discussing the application of ergonomics at a recent conference, Murrell (1961) quotes the case of a heavy hydraulic press operated by a lever which had to be moved down in order to raise the ram. One day an emergency occurred, the operator became confused and pulled the lever up to raise the ram. It moved down and wrecked the press.

When accidents like this happen, the operator is apt to be blamed for having made a mistake, and the question why the mistake occurred is not pursued. In the present instance, it is clear that the mistake was made because it is in some sense 'natural' to raise a control lever in order to bring about an upward movement of the part which it controls. Part of the responsibility for the accident rests therefore with the designer of the machine, who overlooked this psychological factor.

From the designer's point of view, the decision as to what direction of motion of a control shall produce a given movement of the controlled element is often a matter of indifference, and indeed it is common to find no uniformity of usage, even on the same machine (Bartlett, 1943). To the operator, however, this decision may not be a matter of indifference, and the directional relationship may be a variable which has a considerable influence upon his speed and accuracy. In a survey conducted by Fitts and Jones (1947), 17 per cent of errors made by pilots interpreting aircraft instruments resulted from operating the control in the wrong direction in response to a visual cue.

In the case of the hydraulic press, the 'natural' relationship is intuitively obvious, once attention is called to the question. In many cases, however, the relationship is not obvious, and needs to be discovered by psychological experiment. Experiments have also shown that with some arrangements of control and display the psychological factors are more complex than might have been expected.

The quantity of published material bearing on this question is now quite large. Useful bibliographies have been provided by Andreas and Weiss (1954) and Simon (1958), a good discussion of the early work is given by Mitchell and Vince (1951), and some of the principal findings are summarized by Holding (1955). There is, however, no up-to-date account in a readily accessible form, and it is the aim of the present paper to meet this need.

In preparing this paper studies of rather limited interest, such as those concerned with the aircraft attitude indicator, have been omitted unless they had a bearing upon a more general problem. Studies have also been omitted in which the evidence is no more than suggestive, because the relevant variable was confounded with others, or for some similar reason. Clearly confirmatory evidence of points made in earlier studies has, on the other hand, been felt to be valuable, especially since the experiments in question are never exact replications, and has been included.

2. The Effect of Directional Relationship upon Performance

The relationship between a control movement and its effect which is expected by most of the population is known as a 'population stereotype' (Fitts, 1951), and control-display relationships which conform to a stereotype are said to be 'compatible' (Fitts and Seeger, 1953).

Some stereotypes, in that they arise from normal spatial relationships (Gibbs, 1951), may properly be termed 'natural'. For example, where a pointer and a control lever move in the same direction, the operator appears to expect that a given control movement will result in a pointer movement of the same sense ('direct' relationship), and may be disturbed if it results in one of opposite sense ('reversed' relationship). This stereotype is clearly related to eye-hand co-ordinations practised from birth, and the difficulty of the reversed relationship resembles that encountered in mirror drawing, or when wearing inverting spectacles. Other stereotypes do not appear to be 'natural' in this sense, but may reflect the conventions prevalent in the culture to which the operator belongs. Such stereotypes may be more cautiously referred to as 'expected', 'preferred' or 'dominant'.

The extent to which an operator's expectations influence his performance may vary somewhat with the demands of the task. Some of the early investigators (Grether, 1947; Mitchell, 1948) found that in a simple continuous tracking task, performed with the preferred hand, the directional relationship might have little effect upon speed and accuracy; it was even possible to reverse the direction during the test without disrupting the operator's performance, and without his being aware of the reversal (Vince, 1945). Mitchell and Vince (1951) considered that directional factors might be less important in continuous tasks than in tasks requiring a series of discontinuous responses; perhaps because the operator was better able to anticipate direction and rate of display movement, had clearer knowledge of the results of his own movements and had more control over his response rate. It should, however, be pointed out that the design of the experiments quoted was not altogether satisfactory; and that in Mitchell's experiment the continuous task differed from the discontinuous in its use of lever controls, whose rotary motion may well have affected the operator's expectations. Fitzwater (1948), using the same apparatus as Grether, found display-control relationships to affect performance in a continuous task.

Whatever may be the case in relatively easy tasks, there is general agreement that the effect of incompatibility becomes more prominent in tasks requiring the use of the non-preferred hand or both hands, or performance at high speed (Vince, 1945; Mitchell, 1948; Norris and Spragg, 1953; Carter and Murray, 1947; Gibbs, 1950). It will also be shown below that the mechanical reversal of display-control relationships may sometimes fail to produce any apparent effect, not because no stereotype is involved, but because two antagonistic stereotypes are balanced against each other. It must also be remembered that although motion relationships may sometimes have little effect once the operator has become engaged in a continuous task, they are very likely to determine his initial response, which may be critical in the case of sensitive or dangerous equipment.

Designers are apt to argue that even where stereotypes are clearly reflected in behaviour, they are of little practical importance, since the operator will quickly adapt himself to an unexpected relationship. Stereotypes are largely, if not entirely, the result of learning, and the effects of learning can presumably be reversed. Even animals, given sufficiently extensive training, can learn to switch smoothly back and forth between conflicting patterns of response (Harlow, 1951); and experiments showing that direction-of-motion stereotypes become stronger as a function of age, as we should expect, have also suggested that experience develops a facility in adjusting to incompatible relationships (Humphries and Shephard, 1959). Again, while the time required to reach a given criterion of accuracy may be considerably longer for the incompatible relationship (Gibbs, 1951), especially for older or less intelligent subjects (Vince, 1945), the difference in learning time may not be of much practical importance.

Psychologists have nevertheless maintained that the use of incompatible arrangements should be avoided. Two main reasons have been given for this recommendation. Firstly, there is some doubt whether even extensive practice will achieve a level of performance equal to that obtained with a compatible arrangement. Secondly, there is the possibility that even if the established habit can be completely reversed under normal conditions, 'regression' to that habit may occur in circumstances generally described as 'stressful'. These two questions are related and will be discussed together.

While a number of investigators (Morin and Grant, 1953; Fitts and Seeger 1953; Crossman, 1955) have suggested that systems yielding an initially poor performance are not readily brought to the level of better arrangements, there seems to be relatively little direct evidence to support this contention. Gardner (1954) and Gardner and Lacey (1954), in a comparison of aircraft attitude indicators, showed that with the less favourable ('fly-to') relationship, there was a distinct tendency for errors to occur, even after hundreds of hours of practice. On the other hand, Simon (1954a), who wished to compare the effects of stress on a dominant and a non-dominant arrangement, succeeded in equalizing performance fairly adequately in about 200 half-minute trials, spread over two days. However, it should be noticed that in this experiment practice was highly concentrated, and that some regression was evident between days. It is therefore possible to doubt the permanence of the effect in this experiment, and perhaps more generally, where practice on the non-dominant task is distributed and separated by periods during which the dominant habit may recover strength. Reversing a habit is not like reversing an electrical connexion. The old habit is not so much replaced by the new as overlaid by it. During training, the old response is weakened sufficiently to allow the new response to appear, and the latter is then strengthened by further practice; but the old habit has been suppressed rather than eliminated. The suppression is likely to be in part only temporary, so that the old response may reappear after a period away from the task (Adams, 1952). Even with extensive practice, it may be difficult to ensure that the new response has more than a precarious margin of dominance.

It should further be remarked that the fact that the performance of two tasks has been equated on a given criterion by no means guarantees their complete functional equivalence. Differences in performance may still be revealed when a different criterion is used. Thus, Vince (1950) has shown that a non-dominant arrangement may be brought to a level of *accuracy* closely approximating that of a dominant arrangement, but may still be inferior in *speed of reaction*.

Again, differences in habit strength which are not apparent under normal conditions may come to light in special circumstances. As noted above, one of the difficulties in permanently reversing a response based on a population stereotype is the likelihood that the suppressed habit may be revived in strength by experience outside the working situation. A similar effect may be produced when display-control relationships within the working situation are inconsistent. Interference will be mutual, but is likely to have the greater effect upon the non-dominant response (Warrick, 1949; Gardner, 1950; Gibbs, 1951; Andreas, Green and Spragg, 1954).

It can also be predicted on theoretical grounds that habit regression will occur when the operator's motivation is decreased, when he is fatigued, and when he is subjected to any novel change in the working situation (Loveless, 1959a). Very similar predictions are made in somewhat different terms by Broadbent (1958), who stresses the role of immediate memory. A given level of performance may be due partly to long-term and partly to short-term storage of information. When an old habit is replaced by a new one, it is the latter which benefits most from the short-term storage. But short-term storage is of limited capacity, and if it is required to deal with additional incoming information, this will interfere with storage of the new habit. Thus under distraction or similar stresses there may be reversion to the old way of performing the task, even though stress-free performance is satisfactory. This danger could be overcome by giving more practice, until the new relationship is also established in long-term memory. But when the new relation to be learned is one which contradicts everyday experience it cannot be established unconditionally. Correct performance can only be attained by short-term storage of the fact that 'this is not the usual situation'. Once again, interference with short-term storage may cause disruption of the established performance.

These theoretical arguments are plausible, but it is valuable to have empirical evidence confirming the vulnerability of incompatible arrangements.

Vince (1945) found little difference between compatible and incompatible arrangements at low speed, but a conspicuous difference when a high response rate was required. Gardner (1957), in another study of attitude indicators, found that when the operator was required to track a slowly-changing course, very little practice was required to equalize performance on 'fly-to' and 'fly-from' systems; but at high rates, the 'fly-to' arrangement was clearly inferior, and showed no sign of catching up, even with extensive practice. Castaneda and Lipsitt (1959) conclude that the effect of speed stress may be reduced with practice, but that it is difficult to eliminate entirely.

Vince (1950) studied performance on dominant and non-dominant systems under conditions of stress involving speed, distractions designed to startle the subject, and the addition of a secondary task. Although her results are in the expected direction, she does not consider them conclusive, since she did not succeed in equalizing performance on the two systems. Mitchell (1947) found that a secondary task performed with the left hand appeared to have more effect upon incompatible arrangements. Simon (1954a) used a secondary task as a distracting condition. Both mild and severe degrees of stress resulted in significantly more reversal errors being made by subjects performing on the originally non-dominant task than by those performing on the originally dominant one, although both groups had practised to apparently equal performance. A group which had additional practice on the non-dominant task was no less affected. Garvey (1957) made a comparison of tracking with an acceleration-control system and an acceleration-aided control system. Where no special training is given, the second system is easier to use, but Garvey equated performance on the two systems by training. The subjects were then submitted to a variety of 'stressful' conditions: prolonged operation, use of the left hand, tracking with two hands or in two dimensions, performance on secondary tasks involving visual search or mental arithmetic. It was found that both systems deteriorated under the changed conditions, but the deterioration was greater for the originally poorer system. Garvey concludes that fitting the operator to the machine by training gives less stable improvement than arranging the machine to conform to the habits of the operator.

3. Methods of Determining Population Stereotypes

The evidence quoted above appears to justify the recommendation that designers should ensure that compatible motion relationships are incorporated in equipment designed for human operation. Before considering what relationships have in fact been shown to be compatible, it is well to discuss the methods which may properly be used to answer such questions. The designer may easily be tempted to settle problems of this kind by questioning a few of his colleagues. It must therefore be emphasized that investigations of population stereotypes need to be conducted with considerable care.

Not only does the response of a single operator vary from time to time (Warrick, 1947), but differences between operators may be very wide, particularly with the more unusual arrangements, though any operator tends to believe quite strongly that his own response is the only 'natural' one, and to have difficulty in believing that others may respond differently (Holding, 1957a). It is therefore dangerous to rely on a few opinions, however confident, and investigation must be conducted with the precautions appropriate to a statistical survey. The subjects must be an adequate and representative sample of the population which will use the equipment. Since some stereotypes are based on convention, subjects must be drawn from the appropriate culture. Previous mechanical experience is evidently a relevant factor, and will probably include sex differences. Age, intelligence and handedness may also be relevant variables (Vince, 1945; Mitchell, 1948; Simon, 1952a; Humphries and Shephard, 1955; Holding, 1957a).

The task employed should also be representative of the operational task. Murrell (1951), discussing the uses to which indicators may be put, classifies those uses which also involve the manipulation of controls into 'tracking' and 'setting' tasks. The former may again be divided into two types: in 'pursuit' tracking, the operator uses his control to maintain a pointer in alignment with a second pointer registering externally produced variations; while in 'compensatory' tracking, these variations and the subject's control movements are differentially fed to the pointer, and the task consists in keeping the pointer aligned with a stationary 'target'. In setting tasks, the control is used to move the pointer to a given dial reading. The dial graduation here introduces an additional directional feature, which requires separate consideration.

Tracking tasks are commonly arranged to give an integrated error score which takes account of both speed and accuracy of performance. It appears, however, that differences between arrangements in terms of speed are likely to correlate highly with differences in accuracy (Graham, 1952; Loveless, 1959a). If this is true, performance may be adequately scored by noting the number of times the control is turned in a direction which increases the error. This suggests that it may be legitimate to use the simple and speedy single-response technique, in which each subject is given a single trial, being asked simply to produce a certain movement of the display; the experimenter notes how many operators move the control in each of the two directions.

Some investigators have attempted to achieve the same object by paper-and-pencil tests, but most psychologists would treat results obtained in this way with some reserve, not only because of the lack of realism, but because such tests are likely to be used to study the subject's response to a number of successively presented arrangements. There is therefore the danger that the response is influenced by the answer given to previous questions. This danger applies to apparatus tests also, in that the results of a number of tests on the same subject may depend upon the order in which they are given. Despite ample evidence that such serial effects occur, much research on display-control relationships has failed to take account of them. It is clearly desirable to use a procedure which tests each subject on one arrangement only, despite the increase in the number of subjects which may be needed.

Where single-response procedures are used, two groups of subjects are necessary in order that both directions of display movement may be studied. It cannot safely be assumed that the operator's expectations are 'reversible'. A subject who turns a knob clockwise to move a pointer to the right will not necessarily turn it anti-clockwise to move the pointer to the left. Several investigators (Warrick, 1947; Holding, 1957a; Bradley, 1959) have noted a significant tendency to turn a knob clockwise to produce *any* required result, particularly when the system involves some ambiguity (a finding which can be put to practical use when controls have a non-reciprocal function, such as resetting a counter to zero). This tendency does not apparently occur when the left hand is used, and is perhaps attributable to the fact that clockwise rotations of the right hand are somewhat easier to perform.

4. Survey of General Investigations of Stereotypes

This section aims to outline those direction-of-motion relationships which seem reasonably well established under the most
general conditions – that is, when the display is not graduated,
the operator directly faces the display and uses his preferred hand.
It will be convenient to deal separately with rotary and linear
motions of either indicator or control.

(a) Linear indicator, translatory control

It might be supposed that the most obvious field for investigation
was the case in which both control and display move in straight
lines. In fact, evidence on this class of motion relationships is
scanty.

One reason for this may be that for the most common arrangement, where the lines of movement of display and control are
parallel, the solutions seems intuitively obvious. It is natural to
assume that a control movement is expected to produce a display
movement in the same sense. Thus, Vince (1945) verified that an
upward control movement is expected to displace a pointer
upwards (Figure 1(a)). It will be shown below, however, that
there may be some danger in generalizing this assumption to all
cases where it might seem to apply.

Where lines of movement are not parallel, empirical evidence is
more clearly necessary. Vince and Mitchell (1946) measured
performance on a discontinuous tracking task in which upward
pointer movement might be produced by moving the control

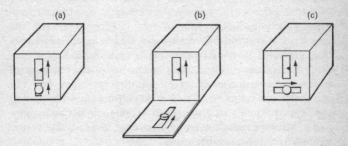

Figure 1 From Vince and Mitchell(1946) and Mitchell (1947)

up, down, forward, backward, right or left. The best results were obtained with upward control movement (Figure 1a), the second best with forward movement (Figure 1b), the third best with movement to the right (Figure 1c). The opposite arrangements yielded the worst performance, and differed little among themselves. The forward-for-up stereotype appeared quite strong, though it would be useful to know how far it depends upon the relative positions of display and control; the operator's response might be less certain if the lines of movement did not lie in the same vertical plane and suggest a continuity of movement. The right-for-up stereotype was not at all well marked, and was not confirmed in a further experiment by Mitchell (1947), in which the operator had to perform a secondary task with the left hand. The first two stereotypes were verified under this condition.

The only additional evidence on this point which needs to be considered comes from a paper-and-pencil test administered by Ross *et al.* (1955). The investigators tried to reduce one of the dangers of such tests by severely limiting the number of responses obtained from each subject; but the experiment is poorly reported, since there are numerical discrepancies in the table of results, and some of the arrangements tested are not clearly described. The aim was to determine what linear display movements were expected to result from operation of a push–pull knob, a rotary knob and a short lever. The results applying to the push–pull control are shown in Figure 2. Of the six arrangements tested, five yielded preferences which were either insignificant or non-reversible.

The exception was arrangement (b), in which a downward movement of the knob was expected to move the display upward. The reason for this surprising result is not clear; the operators may have perceived the moving elements as opposite ends of a 'see-saw' mechanism, or the pushing-in of a knob as producing an increase (upward movement) of the displayed function. The preference was rather weak, and evidence from this investigation should perhaps not be given much weight; but it does suggest that a stereotype which is normally strongly expected may cease to apply with some configurations.

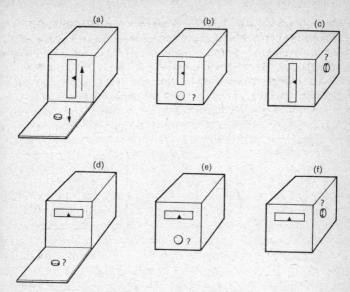

Figure 2 From Ross, Shepp and Andrews (1955)

(b) Linear indicator, lever control

Levers and joysticks are usually treated in the literature as translatory controls, their movements being spoken of as right or forward. This is a somewhat doubtful assumption. Mechanically, the lever is a rotary control, and may be perceived as such by the operator, particularly when it is short, so that considerable angular displacement is required in operation. It will be shown in a later section that, at least when associated with rotary displays, short levers may be affected by the stereotypes typical of rotary controls, and this may well apply also to arrangements involving linear display movement.

This may have been the case in an experiment by Mitchell (1948) which was intended to be a repetition of that by Vince and Mitchell (1946) described above, but substituting a continuous for a discontinuous task. Motion relationships were found to have no significant effect for right-handed operation, and the experimenter attributed this to the change in the nature of the

61

task. There was also, however, a change of controls from sliding knobs to short levers, and it seems possible that the rather odd control movements which resulted may have influenced the results.

The paper-and-pencil test by Ross *et al.* (1955) pictured a short lever protruding through a slot. Six arrangements tested are shown in Figure 3. Surprisingly, arrangement (b) yielded a

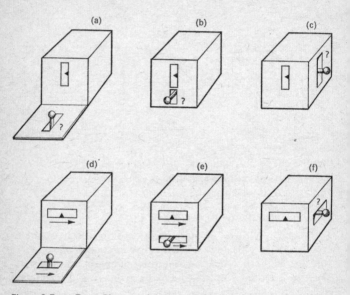

Figure 3 From Ross, Shepp and Andrews (1955), Loucks (1949) and Gardner (1950)

stereotype which was not fully reversible; operators expected to move up-for-up, but the down-for-down association was not significant. The results for (c) appear to have been similar, but are unclear because of a discrepancy in the figures given; this is also true of (f), where in any case there seems to have been no strong stereotype. The right-for-right stereotype is strongly marked in two spatial arrangements (d and e). In arrangement (a), forward lever movement is not significantly associated with vertical indicator movement.

Long joysticks with a small angle of movement seem more likely to be treated as translatory controls. Loucks (1949) and Gardner (1950) confirmed the right-for-right stereotype (Figure 3d). Gardner also confirmed the lack of association between forward joystick movement and vertical indicator movement (Figure 3a).

In summary, present knowledge about direction-of-motion relationships between linear displays and lever controls leaves much to be desired. It can fairly be assumed that where the lines of movement are parallel, movements are expected to be in the same sense; the only evidence throwing doubt on this comes from a paper-and-pencil test. Where the lines of movement are perpendicular, it is unsafe to assume the existence of any stereotype, and reactions are likely to be inconsistent.

(c) Linear indicators, rotary controls

Relationships in this group have been more thoroughly explored than any others.

Warrick (1947) investigated the five arrangements shown in Figure 4, using a single-response technique in which the operator was required to centre an indicator set off to one side; the subjects were however tested on more than one arrangement. His

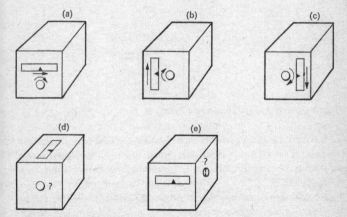

Figure 4 From Warrick (1947)

findings can be grouped under two headings. Where the axis of rotation of the control was perpendicular to the line of movement of the display (Figure 4a, b and c), there was a strong tendency to expect the indicator to move in the same direction as that part of the control nearest the display. Where the axis of the control

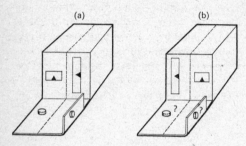

Figure 5 From Carter and Murray (1947)

was parallel to the line of movement of the display (Figure 4d and e), there were no marked stereotypes, and subjects tended to turn the control clockwise to produce display movements in either direction.

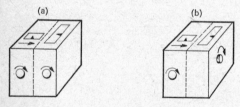

Figure 6 From Norris and Spragg (1953)

Carter and Murray (1947) used a two-handed task, and their investigation was not ideally designed from a theoretical viewpoint, but their results tend to confirm Warrick's findings (Figure 5).

A clear confirmation comes from an investigation by Gibbs (1949), using a single-response technique. The stereotypes shown in Figure 4(a) and Figure 4(b) were verified, while two arrange-

ments in which the control axis was parallel to the line of movement of the display showed no movement preference. This
experiment is of particular interest because it used a large handwheel instead of a small knob, and showed that the initial
position of the handle had no influence on the response.
Apparently it is the direction of rotation of the control, not the
motion of the operator's hand, which is perceptually important.

Norris and Spragg (1953) used a two-handed tracking task in
which the right-hand control rotated either in the frontal plane
or in the vertical plane perpendicular to it. All combinations of
display and control movement were studied. Figure 6 shows the
best combination for each control position. There were no
significant differences between the other combinations within

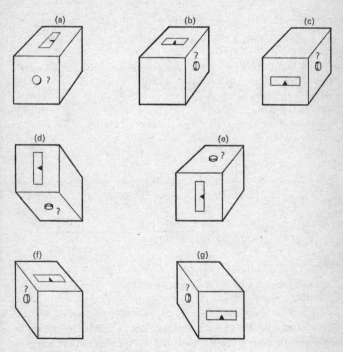

Figure 7 From Holding (1957a)

each position. Performance was however generally better with the control in the position shown in Figure 6(b).

Holding (1957a) made a careful investigation, using a single-response technique, of seven arrangements in which the pointer moved in a line parallel to the axis of the control. He included all the arrangements which seemed likely to be of practical use, including two involving the left hand (Figure 7). As far as any stereotype was found, it was for clockwise rotation of the knob to move the pointer away from the control; but this was strongly overlaid by a general tendency to respond clockwise regardless of the required direction of display movement, a tendency similar to that found by Warrick. The result was that none of the seven arrangements yielded a strong and reversible association.

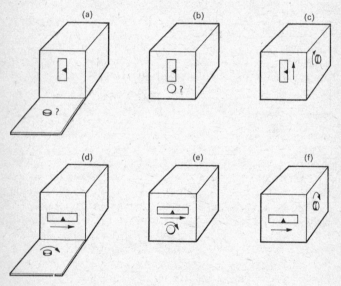

Figure 8 From Ross, Shepp and Andrews (1955)

Rotary controls also figured in the paper-and-pencil test by Ross *et al.* (1955). The six arrangements studied are shown in Figure 8. In three arrangements (c, d, e), the axis of the control is perpendicular to, and to one side of, the line of movement of the display; in these cases, Warrick's principle, that the display should move in the same direction as the nearest part of the control, can be applied and was supported, though in arrangement (d) the association was not very strong. The stereotype found in arrangement (c) was confirmed by Holding (1957b) in an apparatus test. In two arrangements (a, f), the control axis was parallel to the line of movement of the display. In arrange-

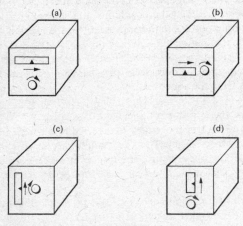

Figure 9 From Loveless (1959)

ment (f) a stereotype was found, namely that clockwise control rotation should move the pointer to the right. In arrangement (a), clockwise control rotation was expected to move the pointer up, but this stereotype failed to reverse. The same is true of arrangement (b), where for the first time we meet a situation in which the control axis, though perpendicular to the line of movement of the display, passes through that line, so that Warrick's principle cannot be applied. There is a suggestion in the last three cases (a, b, f) that there are stereotypes of clockwise-for-right and clockwise-for-up, though the latter is overlaid by the general tendency of clockwise-for-anything.

Loveless (1959a) investigated compensatory tracking performance with horizontal and vertical displays, when the control knob was either below or to the right of the display (Figure 9).

In two of these arrangements (b, d), the line of movement of the display passes through the centre of rotation of the control, and in these cases better performance was found when clockwise rotation of the control moved the pointer up rather than down, and to the right rather than to the left. The same was found to be true of the other two arrangements (a, c), but even more prominently, presumably because the same tendencies were reinforced by Warrick's principle, which operates in the same direction. The orientation of the display and the position of the control knob were found to be unimportant in themselves; it was the relationship between them that mattered.

While there is still a need for systematic investigation of stereotypes in this group, it does seem possible to draw some general principles from the above evidence:

(i) Irrespective of the position of the control relative to the display, a clockwise control movement is expected to displace a pointer upwards or to the right. This expectation may very well derive from the fact that these control and display movements are conventionally associated with an increase in the indicated function.

(ii) Where the axis of rotation of the control is perpendicular to the line of movement of the display and passes to one side of it, the pointer is expected to move in the same direction as that part of the control nearest the display.

Where principles (i) and (ii) are in conflict, principle (ii) appears to be dominant (Figures 4c and 5a). Where these principles act together, particularly consistent responses are likely. The stereotypes shown in Figure 9(a and c) are probably the most dependable in this group.

(iii) Where the axis of rotation of the control is perpendicular to the line of movement of the display and passes through it, principle (ii) cannot be applied, and the response is determined by principle (i). Response may be less consistent than with the arrangements just mentioned, but such stereotypes may nevertheless prove useful. Loveless (1959b) found the arrangement shown in Figure 9(b) to give a level of performance little below that of Figure 9(a and c). This layout is particularly valuable where a number of control-display units are to be mounted in a panel, since it is economical of space, allows the pointers to be aligned for check-reading, and associates each control unequivocally with its own display.

(iv) Where the axis of rotation of the control is parallel to the line of movement of the display, there is some evidence that clockwise control movement is expected to move the pointer away from the control; but there is also evidence to the contrary, and it is not clear what happens in the case of conflict with principle (i). The most reliable finding is that operators respond inconsistently to arrangements of this kind.

(d) Circular indicators, rotary controls

The preference for motion correspondence found with translatory displays and controls suggests that operators will expect clockwise rotation of a knob or handwheel to result in clockwise displacement of the pointer on a circular dial.

Warrick (1948) attempted to confirm this hypothesis, using a paper-and-pencil test. The test consisted of thirty-two diagrams, each showing a control knob and a quadrantal dial with pointer and reference mark. The upper, lower, left and right quadrants were studied, each in combination with a control which might be above, below, to right or left of the display, giving sixteen arrangements in all. For each arrangement there were two items, one requiring the pointer to be moved clockwise to reach the reference mark, the other requiring a counter-clockwise pointer movement. The results clearly supported a clockwise-for-clockwise stereotype for all arrangements. Unfortunately, they were inadequate to show whether the stereotype was more pronounced with some arrangements than with others. A later experiment by the same author (Warrick, 1949), though primarily an investigation into the importance of consistency in motion relationships, suggested that this stereotype was not in fact equally strong in all segments of a circular indicator. With the control knob below the display, the stereotype appeared to be strong when the indicator was the upper half of a circle, but weak when it was the lower half.

Other investigators have found variations in tracking performance according to the sector of the dial in use, when the mechanical linkage was clockwise-for-clockwise. Graham (1952) found that the error of compensatory tracking was smaller, and the control was turned the wrong way more frequently, when the target was in the upper quadrant of the dial than when it was in the other three quadrants. Fitts and Simon (1952), using two simultaneous tracking tasks, one controlled by each hand, found better performance in the upper and left-hand quadrants.

These experiments were not aimed at exploring display-control relationships, and their results are open to a number of explanations. One plausible hypothesis rests on the possibility that operators may perceive rotary motion of a pointer in translatory terms. It has been shown above that a clockwise control movement is expected to result in movement of a linear indicator upwards or to the right. It seems possible that operators may transfer these stereotypes to a circular indicator, in addition to the clockwise-for-clockwise stereotype. Motion relationships on a circular indicator will then be ambiguous in the sense that the operator may regard the pointer movement as both rotary and translatory. He expects not only that a clockwise control movement will move the pointer clockwise, but also upwards or to the right, depending upon its initial orientation (Figure 10). In the upper and left-hand quadrants, both expectations lead to the same response; in the bottom and right-hand quadrants, they lead to antagonistic response tendencies, whose conflict will be reflected in poorer performance. Variation in tracking performance between different sectors of the display could then be accounted for on the hypothesis that both 'rotary' and 'translatory' stereotypes are present.

This hypothesis can be tested directly by comparing tracking performance on diametrically opposite targets, with both mechanical linkages between control and display. Simon (1954b) made such a comparison between targets at the upper and lower cardinal points of a dial, and showed that both stereotypes were present, although the rotary was the stronger. He used an experimental design in which the same subjects were tested on several arrangements. His findings were however confirmed by Loveless (1956), using a more satisfactory design in which each subject was tested on one arrangement only. Loveless also made a comparison between targets at the right and left cardinal points, with a similar result; both stereotypes were present, but the rotary was the stronger. The rotary stereotype appeared to be more marked when the pointer was horizontally aligned than when it was vertically aligned; this difference may perhaps be related to the position of the control knob, which in these experiments was below the display.

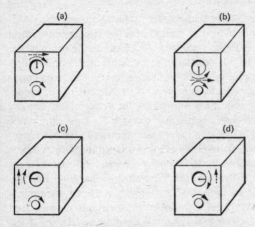

Figure 10 From Simon (1954b) and Loveless (1956)

The practical conclusion to be drawn from these experiments is that direction-of-motion associations between a circular indicator and a rotary control are unambiguous only when the correct response conforms with both stereotypes: that is, when a clockwise-for-clockwise linkage is used, and when the pointer lies in the upper and left-hand quadrants. Because of the dominance of the rotary tendency, the clockwise-for-clockwise linkage should still be used when the pointer is in the bottom and right-hand quadrants, but there is an increased risk that the operator will turn the control in the wrong direction. Where such errors are undesirable, half the scale-length of a circular dial would have to be sacrificed, and the advantage of compactness, as compared with a linear display, would be largely lost. Loveless (1959a) was able to make a direct comparison of tracking performance on circular and linear displays. The most favourable quadrants of the circular display gave no better performance than the most favourable linear arrangements. There is thus a good case for the use of linear indicators where directional errors are to be avoided. Eccentric dials are probably equally acceptable, provided that the scale is convex upwards or to the left.

(e) Circular indicators, translatory controls

It has been shown above that pointer motion on a circular scale can be perceived in two ways, and that as a consequence of this ambiguity control-display association varies with the orientation of the pointer. There is no reason to expect that this ambiguity is confined to the case where the control is rotary. Unfortunately, no research appears to have been aimed at determining stereotypes for circular indicators and translatory controls, although such combinations certainly occur in practice.

Incidental findings from a number of studies of check-reading (Warrick and Grether, 1948; Connell and Grether, 1948; White, 1951; Morley and Suffield, 1951) do however suggest that pointer orientation is a significant factor. Where the primary function of an instrument is to indicate some deviation from a normal operating condition, and a number of such instruments are mounted in a panel, deviations are more readily detected if in normal operation all the instrument pointers are aligned to the same position. On a circular instrument, best performance is probably obtained when the pointers are aligned in one of the four cardinal positions. The investigations cited were intended to determine whether any particular cardinal position is superior.

It is doubtful whether in fact any cardinal position is superior in itself; but differences in speed and errors have been found when the response was registered manually. If, for example, a clockwise deviation was to be responded to with an upward movement of a switch, performance was likely to be particularly good at the left cardinal point, where the motion of switch and pointer corresponded, and particularly poor at the right cardinal point, where they were in opposition. These differences disappeared when the direction of pointer deviation was not relevant to the response, when the response was verbal, or when the switch moved in a different plane from the display.

It would appear, therefore, that translatory control movements induce an expectation that they will result in pointer movement of the same linear sense. It is quite possible that they also carry expectations of clockwise or counter-clockwise motion; this question needs investigation. In any case, it is clear that stereotypes are unlikely to be equal in strength over the whole circumference of the dial, and better performance is likely to be obtained with a linear indicator (Connell and Grether, 1948).

(f) Circular indicators, lever controls

In this group also it is to be expected that control-display associations will depend upon pointer orientation. Simon (1954b) repeated the experiment described above, substituting an upward-pointing lever for the rotary control knob, and again comparing tracking performance in the upper and lower quadrants, with both direction-of-motion linkages between control and display. When the pointer was in the upper quadrant, performance was superior when the motions of lever and pointer were in correspondence. When the pointer was in the lower quadrant, however, there was no significant difference in performance between the two linkages.

This result suggests that directional relationships between rotating pointers and levers involve some ambiguity, but is insufficient to allow of its analysis, since the motion of a lever, no less than that of a pointer, may be perceived as either rotary or translatory. It is therefore to be expected that performance will vary with the orientation of the lever, as well as of the pointer.

This expectation was confirmed in another experiment (Simon, 1952b). The same compensatory tracking task was used, the mechanical motion relationship being clockwise-for-clockwise throughout. Four targets were used, at the cardinal points of the dial. There were also three control positions:

(i)   lever below dial, extending upward from pivot,
(ii) lever below dial, extending downward from pivot,
(iii) lever above dial, extending downward from pivot.

As might be expected, better performance was obtained when the pointer was aligned with the vertical lever than when it was horizontal (cf. Gagné and Foster, 1948). Alignment alone did not lead to maximum efficiency; it was also necessary that both pointer and lever should extend in the same direction from their pivots, so that their motions corresponded exactly. This, of

73

course, agrees with the finding of Simon's other experiment (1954b).

Rather more surprisingly, there appeared to be an effect due to control position. Performance was found to be better when the free end of the lever, rather than its pivot, was near the display. The best performance was therefore obtained with the arrangements shown in Figure 11(a and b), where the lever is below the

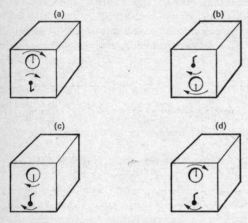

Figure 11 From Simon (1952b)

dial extending upwards, or above the dial extending downwards. Where the lever was below the dial and extended downwards, the average level of performance was significantly poorer; this is a case, however, where the process of averaging is misleading. Operators fell fairly clearly into two distinct groups: those performing better when the pointer was in the bottom quadrant (Figure 11c) and those performing better when it was in the upper quadrant (Figure 11d). For the former group, the motion correspondence of pointer and lever was presumably the governing factor. Those in the latter group, however, seemed able to modify their perception of the situation so as to enable them to track successfully. Interrogation suggested that they achieved this in one of two ways. Either they perceived the pointer and lever as having a common pivot, so that the pointer was imagined as a direct extension of the lever; or else they perceived the lever as pivoting about its point of grasp, so that the motions of lever and pointer were imagined as corresponding. These descriptions are of considerable interest as an indication of the complex way in which the human operator may interpret control-display configurations. At the same time, it seems probable that arrangements which allow of such multiple interpretations are better avoided.

Neither of the above experiments offers a complete analysis of stereotypes in this group. If we allow that the motion of both lever and pointer can be perceived in two ways, it is theoretically possible that four sets of stereotypes may be operating in the same situation:

 (i) translatory control motion, translatory pointer motion (up-for-up, right-for-right),

 (ii) rotary control motion, rotary pointer motion (clockwise-for-clockwise),

(iii) rotary control motion, translatory pointer motion (clockwise-for-up, clockwise-for-right),

(iv) translatory control motion, rotary pointer motion (?).

If, as Simon's results suggest, performance is also affected by the position of the control relative to the display, a very extensive investigation is called for.

Meanwhile, it is possible to recommend some practical arrangements as least likely to cause difficulty. For levers and dials rotating in the same plane:

 (i) lever and pointer should extend in the same direction from their pivots, and have motion correspondence,

 (ii) the lever should be mounted with its free end towards the display,

(iii) motion should preferably be confined to the upper and left-hand quadrants.

Nothing is known of levers and dials rotating in different planes.

5. The Effect of Body Position

When directions of motion are described as 'forwards' or 'to the right', it must be remembered that these descriptions may relate either to some standard frame of reference, or to one determined by the orientation of the operator's body, and that the two do not necessarily coincide. Further, if the operator turns his head, descriptions relative to his body no longer coincide with descriptions relative to his line of regard.

Humphries (1958) has shown that these discrepancies may affect direction-of-motion stereotypes. When the operator used a vertical joystick to control the vertical and horizontal movements of a display, stereotypes were altered when the operator

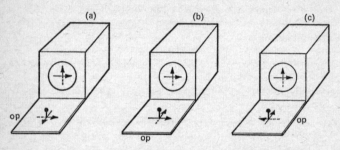

Figure 12 From Humphries (1958). The operator position is shown by the letters OP

moved from the normal frontal position to positions which required him to view the display over his right or left shoulder (Figure 12). A detailed analysis of the effect is not yet possible, since in this experiment both directional linkages were always changed at the same time; but the results certainly suggest that the operator refers display movements to his line of regard, and control movements to the orientation of his body. He appears to expect that a control movement to the right of his body will produce a display movement to the right of his line of regard; and that a control movement away from his body will produce an upward movement of the display.

Shephard and Cook (1959) used the same apparatus, arranged so that control movements to the right and towards the display moved the indicator up and to the right respectively. Body position was varied between 6 o'clock (facing the display) and 9 o'clock (on its left). Performance at the 9 o'clock position was markedly superior to performance at the 6, 7 and 8 o'clock positions, which did not differ among themselves. It would therefore appear that the effect of variation of body position is not progressive; rather at some point the relationships perceived by the operator undergo a relatively sudden transformation. It was also shown that change in position during the course of practice might have a disruptive effect, especially if the change was abrupt rather than gradual.

It should be noted that all the above results were obtained in situations where the planes of movement of control and display did not coincide, so that the most compatible motion relationship was not possible. Humphries (1958) repeated his experiment using a joystick mounted horizontally, so that the planes did coincide, and found that changes in the operator's position now had no effect whatever. Arrangements of this kind therefore seem clearly preferable where the operator has any freedom of movement. However, these studies do little more than demonstrate that the effects of body position are important and complex. More systematic investigations are still required.

6. The Effect of the Hand Employed for Response

In most of the studies reviewed above, the operators appear to have been unselected for handedness, and to have been free to use whichever hand they preferred. While this procedure probably gives the most generally useful results, it leaves unanswered questions about possible differences between the preferred and the non-preferred hand, and between right-handed and left-handed operators.

It is necessary to raise such questions because the bilateral symmetry of the human body makes it conceivable that directional training given to one hand will facilitate symmetrical rather than corresponding movements of the other, and there is evidence which supports this hypothesis. It has long been known that people trained to write with one hand may spontaneously produce 'mirror-writing' with the other, and a careful study by Clark (1957) showed that this phenomenon was quite common among school-children. Simon (1948) has shown that, for both right-handed and left-handed subjects, the non-preferred hand is superior in mirror-drawing. Milisen and Van Riper (1939) trained subjects in tracing a clover-leaf pattern with the right hand, and found that while the effect of training was in part to produce a general improvement in technique, it was also in part directionally specific, and the specific training transferred to symmetrical movements of the left hand.

Effects of this kind are likely to influence direction-of-motion stereotypes in several ways. Firstly, something is likely to depend upon the handedness of the subject. If it is accepted that stereotypes derive largely from experience of natural phenomena or of cultural conventions, there is little reason to suppose that left-handed and right-handed subjects are not exposed to similar training. As far as the results of direct practice go, we should not therefore expect handedness to be a significant factor. Handedness is not, however, a unitary factor, and people who regard themselves as left-handed commonly use the right hand for some purposes (Clark, 1957); indeed, in a right-handed culture, they will frequently be forced to do so. It follows that conventional control-display associations may be weakened in left-handed operators to the extent that they have had experience of right-handed operation. Differences in the strength of stereotypes have certainly been found. Holding (1957a), for example, found that the tendency to turn clockwise-for-anything was less marked in left-handed subjects. Much however probably depends upon the amount and consistency of the training received by each hand, so that a strong stereotype may be little affected. Holding (1957b) found that the above effect was not present in an arrangement chosen for its well-established control-display association. Simon *et al.* (1952) found no effect of handedness on tracking skill using the strong clockwise-for-clockwise association. Grant and Kaestner (1955) and Hartmann, Jaynes and Herbert (1957) found no over-all differences in pursuit tracking between right-handed and left-handed subjects using a right-for-right association.

Similar considerations apply to the use of the non-preferred hand. Differences in performance between the preferred and the non-preferred hand vary considerably from one task to another, sometimes because of anatomical features, sometimes because of differential training (Provins, 1956). Here again, the effect of control-display factors are likely to depend both upon direct training and upon transfer from the other hand, and it is difficult to predict the outcome. Holding (1957a) found the clockwise-for-anything tendency on all the arrangements shown in Figure 7 which employed the right hand, but not on the two arrangements which required left-handed operation, where it seems possible that the effects of direct practice and of transfer may have cancelled out. The arrangements tested in this experiment, however, used controls and displays moving in different planes; where stronger stereotypes are involved there is no evidence of difference between the two hands (Simon *et al.*, 1952; Hartmann *et al.*, 1957).

On the present evidence, therefore, it would seem that as long as well-marked stereotypes are used, there is little risk in assigning controls to the left hand; though in view of the known effects of stress, it might be wise to assign critical controls to the right hand wherever possible.

There is perhaps a stronger case for a symmetrical arrangement when both hands are to be used simultaneously, but no evidence on this point seems to be available. It has however been shown that in a two-handed task the control-display linkage assigned to one hand may affect the directional preferences associated with the other. Mitchell (1949) found that when a forward-for-up linkage was provided for the left hand, a similar arrangement was best for the right, and that when the left-hand linkage was changed to backward-for-up, the right-hand linkage should be reversed also. However, the same left-hand changes had no effect upon performance with the right hand when its movement was lateral or vertical. It is perhaps not surprising to find that when the layouts for both hands are the same, the motion relationships should be consistent; but it would be unwise to extend this principle to the case in which both hands are moving laterally, or using rotary controls.

7. The Effect of Pointer Position

In the kind of situation which has been under discussion, the operator uses the control to bring about some required movement of an indicator from its initial position. There is some evidence to suggest that this initial position of the indicator influences the probability of a given control movement. An experiment by Bilodeau (1951) appears to show a continuous decrease in the preference for lever movement in the dominant direction, as the position of the indicator approaches the end of a linear display. Several features of Bilodeau's experiment were rather unusual, and Holding (1957b) investigated this problem more extensively and under more conventional conditions. He confirmed that the proportion of responses in the dominant direction was reduced towards the end of the scale (76 per cent at the ends compared with 90 per cent in the middle), but found that only the extreme positions were greatly affected. It is to be emphasized that this result was obtained in a situation where a strong stereotype exists; the effect might be more marked with a weaker stereotype.

Since in many applications the effect of an incorrect control movement is likely to be especially dangerous when the indicator shows an extreme reading, the importance of a strong stereotype is emphasized. It might also be wise to provide a scale some 10 per cent longer than the most extreme reading likely to be met with.

8. The Effect of Scale Numbering

Scale numbering introduces an additional directional element which may affect control-display relationships through the association of both display and control movements with an increase or decrease in the indicated function. On the display, the usually recommended convention is that scale numbers should increase from left to right, from bottom to top, or in a clockwise direction. In most cases similar movements of the control are expected to produce an increased reading.

It seems possible that the direction of scale numbering may affect the probability of the initial movement errors with which we have so far been concerned, but there appears to be no direct evidence bearing on this possibility. There is evidence, however, suggesting that this factor may influence the probability of terminal setting errors. A number of studies of scale reading have reported an increased incidence of errors in the right and bottom quadrants of circular dials. Long and Grether (1949) obtained verbal reports of the direction of change of pointer movements, and found a greater number of errors in these quadrants than in the left and top quadrants. In a preliminary study of quantitative reading, Kappauf, Smith and Bray (1947) considered that correct interpretation was more difficult in that part of a circular dial where the numbers increase from right to left. This suggestion was confirmed by a later investigation (Kappauf and Smith, 1950). In a general discussion of scale-reading habits, Kappauf (1951) quotes his own results and those of Christensen (1948) as showing that reversal errors (readings made in the wrong direction from a numbered graduation) may occur in any part of the scale, but more frequently when the scale direction opposes the left-to-right convention. Christensen (1948) has also shown an increase in reversal errors when scales are numbered in a counter-clockwise direction. It is thus fairly well established that violation of scale-numbering conventions, or conflict between them on the circular dial, leads to an increased probability of reversal errors. Where a control is used with the display, the same factors may be expected to produce terminal setting errors due to settings being made on the wrong side of a numbered graduation.

The only direct study of these problems is an investigation by Bradley (1954), who wished to determine the optimum control-display linkage for moving-scale instruments. He recognized that three conventions were involved:

 (i) a clockwise rotation of the control should result in clockwise rotation of the dial,
 (ii) the scale numbers should increase from left to right,
(iii) the control should then turn clockwise to increase settings.

The four possible forms of the moving-scale assembly are shown in Figure 13. It is clear that each violates at least one of the conventions. Bradley was therefore concerned to determine which convention was the least important. Subjects were required to make a series of settings on each of the four assemblies, and a record was made of the types of error which occurred; the subjects were also asked to rank the assemblies in order of preference. Assembly (d), which violates all three conventions, was the worst on any count. Assembly (c), which violates the first convention, was liable to produce initial movement errors. On assembly (b), which violates the second convention, operators tended to make reversal errors in their final setting. The best results were obtained with assembly (a), which appeared to produce no special type of error, and was also most frequently preferred. Although this assembly violates the third convention,

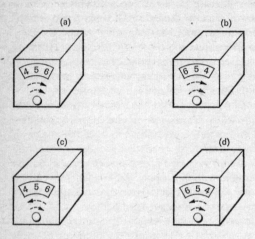

Figure 13 From Bradley (1954)

subjects immediately turned counterclockwise-to-increase even if they had been strongly indoctrinated with the principle of clockwise-to-increase. It was therefore recommended that this type of moving-scale assembly might safely be used, as long as the operator was not likely to make crucial control adjustments without looking at the display. It may be concluded that, with the same proviso, infringement of principle (iii) is of no importance; the relative importance of the other two principles depends upon the relative weight attached to initial movement errors and terminal setting errors.

In the absence of direct evidence, it seems reasonable to extend these principles to linear moving-scale instruments and to moving-pointer instruments. It may be noted that a circular moving-pointer instrument, even with the best arrangement, is liable to produce both types of error in the right and bottom quadrants. There are therefore grounds for preferring linear displays wherever possible.

The convention that controls should turn clockwise to increase has an important exception in the case of hydraulic valves. Bradley's results suggest that this is in itself of small importance; but since the associated pressure-gauge is normally a circular moving-pointer instrument whose scale increases clockwise, the control-display linkage violates the usual rule, and there is therefore a danger that attempts to reduce an undesirably high pressure may momentarily increase it still further.

Considerable ingenuity has been exercised on this problem. Murrell (1951), assuming that the correct control-display linkage in the bottom half of a circular dial was clockwise-for-right, recommended that the gauge should be arranged so that the normal working pressure lay in this region. However, subsequent research has shown that this assumption is not in general correct, and Murrell and McCarthy (1952), using a printed test, found the recommended solution ambiguous, even to experienced steam engineers. They felt that this was an argument against any use of circular dials with hydraulic controls, and investigated several assemblies with linear indicators. As far as initial movement errors are concerned, the best performance was obtained when the valve was placed below a horizontal scale numbered from right to left. Bradley's results indicate, however, that such an assembly would produce terminal setting errors. No moving-pointer instrument is likely to be entirely satisfactory. A better solution might be the use of the moving-scale assembly shown in Figure 13(a), which has both a correct control-display linkage and a correct direction of scale increase. The display might, however, prove unsuitable if it is also to be used for check-reading, since moving-scale instruments are not recommended for this task (Connell and Grether, 1948; Murrell, Murch, Suffield and Morley, 1952). Any proposed solution needs to be verified for the appropriate population.

9. Conclusion

It is satisfactory to have experimental confirmation of the long-held conviction that incompatible motion relationships have more than a transitory effect upon an operator faced with unfamiliar equipment. There seem now to be good grounds for believing that performance may still be affected after extensive experience, and that there is a particular danger of error under conditions of fatigue, stress or distraction.

In view of this demonstration of the practical importance of conforming to the operator's expectations, our current ability to predict these expectations is distinctly disappointing. A review of the literature shows some surprising gaps. Methodology has often been less than satisfactory, and has varied widely from one investigation to another. Few psychologists seem to have had the patience to conduct extensive surveys with a uniform technique. As a result, there is not only, as Fitts (1958) complains, a dearth of general theory in this area, but it is difficult even to formulate low-level generalizations with any confidence.

What does seem clear is that there is rather little hope of providing a few simple rules to guide the designer. Early attempts at such generalizations, which still seem to be in circulation, have proved vulnerable to increasing evidence of inconsistencies and ambiguities. As Welford (1961) hints, the factors which influence the operator shade from the 'natural' schemata of eye-hand co-ordination into more elaborate 'mental pictures' or 'models' (not necessarily consciously formulated) of the relationships between the moving parts of a machine. These models are likely to be based on familiarity with such devices as the lever, gear-wheel, the rack-and-pinion, and the screw-thread, and will be affected by such conventions as the use of right-hand threads. Difficulties may be expected when a piece of equipment does not readily evoke any familiar schema, or evokes more than one. The ambiguity which has been shown to reside in rotary components indicates that even in apparently simple situations the operator may be influenced by more than one set of habits. It also seems likely that his response may be disproportionately affected by rather slight differences in mechanical arrangement or layout: for example, the difference between a slightly curved or strictly linear path of movement.

It seems desirable, therefore, that designers should adhere wherever possible to those relationships whose dominance and lack of ambiguity have been most firmly established, and should endeavour to enhance the strength of these stereotypes by the appropriate design of components. Strong stereotypes are likely to be less vulnerable, not only to stress, but to changes of body position, use of the non-preferred hand, operation by left-handed subjects and end-of-scale effects. Direction of scale numbering is also to be taken into account.

However much thought is given to design, the apparent vulnerability of motion stereotypes to minor configural changes makes it desirable to consider performing a confirmatory check upon the actual design of any piece of equipment. Such a check, though it needs to be carefully done, need not be very onerous.

References

ADAMS, J. A. (1952), The influence of the time interval after interpolated activity on psychomotor performance, *USAF ATC Res. Bull.*, no. 52–11.

ANDREAS, B. G., GREEN, R. F., and SPRAGG, S. D. S. (1954), 'Transfer effects in following tracking (modified SAM two-hand coordination test) as a function of reversal of the display-control relationships on alternate blocks of trials', *J. Psychol.*, vol. 37, pp. 185–97.

ANDREAS, B. G., and WEISS, B. (1954), Review of research on perceptual-motor performance under varied display-control relationships, *University of Rochester Scientific Rep.*, no. 2.

BARTLETT, F. C. (1943), The task of the operator in machine work, *MRC APU Rep.*, no. 30.

BILODEAU, E. A. (1951), Modification of direction of movement preference with independent variation of two stimulus dimensions, *Human Resources Research Center Res. Bull.*, no. 51–12.

BRADLEY, J. V. (1954), Desirable control-display relationships for moving-scale instruments, *USAF WADC Tech. Rep.*, no. 54–423.

BRADLEY, J. V. (1959), 'Direction-of-knob-turn stereotypes', *J. appl. Psychol.*, vol. 43, pp. 21–4.

BROADBENT, D. E. (1958), *Perception and Communication*, Pergamon.

CARTER, L. F., and MURRAY, N. L. (1947), 'A study of the most effective relationships between selected control and indicator movements', in P. M. Fitts (ed.), *Psychological Research on Equipment Design*, U.S. Government Printing Office.

CASTANEDA, A., and LIPSITT, L. P. (1959), 'Relation of stress and differential position habits to performance in motor learning', *J. exp. Psychol.*, vol. 57, pp. 25–30.

CHRISTENSEN, J. M. (1948), The effect of the staircase scale on dial reading accuracy, *USAF AMC Memo. Rep.*, no. MCREXD-64-1-P.

CLARK, M. M. (1957), *Left-handedness*, University of London Press.

CONNELL, S. C., and GRETHER, W. F. (1948), Psychological factors in check-reading similar instruments, *USAF AMC Memo. Rep.*, no. MCREXD-694-17-A.

CROSSMAN, E. F. R. W. (1955), 'The information capacity of the human operator in symbolic and non-symbolic control processes', in J. Draper (ed.), *The Application of Information Theory to Human Operator Problems* (W. R. D. Report No. 2/56).

FITTS, P. M. (1951), 'Engineering psychology and equipment design', in S. S. Stevens (ed.), *Handbook of Experimental Psychology*, Wiley.

FITTS, P. M. (1958), 'Engineering psychology', *Ann. Rev. Psychol.*, vol. 9, pp. 267–94.

FITTS, P. M., and JONES, R. E. (1947), Analysis of factors contributing to 460 'pilot-error' experiences in operating aircraft controls, *USAF AMC Memo. Rep.*, no. TSEAA-694-12.

FITTS, P. M., and SEEGER, C. M. (1953), 'S–R compatibility: spatial characteristics of stimulus and response codes', *J. exp. Psychol.*, vol. 46, pp. 199–210.

FITTS, P. M., and SIMON, C. W. (1952), 'Some relations between stimulus patterns and performance in a continuous dual pursuit task', *J. exp. Psychol.*, vol. 43, pp. 428–38.

FITZWATER, J. T. (1948), A study of the effects of rest pauses in perceptual-motor learning involving compensatory pursuit. (Quoted in Fitts, 1951.)

GAGNÉ, R. M., and FOSTER, H. (1948), A study of transfer in a motor task with varying display-control relationships, *Special Devices Center, US Med. Res. Lab. Rep.*, no. 316-1-3.

GARDNER, J. F. (1950), Direction of pointer motion in relation to movement of flight-controls: cross-pointer type instrument, *USAF AMC Tech. Rep.*, no. 6016.

GARDNER, J. F. (1954), Speed and accuracy of response to five different attitude indicators, *USAF WADC Tech. Rep.*, no. 54-236.

GARDNER, J. F. (1957), The effect of motion relationship and rate of pointer movement on tracking performance, *USAF WADC Tech. Rep.*, no. 57-533.

GARDNER, J. F., and LACEY, R. J. (1954), An experimental comparison of five different attitude indicators, *USAF WADC Tech. Rep.*, no. 54-32.

GARVEY, W. D. (1957), The effects of 'task-induced stress' on man–machine system performance, *US NRL Rep.*, no. 5015.

GIBBS, C. B. (1949), Progress report on the first year's work, *MRC APU Rep.*, no. 113.

GIBBS, C. B. (1950), Factors in the initial learning and transfer of serial motor skills, *MRC APU Rep.*, no. 129.

GIBBS, C. B. (1951), 'Transfer of training and skill assumptions in tracking tasks', *Quart. J. exp. Psychol.*, vol. 3, pp. 99–110.

GRAHAM, N. E. (1952), 'Manual tracking on a horizontal scale and in the four quadrants of a circular scale', *Brit. J. Psychol.*, vol. 43, pp. 70–77.

GRANT, D. A., and KAESTNER, N. F. (1955), 'Constant velocity tracking as a function of S's handedness and the rate and direction of the target course', *J. exp. Psychol.*, vol. 49, pp. 203–8.

GRETHER, W. F. (1947), Direction of movement in relation to indicator movement in one-dimensional tracking, *USAF AMC Memo. Rep.*, no. TSEAA-8-4C.

HARLOW, H. F. (1951), 'Primate learning', in C. P. Stone (ed.), *Comparative Psychology*, Prentice Hall.

HARTMANN, B. O., JAYNES, W. E., and HERBERT, M. J. (1957), Analysis of abductive and adductive phases of movement in continuous tracking, *US Army Med. Res. Lab. Rep.*, no. 314.

HOLDING, D. H. (1955), Display-control relationships, *C.E.P.R.E. Tech. Memo.*, no. 31.

HOLDING, D. H. (1957a), 'Direction-of-motion relationships between controls and displays moving in different planes', *J. appl. Psychol.*, vol. 41, pp. 93–7.

HOLDING, D. H. (1957b), 'The effect of initial pointer position on display-control relationships', *Occup. Psychol.*, vol. 31, pp. 126–30.

HUMPHRIES, M. (1958), 'Performance as a function of control-display relations, positions of the operator, and locations of the control', *J. appl. Psychol.*, vol. 42, pp. 311–16.

HUMPHRIES, M., and SHEPHARD, A. H. (1955), 'Performance on several control-display arrangements as a function of age', *Canad. J. Psychol.*, vol. 9, pp. 231.

HUMPHRIES, M., and SHEPHARD, A. H. (1959), 'Age and training in the development of a perceptual-motor skill', *Percept. mot. Skills*, vol. 9, pp. 3–11.

KAPPAUF, W. E. (1951), A discussion of scale-reading habits, *USAF AMC Tech. Rep.*, no. 6569.

KAPPAUF, W. E., and SMITH, W. M. (1950), Design of instrument dials for maximum legibility: III. Some data on the difficulty of quantitative reading in different parts of a dial, *USAF AMC Tech. Rep.*, no. 5914.

KAPPAUF, W. E., SMITH, W. M., and BRAY, C. W. (1947), Design of instrument dials for maximum legibility: I. Development of methodology and some preliminary results, *USAF AMC Memo. Rep.*, no. TSEAA-694-1-L.

LONG, G. E., and GRETHER, W. F. (1949), Directional interpretation of dial, scale, and pointer movements, *USAF AMC Tech. Rep.*, no. 5910.

LOUCKS, R. B. (1949), An experimental study of the effectiveness with which novices can interpret a localizer-glidepath approach indicator, *USAF AMC Tech. Rep.*, no. 5959.

LOVELESS, N. E. (1956), 'Display-control relationships on circular and linear scales', *Brit. J. Psychol.*, vol. 47, 271–82.

LOVELESS, N. E. (1959a), Psychological factors in the design of display-control systems, *Unpublished thesis, University of Durham*.

LOVELESS, N. E. (1959b), 'The effect of the relative position of control and display upon their direction-of-motion relationship', *Ergonomics*, vol. 2, pp. 381–5.

MILISEN, R., and VAN RIPER, C. (1939), 'Differential transfer of training in a rotary activity', *J. exp. Psychol.*, vol. 2, pp. 640–6.

MITCHELL, M. J. H. (1947), Direction of movement of machine controls. III. A two-handed task in a discontinuous operation, *Min. of Supply Rep.*, no. SM 10018 (S).

MITCHELL, M. J. H. (1948), Direction of movement of machine controls. IV. Right or left-handed performances in a continuous task, *MRC APU Rep.*, no. 85.

MITCHELL, M. J. H. (1949), Direction of movement of machine controls. V. A two-handed performance in a continuous task, *MRC APU Rep.*, no. 110.

MITCHELL, M. J. H., and VINCE, M. A. (1951), 'The direction of movement of machine controls', *Quart. J. exp. Psychol.*, vol. 3, pp. 24–35.

MORIN, R. W., and GRANT, D. A. (1953), Spatial stimulus-response correspondence, *USAF WADC Tech. Rep.*, no. 53-292.

MORLEY, N. J., and SUFFIELD, N. G. (1951), The effect of pointer position on the speed and accuracy of check-reading groups of dials, *NMSU Rep.*, no. 46.

MURRELL, K. F. H. (1951), The design of dials and indicators, *NMSU Rep.*, no. 48.

MURRELL, K. F. H. (1961), 'Discussion', in *Proceedings of Conference on Ergonomics in Industry*, H.M.S.O.

MURRELL, K. F. H., and MCCARTHY, C. (1952), Direction of motion relationships between valves and gauges when mounted in panels, *NMSU Rep.*, no. 51.

MURRELL, K. F. H., MURCH, S. J., SUFFIELD, N. G., and MORLEY, N. J. (1952), A comparison of three dial shapes for check-reading instrument panels, *NMSU Rep.*, no. 40.

NORRIS, E. B., and SPRAGG, S. D. S. (1953), 'Performance on a following tracking task (modified SAM two-hand coordination test) as a function of the relations between direction of rotation of controls and direction of movement of display', *J. Psychol.*, vol. 35, pp. 119–29.

PROVINS, K. A. (1956), '"Handedness" and skill', *Quart. J. exp. Psychol.*, vol. 6, pp. 79–95.

ROSS, S., SHEPP, B. E., and ANDREWS, T. G. (1955), 'Response preferences in display-control relationships', *J. appl. Psychol.*, vol. 39, pp. 425–8.

SHEPHARD, A. H., and COOK, T. W. (1959), 'Body orientation and perceptual-motor performance', *Percept. mot. skills*, vol. 9, pp. 271–80.

SIMON, C. W. (1948), 'Proactive inhibition as an effect of handedness in mirror-drawing', *J. exp. Psychol.*, vol. 38, pp. 697–707.

SIMON, C. W. (1952a), 'The effect of age and experience on direction of movement stereotypes', *Amer. Psychol.*, vol. 7, p. 391.

SIMON, C. W. (1952b), Instrument-control configurations affecting performance in a compensatory pursuit task, *USAF WADC Tech. Rep.*, no. 6015.

SIMON, C. W. (1954a), The effects of stress on performance in a dominant and a non-dominant task, *USAF WADC Tech. Rep.*, no. 54-285.

SIMON, C. W. (1954b), The presence of a dual perceptual set for certain perceptual-motor tasks, *USAF WADC Tech. Rep.*, no. 54-286.

SIMON, C. W. (1958), Bibliography of control-display relationships. I. Direction of movement, *Hughes Aircraft Co. Rep.*, no. 4112.40/103.

SIMON, J. R., DE CROW, T. W., LINCOLN, R. S., and SMITH, K. U. (1952), 'Effects of handedness on tracking accuracy', *Percept. mot. Skills Res. Exch.*, vol. 4, pp. 53–57.

VINCE, M. A. (1945), Direction of movement of machine controls, *F.P.R.C. Rep.*, no. 637.

VINCE, M. A. (1950), Learning and retention of an 'unexpected' control-display relationship, *MRC APU Rep.*, no. 125.

VINCE, M. A., and MITCHELL, M. J. H. (1946), Direction of movement of machine controls. II, *Min. of Supply Rep.*, no. SM 2861 (S).

WARRICK, M. J. (1947), Direction of movement in the use of control knobs to position visual indicators, *USAF AMC Rep.*, no. 694-4C.

WARRICK, M. J. (1948), Direction of motion stereotypes in positioning a visual indicator by use of a control knob. II. Results from a printed test, *USAF AMC Rep.*, no. MCREXD-694-19A.

WARRICK, M. J. (1949), Effects of motion relationships on speed of positioning visual indicators by rotary control knobs, *USAF AMC Tech. Rep.*, no. 5812.

WARRICK, M. J., and GRETHER, W. F. (1948), The effect of pointer alignment on the check reading of engine instrument panels, *USAF AMC Memo. Rep.*, no. MCREXD-694-17.

WELFORD, A. T. (1961), 'Implications of psychological research', in *Proceedings of Conference on Ergonomics in Industry*, H.M.S.O.

WHITE, W. J. (1951), The effect of pointer design and pointer alignment position on the speed and accuracy of reading groups of simulated engine instruments, *USAF WADC Tech. Rep.*, no. 6014.

4 R. A. McFarland

Applications of Human Engineering to Highway Safety

Excerpt from R. A. McFarland, 'The role of human engineering in highway safety', in E. Bennett, J. Degan and J. Spiegel (eds.), *Human Factors in Technology*, McGraw-Hill, 1963, pp. 213–24.

The Scope of Human Engineering in Highway Safety

One of the primary objectives of human engineering is that of improving safety by designing equipment in terms of human capabilities and limitations. From the standpoint of human engineering, it is essential that the mechanical design of automotive equipment be compatible with the biological and psychological characteristics of the driver. The effectiveness of the automotive man–machine combination can be greatly enhanced by treating the operator and the automobile as a unified system. Thus, the instruments should be considered as extensions of the driver's nervous and perceptive systems, the controls as extensions of the hands and the feet as simple tools. In general, any control difficult to reach or operate, any instrument dial of poor legibility, any seat inducing poor posture or discomfort, or any unnecessary obstruction to vision may contribute directly to an accident (5).

When the vehicle driver is viewed as one component of a man–machine system, the general human characteristics pertinent to design are: (a) physical dimensions; (b) capability for data sensing; (c) capability for data processing; (d) capability for motor activity; (e) capability for learning; (f) physical and psychological needs; (g) sensitivities to the physical environment; (h) sensitivities to the social environment; (i) capability for coordinated action; (j) differences among individuals (16). Quantitative information about these human characteristics must be coordinated with the data on vehicle characteristics if maximum man–machine integration is to be achieved.

Unfortunately, much of the biological and psychological information needed for this purpose is not yet available, although pertinent human factors research is currently being carried out by many organizations. One of the most significant developments consists of the technological advances that have been made in electronics, especially in regard to high-speed monitoring, recording and computing procedures, which make possible the effective and quantitative study of the human component in relation to the other components of the system and to the output of the total system. The application of digital and analog computers in simulating the performance of aircraft and submarines is one example of the progress made in this area. These techniques may soon be available for the study of the driver–vehicle–roadway system.

In any such approach the driver would be considered a unique servomechanism in the man–machine system that alters the performance output of the system in accordance with the continuous sensory and perceptual input derived from the vehicle's responses, the environment and the driver's judgements. The functioning of the nonhuman components of the system can be expressed in precise mathematical terms, but it would be difficult to include the human operator in these formulations. Except for a small number of activities, the human operator behaves in a nonlinear fashion, i.e. his output does not necessarily equal the sum of his inputs. The important point for this discussion, however, is that with the new electronic techniques the performance of the vehicle and the environmental factors relevant to driving could be simulated and operator performance could be closely monitored and objectively measured. This procedure would provide the basis for a precise quantitative study of the human problems in highway transportation.

The initial phase of the application of human engineering to highway safety should be an analysis, in advance of manufacture, of all design aspects involving human behavior, or an operational job analysis. This concept of design is relatively new and unexplored in the automotive field, partly because accident reports generally have failed to identify difficulties in man–machine integration as accident causes. Design failures may be so subtle that those responsible for reporting accidents may not be aware of them, particularly if the personnel are not trained in human engineering. However, if defects are present, it is only a matter of time before some driver 'fails' and has an accident (5). The following is an outline of the chief considerations in the advance analysis of equipment for design faults (4):

1. Operational job analysis
   a. Requirements of driving
   b. Driver's area in the vehicle
   c. Characteristics of instruments, displays and controls
2. Blueprint phase
   a. Prediction of performance
   b. Human limitations
   c. Anticipation of errors
3. Mock-up stage
   a. Performance of duties
   b. Physical size of drivers
   c. Skill requirements
   d. Age considerations
   e. Interfering structures
   f. Physiological stress
   g. Errors or near accidents

There are many examples of ways in which automotive engineers have already improved safety by designing equipment to compensate for human limitations. These include improved braking and steering systems, lighting, tires and automatic shifting. However, carefully controlled mock-up studies for testing the nature and range of human abilities might aid in making the most of these advances. How fast should the brakes operate in relation to the age, sex, size and strength of the driver? How much feedback should be provided by the power-steering system? How should the automatic shifting device be designed for greater standardization and ease of operation? If the biological scientist were present during the mock-up stages, he might well be able to advise the engineer about the range of abilities of the driving population (4).

The specific features of vehicle design that deserve the attention of the human engineer are: (a) the layout of the workspace, including spatial accommodation and seating; (b) the design and arrangement of controls; (c) the design and arrangement of displays; (d) the design of window areas for maximum vision from the vehicle; (e) the design of the vehicle to provide maximum occupant protection during an accident; (f) the control of those aspects of the physical environment which influence the driver; (g) the prediction of error and the provision of margins of safety.

A series of human engineering evaluations of this sort has been carried out on commercial vehicles (14) and, more recently, on twenty domestic and twenty-two foreign passenger cars (9). Some of the findings of these studies are presented in the following discussions of specific applications of human engineering to vehicle design.

The Layout of the Workspace

In order to ensure the proper layout of the workspace, the dimensions of both the operator and the vehicle (Figure 1 and 2) must be known. The body dimensions necessary for establishing the dimensions of the workspace and for locating the controls

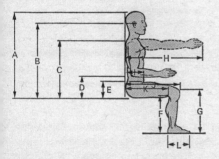

Figure 1 Human body measurements relevant to vehicle design. (See also Table 2 and ref. 12)

are: (a) the maximum arm reaches attainable without alteration of body position; (b) the extension of these reaches which can be attained by movement of the trunk or body; (c) the eye level of the man in the operating position; (d) the body dimensions in the operating position, i.e. sitting heights and fore-and-aft and lateral measurements at various levels; (e) the leg reaches attainable without alteration of posture (3).

Whereas a great deal of human-sizing data has been obtained for pilots in connexion with cockpit design, little specific information is available for motor-vehicle drivers. In surveys conducted by the Harvard School of Public Health, measurements of thirty-two body dimensions were made on a representative sample of approximately 360 bus and truck drivers in all parts

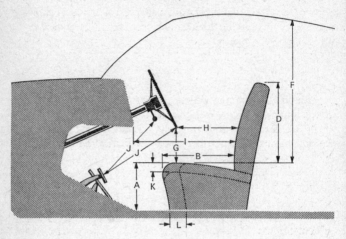

Figure 2 Some vehicle dimensions related to human body measurements. (12)

of the country, including 100 champion truck drivers competing in a National Roadeo of driving skill. These data were supplemented by measurements taken on a large sample of military drivers. However, suitable comparable data on the general driving population for the design of passenger vehicles are still unavailable, although approximations of the body measurements of this group have been interpolated from selected anthropometric studies of various segments of the United States population. Admittedly, direct measurements of the driving population are preferable; however, the tentative values presented in Table 1 should indicate the true measurements closely enough so that they may be used as interim values with some confidence. Many of the needed body measurements are currently being taken by the National Health Survey of the U.S. Public Health Service on a statistically representative sample of the entire United States population, and these data should be available within the next

Table 1

Approximations of Body Measurements Related to Vehicle Design for the General Driving Population

Body measurements, inches	Male Drivers percentiles			Female Drivers percentiles		
	5th	50th	95th	5th	50th	95th
Stature	64·1	68·4	72·6	59·5	63·4	67·3
Weight, lb	131	166	216	105	136	190
A.*Sitting height	33·8	36·0	38·2	31·6	33·7	35·6
B. Eye height	29·3	31·6	33·7	27·2	29·3	31·1
C. Shoulder height	21·4	23·3	25·2	19·3	21·1	22·9
D. Elbow height	7·7	9·3	10·9	8·2	9·4	10·9
E. Thigh height	4·8	5·7	6·8	4·9	5·8	6·7
F. Popliteal height	15·5	16·9	18·1	13·9	15·2	16·2
G. Knee height	19·8	21·6	23·5	17·9	19·5	20·8
H. Anterior arm reach	32·0	34·9	37·5	28·5	30·9	33·4
I. Abdomen depth	8·4	10·1	12·4	7·9	9·0	11·1
J. Buttock-knee length	21·6	23·5	25·5	20·7	22·4	24·0
K. Buttock-popliteal length	17·4	18·9	20·8	16·8	18·2	20·0
L. Foot length	9·6	10·4	11·3	8·8	9·6	10·2
M. Shoulder breadth	16·4	17·7	19·4	14·3	15·6	17·5
N. Elbow breadth	15·0	17·4	20·6	13·4	15·0	16·8
O. Seat breadth	13·0	14·4	16·2	13·6	15·1	17·2
P. Foot breadth	3·6	3·9	4·3	3·3	3·6	3·9

* Letters refer to the dimensions shown in Figure 1.

year or two. In the meantime, on the basis of existing anthropometric data it has been possible to specify dimensions for certain distances within the driver's workspace to accommodate the middle 90 per cent of the drivers with respect to body size (8, 12).

Table 2 gives examples of percentile distributions for three body measurements known to be useful in the design of the driver's workspace. It should be noted that these data are not presented in terms of averages: the use of average values may account for many defects in vehicle design, since arrangements for the person of 'average size' might be suitable for only 50 per

Table 2

Percentile Distributions of Three Selected Body Measurements of Commercial Truck and Bus Drivers

Percentile	Sitting height	Knee height	Anterior arm reach
5	34·3	20·1	33·0
10	34·8	20·4	33·5
15	35·1	20·6	33·9
20	35·3	20·8	34·3
25	35·5	21·0	34·7
30	35·7	21·2	34·9
35	35·9	21·3	35·1
40	36·0	21·4	35·3
45	36·2	21·6	35·5
50	36·3	21·7	35·8
55	36·5	21·8	35·9
60	36·7	21·9	33·1
65	36·8	22·1	36·4
70	36·9	22·2	36·6
75	37·1	22·2	36·9
80	37·3	22·4	37·1
85	37·6	22·6	37·4
90	37·8	22·8	37·9
95	38·2	23·5	38·4
	$N = 310$	$N = 301$	$N = 312$
	Range	Range	Range
	= 33·1–39·0	= 19·3–26·0	= 30·7–41·7

cent of the operators in a normally distributed group. Provision for 90 or 95 per cent, or any other predetermined proportion, of potential operators requires identification of the correct cut-off points. When arm reach for the operation of controls is under consideration, the cut-off point should be well below the average reach.

In several of the commercial vehicles evaluated, for example, only 5 per cent of the drivers could comfortably reach and operate the hand brake. In other vehicles, only 60 per cent of the drivers could be accommodated for knee height between the pedals and the steering wheel. Many tall drivers were unable to adjust their sitting positions to obtain maximum visibility in relation to their instruments and the road ahead (14).

Failure to provide for adequate seat adjustment to allow for variations in human size was frequently reported by the drivers and was evident from the objective studies of work areas. Probably the most striking defect was that the front of the seat could not be lowered to enable shorter individuals to operate the pedals without excessive pressure under the knees. Some of the medical problems frequently observed in truck drivers are believed to be related to poor seat design and to failure to provide adequate shock absorbers (11).

Integrating anthropometric data with the static dimensions of the cab is not always easy, however, since most body measurements are made under static conditions and driving is a dynamic situation. As a result, static data cannot always be applied without additional study using mock-ups and subjects representing known points in the distribution of body measurements. For example, when one truck model was evaluated, it was discovered that the taller drivers could not operate the foot brake when the gear lever was in either of the two left positions. It was impossible for a larger driver to put his foot on the brake pedal without first shifting gears. The distance between the brake pedal and the bottom of the steering wheel was too short to permit the leg to move high enough to put the foot on the pedal, and the gearshift in either of the left positions was too close to the wheel to allow the leg to slip between. As a result, the foot was trapped on the floor until the driver shifted gears (14). This defect should have been eliminated in the preproduction stages of the vehicle

The principle that static dimensions require supplementary techniques involving the dynamic setting of the driver at his task was applied in an additional experiment in which the objective was that of determining the ranges of adjustability in seating and controls for optimal accommodations for individual operators. Subjects representing the 5th, 50th and 95th percentiles of drivers 'drove' an adjustable mock-up in a simulated driving task. The interrelations between the various items in the cab were determined by statistical analysis, and recommendations were made for their location and ranges of adjustability. A significant finding of the experiment was that fewer errors were made in the driving task when the settings in the apparatus were those at which the driver was most comfortable (2).

The Design of Controls

If controls were so designed and located that they could be operated easily, accurately and rapidly, many driver errors leading to highway accidents could be prevented. For example, one serious accident resulted when a driver, while proceeding at high speed in a modern car, shut off his headlights in the belief that he was operating the cigarette lighter. The knobs for these two controls were identical in shape and size and were located near each other on the dashboard. In two truck models the dimmer switch was located directly beneath the foot pedals and close to the steering post. It is likely, therefore, that the driver might operate other switches or equipment while attempting to dim the head lamps. Even when he operates correctly, complex motions and long movement times are required for avoiding the pedals. Adequate shape coding for the accurate identification of knobs and switches by touch and increased standardization in their location would probably aid in the reduction of accidents caused by the inadvertent operation of wrong controls.

The brake and accelerator pedals also require study and improvement. In some vehicles these pedals are so placed that the driver must make lengthy movements in three directions before the brake can be activated, i.e. up, over and down. Sometimes the two pedals are of identical design and material, and therefore it is impossible for the driver to distinguish the pedals by touch alone. Undoubtedly this defect has been responsible for many critical situations, especially with drivers new to the vehicle, and has probably caused a number of accidents.

During the operation of pedals, various muscle groups may become acutely fatigued from holding a steady position. The lower right leg and foot, for example, may react slowly in emergency situations after maintaining continuous pressure against the accelerator pedal. In some situations, as on runs in mountainous country, continuous turning and shifting are required. Mechanized or hydraulic aids to steering will continue to reduce the possibility of errors during such maneuvers.

The more important considerations in the design of controls may be summarized as follows: (a) location of controls for ease, and accuracy of reaching; (b) direction of movement for greatest efficiency; (c) amount of force that must be applied; (d) rate of movement from point to point; (e) speed and amount of rotary or wrist movement required in wheels or knobs; (f) size and shape; (g) frequency of use; (h) the degree to which the control performs a critical function. A considerable amount of data on these factors is currently available and may be applied to problems of automotive design (6, 7).

The Design of Instruments

A driver can successfully control his vehicle only to the extent that he receives unambiguous information on all pertinent aspects of his task. Sometimes accidents, or operational errors, occur because a driver misinterpreted, or was unable to obtain, information from his displays concerning the functioning of the equipment. The three basic types of indicators supplying the driver with information are: (a) the check display, which indicates whether or not a given condition exists, e.g. a red light to show failure, danger or faulty operation; (b) the quantitative display, which indicates an exact numerical value to be read, e.g. a speedometer or clock; (c) the qualitative display, which indicates whether, and in what direction, an operation has deviated from a desired level, without presenting precise quantitative data, e.g. a temperature gauge (1). Many quantitative displays could profitably be changed to the qualitative type of indicator. Whenever possible, instruments should have the least complex type of display consistent with the degree of precision required.

For best possible efficiency, all instruments should possess the following characteristics: (a) can be read quickly; (b) can be read as accurately as is required – and preferably no more accurately; (c) presents no ambiguity or likelihood of gross reading errors;

(d) the information is provided in the most immediately useful form and does not require mental translation into other units; (e) changes in value are easily detected; (f) can be easily identified and distinguished from other instruments; (g) the information is as current as possible; (h) if inoperative, either cannot be read or the operator is properly warned (15). The specific factors that influence the ease, speed and accuracy with which instruments can be read include location with reference to the operator, the size, shape and spacing of the critical detail, and the brightness and contrast of the display. Design specifications for most of these factors have been determined experimentally (1).

The Design of Window Areas

The design of windshields, side windows and rear-vision mirrors is an important area for human engineering research. There has been developed an instrument that precisely delineates the area outside the vehicle that is seen by the driver and thus permits accurate evaluations of the relative efficiency of various configurations of windshields, windows and supporting structures (18).

One important problem is that of evaluating tinted windshields, which have been widely accepted in the United States. There are certain advantages in reducing the glare from bright sunlight and aiding in the control of temperature within the car. However, since the National Safety Council reports that accident rates are three times higher at night than in the daytime, this design feature deserves careful consideration. In the evaluation of tinted windshields the age of the driver is an extremely important factor, since it has been established that with increasing age there is a decrease in the retina's sensitivity to light under low levels of illumination. If during night driving this decrease in light sensitivity is combined with the reduced transmission of light through tinted glass, a serious safety problem may arise. (Ordinary safety glass absorbs 12 per cent of the light, whereas tinted glass absorbs 28 per cent.)

Studies have indicated that at any age the effect of the tinted glass at night is a reduction in the visibility of lights and other objects near the threshold of perception. Figure 3 illustrates these findings. The first portion of the curves shows the course of the sensitivity threshold for groups of subjects in the age range sixteen to eighty-nine years during 40 min of dark adaptation. The slight rise in the thresholds at 41 min resulted from the introduction of clear windshield glass; the substantial rise at 46 min

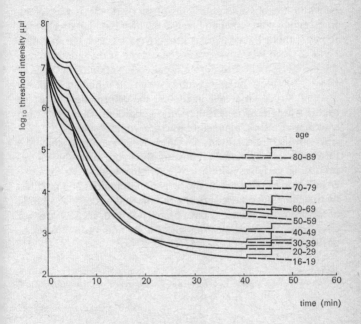

Figure 3 Dark adaptation as a function of age and tinted windshield glass. Age range = 16–89; N = 240. (10)

followed the viewing of the test lights through tinted windshield glass (10). In these experiments, age was shown to be highly correlated with dark-adaptation thresholds at time intervals of 2 to 40 min. The correlations ranged from 0·71 at the second minute to 0·84 at the 40th minute. They are among the highest correlations reported between age and biological function (13).

Crash-Injury Protection

Research by De Haven, Stapp, Ryan and others on the ability of the human body to withstand sudden deceleration and impact forces has indicated that the force of many fatal accidents may be within the physiological limits of survival (17). It was found, for example, that a human being can withstand high decelerative forces without injury if he is properly restrained. On the other hand, a speed of 15 m.p.h. can cause death if the momentum of the head is not checked during rapid deceleration of the vehicle. If a 10-lb object, the approximate weight of a human skull, fell 1 ft and struck an area 1 in square, the deformation would be slight, whereas, if under the same conditions an object 1 cm square were struck, a puncture fracture would result.

Controlled research in this area is defining not only the tolerances of the human body to force but also the injury-producing variables within a decelerating vehicle. Automotive engineers can contribute to the reduction of injuries and fatalities by designing the vehicle according to the findings of such studies. Some protective measures have been developed, such as stronger door locks, recessed steering-wheel hubs and various types of dashboard padding.

References

1. C. A. BAKER and W. F. GRETHER, Visual presentation of information, *USAF WADC Tech. Rep.*, no. 54-160, 1954.
2. N. C. KEPHART and J. W. DUNLAP, *Human Factors in the Design of Vehicle Cab Area*, Occupational Research Center, Purdue University, 1955.
3. B. G. KING, 'Measurements of man for making machinery', *Amer. J. phys. Anthrop.*, vol. 6 (1948), pp. 341–51.
4. R. A. MCFARLAND, 'Human engineering and automobile safety', *Clin. Orthopaed.*, vol. 9 (1957), pp. 260–76.
5. R. A. MCFARLAND, 'Human engineering, a new approach to driver efficiency and transport safety', *Trans. SAE*, vol. 62 (1954), pp. 335–45.
6. R. A. MCFARLAND, *Human Factors in Air Transport Design*, McGraw-Hill, 1946.
7. R. A. MCFARLAND, *Human Factors in Air Transportation – Occupational Health and Safety*, McGraw-Hill, 1953.
8. R. A. MCFARLAND, A. DAMON and H. W. STOUDT, 'Anthropometry in the design of the driver's workspace', *Am. J. phys. Anthropol.*, vol. 16 (1958), pp. 1–24.

9. R. A. McFarland and R. G. Domey, 'Biotechnical aspects of driver safety and comfort', *Trans. SAE*, vol. 66 (1958), pp. 630–48.

10. R. A. McFarland and R. G. Domey, 'Experimental studies of night vision as a function of age and changes in illumination', *Highway Research Board Bull.*, vol. 191 (1958), pp. 17–32.

11. R. A. McFarland and A. L. Moseley, *Human Factors in Highway Transport Safety*, Harvard School of Public Health, Boston, 1954.

12. R. A. McFarland and H. W. Stoudt, Human body size and passenger vehicle design, *SAE spec. Publ.*, no. 142A, 1961.

13. R. A. McFarland et al., 'Dark adaptation as a function of age: I. A statistical analysis', *J. Gerontol.*, vol. 15 (1960), pp. 149–54.

14. R. A. McFarland et al., *Human Factors in the Design of Highway Transport Equipment*, Harvard School of Public Health, Boston, 1953.

15. V. L. Senders and J. Cohen, The influence of methodology on research on instrument displays, *USAF WADC Tech. Rep.*, no. 53–93, 1953.

16. H. W. Sinaiko and E. P. Buckley, Human factors in the design of systems, *Naval Research Lab. Rep.*, no. 4996, 1957.

17. *Summary Report of Automotive Crash Inquiry Injury Research at Cornell University*, Commission on Accidental Trauma, Armed Forces Epidemiological Board, Washington, 1961.

18. P. J. Sutro, H. O. Ward and C. A. Townsend, *Human Visual Capacities as a Basis for the Safer Design of Vehicles*, Commission on Accidental Trauma, Armed Forces Epidemiological Board, Washington, 1958.

Part Two **Maintenance**

Keeping equipment in service is in many ways as important as designing it efficiently. With the rising complexity of machinery the demands upon maintenance grow disproportionately, so the part played by maintenance and fault-finding skills can only increase as the automation of industrial plant proceeds. Psychological research on these skills may take the form of analysing people's behaviour in fault-finding situations, or of attempting to discover optimal procedures and train people in their use.

Reading 5 by Dale, which incidentally contains many useful references to unpublished technical reports, deals with both of these problems in the context of identifying electronic faults. Stolurow, Bergum, Hodgson and Silva (Reading 6) suggest a modification to the dominant 'half-split' strategy of fault-finding, introducing the factor of cost, and provide some statistical support from records of aircraft engine maintenance.

5 H. C. A. Dale

Fault-Finding in Electronic Equipment

Excerpts from H. C. A. Dale, 'Fault-finding in electronic equipment', *Ergonomics*, vol. 1 (1958), pp. 356–85.

The problem of training men to locate faults quickly and correctly has only recently been recognized. In the past it was thought that the acquisition of knowledge of electronic theory was a sufficient preparation for the job. But observation shows that in general men trained in this way do not search for faults in the best possible ways; they frequently make serious errors of strategy. The use of laboratory tasks (in which the secondary difficulties associated with the real job through poor human engineering and a lack of suitable data books and diagrams are eliminated) shows that men do not search efficiently. Their behaviour is influenced to a considerable extent by irrelevant factors; it changes if tasks are presented in different ways; and in a given task irrelevant features of the display affect their procedure.

The appropriateness of a man's strategy appears to be positively correlated with his intelligence. This suggests that if the intelligence level of men recruited for fault-finding training is reduced, then not only will they experience more difficulty in assimilating electronic theory but when they come to the actual job they will use less effective strategies in their fault-finding. The problem of training them to use better strategies is discussed.

Experiments by the author are described and set in relation to previous work.

1. Introduction

The key to the effective maintenance of most present-day electronic equipment lies in the rapidity with which faults are located once they have occurred. This is also true to some extent of mechanical, pneumatic, hydraulic and other kinds of equipment. Although it is possible to design self-monitoring devices the task of fault-finding is likely to be of importance for some time to come, if not for always. Self-monitoring devices are expensive and, in any case, the fault-finder is needed whenever the monitor itself becomes faulty.

Observations of fault-finders at work on electronic equipment made by Crowder (1954), Dale (1958a), and Saltz and Moore (1953) have revealed a low standard of proficiency. Crowder, whose study is probably the most adequate, comments the most strongly: 'The mechanics appeared to work to a great extent by trial and error . . . they made a sufficient confirmatory check before replacing a subunit in only 203 of 600 problems where such a check was possible and necessary' (see p. 28). If, by coming to understand the behaviour of fault-finders, we can reduce this lack of proficiency, research will be well worth while. Attempts to gain an understanding of this behaviour are reported in this paper, but before they are described a brief account of the task of fault-finding is given.

The writer has drawn to a considerable extent upon the review by Standlee *et al.* (1956) in which synopses of 108 papers are given. It is recommended as a source.

2. The Nature of the Task

Rulon and Schweiker (1956) have pointed out that fault-finding, or trouble-shooting to give it its American name, has long been considered an art. A U.S. Navy training manual (Anon, 1952) confirms this view: 'Trouble-shooting ability is a sort of "sixth sense" that you develop with experience' (p. 192). No single recognized way of setting about the task exists. Indeed, the fact that it is regarded by some workers as problem solving (Gagné, 1954; Ray, 1955) is implicit recognition that the individual finds his own way and does not directly apply previously learned rules. But this is not always the case. Bryan *et al.* (1956) prefer a broad definition of the task to include

. . . any activity which is directed expressly to the correction of certain classes of malfunctions. A problem exists when a goal is recognized but the meaning or route to the goal is not immediately clear . . . all trouble-shooting is not problem solving, since for many trouble shooters the path to the goal is quite clear-cut and routinized. Nevertheless a considerable overlap exists . . . in so far as a trouble-shooting attempt contains exploration of the situation to determine the crucial elements, alternative approaches, and the relationships between them, then it involves the type of behavior usually called problem solving (p. 121).

The task encountered by a man then will depend upon the way he sets out to do the job rather than upon the job itself. Miller (1953) has, on these lines, offered two descriptions and the writer has said elsewhere (Dale, 1958c) that the task can be reduced to a simple routine (although this course is not to be recommended).

Although we cannot define the task strictly it is possible to describe the demands of the job, at least in broad terms. It is essentially a form of searching. An equipment will usually contain many parts, perhaps hundreds or thousands, and a failure which leads to its breakdown is commonly caused by a failure of just one of these. The job is to locate it as rapidly as possible. At this point the most efficient ways of searching will be described but these are ideal in a logical rather than a psychological sense. (This point will be brought up again later.)

It is best in a search of this kind to begin by asking general questions if this is possible. Questions about particular parts of an equipment will on the whole yield little information early in the search, for the same reason that it is unwise to ask in the game of '20 Questions', knowing only that the 'thing' is mineral, 'Is it the brass door knocker at No. 10 Downing Street?' This point has been made by Broadbent (1955) and by Miller et al. (1953a). Whether or not it is possible to ask general questions at all depends upon the nature of the system to which the parts belong and the nature of the tests which it is possible to make. If the parts can only be examined one by one, either by virtue of their independence or the nature of the available test-gear, then clearly no general questions can be asked. But where they belong to groups and the over-all performance of these groups can be measured then it is indeed possible to ask general questions.

The over-all function of an electronic equipment is to transform a signal in some way. A simple commercial radio set transforms a signal in the form of weak electromagnetic waves into the form of powerful electrical waves which will drive a loudspeaker. This is not done in one step. Within the radio there are a number of functional units called stages. Each of these will by itself effect only a small change in the form of the signal. The over-all result is achieved through a succession of small changes and the structure of the simple radio reflects this; it consists basically of a single chain of stages. In more complex equipments the flow system will be more involved; there may be several signals; some generated within the equipment, which may be mixed together and separated again at another point; there may even be loops, the signal being tapped off at one point, modified and then fed back into an earlier part of the chain. But in all these cases stages are used as functional units which modify the signal sequentially.

In isolating a faulty stage the fault-finder can test chains of stages by checking that they function correctly as a whole. If when an appropriate signal is fed into one end of a chain it appears correctly transformed at the other end, then all the parts within the chain must be functioning correctly. It is by making this kind of functional test that the fault-finder can ask general questions.

When the faulty stage has been found it is necessary to search within this stage for the part which has failed. Although the parts within a stage are functionally related they cannot be examined in groups in the way that the stage can be tested, and the location of a faulty part is generally a matter of testing each part and each connexion in turn. Searching for a faulty stage can be described as searching in a structured system, for it is by using knowledge of the structure of the system that a faulty stage can be most rapidly located. Searching for a faulty part within a stage can be described by contradistinction as searching in an unstructured system.

The best way of searching for a fault in a structured system containing units (or stages) which are equally likely to be at fault, is to ask questions which each reduce the number of possibilities by a half (see Miller *et al.*, 1953a). If some units are more likely to be faulty than others the question should be such that it divides the possibilities into two equi-probable groups and determines which of these is faulty. But probability is not the only extra factor which should ideally be taken into account. Some tests may be made more easily than others and, if the time taken to locate a fault is to be used as a criterion of efficiency, it might be better to make a rapid test which divides the probabilities unequally rather than to make a lengthy test which is otherwise ideal. Thus effort is a third variable. Hoehn and Saltz (1956) have discussed this matter in more detail, as have Stolurow *et al.* (1955).

From this it can be seen that the choice of an ideal test is a complex matter. The main point, however, is that the search should proceed from the general to the particular. Gross divergencies from this rule, such as those quoted above from Crowder, lead to considerable waste of effort, but a failure to choose ideal tests on the basis of structure, probability and effort, is not generally serious. When the units are treated separately, as are the parts within a stage, the basic requirement is that the search should be systematic. If the units are equally likely to be at fault, then any one order is as good as any other; the only possible cause of inefficiency is that the results of some tests might be forgotten and then have to be repeated. If some parts are more likely to be faulty than the rest or are easier to test, then it is clearly best to examine these first.

The presence of a fault in an equipment is indicated by some change in its over-all function. By careful examination of this change it is sometimes possible to determine which region is faulty. This is especially clear when the equipment has multiple functions such as the domestic television receiver which reproduces both sound and vision. If the sound is faulty while the vision is normal then the fault must be in the chain which leads to the loudspeaker rather than that which leads to the tube. Diagnosis from the change in over-all characteristics in this way can proceed just as the process already described. It is commonly the best first step in fault location since the effort involved in checking performance is usually small and because it provides a means of examining the most general questions. Sometimes the fault can be localized to a very considerable extent by using very fully the information present in the symptoms, so that in some cases it is possible to go straight from symptom to the faulty stage or even the faulty part. To sum up: logically efficient fault-finding proceeds through three phases, an initial deduction based upon the change in an equipment's over-all functional characteristics; a search for the faulty stage, in which use is made of the signal flow path; and finally a search within the faulty stage for the faulty part.

Instead of searching in the way described above it is possible to attempt the job of fault-finding by learning symptom–cause associations by rote. This approach to the job has formed the basis of research by Stolurow *et al.* (1955) into determining the best way to teach these associations. When an equipment is of any size, however, it is clearly pointless to attempt seriously to learn all possible symptom–fault associations.

This criticism, based as it is upon psychological grounds, brings us back to the fact that the logically ideal methods of fault-finding may differ from what are psychologically ideal. This is an empirical matter which has yet to be investigated. The task of fault-finding, i.e. the best method from the engineer's point of view, cannot, therefore, be defined, but one thing is clear and that is that it is some form of searching.

Sources of difficulty

The choice of the best strategy of searching presents the essential difficulty of the task. But apart from this it is found that there are also secondary difficulties. It has been assumed so far that all-or-none tests (which indicate presence or absence of a correct signal) can be made to check signal flow in an equipment, but this is not always the case. Sometimes, when the effect of a fault is to distort the signal, it is possible to measure a number of parameters of the signal, some of which give more sensitive indications of its state than others. At present the onus is upon the engineer to learn by rote the best testing techniques. Handbooks are prepared for equipments but the data are commonly in such a form that it cannot be found quickly unless the handbook has previously been studied extensively. In a complex equipment where it is virtually impossible for the engineer to learn all the best techniques by rote this is a serious matter. Lack of adequate data manuals were given specific mention by both Dale (1958a) and Saltz and Moore (1953). Another difficulty is that diagrams often are not as clear as they might be; they sometimes even fail to show test-points (see Dale, 1958a). [Rulon and Schweiker (1956) have also noted the need for adequate diagrams.] Test-gear is often poorly designed. Bryan *et al.* (1956, p. 171) noted in some field observations: 'Almost every performance contains minor errors of test instrument usage.' Since this was found in the activity of experienced men it is a reflection upon the test-gear rather than those using it.

These secondary difficulties are very real and important; they certainly deserve urgent attention but they will not be further discussed in the present paper which is concerned rather with the essential difficulties of fault-finding. Recommendations for reducing these secondary difficulties are to be found in Miller and Folley (1951), Miller *et al.* (1954), Shackel (1957) and Spector *et al.* (1955). The development of special diagrams (diagnostigrams) is reported by Ellis (1958).

3. Basic Questions and Method

In order to discover how to train efficient fault-finders answers must be found to three fundamental questions. (1) What should the men do; (2) What do they do without any special training; (3) How best can they be trained?

As the above discussion has shown, no definite answer to the first question can yet be given. The men would be most effective if they were to use the logically ideal methods of searching. There is no reason to suppose that these methods impose any great strain upon the searcher's abilities and in the absence of evidence it seems reasonable to accept the method described above as being the best way of doing the job. It was pointed out then that where differences of probability and effort complicate the issue it would be difficult to compute the ideal choice of a checkpoint. But efficiency is not noticeably impaired if the choice is slightly imperfect, so perfection does not matter a great deal. Provisionally it can be said that men should approximate to what is logically the ideal strategy.

An alternative answer to this first question has been offered elsewhere; this is that all men should do what the best of them do already. The study by Warren *et al.* (1955) and the subsequent proposals made in it, are based upon this approach. There are serious disadvantages to this way of tackling the problem. For one thing, there is no guarantee that the best men, in the sense of the most successful or useful men in the eyes of their superiors, have found the best methods. They might do better still with other, untried, techniques. The method advocated by Warren *et al.*, although sufficient, is certainly not very efficient. Then there is the other possibility that these men have evolved methods which best suit themselves but which would not suit others.

The experiments to be reported are concerned with the second fundamental question: 'How do persons search without special training?' Laboratory tasks which are analogous to the searching tasks encountered in fault-finding, have been devised in order to study the strategies subjects adopt under different conditions. This technique can be used to study the behaviour of trained fault-finders working in controlled conditions and to relate their performance to their ability on the job but this has not yet been done.

Compared with on-the-job studies this method has certain advantages:

(a) The laboratory task is free of what have been referred to as secondary difficulties.

(b) The factors which govern the ideal choice of strategy can be readily controlled; the relative probabilities of fault locations can be stated, the relative effort required to make different tests can be indicated and the structure of the simulated equipment can be very clearly displayed. This is not the case if we study men at work on real equipment.

(c) The experience subjects encounter with the tasks can be readily controlled. They will not have met the task before they arrive in the laboratory and their orientation to it can be manipulated by varying instructions. By using the apparatus to be described below the success they achieve when they use a given strategy can also be controlled.

(d) A much wider range of subjects can be used, since specialized knowledge is not required to perform the laboratory tasks. This means that broad questions can be examined. Trained engineers have been selected (if only by attrition). If their strategies are examined the results might only apply to a small subsection of the population. By using a simple task it is possible to examine a larger section of the population and to answer questions about the strategies than can be expected of the population as a whole. (e) By using subjects who have not had specialized training a clearer picture can be gained of the way persons search. Observations of trained engineers might depend to a considerable extent upon their training. Furthermore, if we wish to examine the factors which are important in training, it is better to start with untrained subjects. Relearning differs in some ways from initial learning and the results obtained from relearning experiments might be misleading if applied in an initial learning situation.

(f) It is practically more convenient to work with a laboratory task. The equipment involved is far less complex and requires less attention. What is more, far more subjects are available who can perform the laboratory tasks than could be found from studies on the job.

The serious disadvantage to the method, however, which must always be borne in mind is that the results obtained might be artefacts of the laboratory situation and the conditions of the experiments. In psychological experiments subjects are often suspicious, they expect to be tricked and will consequently look for clever ways of performing simple tasks. But to some extent this attitude always results when subjects are under observation and know it. This factor is also present, therefore, in on-the-job studies.

Another way of studying the way men who have had no special training search, is simply to study the behaviour of men on the job. This is not a facetious statement; it so happens that fault-finders are rarely taught fault-finding. To quote one source: 'The test students showed very little ability in the planning of trouble-shooting. They stated that they had not received instructions on any particular method for trouble-shooting' (Anon, 1953). There is no reason to believe this to be an isolated instance.

In these on-the-job studies, however, the secondary difficulties confound the issue. They are reduced in studies such as those by Bryan *et al.* (1956) and Glaser and Phillips (1954) who used simulated 'real' situations. But with these tasks, knowledge of electronics was necessary and many of the secondary difficulties such as the lack of adequate diagrams were still present. Furthermore all studies of this kind suffer from the limitation already mentioned that they must be carried out on a highly selected group of individuals. In the future recruitment difficulties are likely to arise and potential fault-finders will be less highly selected. These studies cannot contribute to more general questions such as that of whether a different training problem is likely to be presented when these less intelligent personnel are inducted. Laboratory studies are not restrained in this way.

The third basic question, that of how men should be trained, can only be examined when the first two have been answered. It is discussed, however, at a later point in this paper and some tentative suggestions are put forward.

An account will now be given of the laboratory experiments. These are exploratory rather than conclusive and represent the early work in a research project which is continuing. They are presented in four groups. The first consists of a fairly detailed analysis of the way naïve subjects search for a fault in a complex flow system. In the second the strategies used in simple flow problems and those used in searching for a faulty member of a set of unconnected units are examined. (These tasks are presented under differing conditions which affect the ideal choice of strategy so that it is possible to see whether subjects shift their strategies appropriately.) Some different ways of presenting the task of searching among unconnected units are then compared in the third group. In the fourth, learning in the laboratory situation is studied. A final section contains some data on the way individual differences are related to the choice of strategy.

4. Experiment I. A Complex Flow Problem

The purpose of this experiment was to examine the strategies which naïve subjects would employ when searching in a complex flow system in which the units were equally likely to be faulty and tests were equally difficult to carry out.

Figure 1 shows the structure which was used. There were six problems. In three the structure was displayed exactly as in the figure; in the other three the layout was changed by removing all the bends so that, for instance, stages 26, 25, 23 . . . 17, 16, 13, 10, 5, 1 were lying all in a straight line. Problems were created by making one of the 56 stages faulty. The effect of such a fault was to make the signal faulty at all points beyond this stage, i.e. from the faulty stage to the output (or outputs). The faulty stage was either number 9, number 17 or number 51 (see Figure 1). Each fault was met twice by each subject, once with each layout. The apparatus used in this experiment was very primitive. Each stage was represented by a small square of cardboard. If the signal was correct both when it entered and when it left the stage, the

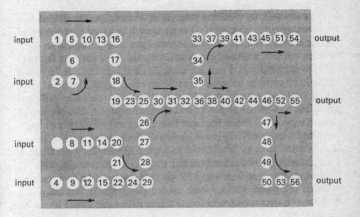

Figure 1 The flow system used in Experiments I and VII. The stages are numbered. Signals flow from the four inputs to the three outputs, the direction of flow is shown by arrows

square was marked with two ticks. If the signal was correct on entry but faulty on leaving, it was marked with a tick and a cross. If it was faulty when both entering and leaving, it was marked with two crosses. The squares were placed face downwards. To make a test the subject had to examine a stage, and his moves were recorded by observing which squares he lifted. After examination, each square was replaced face downwards.

There were twenty-four subjects. Before solving the six test problems, they were given instructions describing the nature of a flow system, and nineteen graded familiarization problems which included simple chain structures, structures with two inputs and one output, and structures having one input and two outputs.

They were therefore thoroughly familiar with the effects that faults would have upon signal flow.

When stage 9 was faulty all three outputs registered faults. This was shown by colouring the backs of the squares representing stages 54, 55 and 56. The best way of locating this fault would be as follows: since all outputs are faulty the fault must lie in, or to the left of, stage 36; thus there are 29 possible loci (the input stages were all marked by colours to show that they were functioning correctly and did not need to be examined); by checking stage 23 or 26 these can be divided into two roughly equal groups; if 23 is checked it is found that the signal leaving it is correct, therefore the chain from stages 1 and 2 up to 23 must be correct; a second check at 24 would show that the fault lay between inputs 3 and 4 and the stage 24; a third check at 21 would show that it must be between 4 and 24, by checking at 15 then at 12 or 9 it would finally be located. Five or six checks would be sufficient according to whether or not 12 was checked before 9. (An element of chance is present.) When the fault is at 17 a good strategy is to begin at 26 and then test 17. This will lead to the fault in two moves, but an equally good strategy would lead to testing 23 then 13, then 18, then 16 and finally 17 which involves five moves. On an average, with the fault at either stage 9 or stage 17 4·4 moves would be required per problem if the best strategy were used; when stage 51 was faulty the number of moves required to locate this specific fault would be, on an average, 3·3.

Results

The results are considered from three points of view.

The number of moves taken to locate the fault. The average number of moves per problem for the four problems when stage 9 or 17 was faulty, was 7·0, 6·0, 5·9 and 6·5 (in temporal order). In each case this is significantly greater than 4·4, the mean number of moves which would have been required if the best strategy has always been used ($P < 0.01$ using a 2-tailed t-test). The greatest number of moves which would be required on any one problem, if the best strategy were used, is six. All but one subject used seven or more moves on at least one problem; eight subjects used ten or more at least once; and one subject took fifteen moves on one occasion.

On the problems where only one output was faulty, the number of moves was closer to that which would be required using the ideal strategy. The means were 3·7 and 3·6 which are not significantly different from 3·3, but eight subjects took more moves than the maximum of four which would have been needed with the best strategy on at least one problem.

The number of moves does not give a very clear picture of the general adequacy of the subjects' behaviour, since it could be dependent upon specific features of the problems which were used. By examining the subjects' strategies it is possible to generalize to other problems and to predict the efficiency with which they would solve them. The strategies are examined in two ways: by looking at the way subjects began the problems, and by analysing all their moves.

The way subjects began the problems. The first move in these problems is the most important, since it reduces the number of possibilities by the greatest number. This section is therefore of particular interest. The data have been examined in two ways: Table 1 shows the number of subjects who began with good moves (in the light of the ideal strategy described above), and Tables 2 and 3 show the frequency with which different points were chosen.

Table 1

Number of Subjects making Good Beginning Moves

	1	2	3	4
Frequency of good beginnings				
Number of subjects: fault at 9 or 17	9	0	0	1
fault at 51	13	6	–	–

From Table 1 it can be seen that only one subject began all the four problems when the fault was at stage 9 or 17 in the best way, and only six did so on both of the other problems. When Table 2 is examined what is most striking is that eighty-five of ninety-six problems were begun at one of six points, seventy-three of them at points which left the number of alternatives (it began at 29) as large as or greater than 24. The two most commonly chosen points were the junctions (stages 25 and 36); nearly half the beginning moves were at these two points. Most of the stages at which subjects began were in the middle of the complete array, but, of course, this was not the important factor in these problems. It might mean, however, that the subjects were attempting to halve the possible loci, but were misled by the display.

Table 2

First Checks on Problems with the Fault at Stage 9 or 17

Number of subjects beginning at a given stage					
Stage	*1st problem*	*2nd problem*	*3rd problem*	*4th problem*	*All problems*
23 or 26	1	4	3	4	12
25	4	7	11	5	27
30	5	4	5	4	18
31	3	1	0	0	4
32	4	3	1	3	11
36	6	4	3	4	17
22	0	1	1	1	3
19	0	0	0	2	2
16	1	0	0	0	1
28	0	0	0	1	1

With the fault at stage 51, subjects tended to begin either at the middle of the chain or near the input. The first stage in the chain (stage 35) was chosen eleven times out of a possible forty-eight. The way of beginning this problem can be compared with the way subjects began their first two familiarization problems (which were also straight chain problems). When this is done it is seen that the stage in an equivalent position to stage 35 was never chosen; the difference is significant at the 1 per cent level using McNemar's (1949) test. This difference means that a chain which is part of a larger structure is not responded to in the same way as an isolated chain. In this case it would seem that those subjects who checked stage 35 were confirming the deduction, which they must previously have made from the state of the outputs, that only this one chain was relevant.

A final general point about this data is that although comparatively few beginning moves were as good as they could have been, only four were completely useless (see Table 3).

Table 3

First Checks on Problems with the Fault at Stage 51

Stage	Number of subjects beginning at a given stage	
	1st problem	2nd problem
33	0	5
34	1	2
35	6	5
36*	1	1
37	1	2
39	8	5
41	4	3
43	0	0
45	2	0
51	0	0
54	0	0
Other*	1	1

* These stages are not in the faulty chain.

The kinds of checks the subjects made. After the first move the problem was no longer the same for each subject; for the remaining alternatives depended upon where the first check was made. Because of this it was not possible to consider all the subjects together. Instead each of the later moves has been considered in the light of the alternatives from which it was chosen, and classified. By examining the frequency with which different kinds of move were made, some idea can be gained of the strategies employed.

Eleven kinds of move have been distinguished, although they are not all mutually exclusive categories. The first nine categories can be considered to describe poor moves; the last two categories, good moves. Grouping in this way reveals that there were altogether 406 poor checks and 383 good ones. The data are shown in Table 4.

There were few errors or repetitions. The number of errors

Table 4

Classification of all Checks made in the Solution of All Problems by Twenty-Four Subjects. (If a check falls into more than one category it is counted in each. A correction is given for the number counted twice. None were counted more than twice)

Category/Description	First 3 problems	Last 3 problems
Confirms a deduction	23	17
Checks at a junction when it would be better to check next to it (i.e. checks 25 instead of 23 or 26)	49	46
Checks a junction at other times	22	16
Checks at a stage adjacent to one already checked	68	37
Checks close to but not adjacent to a stage already checked	27	31
Checks a stage in an input chain before ascertaining that there is a fault in the chain (e.g. beginning a problem with 3 faulty outputs at 28 or 17)	39	37
Makes a check that cannot yield information (e.g. begins a problem with 3 faulty outputs at 40)	13	24
Repeats a check	5	1
Avoids the above listed kinds of moves but does not make the best possible check	43	41
Total	289	250
Number counted twice	63	70
Good. A check that would be made in the light of the best method (as described in the text)	109	130
Good, but restricted in so far that no alternative move could be compatible with the evidence already available, e.g. checking 9 after a check at 15 has shown the fault lies between 4 and 15	65	79
Total	174	209

shown can be a little misleading since they were not independent of each other. What happened was that some subjects began to move in the wrong direction, as if they read tick for cross or vice versa when they made their checks. They sometimes did this for a number of moves. Some subjects seem to be more prone to make reversals of this kind than others as can be seen from Table 5.

Table 5

Reversals

Frequency of reversals made	0	1	2	3
Number of subjects	13	5	4	2

Wastage of moves would seem to be largely due to the tendency to check junctions and to move in small steps from a point already checked. A check made at a junction often yielded very little information, since if two input chains led into it the check would not show which was faulty. The subjects must have been aware of this because they had met problems of the same kind during their familiarization series. The tendency might have been due simply to the perceptual prominence of junctions or it might have been that subjects chose these points because these checks could be remembered more easily. Other results, to be discussed below, suggest that the first of these reasons is most likely the correct one.

Although it is dangerous to emphasize particular results, an idea of the way some subjects were attracted to junctions can be given by quoting the actual moves made by one subject. The fault was at stage 17 and this subject's moves were: 36, 25, 5, 22, 23, 10, 16, 19 and finally 17 (this subject also shows a tendency to move in small steps from points already checked).

Moving in small steps yielded little information, it reduced the number of possible loci by only a small amount. It could be that these moves were regarded by the subjects as slow but sure. They were sure in the sense that they were likely to give the same results as the previous check and hence confirm it. Alternatively the opposite could have been the case; the subjects might have argued when they took a small step, that, if the faulty stage were encompassed by the step, then it would have been located very quickly. This second interpretation equates this kind of move with gambling.

Checks which were quite clearly confirmatory, such as beginning moves at stages 36 or 35 (according to the problem), were less common than most other kinds. That they occurred as frequently as they did is perhaps surprising, since the simple deductions involved in the task were very rarely made incorrectly. As mentioned above, on only four occasions did any subject begin by checking a stage which was irrelevant to his problem.

One kind of confirmatory check is of special interest. Sometimes, where two input chains led to a junction, a subject checked the ultimate stage in one chain and then the ultimate stage in the other (viz. beginning, when the fault is at 17, by checking 26 and then 23). Twenty-one subjects were in a position to make this kind of confirmation at least once; of these, twelve did so on one or more occasions. The interest in this phenomenon is that it shows how these subjects, after eliminating some possibilities, fail to see the remainder as an independent group. Instead of re-assessing the situation (after it has been found that the signal leaving stage 26 is correct, the remaining stages from 5 through 10, 13, 16 . . . to 36 are best considered as a simple chain) they seem to have been bound by their earlier way of looking at the problem (viz. stage 25 is still regarded as a junction, and stage 23 as a member of a limb).

The analysis presented here has the disadvantage that it does not show any strategies as a whole. It is clear that the best strategy was not used frequently. In fact only one subject used 'good' moves throughout a problem where the fault was at 9 or 17. Nine subjects used good moves throughout one of the other problems (with the fault at 51); four of these did so for both. While it is possible to separate out these instances it would be impossible to classify the other strategies since they were so varied.

The data has been analysed for evidence of improvement. Table 4 shows, separately, the checks made in the first three problems and those made in the last three. (The experiment was designed to permit this comparison.) It can be seen that more good checks and fewer poor ones were made in the second half of the test than in the first half. This difference, examined per subject, is not statistically significant.

Subject differences: twelve of the subjects were Naval Ratings, the other twelve were members of the staff of the A.P.U. The total number of moves made by each group was not very different, although the laboratory group required slightly fewer. More members of the laboratory group used the best strategy; seven used it at least once, whereas only two of the ratings ever did so. This difference, viewed as the difference between two binomial proportions, is significant ($p < 0.05$).

Summary

To summarize very briefly: in a complex flow problem naïve subjects did not use what is theoretically the best strategy of searching. They took more moves than they need have done because of their inefficient technique. They seem to have been influenced by perceptually striking features of the display; this might be due to the value of prominent points as aids to memory but later evidence (see below) does not favour this interpretation. Where deductions were necessary in the initial phase of the search they were rarely made incorrectly; but subjects commonly confirmed them with an otherwise redundant check.

This experiment was first reported in somewhat different form (Dale, 1955). An experiment in many ways similar to it has been reported by Goldbeck et al. (1957), but this communication contains no description of strategies. Goldbeck et al. were mainly interested in the effect of instructing subjects to use the half-split technique (this is the American term for dichotomy, see Miller et al., 1953a, b) and their results will be mentioned below. A point of interest is that by using a particularly confusing display they were able to upset their subjects' performance in the initial, deductive, phase of the search.

5. Experiment II. A Simple Flow Problem Compared with a Search among Unconnected Units

The purpose of this experiment was to compare the strategies subjects employed when searching for a fault in a simple flow task under various conditions, with those they employed when searching for one of a number of independent units under similar conditions.

The conditions varied were:

(a) The presence or absence of an *aide-mémoire*. In one condition the subjects had to remember their moves as in Experiment I; in the other condition they were able to record them.

(b) The relative probabilities that units would be faulty. There were altogether seven problems for each subject; subjects were paired, and for one member of each pair the same unit was faulty for problems 2 to 7; it was so arranged that the other member of the pair would take roughly the same number of moves to locate a 'fault' which had not been pre-assigned in this way. Thus for half the subjects one unit was more often faulty than the others.

(c) The time allowed. There was no time limit for the first five problems. In these, as in Experiment I, subjects were instructed to locate the fault in as few moves as possible. On the last two problems, however, a limit of two minutes was set, and subjects were warned that, if the fault had not been located, they would be stopped at the end of this period.

Table 6 shows the number of subjects in the different groups. (All subjects solved seven problems, the last two being under a time limit.) Eighty fresh subjects were used in this experiment.

Table 6
The Design of Experiment II

	Flow Task				Unconnected Units Task	
	Sockets represent stages		Sockets represent test-points		Sockets represent equipments	
	Record of moves	No record	Record of moves	No record	Record of moves	No record
Equal probabilities	5 subjects	5 subjects	5 subjects	5 subjects	10 subjects	10 subjects
One part more often faulty than the rest	5 subjects	5 subjects	5 subjects	5 subjects	10 subjects	10 subjects

A special apparatus (see Figure 2), which is described in detail elsewhere (Dale and Brown, 1958), was used for this experiment. It was constructed so that it could be used to present a large variety of searching tasks. As in the real job, there is an 'equipment', and test-gear. (A signal generator can also be introduced.)

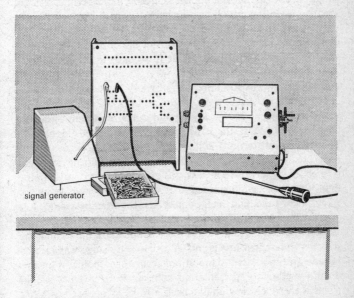

signal generator

Figure 2 The apparatus used in Experiment II as seen by the subject. The display, which represents the equipment or equipments, is on the left; the test-gear on the right. The pegs in the tray in the foreground can be plugged into the sockets to record checks which have been made; they are coloured red or green. (The signal generator was not used in the experiments reported here)

The test-gear is simplified to provide an all-or-none, i.e. 'good' or 'bad' indication. In order to make tests dials first have to be turned to particular settings; each dial is set by turning a screw which moves the dial through a low-gear worm drive. The subject is provided with a screwdriver with which to turn the screws. After setting the dials a lever is depressed to make the test. Depressing the lever returns the dials to their resting position so

127

that in order to make a second test they must be reset. The test-gear can be set in various ways, some settings require only a little effort (i.e. the dials do not have to be turned very far), others require a considerable amount of effort. (The test-points on the 'equipment' are marked to indicate the setting required.) The subject works alone in a cubicle. Outside the experimenter can see from a display which test the subject is making. He controls the result of each test and thus can manipulate the situation to a considerable extent. In this experiment the effort was held constant at a low level; it took about 15 seconds to set up the test-gear to make a check.

The display was the same for all problems except for minor changes. It consisted of a row of nineteen sockets which could be tested by plugging in a jack plug and operating the test-gear. In the simple flow task the left-hand end was marked 'input', the right-hand end 'output' and, as in Experiment I, subjects were instructed that it represented an electronic equipment and were told about signal flow. The task was presented in two ways. In the first, the sockets represented the actual stages and as in the Experiment I the faulty stage could be recognized by a single test (the test gear was made to indicate *both* 'good' and 'bad' simultaneously when the faulty stage was examined). In the second, the sockets represented test points and the faulty stage was located between a 'good' point and an adjacent 'bad' point. With this second method of presentation subjects were given a special tester with which they could check a stage as opposed to a test point. They were told to use it only to confirm the location of the fault; but, as can be seen below, they sometimes used it prematurely. In the searching task where the units were independent, subjects were told that the sockets represented a batch of separate equipments, one of which was faulty.

Results

The simple flow problem. Three 'pure' strategies have been distinguished, and two recurring mixed strategies. These are described in Table 7 which shows the frequency with which they were used. The data are pooled to some extent in this Table, because the recording of non-recording of moves, and the different ways of presenting the task, did not lead to significant differences in

Table 7

The Number of Subjects using each Strategy in the Simple Flow Problem

Strategy	1st problem	2nd problem	3rd problem
Dichotomizing (successively halving the array) *	8	11	12
Bracketing	5	4	3
Moving in steps from a point already checked:			
All steps (up to six units)	15	13	13
steps of 3 units or less	12	10	8
steps of only 1 unit	7	2	1
Dichotomizing at first and then stepping	3	3	2
Bracketing and then stepping	1	1	1
Other strategies	8	8	9

* Six subjects dichotomized on all three problems. Twenty-five did so at least once in the complete series of seven problems.

behaviour. (The data from the subjects who recorded their moves are strikingly similar to those from the other subjects.)

A strategy which has not previously been described was used by some subjects. This has been called bracketing. It is similar to dichotomizing but includes a redundant move. In a chain of nineteen items an example of bracketing would be the series of checks: 10, 19, 14, 17 and 16. Sometimes the first two moves would be followed by stepping; this is described as 'bracketing and then stepping'.

Only the data from the first three problems are shown in Table 7. All subjects had been treated alike up to this point with regard to probabilities. When subjects began their fourth problem, however, some had evidence that one stage had been faulty twice. If this is treated as evidence of differential probability then, for these subjects, the ideal strategy would be to begin at a point between the middle and the twice-faulty stage. (The often-faulty stage was always close to one or other end of the chain so that it would be prominent.)

The tendency to move along in steps was quite wrong; on the third problem thirteen subjects stepped and three others used stepping as a partial strategy (see Table 7). This result is comparable to that of Experiment I, which showed a similar tendency. Stepping cannot be the result of an attempt to avoid forgetting, since as many of those subjects who recorded their moves adopted this kind of strategy as did those who had to remember them. A possible reason for this behaviour is that these subjects failed to distinguish clearly this task from that of searching among unconnected units. This assumes that the stepwise strategy would be adopted quite generally in the other task (where it is the most sensible strategy) and that these are the only subjects who fail to see that it is inappropriate here. Evidence cited below, from the unconnected units task, however, indicates that this is an unlikely explanation.

These data contain evidence of learning. More subjects dichotomize, and fewer proceed in small steps, on the third problem than on the first. Examined subject-wise by McNemar's (1949) technique, the reduction in the number using small steps is shown to be statistically significant ($p < 0.02$). On later problems still more subjects dichotomize (regardless of the fact that for half of them it is no longer the best strategy). The numbers are 15, 21, 18 and 18, on the 4th, 5th, 6th and 7th problems respectively. The increase from the first to the last problem is statistically significant ($p < 0.02$ using McNemar's test). On the last problem, eight of the eighteen subjects who dichotomized had experienced unequal probabilities; this clearly had not greatly affected the over-all number choosing this strategy.

When one stage was repeatedly faulty, some subjects adjusted their strategy so that they began closer to this stage. On the 5th problem, three of the twenty subjects responded to it in this way; on the 7th problem, eight did so (this difference is not statistically significant; $p > 0.05$). This increase, if real, could have been due either to the time limit set on the last problem, or to the fact that, after observing more instances, the subjects had stronger evidence that this stage was more likely to be faulty than the others. Theoretically the provision of a time limit favours the use of a strategy in which the most probable parts are checked first. Our results suggest, since only eight of the twenty showed any influence, that only some subjects were aware of this fact. But the evidence is not conclusive since it can be argued that the time limit was not sufficiently stringent. Some subjects, in fact, commented that two minutes provided them with plenty of time for a thorough search. The other group, who had no evidence of differential probabilities, were unaffected by the time limit.

Those subjects for whom the sockets represented test-points had to confirm that they had successfully located a faulty stage. They did this by using a special tester. It took considerably longer to operate this tester than to make an ordinary check. A confirmatory test in this way parallels the removal of a sub-unit in the real job; it pays not to do it until sure that it will give the expected results. Nine out of nineteen subjects used this tester prematurely (i.e. before they had sufficient information to be sure of the locus of the fault) on at least one occasion, despite instructions to first make sure they had located a faulty stage. (The twentieth subject used it prematurely because he had a special hypothesis about the way the problems were being scored.) This behaviour was not influenced by the time limit; six of the nine made premature confirmatory tests only when there was *no* limit.

Searching among unconnected units. Here again the first three problems have to be considered separately. Three kinds of strategy have been distinguished: (a) Stepwise – beginning at one end checking each unit in turn; (b) Pattern – following some more complex order such as checking the first then the last, then the 18th, then the 2nd and so on; (c) Random – following no perceptible system.

When the fault was located rapidly there was so little data that in some cases it was not clear whether the subject was using a pattern or a random strategy. A fourth, 'other', category has been used for these instances.

Recording moves again made no difference and the results of those subjects who recorded their moves and those who did not, have been pooled. (Table 8 shows the number who adopted each strategy.) These data show an apparent deterioration, since the number of subjects using the straightforward, stepwise, strategy is lower on the later problems that on the first one. Some of the subjects, however, stated in retrospective reports that they adopted this strategy on the first problem because they believed then that they were obliged to use it. The results of the first problem, therefore, give a misleading impression. The number in the 'other' category is zero on the first problem because, on this problem, all subjects were forced to take ten moves, and enough data was therefore obtained to distinguish between pattern and random strategies.

Table 8

Searching among Unconnected Units: the Number of Subjects Adopting each Strategy

Strategy	1st problem	2nd problem	3rd problem
Stepwise	17	9	9
Pattern	9	14	12
Random	14	12	12
Other	0	5	7

It is clear from Table 8 that comparatively few subjects used the stepwise strategy. Excepting the first problem, there were more subjects working with the random than with the stepwise strategy.

One implication of this result is that the tendency to move along in steps noticed in the Simple Flow experiment is unlikely to be due to a failure to distinguish between that task and this one. It was not a general tendency here. But the criterion of stepwise is different in each case and it might be argued that these subjects would perform both tasks in the same way. If the data are re-analysed and a broader category of stepwise defined to include those subjects who moved in from one or both ends in steps of three or less units, it is found that twenty-four subjects used this strategy on the first problem, eighteen did so on the second and eleven on the third. The number of extra cases included, therefore, by this change of definition, is not great. Later evidence (see below) shows that those subjects who proceeded in unit steps in this task were the more intelligent ones, whereas those who 'stepped' in the flow problem were the less intelligent. Thus subjects who use the strategy in one task differ from those who do so in the other.

On the later problems, where one unit was more often faulty than the rest, most subjects adapted their strategy so that they inspected this unit early in their search; a few began by checking this more-probable unit (see Table 9). There was a tendency for those adapting completely to be subjects who had previously worked at random at least once, but this was not statistically

Table 9

Searching among Unconnected Units: the Number of Subjects Adjusting their Strategies in the Light of Probability Evidence ($N = 20$)

| | Problem | | | |
	4th	5th	6th*	7th*
Inspecting the more probable unit early in the search	11	15	17	16
Inspecting the more probable unit on the first move	3	7	7	6

* There was a time limit on these problems.

significant. The time limit clearly did not affect the issue (see Table 9) and with this task, as opposed to the Flow task, it cannot be objected that the time allowed was sufficient for a thorough search. A complete search would have taken, on average, over 5 minutes.

The time limit had no effect on the other subjects (those for whom the fault might have been at any point). There was no tendency, under time pressure, for those using the stepwise strategy to discard it, or for any other subjects to change their strategies.

6. Experiment III. The Effects of Varying Relative Probability Alone and of Varying Both Relative Probability and Relative Effort

In this experiment eighteen fresh subjects were given the task of searching among a set of unconnected units for one which was faulty, under differing conditions. The apparatus and display were basically the same as those used in Experiment II.

Relative probability was varied by marking some units distinctively and instructing subjects that the marked units were more likely to be faulty than those not marked. Here, as in Experiment II, most subjects (fourteen of the eighteen) began by checking first those units which were more likely to be faulty.

When both probability and effort were varied, no such clear effect was observed. Effort was varied by demanding different settings of the test-gear (see above). Nine different levels of effort were used; the greatest demanded twelve times more work than the least, and most subjects required about 5 minutes to make a test with this (most effortful) setting. It was expected that subjects would begin by testing those units which were more likely to be faulty and those which were easy to test, but the way these two factors would be weighted could not be predicted. Of the eighteen subjects, one checked the more probable units first, regardless of effort, and then checked through from the easiest to the most effortful. Three others began with the more probable but then disregarded effort. Three more took some account of effort, and began with easier tests. The other ten subjects showed no sensible regard for effort or probability, and some even made the most effortful checks first.

Detambel (1956) and Detambel and Stolurow (1957) have shown, in a similar situation, that the probability variable weighs more heavily than the effort variable in determining subjects' choices. In both these studies only a small number of units (three in one case, four in the other) were used, and the subjects learned about effort and probability through familiarity with the material (as in Experiment II).

7. Experiments IV and V. The Effect of Varying the Method of Presentation

The aim of the two experiments to be reported was to see whether the strategies employed when subjects search among unconnected units would differ if the task was presented in different ways.

Two new ways of presenting the task were used. In the first, the letters of the alphabet were used as the units; in the second, the apparatus used in Experiment II was slightly modified, and the nineteen units were nineteen wireless transmitting stations which the subjects had to monitor. Eighty-four new subjects were used in these experiments.

Experiment IV: searching in the alphabet

There were three variants of this task. The first group of subjects were told by the experimenter 'I am thinking of a letter of the alphabet and I want you to discover which one it is with as few guesses as possible.' The subject was told after each guess 'No!' if his guess was incorrect or, when he successfully located the desired letter, 'That's it'. No other information was given. The second group had similar instructions except that the word 'questions' was substituted for 'guesses'. The third group were handed a pack of twenty-six cards each bearing a different letter, they shuffled the cards themselves, then the experimenter cut and instructed them to discover which one was at the bottom of the pack. (Again the wording did not imply that they should guess.) Subjects were given two, or in some cases three, problems. The results considered are for the first problem only; very few subjects changed their strategy for the second problem.

Experiment V: wireless monitors

The nineteen sockets were numbered to represent wireless transmitting stations. When one was tested (using the test-gear) the faulty–correct indicating lamps flashed a short message which was repeated at brief intervals. The subjects were told to locate as quickly as possible the one station which was transmitting a given message. The messages were all rather similar and subjects were warned that they must be sure to get the correct one.

Transfer

Those subjects given the wireless monitoring task were given the alphabet task immediately afterwards (it was presented on cards) so that it is possible to compare the strategies they adopted on each.

Results of Experiments IV and V

The results of these two experiments are given in Tables 10 and 11. It is clear that there was a strong tendency to adopt a Random strategy when searching in the alphabet, whichever variant of the

Table 10
Searching the Alphabet and Searching for a Wireless Station

	Stepwise	*Pattern*	*Random*
Searching in the alphabet:			
'guesses' instructions $n = 26$	2	3	21
'questions' instructions $n = 12$	0	0	12
using cards $n = 28$	2	1	25
Searching for a wireless station:			
results of 3rd problem $n = 18$	7	8	3

task was used. On the Wireless Monitoring task the systematic strategies were preferred, and fewer subjects worked at random than would be expected from the results of Experiment II. This could be due to the selection of subjects, but the transfer experi-

Table 11
Strategies used for the Alphabet and Wireless Monitoring Tasks Compared

		Searching in the Alphabet	
		Stepwise or Pattern	*Random*
'Wireless Monitoring'	Stepwise or Pattern	2	13
	Random	0	3

ment clearly shows that the same subjects shift to different strategies when given the alphabet task (Table II). (The difference is highly significant, $p < 0.001$.) Some characteristic of the Wireless Monitoring task might, therefore, lead to this difference from the result of Experiment II.

Bryan *et al.* (1956) provide supporting evidence for shifts of the kind observed here. They noted that many men who were given two kinds of problem, one in radio equipment the other in radar equipment, did not approach both of them in the same way. Clearly the logical requirements of a task do not determine the strategy which men will use.

8. Experiments VI and VII. A Further Investigation of Learning

Some of the data already presented show that when subjects are given a number of problems there is a tendency for them to use more appropriate strategies on the later ones. Two experiments are reported here. In the first, further evidence of learning in the task of searching among unconnected units was sought; in the second, the success subjects obtained with different strategies in a complex flow was manipulated and the effects observed. Some data is also presented which shows the effect of success upon searching among unconnected units.

Experiment VI: changes in strategy over a long series of searches among unconnected units

Table 12
Changes over a Long Series of Searches among Unconnected Units: the Number of Subjects Adopting each Strategy

Strategy adopted	Stepwise	Pattern	Random	Other
First problem	0	1	8	1
Tenth problem	0	7	2	1

A small group of ten subjects was given ten problems of this kind, with the display used in Experiment II. Table 12 shows the strategies used on the first and last of these problems. The shift from the use of the Random strategy to the Pattern strategy is statistically significant ($p < 0.02$ using McNemar's test). Thus there was a tendency for subjects to become more systematic, but no subjects changed to the Stepwise strategy.

Experiment VII: the effect of success in a complex flow task

It is reasonable to suppose that if a strategy leads occasionally to rapid success it is likely to be used again. If it never does so then it is more likely to be discarded. In a flow task, any strategy other than dichotomizing is risky. If a check divides the alternatives unequally and the fault is in the smaller group, success is more rapid than with dichotomy. Rapid fault location sometimes occurs, therefore, when poor strategies are used. In this experiment, the experimenter so manipulated the situation that if the alternatives were divided unequally the subject would always be unlucky. In these conditions the best strategy *always* led to the fewest moves.

Twelve subjects in an experimental group were given fourteen problems, of the kind used in Experiment I, which were all rigged by the experimenter. Twelve subjects in a control group were given fourteen similar problems; the first two and last two of these were rigged, but in the other ten the fault was fixed beforehand; these subjects, therefore, had a normal run of luck. It can be seen that the first and last two problems were the same for both groups, and could be used for comparing their performances. The number of moves made in these four problems gives an indication of the effectiveness of the subjects' strategies.

Table 13
The Effect of Success in a Complex Flow Task

| | *Number of Moves Taken per Problem* | |
	before 'training'	*after 'training'*
Experimental group:	8·92	8·50
Control group:	9·93 *	8·08 *

* Tested per subject this difference is significant ($p < 0.05$, 1-tail test).

It was expected that the experimental group would improve to a greater extent than the controls, but, as the Table 13 shows, the opposite was the case. The control group improved slightly more than the experimental group. Considerable room for improvement remained for both groups, since, had the best strategy been employed, on the average 4·2 moves would have been required per problem. (In all of these problems the faults were such that all three outputs were faulty.)

Success, and the strategies used for searching among unconnected units

Sometimes when subjects used a Random strategy they got into a muddle; they repeated moves, and sometimes took more moves than there were units to solve a problem. (One subject, for instance, took thirty-six moves to find a letter in the alphabet.) Data from some of the experiments already described have been analysed to see whether such experiences led subjects to change their ways and adopt systematic strategies. Twenty subjects were found to have become muddled in this way at least once. Of these, twelve used the random strategy again at least once, whereas eight changed to a systematic method of searching.

The fact that two-thirds were not influenced by this experience suggests that, just as the gambler does not usually give up when he loses a bet, these subjects were prepared to take the rough with the smooth.

Summary

To sum up this section briefly: subjects improve their strategies when they are given a series of problems but, in the series studied, considerable room for improvement remains. This is true of both the flow problems and the searches among unconnected units. It is possible that further improvement would be observed if the subjects were exposed to longer series of problems.

With both kinds of problems the improvement does not appear to be related in a simple way to success and failure. Faust (1958) has obtained a similar result to this in a study of the game '20 Questions'. [. . .]

9. Discussion of the Practical Significance of the Results

If these results can only be interpreted as a record of the behaviour of persons within a psychological laboratory they are of no practical significance.

It might be argued that those subjects who used random

strategies when searching among unconnected units did so because they expected to find some catch in the experiment. But this is unlikely to be the whole answer, if even a part of it. For one thing, if this were the case why should the more intelligent subjects be less likely to work in this way? For another, there is the evidence that this sort of behaviour occurs on the real job. Crowder (1954) remarked upon it, and elsewhere Rosen (1957) has given a vivid account of it.

The fact that behaviour was influenced by the way tasks were presented can also be interpreted as a criticism of the laboratory studies. The results of the experiments differed according to the method of presentation. Which, then, was the true analogue of the practical task? This is only a criticism if it can be asserted that the practical task is always presented in one way. What is more likely true is that what has been discovered to be a relevant variable in the laboratory is also relevant in 'real' life. It is unlikely that all men on the job look upon it in the same way and these results suggest that we can influence their strategies by changing their viewpoint. However, further analysis of the differences observed are necessary before the key variables can be identified. All that can be safely concluded from the experiments reported is that presentation affects behaviour.

What these results do show clearly is that we cannot expect men to use the best strategies of searching without training; they use them neither in very simple problems nor in more complex ones. The results cannot, therefore, be ascribed to the simplicity or the complexity of the problems used. From the practical point of view it might seem that the criteria of 'good' and 'poor' strategies which have been adopted here are unduly severe. But in Experiment I subjects took about 50 per cent more moves than they need have done because of the inefficiency of their strategies.

The laboratory tasks differed from the real job in that, in most cases, they did not have these two levels of search which are encountered by the electronics fault-finder (who has to isolate first the faulty stage and then the faulty part). For effective fault-finding in electronics it is of prime importance that the search in the flow system should be sufficient. The serious wastage of effort noted by Crowder (1954) and Dale (1958a) resulted when subjects went to the second level of search prematurely; when they checked within a stage which was not faulty. A direct comparison with this kind of behaviour was possible in only one experiment (Experiment II), where it was found that, as in the real job, specific tests were made prematurely in a good number of cases. If it ensures correct identification of the faulty stage, some redundancy when searching in a flow system might be a good thing, as the writer has suggested elsewhere (Dale, 1958a). Its cost is certainly much less than the cost of chasing a false lead to the point of making tests within a stage which is not faulty.

In the task of searching among unconnected units, the strategy of exploring according to some pattern is logically as good as that of beginning at one end of the row and taking each in turn. Only the random strategy is seriously inefficient. Some subjects who followed patterns, however, made them progressively more complex, and it might well be predicted that, had they been forced to explore nearly all the alternatives, they would have forgotten their moves. In this task and in the others more subjects might have used the better strategies had they been forced, before they began, to think out all possible ways of proceeding. This is suggested by the evidence of Moore *et al.* (1955). The evidence, however, is not strong.

The fact that a man's strategy depends, at any rate in certain circumstances, upon his intelligence is of considerable practical importance. It is especially significant since the subjects used in these experiments tended to be of above-average intelligence (Dale, 1958c). The increased demand for maintenance personnel inevitably means that men of lower intelligence than those hitherto accepted will have to be recruited and trained. Under present-day training methods it is known that they will have difficulty in assimilating electronic theory. These results indicate that even if they surmount this hurdle they cannot be expected to use such good strategies of searching as their more intelligent colleagues, at any rate, not without special training. (The effectiveness of the fault-finders of today might well be as high as it is because the men have been selected on the basis of intelligence in order to cope with electronics theory.)

The question arises whether, since men cannot be expected in general to use the best strategies, it might be better if the choice of checks was made for them. Warren *et al.* (1958) and Berkshire

(1954) have developed guides on the assumption that this is so. It is really outside the scope of this paper to answer this question since much depends upon the conditions under which men work, but since learning occurs in the laboratory in a very short time there is good reason to hope that men can be trained to use reasonably efficient procedures.

10. The Problem of Training

The results of the experiments reported here suggest that it is probably possible to train men to search reasonably efficiently. Some other studies have been specifically devoted to training, both in the laboratory and in the field.

In the laboratory, Fattu and Mech (1953) found that subjects who had had a lecture on a specific method of locating faults in a gear train apparatus successfully located more faults than others who had not had the lecture. Goldbeck *et al.* (1957) using an apparatus which presented flow problems of the kind used in the experiments reported above, found that subjects could be taught to dichotomize (at the same time they showed that the subjects could be confused by other aspects of the task). Warren *et al.* (1958) also report successful training using a simple simulated fault-finding task.

These experiments can be regarded as demonstrating the subjects' ability to understand and apply instructions. But more than this may be involved in establishing stable patterns of searching, for, if inefficient strategies are used because of a proclivity for risk-taking, then it will be necessary to thoroughly and effectively convince a man that, in the long run, gambling does not pay. Gambling has a strong and persistent appeal in everyday life, much of which might well lie in the pleasure of risk-taking itself rather than in the expectation of gain associated with the risks. Lord Keynes (1932), on these grounds, equated it with the pleasure of a glass of wine or a visit to the opera. Training men to abstain from risk-taking might, therefore, present a considerable problem. To instruct a man not to gamble is unlikely, by itself, to be effective. The trainee is likely to follow the instructions when tested, but this does not mean that he will continue to do so when he is no longer under observation. The car driving test provides a parallel. In the driving test the trainee must satisfy the examiner that, among other things, he drives cautiously. It is a matter of common observation, however, that this provides no guarantee that he will subsequently abstain from taking risks.

The evidence from field work, e.g. Anon, 1953, and the complex laboratory tasks (Experiment I, Fattu and Mech, 1953; Goldbeck *et al.*, 1957) suggests that persons fail to understand how to set about searching. Instruction should help these persons. Evidence from the simple laboratory task, however (Experiment II), suggests that inefficiency is due to the tendency to gamble. What might well be found, therefore, in the complex task, is that instructions, through giving an insight into the best ways of searching, will lead to an initial improvement; but when subjects master the task they will begin to take risks and inefficiency will result.

French *et al.* (1956) have been able to improve the fault-finding performance of electronics mechanics by specific training in which consideration of the basic signal flow characteristics of an equipment was emphasized. A follow-up was made after six months, to check that the improvement was maintained, but it was inconclusive; supervisor ratings did not distinguish between men with specific training and controls, but a written test did. More and better studies of this kind are badly needed.

In section 2 no definition of the task of fault finding was offered since many approaches to the job are possible. The most efficient was described in order to show the scope of the job and this was then used as an ideal with which the strategies of the experimental subjects were compared. Lacking evidence to the contrary it seems reasonable to believe that men can be trained to approach this ideal method even if they do not match it. There might, however, be an intellectual barrier; it might be possible to train only men of relatively high intelligence.

What is striking about all the evidence discussed in this paper is the need for training which has been revealed by both on-the-job and laboratory studies. It is surprising that courses designed to produce fault-finders should, in fact, produce men who complain that they have not been taught how to set about locating faults. So much emphasis has been placed upon the theory which it has assumed the men will require, that the actual task has been forgotten. Indeed it has only recently been analysed at all. Proposals have been made to correct this bias in training by Rulon and Schweiker (1956) and the writer (Dale, 1959). Experimental training programmes based upon a job-orientated approach are briefly described by Ellis (1958). Unfortunately the research Ellis describes has been discontinued and the training he reports has not been properly evaluated, despite signs of considerable promise. It remains to be seen, therefore, how successful a training programme of this kind can be.

References

ANON (1952), Electrician's mate 3 NAVPERS 10548-A, *Navy Training Courses, Bureau of Naval Personnel*, Washington, D.C.

ANON (1953), Evaluation of graduates of the K bombing systems course, *Final Report. Project No. APQ/SAS/125-A. Eglin Air Force Base*, U.S.A.

BROADBENT, D. E. (1955), 'The concept of capacity and the theory of behaviour', in C. Cherry (ed.), *Third London Symposium on Information Theory*, Butterworth.

BRYAN, G. L., BOND, N. A. JR., LA PORTE, H. R. JR., and HOFFMAN, L. S. (1956), Electronics trouble shooting: a behavioral analysis, *Electronics Personnel Research, Technical Report*, no. 13, Department of Psychology, University of Southern California.

CROWDER, N. A. (1954), Proficiency of Q.24 radar mechanics: V. level of trouble shooting performance observed, *AFPTRC Research Bulletin, 54/102, Lackland Air Force Base*, San Antonio, Texas.

DALE, H. C. A. (1955), Searching in a structured system: a methodological study, *Medical Research Council, A.P.U. Report*, no. 55/247.

DALE, H. C. A. (1958a), A field study of fault-finding in wireless equipment, *Medical Research Council, A.P.U. Report*, no. 58/329.

DALE, H. C. A. (1958b), On the nature of fault-finding in electronic equipment, *Medical Research Council, A.P.U. Report*, no. 58/328.

DALE, H. C. A. (1958c), Fault-finding: approaches to the personnel problem. (Unpublished, available from the author on request.)

DALE, H. C. A. (1959), 'The training of electronic maintenance engineers', *Br. Comm. Electronics*, vol. 6, pp. 10–14, 110–13.

DALE, H. C. A., and BROWN, I. (1958), An apparatus for studying certain aspects of fault-finding, *Medical Research Council, A.P.U. Report*, no. 58/318.

DETAMBEL, M. H. (1956), 'Probabilities of success and amounts of work in a multichoice situation', *J. exp. Psychol.*, vol. 51, pp. 41–4.

DETAMBEL, M. H., and STOLUROW, L. M. (1957), 'Probability and work as determiners of multichoice behavior', *J. exp. Psychol.*, vol. 53, pp. 73–81.

ELLIS, D. S. (1958), Research on general skills and concepts in electronic maintenance training, *Technical Report AFPTRC-TR-58-4, Maintenance Laboratory, Air Research and Development Command, Lowry Air Force Base*, Colorado.

FATTU, N. A., and MECH, E. V. (1953), 'The effect of set on performance in a "trouble-shooting" situation', *J. appl. Psychol.*, vol. 37, pp. 214–17.

FAUST, W. L. (1958), 'Factors in individual improvement in solving twenty-questions problems', *J. exp. Psychol.*, vol. 55, pp. 39–44.

FRENCH, R. S., CROWDER, N. A., and TUCKER, J. A. JR. (1956), The K system MAC-1 trouble-shooting trainer: II. Effectiveness in an experimental training course, *Development Report AFPTRC-TN-56-120, Lackland Air Force Base*, San Antonio, Texas.

GAGNÉ, R. M. (1954), An analysis of two problem solving activities, *Research Bulletin, AFPTRC-TR-54–77, Lackland Air Force Base*, San Antonio, Texas.

GLASER, R., and PHILLIPS, J. C. (1954), An analysis of tests of proficiency for guided missile personnel: III. Patterns of trouble-shooting behaviour, *Technical Bulletin 55-16, Bureau of Naval Personnel, Guided Missile Personnel Research Report no. 5. Contract N7 onr-37008. NR-154-079*, American Institute for Research, Pittsburgh.

GOLDBECK, R. A., BERNSTEIN, B. B., HILLIX, W. A., and MARX, M. H. (1957), 'Application of the half-split technique to a problem-solving task', *J. exp. Psychol.*, vol. 53, pp. 330–38.

HOEHN, A. J., and SALTZ, E. (1956), Determination of the behavioral content of a trouble-shooting guide, *Laboratory Note 56–19, TARL, Chanute Air Force Base*, Illinois (unpublished draft).

KEYNES, J. M. (1932), Evidence given before the Royal Commission on Lotteries and Betting. 1932–3 para. 7822.

MCNEMAR, Q. (1949), *Psychological Statistics*, Wiley, pp. 77–82.

MILLER, R. B. (1953), Anticipating tomorrow's maintenance job, *HRRC Research Review 53/1, Human Resources Research Center, Chanute Air Force Base*, Illinois.

MILLER, R. B., and FOLLEY, J. D., JR. (1951), Recommendations on designing electronics equipment for the job of maintenance, *Research Bulletin, American Institute for Research*, no. 51–33, Pittsburgh.

MILLER, R. B., FOLLEY, J. D., JR., and SMITH, P. R. (1953a), Systematic trouble-shooting and the half-split technique, *Human Resources Research Center Technical Report 53–21, Chanute Air Force Base*, Illinois.

MILLER, R. B., FOLLEY, J. D. JR., and SMITH, P. R. (1953b), *Trouble-Shooting in Electronics Equipment – A Proposed Method*, American Institute for Research, Pittsburgh.

MILLER, R. B., FOLLEY, J. D., JR., SMITH, P. R., and SWAIN, A. D. (1954), *Survey of Human Engineering Needs in Maintenance of Ground Electronics Equipment*, American Institute for Research, Pittsburgh.

Maintenance

MOORE, J. V., SALTZ, E., and HOEHN, A. J. (1955), Improving equipment maintenance by means of a preplanning technique, *Research Report AFPTRC-TV-55-26, Training Aids Research Laboratory; Air Research and Development Command, Chanute Air Force Base*, Illinois.

RAY, W. S. (1955), A problem-solving apparatus note, *Laboratory Note SCRL-55-4, Lackland Air Force Base*, San Antonio, Texas (unpublished draft).

ROSEN, M. W. (1957), *The Viking Rocket Story*, Panther, p. 157.

RULON, P. J., and SCHWEIKER, R. F. (1956), The training of flight-simulator maintenance personnel: a proposed course that emphasises trouble-shooting, *Technical Memorandum ML-TM-56-17, Lowry Air Force Base*, Denver, Colorado.

SALTZ, E., and MOORE, J. V. (1953), A preliminary investigation of trouble-shooting, *HRRC Tech. Report 53/2, Human Resources Research Center, Chanute Air Force Base*, Illinois.

SHACKEL, B. (1957), 'Human engineering and electronics', *Br. Comm. Electronics*, vol. 4, pp. 350–55.

SPECTOR, P., SWAIN, A. D., and MEISTER, D. (1955), Human factors in the design of electronics test equipment, *Report no. RADC-TR-55-83, American Institute for Research*, Pittsburgh.

STANDLEE, L. S., POPHAM, W. J., and FATTU, N. A. (1956), *A Review of Trouble-Shooting*, Institute of Educational Research, School of Education, Indiana University.

STOLUROW, L. M., BERGUM, B., HODGSON, T., and SILVA, J. (1955), 'The efficient course of action in "trouble-shooting" as a joint function of probability and cost', *Educ. psychol. Meas.*, vol. 15, pp. 462–77.

WARREN, N. D., ATKINS, D. W., FORD, J. S., and WOLBERS, H. L. (1955), Development of a training programme for teaching basic principles of trouble-shooting, *Technical Memorandum, ASPRL-TM-55-19. Lowry Air Force Base*, Denver, Colorado.

WARREN, N. D., FORD, J. S., and SCHUSTER, D. H. (1958), Development of a trouble locator and evaluation of a generalized electronic trouble-shooting course, *Technical Report AFPTRC-TR-58-1, Maintenance Laboratory, Air Research and Development Command, Lowry Air Force Base*, Colorado.

6 L. M. Stolurow, B. Bergum, T. Hodgson and J. Silva

The Efficient Course of Action in 'Trouble-Shooting' as a Joint Function of Probability and Cost

L. M. Stolurow, B. Bergum, T. Hodgson and J. Silva, 'The efficient course of action in "trouble-shooting" as a joint function of probability and cost', *Educational and Psychological Measurement*, vol. 15 (1955), pp. 462–77.

The Model

An important personnel problem is the evaluation of performance in both real and simulated trouble-shooting tasks. To accomplish this evaluation it is necessary to have a criterion. The most acceptable criterion is one which is generated by an appropriate general model of the behavior requirements of the situations within which persons must work. This is the general problem to which this study is addressed.

This study has the following purposes: (a) to present a probabilistic model of 'trouble shooting'; (b) to utilize available maintenance records for several aircraft power plants to determine whether the assumptions of the model are generally justified; (c) to propose two methods for combining the probability and time estimates for various repairs associated with a set of symptoms; (d) to demonstrate, with the computationally simpler one of two methods, the efficiency achieved by using both probability and work-time in determining the course of action to follow in locating defects; and (e) to report results of a study of the ability of instructors to estimate the probability and work values associated with defects.

Trouble-shooting can be conceived as a complex skill consisting of several interdependent components. One of these skill components is diagnosis, the deduction of possible causes of a given set of symptoms. Another is the reduction process whereby the mechanic reduces the number of possible causes of a set of symptoms as efficiently as possible in his attempts to isolate the actual cause. A third set of skills is involved in repair.

The present model assumes (a) that the implications about the nature of the defect that can be drawn from diagnostically useful signs have a probabilistic relationship with these signs, (b) that the associated probabilities are frequently *unequal* for a given set of possibilities and (c) that the possible significates (implications or causes) also differ to an important extent with respect to the cost (e.g. effort, time or dollars) each involves.

It is possible to use these assumptions in arriving at a criterion for determining the efficiency of various courses of action available to mechanics in trouble-shooting. In terms of a probabilistic model that also considers time or effort as a parameter, the efficient mechanic would react to a particular set of symptoms by selecting the course of action that would result in the fastest *average* rate of identification of the trouble. This criterion of efficiency is not the usual one. It is more common to define the most efficient trouble-shooter as the mechanic who finds the cause of a particular set of symptoms in either the fewest steps or the least amount of time. From the point of view of a probabilistic model of trouble-shooting, the efficient course of action is one that is determined by the joint consideration of two classes of information in a particular way. The symptom sample considered in arriving at a theoretical criterion for determining the efficient course of action should include all possible causes in the relative frequency obtaining in the population defined by the symptoms. As pointed out, the operational criterion of the efficient course of action from this point of view is the minimum average cost (e.g. time) per discovery of the actual cause of a given symptom. This most efficient course is the one that results in the maximum number of discoveries of the malfunction per unit of time or effort. It is not necessarily the most efficient sequence for each example of the symptom.

Some recent attempts to analyse the trouble-shooter's task have conceptualized his most efficient procedure in terms of a 'half-split' logical stratagem (2, 4). By this procedure the mechanic would make diagnostic judgements in such a way as to reduce the number of probable causes by 50 per cent at each 'choice point'. This 'half-split' conceptual model for determining the behavioral route in the reduction of possibilities does not make the assumptions stated above concerning the inequality of probability and time per possibility. Also it appears to have been applied only to equipment that permits the mechanic the freedom of determining both where in the system he will make his checks, and in what order. In addition, it requires equipment that transmits information along routes that permit 'logical' reduction of component sets of possibilities. Furthermore, the information transmitted by a variety of potential troubles must converge at points that can be checked easily. This 'logical' model (2, 4) might be useful for many electronic devices; it is questionable, however, whether it will always generate the most efficient rate of reduction of possibilities for such devices. In the case of an aircraft power plant, the failure to consider probability and time as joint parameters might be a serious omission, as will be indicated in this study based upon powerplant maintenance records.

Course of action and strategic behavior

Some evidence relating to the behavior of subjects in a laboratory task which had no optimum solution but which was generated by a probabilistic model has been presented by Detambel (1). His results are based upon a simulated trouble-shooting task. They indicate that when the range of effort is very small, the course of action which subjects take is primarily related to the probabilities that obtain for the choices rather than to the work involved. Detambel's subjects turned over cards in each of four decks until they found the one which had been assigned signification as either trouble or a normal operation. The card decks differed in the probability of appearance of cards that signified a trouble and in the number of cards that had to be turned to get the information (i.e. work). Although suggestive, Detambel's study cannot be related directly to the task of trouble-shooting for complex equipment such as reciprocating engines. One reason is that a very limited range of low-value time (or work) differences existed among alternative courses of action. Another is the relative simplicity of the task as compared with engine diagnosis.

A Methodological Study

The data for this study were drawn from maintenance records secured at an air force base. From these records two sets of basic computations were made: (a) probability estimates of repairs

149

associated with sets of diagnostic signs, and (b) the average amount of time required for each type of repair that was performed. The procedures used for computing these values and the results are presented. The probability estimates reported for the different troubles associated with the various diagnostic signs are a small fraction of the total number computed. Since three examples of symptom–trouble relationships appeared to be sufficient for demonstrating the applicability of the probabilistic model, and both the 'complete' and 'simplified' methods for determining an efficient reduction of possible causes derived from it, only the probability values appropriate to those examples were included.

Following a description of the procedures used to obtain the two types of basic data, two methods for combining the empirical probability and time estimates will be described. One of these proposed procedures has been called 'the complete method'. It provides information for deciding upon the most efficient course of action when accurate and representative probability and time estimates are available. This method therefore provides the criterion course of action for evaluating the observed performance of mechanics in solving either real or simulated equipment problems. In addition, it also provides a basis for evaluating the relative efficiency of every course of action a mechanic would take. It is possible, therefore, to determine an objective and quantitative index of the relative excellence of all courses of action taken in attempted solutions of any set of trouble-shooting problems.

The second procedure is called 'the simplified method' because it identifies one of the more efficient courses of action, and frequently the most efficient course. While the 'complete' method is primarily useful in providing a quantitative index of the relative superiority of the possible behavioral routes, it also should be considered as a technique to be taught to mechanics so that they can apply it routinely in their work. A deterrent to the latter use is the difficulty of the computations involved; computation is particularly difficult when the number of possibilities becomes large. This fact led to the development of a simplified procedure that might be used by mechanics. The 'simplified' procedure is one that appears to be more teachable to mechanics, and also one that is more likely to be used in the field in the daily business of finding malfunctions.

Probability and time data

The record of maintenance that was available included dial readings and information on both the prescribed maintenance and the completed maintenance. These data were available for forty-six aircraft, each with four engines. The records were analysed to determine the frequency of various types of repair associated with symptoms of malfunction and the amounts of time involved in performing these repairs.

Procedure for obtaining probability estimates. Objective standards applicable to all aircraft were not available for classifying as either normal or abnormal the dial indications obtained from the power plants. It therefore was necessary to use the available maintenance records to compute norms. These norms permitted the classification of readings from every dial as high, low or normal. With the dial readings classified it was possible to compute the probability estimates for the various repairs associated with the three classes of readings.

The first step in determining norms consisted in selecting the records for aircraft that had, for at least one engine, complete sets of instrument readings, each of which was followed by no maintenance. These records constituted the normative sample for individual aircraft. All of the readings for any one aircraft were combined disregarding engine position, and the semi-interquartile range was computed for each instrument at each of the three recorded power settings. At each power setting three evaluation ranges were identified, viz. high (H), normal (N) and low (L).

The next step consisted in assembling the sample of 'malfunction' readings. The sample selected contained only records from the twenty-one aircraft which supplied the normal sample of readings. Any records indicating that maintenance was performed on one or more engines immediately following the recording of the dial indications were included in this sample. A further restriction was that a record would not be included if the next record also showed that a repair had been accomplished on the same engine. These two restrictions were prompted by the following two assumptions: (a) a set of dial indications followed by a specific repair operation contained signs of the malfunction that was repaired; and (b) dial indications of a particular type of malfunction are more likely to be contained in readings associated with the performed repair when the next set of dial indications for that engine is not followed by an additional repair.

All the readings of the twenty-one aircraft were coded in terms of the H, N or L ranges into which they fell. Readings in the lowest quartile were coded L, in the middle two quartiles N, and in the highest quartile H. These classes of coded readings were then associated with the different types of repair performed after they were obtained. The probability value of every repair associated with a particular coded symptom was computed by using the entire set of records for each of the twenty-one different aircraft (eighty-four engines in all).

In the same way, *patterns* of coded symptoms at particular power settings were related to repairs. These patterns of symptoms are called 'level coded dial patterns' to distinguish them from patterns based upon all three of the power settings that were recorded. The latter are called 'coded dial syndromes'.

Procedure for obtaining time estimates for repairs. All examples of each type of maintenance were collated for all aircraft, and means and standard deviations of the time spent at each type of repair were computed. The assumption was that mean man hours per type of maintenance would represent the best estimate of the combined effects of difficulty of manipulation of the affected parts, accessibility and complexity of task – all of which presumably contribute to the overall efficiency of a course of action. All records were included in order to improve the reliability of estimates.

Method for combining estimates of probability and time

Complete method. Fundamental to the determination of an optimum course of action is the notion of rate. The obvious concern is with the average rate at which troubles are located over a series of occurrences of a set of symptoms. The criterion used to determine the efficiency of a course of action is the average number of man hours required to locate the actual trouble, given a number of occurrences of the symptom. If, for example, the conditions and values presented in Table 1 existed, an efficient course of action could be determined for the probability model by the complete method. In this example, three troubles are assumed to be possible causes of a given set of symptoms. These troubles are assumed (a) to have different frequencies of occurrence and (b) to require different amounts of time for repair (cost).

Table 1

A Hypothetical Example of Probability and Time Estimates for Three Troubles That Could Produce a Set of Symptoms and Total Man-Hour Requirements for the Six Possible Courses of Action per 100 Occurrences of the Symptoms

Trouble	Frequency per 100	p	Time (man hours)	Courses of action	Man hours required for 100 occurrences
A	50	0·5	3	ABC	420
B	30	0·3	2	ACB	410
C	20	0·2	1	BAC	430
				BCA	420
				CAB	400
				CBA	410

It would be possible to determine the optimum course of action by considering the six possible sequences in which the three possibilities could be checked. There are T-factorial sequences or courses of action available to a mechanic if there are T possible troubles for a given set of symptoms. In this example therefore there are six sequences. Each sequence or strategy must be considered in terms of the time required per possible trouble (tA, tB, tC) and in relation to the probability (pA, pB, pC) that each trouble (A, B, C) will be the actual cause in any given instance.

A course of action dictated by following the principle of maximizing probability would be to check troubles A, B and then C. This order would require 420 man hours of checking time over 100 occurrences of the symptoms associated with troubles A, B and C. According to this strategy each possibility is ordered in terms of its likelihood (probability) of producing the observed symptoms, i.e. what Detambel's subjects did. The average time per occurrence required in following this sequence for 100 occurrences would be 4·20 man hours. Is this sequence the most efficient course of action in terms of the average rate of location of the troubles associated with this set of symptoms? The answer is 'no' for these data. CAB is the most efficient, for if the mechanic checks C first (the least probable trouble) then in twenty times out of 100 he finds the trouble in one hour (total 20 hours); in fifty times out of 100 he finds trouble A in 4 hours, i.e. $tC + tA$ (total 200 hours); and in thirty times in 100 he finds the trouble in 6 hours, viz. $tC + tA + tB$ (total 180 hours). This route totals 400 man hours for 100 occurrences which results in an average rate of 4·00 man hours per occurrence of this symptom. The resulting averages for the other courses of action are greater. CAB is therefore the best route on the average. It maximizes the rate at which the troubles will be found or in other words it minimizes the amount of wasted man hours in the long run.

To use this complete method of computation in situations in which there are many possible troubles associated with a symptom would be difficult. For example, if there were seven possibilities, then 7! or 5040 totals would have to be compared; if eight, then $8! = 40,320$; $9! = 362,880$, etc. To accomplish the necessary calculation, even by using an electronic computer, would become a prohibitively difficult task with a large set of possibilities. While these calculations might be made for research purposes it is not likely that a mechanic would be interested in determining the relative efficiency of all permutations. He is more likely to want to know only the most efficient course of action.

A simplified method. Since a large number of possibilities demands a great deal of computation, and since the available data for time and frequency of occurrence are often based upon small samples, there is an obvious need for a simplified method of determining an efficient strategy which would consider the parameters of both time and probability but which would reduce the amount of computation required. One method of combination that would provide the basic data required in determining an efficient action sequence would be to use the 't/p ratio', The quantity t/p is an estimate of the mean amount of time that would be spent in checking a possible trouble, per discovery that it was the *actual* trouble.

A procedural rule which would provide an efficient strategy is to check possible troubles in the order of increasing t/p value. To use this strategy it is necessary to calculate only as many t/p ratios as there are possible troubles associated with a symptom. Using the example in Table 1, the three calculations required are: (a) $\bar{T}A = tA/pA$; (b) $\bar{T}B = tB/pB$; and (c) $\bar{T}C = tC/pC$. These values are 6, 6·7 and 5 respectively, for this example. Having computed the values of $\bar{T}$ the next step is to order them from smallest to largest. The resulting order is the best course of action for this example, i.e. CAB. Separate computation of the mean time per discovery for each possible trouble (t/p ratio) does not also provide an estimate of the average time per discovery of a trouble for every possible sequence of action that could be followed. However, the complete method does provide this information. Therefore, for research purposes, and in particular with respect to problems of the criterion for evaluating observed behavioral sequences, the complete method is necessary. Because of the relative ease with which an efficient course of action can be identified using the simplified technique, it is potentially more useful than the complete method as a procedure that could be both taught to mechanics and used by them in their work.

Use of the t/p ratio

Three examples of the application of the simplified method for finding an efficient reduction sequence will be presented. Two of these examples are at one level and a third is at another level of symptom complexity. The first level of complexity is represented by two examples in each of which six or seven possible troubles were found to be associated with a *single* symptom. At this level of symptom complexity the number of possible troubles is at a maximum and the individual probability values are lowest. In general, a single symptom in isolation presents a minimal amount of diagnostic information.

The third example is one in which the empirical relationships between a set of five troubles are associated with a level coded dial pattern of symptoms. This is a pattern of three symptoms, each obtained from a different dial but all observed at the same power setting (level). It too is a simplified example in that it is customary practice to run an engine at several different power settings to obtain symptom information. This example contains only a part of the information a mechanic would normally obtain in the course of making his diagnosis. But it is more realistic than the 'single symptom' cases as an example of the application of the proposed method of combining probability and time estimates. Further, it illustrates a criterion sequence for evaluating the behavior of a mechanic, and also demonstrates what a mechanic could do if he were taught to use the simplified procedure for deciding upon an efficient course of action.

Probability and time estimates. Suitable records for the normative sample were obtained from twenty-one different aircraft out of the total of forty-six. Each of the selected aircraft had sixteen or more records containing complete dial indications for one or more engines which were not followed by some type of repair. The malfunction sample of records for the same twenty-one aircraft contained eighty-seven sets of readings, each of which was associated with one of thirteen different repairs. In all, sixty-eight different types of maintenance were found within the complete sample of records collected. The mean times, for these types of maintenance, varied from 0·5 hour for 'insert bearings in idle mixture' to 33·5 hours for 'Repair T.O.P.'.

Reduction of trouble possibilities associated with single symptoms. Table 2 indicates the probabilities that each of eleven repairs will be associated with each of three types of readings for three different instruments at a power setting of 2300 r.p.m. Two types of repair stand out as highly probable causes of all of these symptoms, i.e. A and B. They are magneto timing and spark plugs. These two forms of ignition trouble might represent 'maintenance stereotypes' which cause the real trouble to remain undetected and generate a recurring series of repair operations. For example, if the trouble is not due primarily to a spark plug and if the latter is affected by the 'real' trouble, replacing the plug might cause the observed symptoms to disappear. But they would then be likely to reappear one or two flights later. Such circumstances could result in a large number of spark plug 'troubles' in the present sample in spite of the fact that rules were used to exclude records of recurring trouble. Operational research would be necessary to establish the validity and meaning of such figures as those presented in Table 2. However, these data serve the present

Table 2

Probabilities of Eleven Repairs in Relation to Symptoms on Three Engine Dials at a Power Setting of 2300 r.p.m.

Repair Trouble	Mean time (hours)	Symptom probabilities		
		Low torque oil pressure	High manifold pressure	High fuel flow
A	11·1	0·286	0·200	0·220
B	1·5	0·528	0·400	0·440
C	12·8	0·000	0·000	0·037
D	2·0	0·000	0·000	0·037
E	7·1	0·036	0·000	0·000
F	2·0	0·036	0·000	0·000
G	2·7	0·011	0·067	0·037
H	1·3	0·070	0·000	0·000
I	2·6	0·000	0·130	0·110
J	12·0	0·036	0·130	0·037
K	4·1	0·000	0·067	0·070

purpose of illustrating the type of problem situation that confronts a mechanic in deciding upon a course of action. To demonstrate the method of solving this type of situation let us consider two examples.

First example. In column 1 of Table 3 the probabilities of occurrence (from Table 2) of seven troubles with a low torque oil pressure reading (T.O.P.) at a power setting of 2300 r.p.m. are listed. Column 2 indicates the mean time required to perform each type of repair. The t/p ratios (mean repair time divided by the probability of occurrence) for every possible trouble are listed in column 3. In column 4, the best action or checking sequence is listed, with an ordinal number 1 indicating the first trouble to be checked and number 6 the last. This sequence represents the most efficient course of action in response to this symptom.

Table 3

Best Action Sequence to be Followed in Locating the Trouble Producing a 'Low' T.O.P. Reading at 2300 r.p.m. in an Aircraft Engine

Troubles	Probability of occurrence * p (1)	Mean repair time (hours) † t (2)	t/p ratio (3)	Best checking sequence (4)
B	0·528	1·5	2·83	1st
A	0·286	11·1	38·27	3rd
H	0·070	1·3	18·57	2nd
J	0·036	12·0	300·00	7th
E	0·036	7·1	177·50	5th
F	0·036	2·0	50·00	4th
G	0·011	2·7	270·00	6th

* Probability of a trouble based upon maintenance records. These values were rounded to two places when the t/p ratios were computed.

† Time estimates based upon maintenance records.

Mathematical proof is available for the general applicability of this method. In all applications made thus far to the available data, this method has been found to provide the efficient course of action.

Second example. The results of a second application of the t/p ratio to troubles associated with a single symptom of malfunction are presented in Table 4. The data in this case refer to the symptom 'high manifold pressure reading at 2300 r.p.m.'. Interpretation of the table is the same as for Table 3.

Both examples support a conceptual model in terms of which differences in efficiency in trouble shooting are a joint function of the probabilities associating diagnostic signs with possible causes and their repair times. The proposed methods for determining an efficient strategy are therefore potentially useful devices for establishing objective criteria by means of which (a) the efficiency of behavior routes in trouble shooting can be evaluated, and (b) an efficient course of action can be determined.

Table 4

Best Action Sequence to be Followed in Locating the Trouble
Producing a 'High' M.P. Reading at 2300 r.p.m. in an Aircraft
Engine

Troubles	Probability of occurrence * p (1)	Mean repair time (hours) † t (2)	t/p ratio (3)	Best checking sequence (4)
B	0·400	1·5	3·75	1st
A	0·200	11·1	55·50	4th
I	0·130	2·6	20·00	2nd
J	0·130	12·0	92·30	6th
G	0·067	2·7	38·57	3rd
K	0·067	4·1	58·57	5th

* Probability of a trouble based upon maintenance records. These values
were rounded to two places when the t/p ratios were computed.

† Time estimates based upon maintenance records.

*Reduction of trouble possibilities associated with a pattern of
symptoms.* An example of symptom-cause probabilities existing
when level-coded dial indications are available as diagnostic signs
is presented in Table 5. This example serves as an application of

Table 5

Best Action Sequence to Follow in Locating the Trouble
Producing an L.L.L. Pattern of Readings at 2300 r.p.m. in an
Aircraft Engine

Trouble	Probability of occurrence * p (1)	Mean repair time (hours) † t (2)	t/p ratio (3)	Best checking sequence (4)
A	0·276	11·1	40·21	5th
B	0·390	1·5	3·84	1st
D	0·054	2·0	37·04	4th
G	0·167	2·7	16·16	3rd
H	0·110	1·3	11·81	2nd

* Probability of a trouble based upon maintenance records.

† Time estimates based upon maintenance records.

the simplified method to a *pattern* of symptoms at a given power setting. Column 1 of Table 5 lists the obtained probabilities for the five repairs that were effective in removing the indications of malfunction in this example. The symptom pattern consists of 'low' readings for three instruments (M.P., T.O.P., F.F.) at 2300 r.p.m. This example is one of the seventeen level-coded dial patterns found in the available records. The results of this application of the simplified method also are indicated in Table 5, column 4. The course of action for this example, as indicated by t/p ratios, is to check B first, H second, G third, D fourth and A last.

Estimation of Probability and Work-Time

Maintenance records which provide the necessary information for generating an optimum strategy for a particular set of symptoms are not always available. Frequently repairs and work-time data are recorded but the observed symptoms which led to the decision to repair a component are not. Also a real problem exists for relatively new equipment. In the absence of these two types of data it is reasonable to ask whether experienced individuals can estimate these values.

Subjects

Instructors in an advanced reciprocating engine course were asked to estimate probability and time values associated with a variety of repairs. Ten instructors were available for this task.

Method

The instructors served as judges and rated each one of several defects associated with symptoms of malfunction in terms of probability and time.

The end points of the scale used to rate the likelihood of repairs for sets of symptoms were: (5) 'always the cause of the trouble' ..., (1) 'seldom the cause of the trouble'. Those for work-time were: (A) 'an excessive amount of time' and (E) 'very little time'.

Results

A distribution-free technique described by Mood (3) was used to analyse the ratings assigned by these instructors to determine how well they agreed. For three separate sets of ratings the χ^2 values for the appropriate degrees of freedom exceeded the 0·01 level of confidence.

Apparently different instructors have different frames of reference with which they evaluate the probability and work requirements of the various repairs.

Implications

Some important implications can be drawn from these data. One is that experienced personnel may not agree in their estimates of probability and work. Since they do not agree they may impart different information to their students regarding the relative probability and work values associated with repairs. While trainees could be expected to revise rapidly their work estimates with brief experience, they are not likely to achieve this for the probability values. Another implication is that at best the judgements of work and probability values of experienced personnel should be used with a great deal of caution until additional information becomes available on their ability to perform this type of judgement task.

Summary

A probabilistic model of 'trouble shooting' was presented and available maintenance records for forty-six four-engine aircraft were analysed to obtain estimates of the probability of each possible cause of a particular set of diagnostic signs. The mean repair times also were computed for each type of repair. The mean time estimates ranged from 0·5 hour for 'insert bearing in idle mixture' to 33·5 hours for 'repair T.O.P.'. Both the probability and time estimates obtained for the different symptom-cause relationships confirmed the basic assumption of the model that for a set of possible troubles associated with a symptom, the probability and/or time values are unequal.

Many of the implications of the model were discussed. One important one for future research was the definition of the criterion of the efficient strategy or course of action for a given set of diagnostic signs. The efficient mechanic, from the point of view of the probabilistic model, would be the person who, when given a particular set of symptoms, selected the course of action which, if it was followed whenever the particular set of diagnostic signs appeared, would result in the fastest average rate of identification of the cause of a trouble.

A complete method and a simplified method were described for determining an efficient course of action to be followed in reducing a set of possible causes of malfunction to the actual cause. These methods, generated by the model, utilize both probability and time estimates for each of the possible malfunctions. To illustrate the complete method a simple hypothetical example was used. This method permits a determination of (a) the comparative efficiency of all possible course of action, (b) an objective and quantitative scale for the evaluation of observed strategies and (c) the separate identification of the most efficient course of action. However, it is cumbersome to use when there are several possible malfunctions for a given set of symptoms, since it is necessary to make T-factorial sets of computations of man-hours if there are T-possible troubles.

To overcome this limitation, a simplified method was proposed. Three examples of the application of this procedure for finding an efficient course of action without determining the efficiency of *all possible* behavior routes were presented. The data used for these examples came from the analyses of maintenance records. This technique uses the mean repair time and probability values, i.e. the t/p ratio, to determine the course of action to follow in reducing the list of possible troubles.

The results of the analyses of maintenance records were sufficiently encouraging to suggest that further research of this type be done for a variety of complex devices. In particular, operational research is required (a) to provide more evidence for the variations among the probability and time estimates associated with sets of possible troubles, and (b) to validate the assumptions concerning the efficiency of the proposed methods for determining the trouble which produces diagnostic symptoms in complex devices such as aircraft power plants, television sets, radar equipment, etc.

Experienced instructors showed a statistically significant amount of disagreement among themselves in their judgements of probability and time associated with repairs. This result indicates the potential hazard of employing personnel to obtain this type of data. Objective records of maintenance appear to be required to accomplish this.

References
1. M. H. DETAMBEL, 'Probabilities of success and amounts of work in a multi choice situation', *J. exp. Psychol.*, vol. 51 (1956), pp. 41–4.
2. R. B. MILLER, J. D. FOLLEY and P. R. SMITH, *Trouble-Shooting in Electronics Equipment: A Proposed Method*, American Institute for Research, Pittsburgh, 1953.
3. A. M. MOOD, *Introduction to the Theory of Statistics*, McGraw-Hill, 1950.
4. J. L. SAUPE, *Trouble-Shooting Electronic Equipment*, Bureau of Educational Research, College of Education, University of Illinois, 1954.

Part Three Monitoring and Inspection

One of the consequences of automation is that less time will be spent in manual production skills and more in watching dials and meters. This raises the problems of detection efficiency and human alertness which first appeared in the wartime context of maintaining radar watch. There is now a wide literature on these topics, which Broadbent reviews in Reading 7.

At the same time, it can be predicted that the importance of inspection techniques will grow. Colquhoun's article (Reading 8) demonstrates the ways in which existing knowledge can be applied to practical inspection problems. Reading 9 by Thomas discusses the changes in perception which occur in experienced industrial inspectors, taking examples from the quality control of paint finishes, domestic cleaners and castings. The inspector's task is sometimes poorly defined; in one such case Chaney and Teel (Reading 10) are able to show the improvement in efficiency obtained by providing visual aids and specific training.

7 D. E. Broadbent

Vigilance

D. E. Broadbent, 'Vigilance', *British Medical Bulletin*, vol. 20 (1964), pp. 17–20.

Vigilance is the name given to human performance in situations where a faint and infrequent signal has to be detected at an uncertain time. Practical examples of this kind of task are to be found in the work of radar operators keeping a watch for aircraft or ships appearing on their screens, and in the work of industrial inspectors monitoring a continuous flow of finished products in search of a faulty article.

1. History of the Problem

Mackworth demonstrated during the war that performance in such tasks could be studied in the laboratory and revealed interesting changes in efficiency. In his early experiments he studied a task in which a clock pointer moved in a series of jumps (Mackworth, 1950). Occasionally the pointer gave a double jump which the human observer had to detect and report. Mackworth discovered a rapid decline in the proportion of such signals which were detected, so that in a two-hour period of watch the first half-hour gave substantially better performance than any of the succeeding half-hours. This rapid fatigue-like drop in efficiency was of obvious practical importance, as well as being an apparent instance of deterioration in work which did not involve much muscular effort. Much attention was therefore paid to ways of preventing the decline from appearing. Mackworth showed that it could be markedly reduced by rest pauses, by amphetamine, by providing immediate knowledge of results whenever a target was detected or missed, and by various other changes in the experimental situation.

Subsequent investigators used a variety of tasks different from

Mackworth's in various respects: thus, a number of sources of signals might require watching, the signal might remain visible until dealt with, the signal might be a change in some stimulus which occurred regularly or might be the occurrence of some event which did not take place at all at other times, and so on. Broadbent (1958) has reviewed in detail most of the experiments up to that date; recent surveys have been undertaken by Frankmann and Adams (1962), by McGrath, Harabedian and Buckner (1959) and by Bergum and Klein (1961).

2. Effects of Probability of Signals

It early appeared (Deese, 1955; Jenkins, 1958) that the higher the rate at which signals occurred, the more efficient the observer was in detecting them. This observation by itself might imply simply that an increase in the general level of stimulation served to keep the observer awake; but it seems rather that the observer is particularly good at detecting signals at a time when they are particularly probable. Thus Baker (1959a) found that the rapid deterioration during a watch, shown by Mackworth, depended upon the wide range of inter-signal time intervals employed by Mackworth. Some of the latter's signals were separated by intervals of only 45 seconds, and others by 10 minutes. If signals occurred at about the same over-all average rate, but with the longest interval only 150 seconds, the second half-hour of a watch was just as efficient as the first. Baker (1959b) has since shown that a completely regular sequence, in which a signal occurs every 150 seconds exactly, shows no significant decrement in performance during a period of an hour. The point of such a sequence is of course that the signal becomes extremely probable at the time when it is in fact just about to arrive; and thus it is efficiently detected. Baker (1959b, 1962) has also analysed the detectability of signals which occur at various times since the last signal, and concluded that a signal is more likely to be noticed if it occurs at about the average interval between signals that has already been experienced. A number of other investigators have, however, performed similar analyses (see Frankmann and Adams, 1962) and have come to negative conclusions about the effect of inter-signal interval. It seems clear that the time since the last signal may or may not affect performance, depending on a number of other conditions: but it is equally clear that increases in the average probability of the whole series of signals will increase the efficiency of detection.

Performance also changes with changes in the conditional probability of occurrence of a signal, given that some other event has occurred. Thus Colquhoun (1961) presented objects for inspection at various rates, and with varying proportions of objects containing a signal that was to be detected. The important determinant of behaviour was the probability that a signal would occur, given that an object had been presented for inspection – and not the over-all rate of presentation of objects or of signals. Correspondingly, when there are several places in which signals may occur, it is more likely that any given event will be detected if it happens in the place where the majority of signals have occurred in the past (Blair and Kaufman, 1959; Nicely and Miller, 1957).

The generalization that a low signal probability means a low probability of detection does not necessarily imply that a situation in which signals are very infrequent will be one in which the efficiency of the observer will be lower at the end of a work period than it is at the beginning (cf. Buckner and McGrath, 1963). Although such an effect of signal probability upon the rate of decline has been reported in the past (Kappauf and Powe, 1959), this has usually been under circumstances in which the experimental subjects were trained before the experiment with a fairly high frequency of signals and then tested with a low frequency. The readjustment of their subjective probabilities from high to low as the period of watch continued might well be expected to produce a downward trend in performance. The effect of the prior training of the subjects has been demonstrated by Colquhoun and Baddeley (1963), and it would appear that when this preliminary training is held constant there is no greater deterioration during the run in people who are experiencing a low frequency of signals than there is in people who are experiencing a high frequency; although, of course, the former are less efficient than the latter even at the beginning of the run.

Because of the beneficial effect of a high signal probability, it has often been suggested that in practical situations the efficiency of radar monitors or industrial inspectors could be improved by the insertion of artificial signals interspersed among the real ones. Experiment shows that such artificial signals are indeed helpful (Baker, 1960; Wilkinson, 1964; Faulkner, 1962). It is, however, essential that the artificial signal be introduced unexpectedly as part of the real task, and not as a clear interruption in the normal job of looking for real signals (Wallis and Newton, 1957).

A particular advantage of artificial signals is of course that they can be used to provide immediate knowledge of results to the observer, and this, as already indicated, is helpful to him. In addition there appears to be some effect upon his general state of arousal or alertness (cf. Baker, 1961; Loeb and Schmidt, 1963).

3. Effects of the General State of Alertness

Since the early work of Bjerner (1949), who showed that a man lying relaxed and listening for an auditory signal would be unduly likely to fail to respond to the signal if his electro-encephalogram (EEG) were showing signs of lowered arousal or sleep, it has frequently been urged that efficiency in vigilance tasks is determined by a general state of excitability, alertness or arousal. It is plausible to suppose that the downward trend in efficiency from the beginning of a watch to the end might in some cases be due to a lowered state of arousal because of the monotony and un-stimulating quality of the surroundings of the task. Certainly, physiological measures may show a tendency towards lowered arousal as the task proceeds (Dardano, 1962) and, although observation of simultaneous changes in performance and physiology does not prove that the latter cause the former, it encourages that belief. There is evidence too that individuals who show least effect in vigilance tasks after loss of sleep may be those who show least drop in physiological measures of arousal (Corcoran, 1963).

An alternative line of proof comes from attempts to change the level of arousal by various experimental treatments, such as testing the observer at various times of day when he might, through his normal diurnal rhythm, be supposed to be at varying levels of arousal. Tests of this kind have indeed shown a higher level of efficiency later in the day rather than earlier, which is what we would expect (Colquhoun, 1962). From other findings it would seem that this difference may be much greater in some individuals than in others, since the direction of correlation between a vigilance task and a personality test changed as the day proceeded (Colquhoun, 1960); but this does not affect the implication that some general state of arousal was affecting the vigilance performance. Sleep-deprivation also causes lowered efficiency at vigilance tasks (Corcoran, 1962; Wilkinson, 1960; Williams, Lubin and Goodnow, 1959), and this also is a treatment which may be supposed to lower the general level of arousal (Broadbent, 1963, p. 184). McGrath (1960) has found that a variety of auditory stimuli presented during the performance of a visual vigilance task improved performance; and equally that people did an auditory task better if allowed to look at a variety of visual stimuli while working. It appears therefore that if arousal is allowed to drop to a low level, poor performance in vigilance will result.

But it does not necessarily follow that an increase in the level of stimulation will always be beneficial. Beyond a certain point, further increases in arousal may not be helpful. Corcoran (1963) found his correlations between performance and physiological measures only in subjects who had been deprived of sleep. McGrath and Hatcher (1961) found no advantage from varied auditory stimulation when the signal frequency in the task was higher than that previously used by McGrath; and Adams and Boulter (1960), using a complex task, found no beneficial effect from an increase in signal rate itself. Corcoran (1963) found an improvement from increasing the rate of signals in the task itself only when the subjects had been without sleep. In general, therefore, although low arousal means bad performance, it does not follow that increasing arousal beyond a certain point will improve performance.

4. Effects of Distracting and Competing Stimulation

The presence of noise of high intensity may in some circumstances cause deterioration in vigilance. This has been found by Broadbent (1954) and by Jerison (1959). The combined effects of noise and vibration also produced deterioration in subjects studied by Loeb and Jeantheau (1958). In all these studies the task was one involving a number of different possible sources of signals, and it may therefore be that the level of arousal produced by the task itself was reasonably high. Indeed, Jerison (1957) found that noise had no effect on a vigilance task involving only one source of signals and a low rate of presentation of signals – such a task might well be unarousing. Unpublished work by myself has shown a similar result, while also demonstrating that it is possible to obtain a harmful effect of noise on a vigilance task by using only one source of signals, provided that the signal rate is high. It has also been shown by Corcoran (1962) that the harmful effects of loss of sleep on vigilance may actually be reduced by the presence of noise of high intensity. In general, therefore, it seems to be true that an intense competing stimulus may be harmful, but only if the observer is already in a fairly aroused and alert state. If he is relaxed and unstimulated, external irrelevant stimuli in addition to those from the task itself may simply serve to wake him up.

5. Inspection at One's Own Speed

If the bad effect of such competing stimulation is due to a distraction of attention, it might be expected that the distraction would not have a continuous effect throughout the work period, but would make the man inefficient at some times and not at others. To the extent that a similar process occurs in any vigilance situation, one might expect that the response time for detecting a signal would show a variability which might be increased or decreased by suitable conditions; and indeed, Faulkner (1962) and Fraser (1952) have found that variability increases as the work period continues. One might also expect that a prolonged duration of the signal would improve the frequency with which it was detected, since it would allow time for the diverted attention to return. But if this general account is correct, then in a situation where a series of objects has to be inspected it should be beneficial to give the subject control over the length of time for which each object is present before he passes on to the next. An unpaced system would allow time for momentary distractions to occur without harming performance; and indeed in continuous work rather than vigilance it has been found that unpaced performance is considerably better than a forced mechanical rate (Broadbent, 1953; Conrad and Hille, 1955).

In the case of vigilance, however, this assumption does not appear to be correct. Studies of the comparison of paced and unpaced vigilance by Colquhoun (1962) and by Wilkinson (1961) have shown that no benefit is secured by allowing a man to inspect at his own rate. A similar conclusion can be drawn from experiments cited by Broadbent (1963, p. 72) using 'observing responses' (Holland, 1957). Holland required his subjects to press a button in order to secure a flash of light to look at the dial which they were watching; and Broadbent, using a similar technique, found that, as a period of watch proceeded, his subjects tended to press the button at an increasing rate but to require more observations of a signal before they would report it as such. Thus it seems that, under certain conditions, the motor response of calling for the next object or display to be observed may become independent of the attentive state of the observer; and hence there is no advantage in letting the man set his own rate of work in this kind of situation.

6. Simultaneous Use of Different Senses

Another possible application of the idea that attention wanders during vigilance is the presentation of signals to the observer by more than one sensory channel. If the operator ceases to attend to his eyes, he may well be attending to his ears. One might therefore arrange that each individual signal is made not only visible but also audible, in the hope that the probability that he will detect it on one channel will be almost independent of the probability that he will detect it on the other. In fact both Buckner and McGrath (1961) and Loveless (1957) have found that this can happen, e.g. if men miss one signal in ten by eye or ear alone, they miss only two or three in 100 when both are used.

Another possible way of using both eyes and ears simultaneously is to give the subject two separate jobs, one to be done using the eyes and the other using the ears, but never with a signal coming in by both simultaneously. Once again, this may do little harm if concentration on vision is almost independent of listening carefully; and extra stimulation through the ears might

173

indeed be helpful to a visual task if the latter were rather un-arousing. Indeed, use of ears as well as eyes in this way has been found quite acceptable in experiments closely simulating real naval situations (Wallis and Samuel, 1961). Other studies by Buckner and McGrath (1961) and by McGrath (1962) have found that combined auditory and visual tasks were performed on the average just about as well as each was done when alone. An interesting qualification of this statement is that performance of the easier task improved and of the harder one got worse. McGrath suggests that the effect may be due to a beneficial effect of arousal on the easy task and a harmful effect on the more difficult one. If this is so, it might well be that two fairly easy tasks would both be improved by simultaneous performance.

Because of the effect of the difficulty of the task, it is hard to draw firm conclusions about the relative merits of the eyes, ears, or other senses for vigilance. In general, hearing seems less frequently to have shown a decrement during the watch period, and this has been found again by Loeb and Hawkes (1961) who compared auditory with cutaneous stimuli at equal subjective intensity. The cutaneous task showed a more rapid deterioration. In this case the auditory stimulus was a noise covering a wide band of frequencies and, as Loeb and Hawkes point out, this type of signal may be much easier to detect under vigilance conditions than is a pure tone of a single frequency.

7. Effects of Caution or Riskiness in Reporting

An important new development in the study of vigilance stems from the work of Tanner and Swets (1954). In all the studies mentioned so far, the observer's report has been treated as if he either detected the signal or completely missed it, without any intermediate category; but there may be a whole range of states, from complete confidence that a signal is present, through complete uncertainty, to confidence that no signal is present. The precise point along this continuum at which the observer decides whether or not to report a signal may make a great difference to his performance as recorded by traditional methods. Tanner and Swets described the performance of a human signal detector in terms of a randomly varying process inside the brain, whose average value was changed by the arrival of a signal. If a signal was reported whenever a certain critical level was exceeded, a proportion of signals would be reported, but there would also be a proportion of false reports of the presence of signals when none in fact occurred. Shifts in the critical level would affect both proportions, but changes in the rate of detecting signals might be very large for quite small changes in the rate of false reports. If one asks subjects in a vigilance task to record their degree of confidence in their reports, one finds (Broadbent, 1963) that the less confident reports do in fact show a high ratio of detections to false alarms, as Tanner and Swets would predict. This is quite inconsistent with the usual assumption that there is no half-way house between a detection and a failure to detect.

Since this is so, it means that the downward trend during a watch in vigilance tasks may be due either to a shift in the critical level which the observer sets himself for reporting, or to a change in the underlying efficiency of his senses. Both possibilities are being examined by Mackworth and Taylor (1963) of the Defence Research Board Medical Laboratories of Toronto, who have measured detections and false alarms during the watch under different conditions, with various reporting methods. They find that efficiency of the senses declines smoothly throughout watch periods as long as an hour. The evidence for a change in critical level was ambiguous. I have found a definite effect on critical level (Broadbent, 1963, p. 72) and, in unpublished work, have also found that similar changes in critical level underlie effects of intense noise on visual vigilance.

It is to be expected that the position of such a critical level for decision would depend upon the probability of a signal, and hence would explain many of the effects referred to already. It is less clear how changes in arousal would affect the critical level, but it is not inconceivable that they should do so, and hence that the bad effects of states of drowsiness and under-stimulation on the one hand, or of exposure to very high levels of stimulation and distraction on the other hand, should produce a low level of detection.

8. Conclusions

As research on vigilance increases, it has become evident that no one theory will account for all the phenomena. Attempts have been made to explain poor performance as due to low expectancy, low arousal, distraction and the accumulation of inhibition; but each of these explanations is inconsistent with some of the facts. We may, however, be on the verge of combining the various points of view into a single description, using the statistical decision theory of Tanner and Swets.

References

ADAMS, J. A., and BOULTER, L. R. (1960), Monitoring of complex visual displays: I. Effects of response complexity and inter-signal interval on vigilant behavior when visual load is moderate, *Technical Note AFCCDD-TN-60-63*, *Air Force Command and Control Development Division, U.S. Air Force.*

BAKER, C. H. (1959a), *Brit. J. Psychol.*, vol. 50, p. 30.

BAKER, C. H. (1959b), Three minor studies of vigilance, *Defence Research Medical Laboratories Report*, no. 234-2, Canadian Defence Research Board.

BAKER, C. H. (1960), *J. appl. Psychol.*, vol. 44, p. 336.

BAKER, C. H. (1961), *Ergonomics*, vol. 4, p. 311.

BAKER, C. H. (1962), *Science*, vol. 1936, p. 46.

BERGUM, B. O., and KLEIN, I. C. (1961), A survey and analysis of vigilance research, *HRU Report, Human Research Unit, Fort Bliss, Texas*, no. 8.

BJERNER, B. (1949), *Acta physiol. Scand.*, vol. 19, suppl. 65.

BLAIR, W. C., and KAUFMAN, H. M. (1959), Command control – I: Multiple display monitoring; II: Control-display spatial arrangement, *General Dynamics Corp. Report*, *Groton, Conn.*, no. SPD 59-082.

BROADBENT, D. E. (1953), *Brit. J. Psychol.*, vol. 44, p. 295.

BROADBENT, D. E. (1954), *Quart. J. exp. Psychol.*, vol. 6, p. 1.

BROADBENT, D. E. (1958), *Perception and Communication*, Pergamon.

BROADBENT, D. E. (1963), in D. N. Buckner and J. J. McGrath (eds.), *Vigilance: A Symposium Sponsored by the Office of Naval Research Conducted by Human Factors Research, Inc., Los Angeles, California*, McGraw-Hill, pp. 72 and 184.

BUCKNER, D. N., and McGRATH, J. J. (1961), A comparison of performances on single and dual sensory mode vigilance tests, *Technical Report, Human Factor Problems in Anti-submarine Warfare, Human Factors Research, Inc., Los Angeles*, no. 8.

BUCKNER, D. N., and MCGRATH, J. J. (eds.) (1963), *Vigilance: A Symposium Sponsored by the Office of Naval Research Conducted by Human Factors Research, Inc., Los Angeles, California*, McGraw-Hill.

COLQUHOUN, W. P. (1960), *Ergonomics*, vol. 3, p. 377.

COLQUHOUN, W. P. (1961), *Ergonomics*, vol. 4, p. 41.

COLQUHOUN, W. P. (1962), *Bull. C.E.R.P.* (*Bull. Etud. Rech. psychol.*), vol. 11, p. 27.

COLQUHOUN, W. P., and BADDELEY, A. D. (1963), *J. exp. Psychol.*, vol. 68, p. 156.

CONRAD, R., and HILLE, B. A. (1955), *Occup. Psychol.*, vol. 29, p. 15.

CORCORAN, D. W. J. (1962), *Quart. J. exp. Psychol.*, vol. 14, p. 178.

CORCORAN, D. W. J. (1963), Individual differences in performance after loss of sleep, *Ph.D. Thesis, University of Cambridge*.

DARDANO, J. F. (1962), *J. appl. Psychol.*, vol. 46, p. 106.

DEESE, J. (1955), *Psychol. Rev.*, vol. 62, p. 359.

FAULKNER, T. W. (1962), *J. appl. Psychol.*, vol. 46, p. 325.

FRANKMANN, J. P., and ADAMS, J. A. (1962), *Psychol. Bull.*, vol. 59, p. 257.

FRASER, D. C. (1952), A study of fatigue in aircrew. Interim report. I. Validation of techniques, *Report, Applied Psychology Research Unit, Medical Research Council*, no. 185/52.

HOLLAND, J. G. (1957), *Science*, vol. 125, p. 348.

JENKINS, H. M. (1958), *Amer. J. Psychol.*, vol. 71, p. 647.

JERISON, H. J. (1957), *J. acoust. Soc. Amer.*, vol. 29, p. 1163.

JERISON, H. J. (1959), *J. appl. Psychol.*, vol. 43, p. 96.

KAPPAUF, W. E., and POWE, W. E. (1959), *J. exp. Psychol.*, vol. 57, p. 49.

LOEB, M., and HAWKES, G. R. (1961), The effect of rise and decay time on vigilance for weak auditory and cutaneous stimuli, *Report, U.S. Army Medical Research Laboratory, Fort Knox*, no. 49.

LOEB, M., and JEANTHEAU, G. (1958), *J. appl. Psychol.*, vol. 42, p. 47.

LOEB, M., and SCHMIDT, E. A. (1963), *Ergonomics*, vol. 6, p. 75.

LOVELESS, N. E. (1957), Signal detection with simultaneous visual and auditory presentation, *Air Ministry, Flying Personnel Research Committee Report*, no. FPRC/1027.

MCGRATH, J. J. (1960), The effect of irrelevant environmental stimulation on vigilance performance, *Technical Report, Human Factor Problems in Anti-submarine Warfare, Human Factors Research, Inc., Los Angeles*, no 6.

MCGRATH, J. J. (1962), Performance sharing in dual-mode monitoring, *Technical Report, Human Factors Research, Inc., Los Angeles*, no. 740-1.

MCGRATH, J. J., HARABEDIAN, A., and BUCKNER, D. N. (1959), Review and critique of the literature on vigilance performance, *Technical Report, Human Factor Problems in Anti-submarine Warfare, Human Factors Research, Inc., Los Angeles*, no. 1.

MCGRATH, J. J., and HATCHER, J. F. (1961), Irrelevant stimulation and vigilance under fast and slow stimulus rates, *Technical Report, Human Factor Problems in Anti-submarine Warfare, Human Factors Research, Inc., Los Angeles*, no. 7.

MACKWORTH, J. F., and TAYLOR, M. M. (1963), *Canad. J. Psychol.*, vol. 17, p. 302.

MACKWORTH, N. H. (1950), *Spec. Rep. Ser. Med. Res. Coun., Lond.*, no. 268.

NICELY, P. E., and MILLER, G. A. (1957), *J. exp. Psychol.*, vol. 53, p. 195.

TANNER, W. P., and SWETS, J. A. (1954), *Psychol. Rev.*, vol. 61, p. 401.

WALLIS, D., and NEWTON, G. DE C. (1957), An experiment on synthetic signal injection as a method of improving radar detection, *S.P. Report W2/4, Division of the Senior Psychologist, Admiralty*.

WALLIS, D., and SAMUEL, J. A. (1961), *Ergonomics*, vol. 4, p. 155.

WILKINSON, R. T. (1960), *Quart. J. exp. Psychol.*, vol. 12, p. 36.

WILKINSON, R. T. (1961), *Ergonomics*, vol. 4, p. 259.

WILKINSON, R. T. (1964), *Ergonomics*, vol. 4, p. 63.

WILLIAMS, H. L., LUBIN, A., and GOODNOW, J. (1959), *Psychol. Monogr.*, vol. 73, no. 14.

8 W. P. Colquhoun

The Reliability of the Human Element in a Quality Control System

W. P. Colquhoun, 'The reliability of the human element in a quality control system', *Glass Technology*, vol. 4 (1963), pp. 94–8.

Inspection of glassware relies heavily on the human qualities of the sorters and these need to be understood if the best results are to be obtained. The ability to detect faults diminishes as fatigue increases, especially if there are very few faults present, but it is shown that the effect of fatigue can be overcome by the introduction of other tasks which reduce monotony. If there is an unexpected reduction in defects, the sorter is likely to reject good ware, but if the defect-rate increases suddenly the sorter is likely to miss many of them. The boundary between acceptance and rejection can be influenced by the severity of the previous defects and steps may therefore be necessary to keep the 'standard' stable. Other factors can influence the level of the 'standard' such as the tendency of a sorter to use a 'favourite' rejection rate, irrespective of the actual average quality of the output. Social and organizational aspects of the inspector's job are at least as important in determining his efficiency as his level of skill or the difficulty of the task.

Although the age of automatic inspection is approaching, it would seem that for some time to come the responsibility for detecting and classifying faulty products will rest on mere human beings: thus any quality control system is as good as its individual human components. This applies whether we are considering the case of 100 per cent examination or the operation of a sampling scheme; in the latter situation the actual number of operatives required is of course very much smaller, but the problem of human reliability is if anything greater since any errors of assessment are automatically magnified.

Basically the human inspector performs two operations: *detection* of faults in the product and *classification* or grading of the faulty items according to the severity of the defect. Since he cannot carry out the second of these functions without successfully concluding the first, it seems logical to approach the question of human reliability in this kind of work by considering first the efficiency of the human operator as a detector of small changes in his environment, or, as these are termed in psychology, 'signals', and secondly the question of how well people are able to make judgements of perceived variations in the nature of these signals.

The Human Operator as a Signal Detector

Psychological interest in the problem of signal detection was stimulated by the wartime observation that personnel performing watchkeeping duties using equipment such as search-radar and anti-submarine listening devices exhibited an alarming tendency to report fewer and fewer 'targets' as their period on watch lengthened. Since this seemed to be more than coincidence, an investigation was started into the possible reasons for this 'fatigue', in the hope that simple remedies might be forthcoming. A series of experiments showed that fatigue could be observed in a variety of laboratory 'watchkeeping' tasks completely divorced from the stress of active service, and that if certain measures were taken the fatigue could be prevented.

Signal detection in vigilance tasks

The laboratory tasks used in these experiments involved the presentation to the subject of a lengthy series of items, a small proportion of which (the 'signals') differed slightly from the remainder; the subject was required to report the occurrence of these signals. It was found that the efficiency with which signals were detected declined considerably during the early part of a two-hour watch, and that such a decline took place in all but a few of the subjects tested (1). Measures which proved to be successful in preventing or reducing this apparent 'decline in vigilance' include the following:

(a) Alternating 30-minute spells of watchkeeping with 30-minute rests (later evidence suggests that ten or even five minutes' rest after 30 minutes' work may be adequate)
(b) Providing subjects with 'knowledge of results' by informing them whenever they missed a signal

(c) Administering benzedrine (a stimulant drug) beforehand
(d) Interrupting the watch at intervals to encourage the subjects by verbal exhortation
(e) Increasing the signal rate, i.e. the frequency of occurrence of items which are 'signals'.

Inasmuch as all of these remedial measures serve to 'arouse' or motivate the subject, the original hypothesis that watchkeeping tasks are intrinsically 'fatiguing' or 'boring' was substantiated. However, it should be noted that since the effects of the remedial measures were investigated on a single occasion only, the improvement in performance may well have been due to the novelty value of the changing circumstances in each case. If this is so the effectiveness of such measures might decline with repetition: whether this is the case remains to be determined (note: the repeated administration of drugs is not recommended).

Some recent research which provides additional support for the 'arousal' interpretation of performance in vigilance tasks has shown that factors such as the amount of sleep obtained during the previous night (2), and the time of day at which the work is carried out (3), can also affect the level of efficiency, as can the inherent 'wakefulness' of an individual (it appears that people of a certain personality type are, other things equal, at a higher level of arousal than their fellows (4).

On the other hand, other studies have demonstrated that, even under circumstances where the level of arousal is well maintained, detection efficiency is affected by the probability that any item is a signal, that is, in inspection terms, by the 'batch quality' (5). The lower this probability, the less likely it is that any particular signal will be detected. Again, if the object to be examined is a large one, and the signals appear in different parts with differing probability, then those parts where signals are less likely to occur tend to be less efficiently inspected (6). This latter tendency to bias attention towards the more 'rewarding' parts of the search field is independent of a strong effect of spatial location *per se* which makes detection of peripheral signals inherently less probable (5), possibly because of the nature of the scanning movements made by the eyes when searching an area (7).

It should be noted here that the basic 'signal probability' effect

181

occurs only where the subject has learned what the actual probability is. In many laboratory experiments he may expect this probability to be higher than that actually set by the experimenter; in this situation initial detection performance is relatively good, but this efficiency is achieved only at the cost of a substantial error rate, i.e. reporting signals which do not exist (8). As the subject learns the true low probability his 'expectancy' for signal occurrence declines and so does his efficiency at detecting these signals; at the same time his error rate, in most cases, drops to a negligible figure. In the opposite case, where previous experience has led subjects to expect a lower signal probability than the actual one, the process of adjustment may be so delayed that the great majority of signals are not detected at all in the course of a 40-minute session by all but the most intelligent individuals.

The relation between detection efficiency and error rate observed in these investigations suggests that we have been wrong in the past in thinking that the only limits to a man's detection capacity are his own sensory threshold and the viewing conditions obtaining at the point of search. While adverse viewing conditions obviously prevent maximum efficiency from being attained, it seems that even when these conditions are optimal, the concept of an absolute sensory threshold is inapplicable. It appears more likely that the nervous system makes a statistical decision about small signals it receives, accepting or rejecting these as resulting from genuine environmental changes, rather than from random fluctuations in the level of its own internal 'noise', on the basis of a given criterion of confidence (9). If this criterion is set at a low 'risky' level, the real signals are more likely to be detected, but at the same time the probability of making an erroneous decision (i.e. to accept a 'noise peak' as a genuine signal) is increased. Conversely, at a high 'cautious' level, detection probability is much lower, but accuracy is assured in that the number of 'false positives' is minimal. Since the relationship between detection and false positive probabilities is non-linear, a shift in the criterion towards the more risky end of the scale can effect a substantial increase in the probability of true signal detection at the cost of only a relatively small increment to the error rate.

Applications to inspection operations

It seems clear that both the level of arousal of the inspector and the signal probability will be important in determining performance at tasks of visual inspection. Since the relative contributions of these two factors to the final level of efficiency at which the work is carried out is not known, such remedial measures as are possible in any particular inspection situation should aim to take account of both.

In point of fact many actual inspection operations appear to be inherently more arousing than are the laboratory tasks employed in experimental investigations of this field. Since the work is not usually paced by a machine, the inspector is able to take rest-pauses which are not possible in the laboratory situation. Also, in a typical product, the kind of fault encountered varies over a considerable range and this may provide an element of variety in the work that is lacking in the uni-dimensional signal case. A similar reduction in monotony is provided by the necessity to carry out other operations either concurrently with the actual inspection, or separately at frequent intervals, e.g. collection and delivery of batches of material, setting up test rigs, recording faults discovered, manipulating large objects for full viewing coverage, packing and labelling, etc. However, as was pointed out earlier, because these various operations are routine, their effect on arousal may not be all that substantial, the effect of signal variety is unknown and the available evidence on paced versus unpaced performances suggests that there is little difference between the two situations as far as detection efficiency is concerned (3, 10). Nevertheless it would seem well worth while to avoid the risk of loss of arousal by varying the work routine associated with an inspection operation, as far as it is possible to do so without interfering with the smooth flow of the production line.

The problem of low probability signals is less tractable. Since the aim of any production process is to improve the level of quality, or at the least to maintain it at a high level, the fault probability must inevitably be *on average* relatively low. In these circumstances it may be desirable to consider the possibility of introducing 'extra' faults into the flow of material in order to raise artificially the perceived probability. The objects on which such faults occurred would, of course, be invisibly labelled (11), e.g. by fluorescent dyes, in order that they could be subsequently abstracted. A count of these artificial faults that were missed by the inspector could be used to provide him with 'knowledge of results' at the same time as indicating the true level of efficiency of the inspection process. The effect on the inspector of *changes* in signal probability resulting from fluctuations in output quality can of course be completely avoided only by efficient control at the production end, but it is possible that inspectors may in time learn to adjust to these changes more rapidly than experimental subjects are able to do in the laboratory; whether this is so requires investigation.

An alternative approach would be to make use of the relationship between 'false positive' and detection probabilities by deliberately training inspectors to adopt a less cautious criterion for acceptance of a signal than is normal practice. This should result in a higher percentage of detected faults at the expense of a small increase in the number of fault-free items incorrectly rejected; these items could of course be identified by a second-stage examination.

The Human Operator as a Judge of Quality

While it is true that the detection of faulty products is a logically prior operation to the grading or classification of these items, there is little doubt that troubles associated with the running of an inspection department most often appear to arise from alleged failure in the latter function. Usually the same operator performs both the detection and the classification operations, and this must inevitably cause some interaction between the two which complicates the picture. However, there is no theoretical reason why the two operations should not be carried out by different individuals, and in fact there may be distinct advantages in this. In order to simplify the discussion it will be assumed that the two functions are in fact independent. In this situation the accuracy with which detected faults are classified or judged can be affected by two kinds of variable, one of which arises from the perception of the fault distribution itself, the other from the structure of the work situation in which the inspection is performed (this includes the nature of the social relationships existing between the inspector and his workmates). The former is obviously more amenable to experimental investigation than the latter.

Absolute and relative judgements of signal 'intensity'

The non-independence of successive judgements on stimuli of varying intensity is a well-known psychological phenomenon. The effect of the preceding stimuli on current judgement is most marked when the stimuli are judged 'absolutely', i.e. in the absence of any objective reference standard, but can also appear to a much less marked extent, when the judgements are comparative. The general finding is that a stimulus of, say, a given size will be judged larger than it really is when the preceding stimuli are large. The 'adaptation level' or 'neutral' point against which a given stimulus is judged has been shown to be a weighted geometric mean of all the stimuli in the sequence up to that point (12). Recent examples affect the adaptation level to a greater extent than remote items and more extreme stimuli have a greater effect than average ones. Thus in an inspection situation where successive faults are being judged against a subjective standard, the classification of marginal items as 'rejects' or 'accepts' is likely to fluctuate considerably according to the quality of the batch. The 'cure' here is to provide accurate objective reference standards with which each fault must be compared; where this is impracticable, insertion of labelled artificial 'faults' into the flow of material should correct any tendency for the standard to drift. This applies to judgement along a single dimension; where 'faultiness' is a complex of many variables both the judgement process and the remedial measures applicable may be far more complicated, but little is known about behaviour in this kind of situation, which deserves experimental investigation.

Social and organizational factors

An illustration of how social pressures can affect the inspector's classification of marginal faults is given by Belbin (11). He describes how, in a knit-wear factory, inspectors looking for defects reported very few 'seconds'; instead they classified nearly all defective work as 'mendable'. The point was that the knitters lost more pay for 'seconds' than for 'menders', and the inspectors were unable to resist the pressure from the knitters to class most defects as menders. McKenzie (13), referring to Belbin's example and describing several others, points out that the effects of this kind of inter-personal pressure can be reduced by the provision of clear, usable standards, by giving explicit and detailed instructions and training, and by repeated 'calibration' of inspectors in periodical sessions of supervised, corrected practice.

McKenzie also discusses the growth of 'norms of rejection' among groups of inspectors. Once established, these norms may determine the actual percentage of rejects reported irrespective of the true quality of the batch. So long as an inspector's rejection rate stays within the accepted norm his actual accuracy is unlikely to be questioned, though it is obvious that with fluctuating quality his standards must inevitably be varying in order to achieve this constancy. A 'set to pass' or a 'set to reject' can arise in a particular situation and this can be very resistant to attempts to change it. There are many and complex reasons for the existence of sets and norms among inspectors but in many cases the underlying cause of disruptive attitudes is the general structure of the relationship of inspection with production. This relationship is often strained because the nature of the inspection function *vis-à-vis* production is essentially a controlling one, and this means that the two departments are almost unavoidably opposed. Difficulties which arise as a result of this clash of aims can be minimized by endeavouring to make the entire quality control department an independent and 'anonymous' organization; this is no mean task.

Individual Differences

Throughout this paper the emphasis has been on factors that influence the detection and classification operations performed by inspectors in the mass. However, inspection is in fact performed by individual human beings, and as it is a truism to say that no two people are alike, so it is certain that individual inspectors will differ in their efficiency and will also react to the various influences which are brought to bear on their work in different ways. But consistency between inspectors is at least as important for efficiency operation of a quality control system as is the reliability of any given inspector, and it is therefore essential that these individual differences should be minimized. Two approaches suggest themselves: selection and training.

The weeding-out of individuals who are unlikely to make good inspectors is of course only possible where there is a sufficiently extensive labour pool. Even in these fortunate circumstances, however, there is little evidence to suggest what criteria should be used in a selection procedure. Within quite wide limits there appears to be little or no relationship between detection skill and visual acuity, age, sex or general intelligence. Having eliminated those applicants suffering from grossly defective vision, and those with a very low or a very high I.Q., the only grounds for exclusion on the basis of age or sex are the probabilities that older people will be rather slower at the work (but not necessarily less efficient) and that women may not remain with the firm for long enough to justify the expense of the relatively lengthy training period to which inspectors are subject. It is possible that a 'miniature work-test' on a simplified version of the actual inspection job may help to identify different levels of initial skill, but this may be misleading for selection purposes since these differences may well be eliminated by an efficient training procedure. It now seems likely that personality factors are more important than most other things in the specification of a good fault detector, but as yet only hints are available as to which tests are desirable.

The foregoing remarks apply to selection for detection skill. Identification of the best people for work involving grading and classification of faulty material is confused by the multiplicity of social situations in which inspectors have to function. Thus where the job is highly 'relational', i.e. where inspectors have to face production operatives directly with their rejected work, personality is obviously important, but the traits that are desirable in this situation will differ from those where the inspector works in isolation, perhaps in a special testing booth under abnormal environmental conditions. It is possible that skill in judgement is itself related to personality or some other measurable aspect of the operator, but this is not known. In any case, in the typical present-day factory set-up, the situational factors mentioned above are likely to be of over-riding importance, and until the organization of inspection departments has been rationalized there is little profit in pursuing the matter.

A more profitable approach would be through the initiation of efficient training procedures, based on a thorough job-analysis of the inspection operation and the application of the psychological principles of learning. Many current training methods depend on the 'sit by Nelly' technique by which all the faulty techniques and biased attitudes of the 'old hand' are more or less efficiently transmitted to her protégée. This is obviously a lengthy and costly method of producing 'trained' examiners and should be replaced, where possible, by an objective, standard and semi-automatic teaching procedure such as has been outlined by the present writer elsewhere (14). Just as important as the provision of an efficient and standardized initial training scheme is the holding of re-training or calibration sessions at frequent intervals, using the same objective techniques. By these methods individual differences both in detection and in classification skills should be considerably reduced.

Conclusions

Enough has been said to show that the question of human reliability in a quality control system is an extremely complicated one. Although we are now aware of many of the causes of error in inspection operations, it is clear that a great deal of further research is necessary before a full understanding of the problems involved can be achieved. In the meantime it is important that, whenever a quality control scheme is being planned, the limitations imposed on its efficiency by its human operators should be recognized. In practice, the initiation of a scheme often of necessity requires that the inspection operation be studied more closely than has been the case beforehand. The chances are that any alterations to the examiner's task that result from this appraisal will in fact be beneficial: an improvement in reliability can only be assured, however, if these changes are made in the light of existing psychological knowledge.

References
1. N. H. MACKWORTH, *Researches on the Measurement of Human Performance*, Medical Research Council, H.M.S.O., 1950.
2. R. T. WILKINSON, *Quart. J. exp. Psychol.*, vol. 12 (1960), p. 36.
3. W. P. COLQUHOUN, *Bull. C.E.R.P.*, vol. 11 (1962), p. 27.
4. W. P. COLQUHOUN, *Ergonomics*, vol. 3 (1960), p. 377.
5. W. P. COLQUHOUN, *Ergonomics*, vol. 4 (1961), p. 41.
6. P. A. NICELY, and G. A. MILLER, *J. exp. Psychol.*, vol. 53 (1957), p. 195.
7. C. H. BAKER, *Brit. J. Psychol.*, vol. 49 (1958), p. 279.
8. W. P. COLQUHOUN and A. D. BADDELEY, *J. exp. Psychol.*, vol. 68 (1963), p. 156.
9. W. P. TANNER and J. A. SWETS, *Psychol. Rev.*, vol. 61 (1954), p. 401.
10. R. T. WILKINSON, *Ergonomics*, vol. 4 (1961), p. 259.
11. R. M. BELBIN, *Brit. Man. Rev.*, vol. 15 (1957), p. 79.
12. H. HELSON, *Psychol. Rev.*, vol. 55 (1958), p. 297.
13. R. M. McKENZIE, *Ergonomics*, vol. 1 (1958), p. 258.
14. W. P. COLQUHOUN, *Inspect. Engin.*, vol. 23 (1959), p. 80.

9 L. F. Thomas

Perceptual Organization in Industrial Inspectors

L. F. Thomas, 'Perceptual organization in industrial inspectors', *Ergonomics*, vol. 5 (1962), pp. 429–34.

Descriptions of the inspection of painted surfaces, of domestic cleaners for noise, and the surface of castings, are used to illustrate the suggestion that prolonged perceptual interaction with a restricted range of objects produces new figure-ground experiences in the inspector. The paper discusses the observation that the inspector learns to recognize a wide variety of secondary cues as relevant to his task, and is thus enabled continually to adjust his perceptual 'set' to optimize his performance. This perceptual development is compared with that experienced by a subject during prolonged viewing of a distorted room.

1. Introduction

A man starting a new job as an industrial inspector often spends many months acquiring the accepted level of skill. His formal training is not likely to be more than a few weeks, but after this he may be many more months working on the job before he is making consistently reliable judgements about quality, at production speed. As with other types of industrial task, efficient training is the exception rather than the rule.

Effective training for any task involves thoroughly understanding the nature of the task to be learned; the trainer must appreciate the socio-technical context within which the task is to be carried out and the full range of activities that are necessary for it to be done effectively. While most senior inspection staff have an implicit understanding of what each task involves, there is a considerable difference between the formal description of the task which is given to the trainee and the description which can be built up gradually by informed observation and discussion with the people concerned.

A number of inspection tasks have been described by psychologists (e.g. Irvine, 1955; Katz, 1938; Raphael, 1942; Sheppard, 1955). These studies give some idea of the fairly complex psycho-physical skills involved in judging those aspects of the product which are considered to be important determinants of its quality, and often consist of evaluating the inspector's performance against some industrial criteria. Such studies of inspection tasks involving 'the judgement of quality without aid of instruments', usually conclude that the inspector is inconsistent (e.g. Meadows *et al.*, 1959). When, however, the tasks are considered on the basis of psychological criteria, the variations in performance appear much more systematic and may even be quite predictable in certain well-defined situations.

There are two psychological processes which I wish to discuss in this paper and which appear in many of the industrial inspection tasks involving subjective judgement, which we have investigated (Seaborne and Thomas, 1961). These two processes are the semi-permanent perceptual reorganization that is produced in the inspector, and the continuing adjustments of perceptual set that derive from the inspector's understanding of the underlying causal relationships in the work situation, and are, perhaps, similar to those noted by Crossman (1960) in the operators of process plants.

Repeated presentations over protracted periods of similar objects which have to be judged for certain aspects of their appearance bring about semi-permanent changes in the perception of these objects. Certain characteristics of the object which the inspector finds to have relevance to the effectiveness of his performance, gradually acquire perceptual significance and may eventually begin to stand out as 'figures' against the 'ground' of the rest of the object. Scott Blair (1942) has observed that 'learnt Gestalten' seemed to develop in certain skilled operators. Four chief inspectors in different firms have, during our investigations, independently mentioned that the thoroughly experienced inspector seems to acquire a picture of the 'good' product and that defects seem to stand out against this. Inspection staff also report that the really good inspector gets to know what to expect in certain situations. He has considerable familiarity with the product and with the processes whereby it is produced, and he often has a good understanding of the use to which the product will be put. His skill and 'know-how' consist in being able to use effectively the large range of cues which he has found to be relevant to his task. These two aspects of perceptual organization are illustrated in the following descriptions of three inspection jobs.

2. Paint Inspection

In the paint department of an engineering firm the spray booths were situated on either side of an overhead conveyor on which the sprayed articles were hung by the painters. These were taken by the conveyor slowly through a drying oven at the other end of which they were removed from the conveyor by the paint inspector. He inspected the articles for faults which might include runs, blisters, thin sections of paint, occluded dust and 'orange peel' appearance. For each type of article the inspector had learned that certain defects were acceptable if they were not too severe and if they occurred on certain less visible parts, but were unacceptable when they occurred in more obvious places. Similarly, for any one type of defect in any one position, a certain intensity could have led to rejection where a less intense defect would be accepted. Thus the inspector built up a complex understanding of the types, positions and intensities of defect which were just acceptable and just unacceptable for any article.

In discussion, the paint inspectors were able gradually to explain that one of the important factors which affected their performance was their knowledge of the different paint sprayers. It appeared that they were much more likely to do an efficient inspection job when they knew which paint sprayer was currently painting a certain article and when they had a fairly shrewd idea about the general quality of his work. Further discussion showed that the really experienced paint inspector got to know what types of fault were likely to be found on the surfaces of different materials. He also learnt that one type of fault was likely to be produced when objects of a particular shape went through the drying oven in certain positions on the conveyor. Thus, the skilled inspector noted how an article was hung on the conveyor when he took it off, and this led him to look for a certain kind of fault.

The general conclusion to be drawn from observation of these paint inspectors is that they tended to become faster and more reliable in their judgement when they used the whole range of secondary cues to adjust continually their perceptual set.

3. Inspection of Domestic Cleaners for Noise

In a firm manufacturing domestic appliances one man was fully employed inspecting cleaners to ensure that the sound which they made when running was not excessive. He worked at a bench on which he placed the cleaner, plugged it in, and listened to the resulting noise. The firm had attempted to use a simple 'sound energy meter' for this purpose but had found no correlation between the way in which the inspector classified cleaners and the results obtained with the meter. The chief inspector thought that this task was being performed reasonably well and was serving an essential function in the control of the quality of the appliances. Observation of this particular task and discussion with the inspector showed that the man was more concerned with differentiating between 'good' noise and 'bad' noise than he was with the over-all intensity. He could recognize the sounds made by a well-adjusted cleaner and these appeared to provide the background against which he perceived certain types of deviation. Gross deviations led to rejection.

When a cleaner was rejected it was returned to the production section which was thought to be responsible for producing the fault. There the fault was remedied and the cleaner was again sent for inspection. The inspector was thus provided with a continual check on the validity of his inspection. He had by informed experience acquired considerable skill in recognizing the different sounds associated with certain types of maladjustment or defectiveness. He would reject a cleaner for 'motor front bearing fault', or 'motor back bearing fault', 'motor brush chatter', 'fan noise', 'sweeper brush noise', 'sweeper brush bearing noise', etc. The fault having thus been classified, the rejected cleaner was returned to the section responsible, who had to strip it down and rectify it. Any error of judgement by the inspector was quickly brought to his notice by a section which had stripped a machine down and found no fault. In this way the inspector was able to develop the perceptual skills he needed to meet the demands of his job.

Further discussion with the inspector showed that different designs of cleaner were apparently prone to certain types of fault; and that certain types of fault occurring in one item in a batch were likely to recur through the whole batch. He also had some idea of the labour and machinery conditions in the different production sections. When the inspector learned of a change of machine, or of the person running a machine, he began to look out for certain types of fault until he had established stable expectations again. One point that came up particularly in discussion with this inspector was the difference between faults which were random in origin and therefore provided little information which could be used to prepare for subsequent items, and those which were systematic and which were treated as cues to be taken into account in looking at subsequent items in the same manufacturing batch.

4. Visual Inspection of Castings

In the foundry of another light engineering firm, castings were inspected after they had been fettled, and before they were sent to the machine shop. The particular castings with which we were concerned formed the outer case of the product. This case was subsequently machined and sprayed with paint. The inspector's task consisted of looking carefully at the castings and deciding, on the basis of their appearance when raw, whether any of the defects present on the surface would produce appreciable blemishes after the casting had been sprayed. This task was carried out by a fairly elderly woman who had been doing it for many years. Some time prior to our study of her work she had been sick for about three or four months and an attempt had been made to train somebody else to do her job. However, nobody had been found who could do it effectively. Discussion and observation showed that she had developed considerable skill in recognizing the relationship between the raw casting surface and the kind of paint finish it would have after spraying. She ignored, and in fact appeared not to see, all kinds of discolouration and differences of surface appearance, and only attended to the actual detailed surface contours. She was able to differentiate between those types of contour differences which would be covered by the paint and those which would show through or even be accentuated by the paint. We ourselves had great difficulty in understanding what was being seen, and it was only after fairly prolonged discussion and observation that we began to appreciate the kind of perceptual organization which had become 'second nature' to this inspector.

This particular example illustrated the semi-permanent changes in the perception of an object which can gradually come about after prolonged experience of judging it for a particular purpose. Again, in this situation there was information available by which the inspector could assess her performance: rejects at the paint stage could be classified into those that were produced by the painting and those that were produced by the surface under the paint.

5. Summing up of Evidence on Perceptual Changes

In observing inspectors at work, certain characteristics of their performance seem to be evidence for believing that the skilled inspector's perception of the product differs from that of the layman.

These are:

(a) The wording of descriptions of their task given by inspectors implies that they are talking about figure-ground effects. Such phrases as 'faults jump out at you' and 'when you look at the component like this it's easy to see the scratches' seem to be descriptions of figure-ground phenomena in non-psychological terms.

(b) An inspector may have considerable difficulty in recognizing what appears to the layman a gross difference between products if this difference is irrelevant to the quality of the component.

(c) The scanning methods used by inspectors and the high speeds they attain often suggest that they do not have to carry out an elaborate search for defects.

(d) It is consistently reported that even an inspector who has received training takes considerable time to become fully effective. Such long learning periods are often associated with the acquiring of perceptual skills (King, 1947).

(e) A number of independent reports have mentioned that the skilled inspector keeps in mind an idea of a 'good' component and perceives faults in terms of divergencies from this often complex 'good' item.

(f) If an inspector did not realize that he was going to be asked why he rejected a certain object, he would often pick it up and re-examine it before he could name the fault for which it had been rejected. He could tell that it looked wrong, but if the task did not include classification according to type of fault, there was often no memory of the detailed defect. Conversely, when he knew that he was going to be asked to describe the kinds of fault that led him to reject items, he slowed down and his performance lost its rhythm.

6. Discussion

While this evidence for perceptual phenomena is inevitably in-direct, these three descriptions of industrial tasks illustrate the probable existence of the semi-permanent changes in perceptual organization which occur in inspectors judging the quality of similar products over and over again. They also show that around this new, seemingly permanent perceptual organization, there may develop short-term deviations which arise from the current sociotechnical context within which the article is viewed. In psychological terms, these may be taken as examples of learned 'figure-ground' phenomena and examples of the influence of 'set' on perception. They seem very similar to those which have been found by Weiner (1956) in a study of the perception of a distorted room.

In his monograph Weiner describes in some detail what happened to a subject while she was viewing an Ames distorted room for a total of 30 hours. At first the illusion was complete, she saw it as a normal rectangular room; then gradually, with the cues provided by stationary known objects and moving figures, she began to develop slight changes in perception until, aided by tactual information, she was able to learn the 'objective' view of the room. In other words, the organization of the perceptual data provided by the room developed and changed in the course of the subject's experience, giving different weight to the various per-ceptual cues early and later in the session.

Weiner also describes how at different times during the 30 hours the subject suddenly perceived certain parts of the room differently. When the new way of viewing a part was incompatible with her original total view of the room, she described experiences of perceptual oscillation. Such oscillation was often followed by a change in the view of the room as a whole. Weiner goes on to say that 'There is an indication that an undifferentiated "whole perception" plays a part in impeding progress in perceptual change.' Abercrombie (1960), in her study of the interpretation of X-ray photographs by medical students, has commented on a similar phenomenon; she showed that paying attention to particular parts of the X-ray and discussing them in detail may bring about a reorganized perception of these parts and that this in turn may lead to a new way of perceiving the whole X-ray plate. The industrial inspector is forced by the nature of his job to look very closely at particular parts of the article which he is inspecting, and this, linked with the possibilities for checking his judgement which we have mentioned, provide what would appear to be an effective perceptual learning situation – a situation likely to produce changes in the perception of a whole group of sense-data comparable to the changes that occur during prolonged study of the distorted room.

One further point which comes out of Weiner's study is that at one stage during her experimental period, as a result of the perceptual oscillation which was occurring in her view of the room, the subject became very anxious about herself. Pearl King (1947), noticed similar anxiety developing in 'linkers' at a critical point in their training period, and she was able to relate this to a particular kind of 'figure-ground' perceptual learning. Senior inspection staff report similar disturbed periods during the training of inspectors on perceptual tasks which were particularly disturbing.

References

ABERCROMBIE, M. L. J. (1960), *The Anatomy of Judgement*, Hutchinson.

CROSSMAN, E. R. F. W. (1960), Automation and skill, *D.S.I.R. Problems of Progress in Industry*, no. 9, H.M.S.O.

IRVINE, D. H. (1955), An experimental study of human variability in a task involving visual inspection, *Unpublished Ph.D. Thesis, University of London*.

KATZ, D. (1938), 'The judgments of test baker. A psychological study', *Occup. Psychol.*, vol. 12, pp. 139–48.

KING, P. H. M. (1947), 'Task perception and interpersonal relations in industrial training', *Hum. Rel.*, vol. 1, pp. 121–30.

MEADOWS, A. W., LOVIBOND, S. A., and JOHN, I. D. (1959), 'The establishment of psychophysical standards in the sorting of fruit', *Occup. Psychol.*, vol. 33, pp. 217–22.

RAPHAEL, W. (1942), 'Some problems of inspection', *Occup. Psychol.*, vol. 29, pp. 157–63.

SCOTT BLAIR, G. W., and COPPEN, F. M. V. (1942), 'The subjective conception of the firmness of soft materials', *Amer. J. Psychol.*, vol. 51, pp. 127–39.

SEABORNE, A. E. M., and THOMAS, L. F. (1961), 'The socio-technical concept of industrial inspection', *Occup. Psychol.*, vol. 35, pp. 36–43.

SHEPPARD, D. (1955), 'The sensory basis of the cheese-grader's skill', *Occup. Psychol.*, vol. 29, pp. 150–64.

WEINER, M. (1956), 'Perceptual development in a distorted room: A phenomenological study', *Psychol. Monogr.*, vol. 70, no. 16.

10 F. B. Chaney and K. S. Teel

Improving Inspector Performance through Training and
Visual Aids

F. B. Chaney and K. S. Teel, 'Improving inspector performance through
training and visual aids', *Journal of Applied Psychology*, vol. 51 (1967),
pp. 311–15.

An experimental study was performed to evaluate, singly and in combination, the effectiveness of a 4-hour training program and a set of
visual aids designed to improve the performance of twenty-seven
experienced machined-parts inspectors. The criterion used was the
percentage of true defects detected in a selected sample of machined
parts. Findings indicated that (a) use of training alone resulted in a
32 per cent increase in defects detected, (b) use of visual aids alone
resulted in a 42 per cent increase and (c) use of both resulted in a 71 per
cent increase, while (d) performance of the control group did not
change.

Accurate inspection performance is essential to the success of any
organization which manufactures, assembles and sells a product.
It is particularly critical, however, to those organizations that
build precision equipment which is expected to operate for long
periods of time under a wide variety of environmental conditions.
For this reason, the authors have, for the past several years, been
conducting a series of studies designed to improve inspection
performance.

The purpose of the study reported herein was to evaluate the
effectiveness of training and visual aids in improving the performance of machined-parts inspectors.

Machined-parts inspectors are individuals whose job is to
examine precision machined parts for defects which might make
them unsuitable for use. The two items used in this study are
shown in Figure 1; both are typical of the kinds of parts inspected.

These parts are examined for both objective and subjective
defects. Included in the objective category are such defects as
mislocated holes, threaded holes, lack of parallelism and concen-
tricity and improper dimensions. In the subjective category are

such things as poor finish, scratches and nicks. A part may be rejected for either objective or subjective defects; experience indicates, however, that objective defects are far more serious and therefore are the reasons for most rejections. A rejected part is either returned to manufacturing for rework or scrapped.

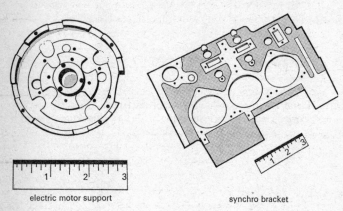

electric motor support   synchro bracket

Figure 1 Sample parts

Although rework and scrappage are expensive even at this point, it is far more expensive to allow a defective part to be incorporated into a delivered product and subsequently to have that product returned by the customer. Thus, while the stated goal of inspection is to maximize the number of legitimate defects detected and to minimize the number of false ones, it appears to be better, when in doubt, to err on the side of rejecting an item rather than accepting it.

One of the reasons machined-parts inspectors were selected for study was that previous informal investigations had indicated that these inspectors were identifying less than 50 per cent of the objective defects in the items reviewed.

Method

Job-sample performance measures were used to divide twenty-seven machined-parts inspectors into four matched groups. One group served as a control. A second was given a specially designed 4-hour training program. A third was given both the training and visual aids, and a fourth visual aids only. Subsequently, equivalent job-sample measures were again obtained for each of the groups. The control group used standard drawings and specifications as inspection aids for both the 'before' and 'after' measurements. The training and/or visual aids were introduced in the other three groups as part of a continuing research program which had been carried out, with full management support, for 2 years prior to the study. Consequently, Ss accepted the experimental treatments as part of their normal work environment, not as implied criticism of their previous performance. All Ss carried out their normal duties during the 6 months between testings. Statistical comparisons were made of the differences in performance among groups, and of the differences in 'before–after' performance within each of the groups.

Subjects

The Ss were twenty-seven machined-parts inspectors, the full population available in the organization. Their median age was 49, with a range from 28 to 62. Their median inspection experience was 8 years, with a range from 3 to 20. Their median tenure with the company was 6 years, with a range of 4–17. Thus, Ss were mature, experienced inspectors whose performance presumably had leveled out. Therefore, it seems safe to assume that incidental learning during the course of the study probably had little or no effect on the final performance levels of the various groups.

Job-sample test

Four machined parts were fabricated for use in the study. Two were brackets; the other two were motor supports. One of each was shown in Figure 1. All four items were fabricated to contain a representative sample of known defects. Each of the items was then inspected independently by four men, two leadmen and two engineering supervisors. The four then met as a group and agreed on master lists of characteristics to be inspected and defects present in each of the four parts. Each of the four parts had approximately 100 characteristics to be inspected and thirty-four defects.

Both the 'before' and 'after' measures for each of the groups were obtained by having each S independently inspect one bracket and one support. The initial measures were obtained with half of the Ss inspecting support 1 (S_1) and bracket 1 (B_1), and the other half inspecting support 2 (S_2) and bracket 2 (B_2). The final criterion measures were obtained by having Ss inspect the alternate parts they had not inspected previously; thus, those who inspected S_1 and B_1 initially, inspected S_2 and B_2 later, and vice versa.

Group matching

The initial job-sample test yielded four measures of performance for each of the twenty-seven Ss. The measures were (a) percentage of objective defects detected, (b) percentage of subjective defects detected, (c) number of false detections and (d) inspection time. Since primary interest was in percentage of objective defects detected, Ss were initially sorted into four equivalent groups on the basis of that criterion alone. Further matching was unnecessary because statistical tests revealed that the groups did not

Table 1

Group Performance Levels before the Study

Performance measure	Group means				Analysis of variance		
	Control (N = 7)	Training (N = 6)	Visual aids (N = 7)	Training plus visual aids (N = 7)	MS groups	MS error	F ratio
Percentage of objective detections	35·7	30·5	37·6	34·3	57·3	97·6	0·59
Percentage of subjective detections	53·6	51·5	47·0	54·0	77·1	75·0	1·03
No. false detections	2·3	7·0	5·0	2·7	30·9	14·5	2·13
Inspection time (hours)	11·4	12·7	12·7	11·1	4·8	8·7	0·55

differ significantly on any of the other three measures. The equivalence of the four groups is illustrated in Table 1.

Training program

The training program consisted of four 1-hour sessions conducted by the inspection supervisor. Each session included a lecture, demonstrations and a question-and-answer period. The four sessions dealt, respectively, with the topics of (a) precision measurement, (b) thread gaging, (c) use of the Sheffield Internal Comparator and (d) interpretation of drawing notes. The sessions were conducted once a week for 4 weeks. Approximately a month elapsed between the end of the training and the administration of the final job-sample test.

The course contained no information on the specific defects contained in the job-sample parts, and none of the Ss saw those parts except during the test sessions.

Visual aids

The visual aids consisted of a series of simple drawings of the sample parts – six for the bracket and eight for the support. One of those drawings is shown in Figure 2.

The dimensions and tolerances for each characteristic to be inspected were placed on the drawings to minimize the need for

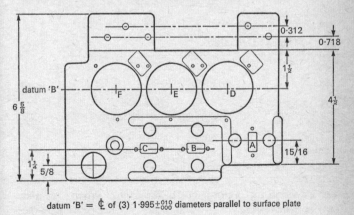

datum 'B' = $\mathbb{C}$ of (3) $1.995 ^{+010}_{-000}$ diameters parallel to surface plate

Figure 2 Sample inspection drawing

calculation or reference to other materials; these data typically had been presented on one master blueprint and in written instructions. Furthermore, similar items were grouped on a single page to encourage the inspector to examine the part fully for one class of defects before reviewing it for others. The visual aids were prepared by an experienced inspector who was not an S in the study and who did not know what specific defects were contained in the sample parts.

No training was given in the interpretation or use of the visual aids. The Ss were simply given the drawings immediately before their final inspection of the two parts and told to use them in carrying out the inspection.

Results

Since four different measures of performance were obtained, the results are presented separately for each.

Objective defects

Results indicated clearly that use of either training or visual aids resulted in significant gains in objective detection performance and that use of both resulted in even greater gains. These findings are presented in Table 2. It will be noted that there was no signifi-

Table 2

Objective Defect Detection

Group	Percentage of defects detected		Percentage of change
	Before	After	
Control	35·7	33·4	—6
Training	30·5	40·3	32
Visual aids	37·7	53·4	42
Training plus visual aids	34·3	56·8	71

cant change in the performance of the control group, but that there were increases of 32, 42 and 71 per cent respectively, in the detection of objective defects in the training, visual-aids and training-plus-visual-aids groups. The F-ratio of 10·2 for differences among the four groups was significant beyond the 0·001 level. 'Before' and 'after' comparisons within groups revealed that the increase in the training group was significant at the 0·05 level, and those in the visual-aids and training-plus-visual aids groups were significant at the 0·01 level. Thus, the experimental treatments clearly resulted in significant gains in detection of objective defects.

Analysis of difference scores revealed that improvement in the performance of the training group did not differ significantly from that of the visual-aids group. It also revealed that improvement of the training-plus-visual-aids group was significantly greater ($p < 0.05$) than that of the training group, but not significantly different from that of the visual-aids group. Thus, the data suggest that the visual aids may have contributed more heavily to the improved performance of the combination group than did the training.

It should be noted that the initial performance levels of the four groups in this study were similar to those noted in previous studies of machined-parts inspection. Lawshe and Tiffin (1945) reported accuracies of 9–66 per cent for twenty different measurement techniques. These and other findings strongly suggest that stated accuracies for many precision inspection techniques have been established under 'ideal' conditions, rather than under those of the typical working environment. Thus, while the initial levels reported in this study may appear low, they probably are representative of those achieved by machined-parts inspectors under normal working conditions. The final levels, on the other hand, reveal how significant improvements in performance can be effected at relatively little cost.

Subjective detections

No significant changes occurred in subjective defect detection performance. Changes ranged from a 3 per cent decrease to a 7 per cent increase; the over-all level remained at approximately 50 per cent detection of subjective defects. The F-ratio of 1·02 for differences among the groups was not significant.

This finding is not surprising, because both the training program and the visual aids were designed solely to improve detection of objective defects. Previous studies conducted at Autonetics have indicated, however, that subjective defect detection performance can be significantly improved by providing inspectors with photographs of items containing such defects; no photographs were furnished in this study.

False detections

No significant differences were noted among the four groups in numbers of false defects reported. Changes ranged from a 1 per cent decrease to an 8 per cent increase; the F-ratio of $2 \cdot 19$ failed to achieve significance. Thus, the gains in objective detection performance apparently were obtained without a corresponding increase in false detections.

Inspection time

No significant differences were obtained in inspection times. The times ranged from $10 \cdot 4$ to $15 \cdot 3$ hours; however, the F-ratio of $2 \cdot 32$ failed to achieve significance ($F_{0 \cdot 05} = 3 \cdot 03$). The gains in objective detection performance, therefore, were obtained without significant increase in inspection time and cost.

Conclusions

These findings demonstrate clearly that inspection performance can be improved by giving inspectors a short training program designed to correct deficiencies identified through use of objective performance measures. They also show that gains can be obtained by providing inspectors with simplified drawings which show clearly the characteristics to be inspected and the tolerances for each. Furthermore, they reveal that even greater gains can be effected by utilizing both the training and the visual aids.

Finally, they highlight the fact that industrial/experimental psychologists can make significant contributions to the solution of inspection problems. Furthermore, the benefits to the company can be measured in dollar terms; in a 2-year period an investment of approximately \$50,000 in research in this area yielded a return of over \$200,000 per year in documented cost savings (Thresh and Frerichs, 1966). It seems safe to assume that the same kinds of results could be achieved in other organizations.

References

LAWSHE, C. H., and TIFFIN, J. (1945), 'The accuracy of precision instrument measurement in industrial inspection', *J. appl. Psychol.*, vol. 29, pp. 413–19.

THRESH, J. L., and FRERICHS, J. S. (1966), Results through management application of human factors, *Paper presented at a Meeting of the American Society for Quality Control, New York*.

Part Four Technological Skills

Apart from the problems of fault-finding and monitoring, modern industrial technology makes a variety of other demands upon human skill. Quite commonly human operators are required to respond at speed, perhaps to several streams of signals. Despite its unitary title, Conrad's paper (Reading 11) deals with both these problems, relating them to practice in cotton textile mills. Mackworth and Mackworth (Reading 12) provide a more detailed analysis of multi-channel displays in a task resembling air traffic control, showing how difficulties occur where signals overlap.

It is increasingly necessary to replace the human operator by his automatic counterpart, although it is not yet clear how far this process must be extended by the development of computers. However, in one of the few available experimental comparisons Shaffer (Reading 13) finds the computer superior in queue-serving decisions. Reading 14 by Conrad presents an assortment of the human performance problems which arise in the telephone and postal services.

11 R. Conrad

Speed Stress

R. Conrad, 'Speed stress', in W. F. Floyd and A. T. Welford, *Human Factors in Equipment Design*, Lewis, 1954, ch. 13.

The term 'display' is usually used with reference to one or more dials or a cathode-ray tube. The term, however, retains its value to experimental psychology when used in a much wider context which has recently been delineated by Welford (1951).

It describes in one word all the sources of sensory information which provide the signals for that kind of action which is called skilled behaviour. It might be a single light, or a series of flashes which, when transcribed, form a message, or (Broadbent, 1952) a collection of verbal messages. It might be a bank of instrument dials, or a football field seen from the point of view of one of the players. It is a convenient term which circumscribes one particular feature of a skill, and which leaves out environmental factors which affect but which do not necessarily belong to the skill.

In most of the skills of life, displays are not designed with a psychological concept of display in mind. Sometimes – as in sailing for example – they occur naturally with no possibility of design. But usually design is present, though incidental to some other aim. For instance, a lathe is built primarily to cut metal, and this production objective in the skill dominates the design of the display features of lathe-operating. But one of the most interesting developments in psychology in recent years has been the discovery that the objective aim might be more easily or more efficiently achieved if displays were designed as much with the human operator in mind as with the objective.

Research arising out of this is now becoming familiar (e.g. Chapanis, Garner and Morgan, 1949). But it has been very largely concerned with the one aspect of display design which refers to the physical appearance of the display. It has examined the effects on performance of different shapes of indicator,

211

degrees of legibility, the relative merits of visual or auditory signals, the advantages of one colour, or one pitch, or one intensity of signal over another. Attention will be drawn here to the possibility of research in a quite different aspect of display design; what Bartlett (1951) has called the *amount* of evidence as distinct from the *kind* of evidence presented.

The attribute that is common to most displays is that they are continuously changing. Objects change position with regular or irregular velocities, sounds change pitch or loudness, signals occur and cease. The skilled operator attending to this changing mass of information is alerted to select those changes which demand a change in his behaviour if the skill is to be adequately maintained. In order to do this he must know which parts of the skill are most worth while attending to, and for how long any part can be safely neglected. This leads to a key question in research in this field. In designing displays, what are the limiting factors which determine how frequently critical signals can be permitted to occur?

The term 'critical signal' itself requires a brief explanation. The changing events of visual displays consist very largely of objects moving along courses or tracks which are often predictable from relatively little information, or of events which develop in fairly predictable ways. Vehicles in traffic, or dial pointers do not normally make frequent sudden and unexpected changes in course. Usually, therefore, not every signal change that occurs is important. What is important though, is that the observer should notice any sudden change and that he should notice when, for example, a moving object is likely to reach some point when action would be desirable. These are the critical signals to which response must be made. In many cases, particularly in industrial skills, the rate at which critical signals occur is known and can often be controlled. What factors must be considered in determining this speed?

Figure 1 shows some laboratory apparatus which involves the exercise of skilled behaviour, the 'know-how' of which can be learned very quickly. It has been described in more detail elsewhere (Conrad, 1951a). Briefly, the operator must attend to several pointers moving at slightly different speeds so as to press a key whenever a pointer coincides with the target marks around the dials. Thus the skill is to make a continuous series of judgements in order to respond correctly when the signal occurs. The response depends not at all on a quick reaction but on quick judgements and decisions, and the only way to perform well at this task is to predict which of the several possible situations is next going to require a response. Signals can occur from several

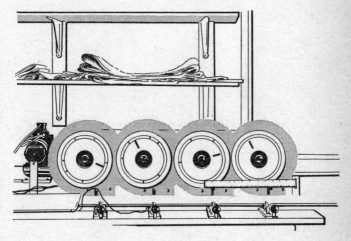

Figure 1 Diagram of the apparatus used in the laboratory experiments

different sources, the number being under experimental control, and the order being quite irregular. Equally the rate at which signals occur can be experimentally varied independently of the number of sources. The apparatus, therefore, can be used to investigate the effects of varying the amount of information along two dimensions, (a) referring to the number of signals per unit time, the speed; and (b) referring to the number of separate independent streams of signals, the load.

Effects of Varying Speed

Considering the relationship between the rate at which signals occur, keeping the load constant, and the rate at which signals are adequately responded to, a number of hypotheses would be

213

possible. One would be that a more or less perfect score would be obtained up to the point at which successive responses could not be made faster, and after that no change in response rate would occur.

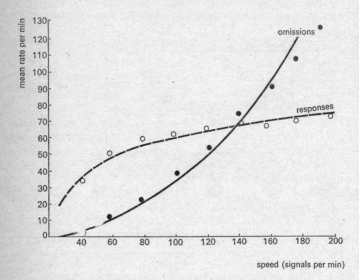

Figure 2 Effect of very high speeds on performance (load constant)

A second debatable hypothesis would be based on the idea of the more haste leading to the less speed. In this case one would expect performance to keep up with the demands of the display up to an optimum point, and then fall off to a level below what had previously been attained. A third possibility is based on a concept of diminishing returns – i.e. as the signal speed increases, so too, does response rate, but the latter lagging farther and farther behind the former.

Figure 2 shows what actually happens with a skill of this kind. The curve is based on the scores of twenty-four naval ratings working for ten minutes under each condition, the order being randomized. It is quite clear that the third hypothesis is most closely supported by the experimental data. In this experiment the signal speed was taken up to 200 per minute, which is nearly as fast as morse keys can be tapped over a long period. But although at the end the response rate is still rising steadily, it has in fact only reached about seventy-five per minute, which is much slower than even a comfortable tapping rate. There is, though, no tailing off at this speed, and it therefore seems justifiable to say that in this task the faster display changes occur the greater will be the 'output' of the operator. It must, of course, be remembered that errors (i.e. failures to respond) are increasing very rapidly, and the desirability of increasing signal speed in any situation must depend on the effect of these mounting errors.

That the effects of errors in this sense do not always outweigh the possible advantages of increased response rate is demonstrated by the results of an experiment carried out in the bobbin-winding room of a cotton textile mill. Two similar experiments were carried out in different mills using exactly the same process and machinery which is shown in Plate 9 (see central inset). The details of this investigation have been reported by the writer (1951b). Briefly, the operator's work consists of replacing empty supply packages, replacing fully wound bobbins and knotting the two ends of yarn in the above cases, and also whenever it breaks.

By far the most frequent operation is the replacing of supply packages and joining up. This operation accounts for about 80 per cent of the total work in this case. It takes 5–6 seconds to perform, and the rate at which it needs to be done can be experimentally varied. Figure 3 shows (in two experiments) the effect of increasing the rate at which the packages emptied, on the rate at which they were replaced. The order of conditions was randomized, each operative working for one working week under each condition. Once again the continued but diminishing rise in the rate of work is observed as the pace is increased.

Now, although the trends of response rates shown in Figure 2 and Figure 3 are very similar, there is an important difference between the nature of the variables represented by the two abscissae. In the first case the abscissa shows the increase in the number of signals occurring per unit time when the number of signal sources was constant. In the second case, the increase in the signal speed was due partly to an increase in the number of spindles, so that each division along the abscissa represents more signals per unit time, and also more spindles – i.e. greater load. This would seem to suggest that the number of sources of signal had little or no effect on performance. Since earlier work by Mackworth (1948) and by the present writer (1951a) had indicated that load increases had a deleterious effect on response rate the problem was investigated further.

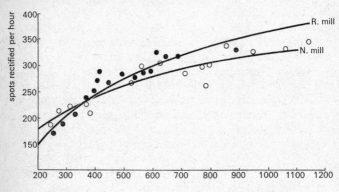

Figure 3 Relation between rate of stoppage and rate of rectifying stops. Dots show means of six operatives at R. mill. Circles show means of three operatives at N. mill

Effects of Varying Load

The apparatus shown in Figure 1 was used, but the number of pointers on each dial was varied between one and six, so that the total variation in the load was between four and twenty-four pointers, and the signal speed was kept constant. Three different speeds were used and the mean response rates and the mean number of signals not responded to for eighteen naval ratings are shown in Figure 4.

Considering the response rate in relation to the load, it will be seen that when the load is relatively light, there is a fairly steep fall in response rate. With the heavier loads, however, this decline tends to level off. For all three curves in Figure 5 the difference in response rates between four and twelve pointers is statistically significant (at the 2 per cent level). whereas between twelve and twenty-four pointers it is not.

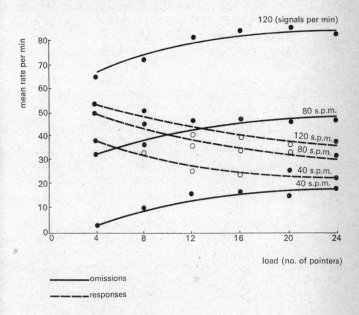

Figure 4 Effect of heavy loads on performance

The result of this experiment provides a possible explanation of the bobbin-winding data of Figure 3. If the variation in the number of spindles occurred within a 'heavy' load range, one might expect the effect of load increases (i.e. lower response rate) to be slight, in relation to the effect of signal speed increases (i.e. increased response rate). The combined effects would then show as a curve not unlike that of Figure 2. (It should, of course, be recognized that the term 'heavy' load has no numerical significance. The 'heaviness', in the sense of the term used here, will depend on the nature of the task.)

In the laboratory, as has been shown, it is possible to vary the speed and the load content of a display independently. Outside the laboratory this rarely happens. When another indicator is added to an existing instrument panel, the speed and the load are simultaneously increased. Similarly, it frequently happens that a four-loom weaver takes on another loom, or a sixty-spindle bobbin winder takes on another fifteen spindles. It very rarely happens in such cases that the speeds of the individual looms or spindles are changed, and so the effect is to increase both the speed and the load by 25 per cent. The net effect on performance will depend on two separate, and to some extent interacting, effects.

An attempt to show what this could mean in industrial practice is illustrated in Figure 5. This shows synthetic values of response

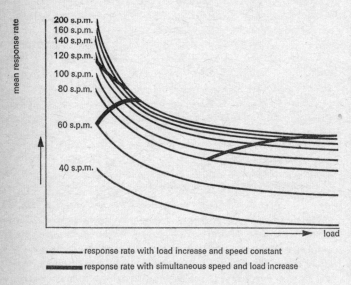

———— response rate with load increase and speed constant
▬▬▬▬ response rate with simultaneous speed and load increase

Figure 5 Hypothetical effect of simultaneous speed and load increases on response rate

rate which could occur over an extensive range of speed and load changed. The heavy lines indicate types of response rate which could occur if the speed and load were simultaneously varied in the manner suggested in the previous paragraph. One curve postulates the response rate that would occur if each unit of load carried few imaginary units of speed. Another curve indicates how different the effect might be if each unit of load carried many units of speed. One can imagine for example two situations, the speed of both of which was 120 signals per unit time. If four units of load were added to the former, response rate would increase. The same absolute increase in load in the latter case, however, would lead to a decrease in response rate.

This, indeed, is the kind of problem that has to be faced once one recognizes that the amount of information inherent in a display is a factor affecting performance, and once one attempts to determine optimum amounts of information that can be reasonably dealt with by a human operator. Speed and load are only two variables which determine the level of performance in relation to the amount of information presented. When any one of several sources might equally provide the next signal to be dealt with, the difficulty of the choice involved is without doubt another factor which has to be considered.

As the sympathetic recognition of man–machine relationships develops in industry, the problems related to the assessment of optimal work-loads will become increasingly important. If the great strides are to be maintained which have already been made in the direction of designing the display side of skills, then considerable attention will have to be given to research concerned with the time limits inherent in the nature of the skill and which are inescapably imposed on the operator. Everyone at some time has had too many things to do in too short a time. The different phenomenal possibilities involved in that situation merit a systematic analysis. This paper has attempted to demonstrate some aspects of this problem.

References

BARTLETT, F. C. (1951), 'The experimental study of skill', *Research*, vol. 4, p. 217.

BROADBENT, D. E. (1952), Failures of attention in selective listening, *Applied Psychology Research Unit Report*, no. 168, Medical Research Council.

CHAPANIS, A., GARNER, W. R., and MORGAN, C. T. (1949), *Applied Experimental Psychology*, Wiley.

CONRAD, R. (1951a), 'Speed and load stress in sensori-motor skill', *Brit. J. indust. Med.*, vol. 8, p. 1.

CONRAD, R. (1951b), 'Preliminary factory studies of the effect of speed and load on cotton winding', *Applied Psychology Research Unit Report*, no. 147, Medical Research Council.

MACKWORTH, N. H. (1948), unpublished.

WELFORD, A. T. (1951), *Skill and Age*, Oxford University Press for the Nuffield Foundation.

12 J. F. Mackworth and N. H. Mackworth

The Overlapping of Signals for Decisions

Excerpts from J. F. Mackworth and N. H. Mackworth, 'The overlapping of signals for decisions', *American Journal of Psychology*, vol. 69 (1956), pp. 28–47.

Objectives

The primary aim of the present paper is to draw attention to certain physical characteristics inherent in visual situations which are simultaneously presenting rapidly changing events overlapping in time. Secondly, an attempt has been made to measure varying stimulus situations of this kind more exactly, to specify the changes that occur from moment to moment during a simple laboratory task. Thirdly, the meaningfulness of the proposed index of task difficulty has been assessed by considering the relationship between momentary changes in this index and fluctuations in average achievement at this work which demands a series of decisions.

Briefly, signal overlap will account for most of the psychological effects of simultaneous visual presentations – but no claim is made that this is more than one chapter in the story. Further possible factors are now being experimentally evaluated.

Speed in decision taking can be a relatively simple concept under *single-channel* conditions. Here a stream of separate problems appears through a single physical gateway, one problem at a time. A new problem arrives every few seconds at approximately regular intervals. The relevant facts appear abruptly and cannot be predicted or considered in any way beforehand. Action demanded by the events must be taken instantly, before the stimulus objects disappear, as the information cannot be remembered. The serial order in which the decisions are to be taken is predetermined by the situation. Single-channel speed stress is easy to measure because the stimulus situation can obviously best be specified in the ordinary way by taking the average rate at which the environment is demanding decisions. The successive events in the single channel are more or less evenly spaced along the time scale, and therefore this average speed at which decisions are demanded is a good index of the difficulty of the task.

With *multichannel conditions* the situation is rather different; here the average speed is quite inadequate as a measure of stress and some other index is needed. A multichannel display has two or more signal sources, each of which is providing a stream of signals. The data appear through more than one physical gateway, hence the demands for immediate action will overlap in time.

An extra channel added to a display without extra time will obviously cause trouble because that channel calls for an increased number of decisions per minute. The main thesis of this paper is that multichannel displays are undesirable for a less obvious reason. Multichannel displays create difficulties even when there is no change in the average rate at which decisions are demanded, i.e. even when time is added directly in proportion to the increased number of channels. For example, if the number of channels is doubled, it is not enough to halve the number of signals that occur over a given period of time in each separate channel. Conrad (1951, p. 4 ff.) has also shown that achievement in multichannel displays cannot be specified by quoting simply the average speed required from S without mentioning the number of sources of signal he has to consider.

An arrangement whereby more gateways supply the same number of signals within a given period will tend to give the effect that action demands are irregularly spaced along the time scale. There are greater opportunities for a large number of signals to occur at once. The speed level varies much more from moment to moment and there is therefore a need for a measure which will estimate rapid changes in speed stress, to assess the speed stress under which each separate signal is considered.

Cox and Smith (1953, p. 1) analysed the problem from a general statistical point of view. They considered the matter largely as a question of the frequency distribution of the time intervals between successive events to be expected when several strictly periodic sequences of events are superimposed on one another to form one final common stream. The variables considered are the number of sources, the relative signal frequency of each source and the average signal frequency of their pooled output. In a later paper Cox and Smith (1954, p. 97) have taken up the problem of the pooled output from several independent sources when the intervals between successive events at any one source are assumed to be independent random variables all with the same distribution. The greater the number of original sources, the closer will the pooled distribution be to an exponential distribution; more very short and very long intervals are found. Conrad (1954, pp. 7–9) has considered these statistical principles in relation to performance at a sensorimotor task.

Problem

The problem is to measure and express temporary bursts of intense activity on the display; this requirement becomes especially noticeable in decision taking when this would be within the limits of ability if the problems were more evenly spread over the available time. The difficulty of a given signal in a multichannel display cannot be assessed only in terms of the time intervals between pairs of successive signals; groupings may occur in which the perception of each signal is influenced by several other signals, as well as by those nearest to it in time. This is particularly so in taking decisions each of which has to be considered over a definite period – for at least several seconds – rather than for a single fleeting instant.

It seems reasonable to estimate the momentary difficulties arising from these close groupings of events by the extent to which any given signal overlaps in time with any other signal in the series. This index of overlap for a given signal is therefore suggested for the assessment of these vitally important and crowded moments in the task, when everything seems to happen at once.

Method and Procedure

The procedure adopted in applying this technique is best indicated by considering its actual use in the analysis of a motion picture display of the type to be described later. Each problem was visible for 14 s and this active period was marked out for every signal in the series along a scale accurate to the nearest second. Separate horizontal lines were allocated to each of the channels in the display, but all the channels shared the same common time base. The total length of time that each signal was overlapped by any other signal could therefore readily be measured from this chart. The *index of overlap* for a given signal was the total sum in seconds of the various periods during which that signal was overlapped by any of the other signals in the series.

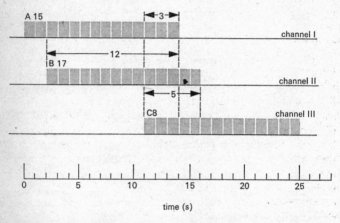

Figure 1 Index of signal overlap

This may be illustrated by considering a series of three signals, A, B and C, each visible for 14 s (see Figure 1). If A overlaps the first 12 s of B, and A also overlaps the first 3 s of C, then the signal overlap index for A = 15 s. Similarly, B will overlap 12 s with A and 5 s with C; therefore the signal overlap index for B = 17 s. As C will overlap 3 s with A and 5 s with B, the signal overlap index for C = 8 s.

Figure 2 contrasts the physical situations that result when this measure a signal overlap has been applied to a four-channel and a twelve-channel display. In either case fifty signals have arrived in 5 min. The average speed stress is, therefore, exactly the same – an average of one problem every 6 s. There are, however, obvious differences between the two forms of the task, despite the

Plates 1 and 2 Old and new methods of processing animal feeding stuffs. With the new method, weighing, mixing and grinding are carried out by a series of machines, most of which are automatic and controlled from the panel shown on the right. The new method involves none of the heavy manual work that characterized the old method illustrated below and also saves man-power, since the seven men formerly required are replaced by one operator at the control panel. The operator is, however, subject to a mental load which the old method did not impose. This load arises because the operator is no longer in contact with the material and cannot see what is happening to it. He deals with it indirectly by means of push buttons which start and stop the several machines. Some help in visualizing the process is provided by the mimic display. The help might have been greater if the push buttons had been mounted at the appropriate points on the display. (Reproduced by permission of R. Silcock and Sons Ltd.) See page 16

Plates 3 and 4 The new signal box shown on this page has many important advantages over the older box shown opposite. Three of these are :

(a) The physical effort of moving heavy levers is no longer required. Instead the signalman presses small buttons on the track diagram at the beginning and end of the route he wishes to set up. Operating two buttons in this way sets all signals and points over a given stretch of line.

(b) The placing of the control buttons on the diagram avoids the difficulty inherent in the old-type box of relating the illuminated track diagram to the levers and signal indications.

(c) In the old-type box, trains coming from the areas controlled by adjacent boxes are described by a system of bell codes and information from these has to be remembered by the signalman. In the new box, descriptions of trains coming from adjacent areas are indicated by lights on the panels at either end of the track diagram. The lights remain illuminated until the trains have passed and thus they relieve the load upon the signalman's memory.

It should be noted that the length of track which can be controlled by one signalman is very much greater with the new type of box than with the old. (Reproduced by courtesy of British Rail.) See page 16

Plate 5 Good and poor designs of speedometers. The figures on the upper example are very much easier to read than those of the lower one. Not only are they of better form but all are oriented so that they are read the right way up. The second example has too many lines of demarcation for clarity, and the use of two sizes of figures is confusing.

Almost all speedometers have the disadvantage that the mileometer counters are partially obscured by the pointer at certain speeds. The fundamental solution would be to remove the mileometer counters from the part of the dial face swept by the pointer. (Reproduced by permission of Smiths Industries Ltd.) See page 25

Plate 6 Old and new versions of a meter dial. The scale of the old version is difficult to read quickly. Not only are there too many marks, but the enclosure of these between parallel lines is confusing. The scale of the new version is much more easily read. The figures of the old version have the advantage that they are not at any time covered by the pointer, but the increased scale length of the new version and the fact that the new figures are all upright more than outweighs this. Both versions transgress good design in placing the legend 'Kilowatts' or 'kW' on the portion of the dial face swept by the pointer.

The heavy, polished black centre and bezel distract attention from the scale and pointer in the old version. The matt grey bezel and white centre of the new version are improvements. The new version would have been better still if the large centre piece had been eliminated and the pointer continued to the centre of the dial face. The new version has the refinement that the scale itself is raised a little above the rest of the dial face, an arrangement which avoids difficulties due to parallax between the pointer and the scale if the meter has to be read at an angle. (Reproduced by permission of G.E.C.–A.E.I. Ltd.) See page 25

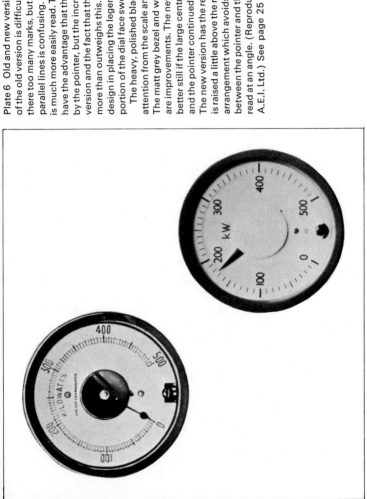

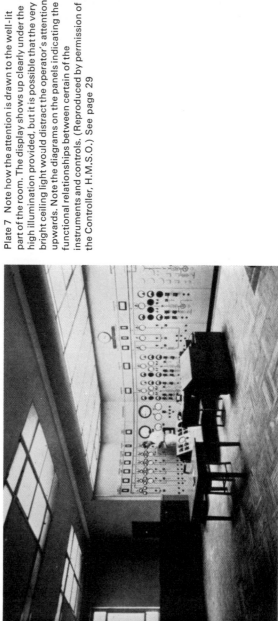

Plate 7 Note how the attention is drawn to the well-lit part of the room. The display shows up clearly under the high illumination provided, but it is possible that the very bright ceiling light would distract the operator's attention upwards. Note the diagrams on the panels indicating the functional relationships between certain of the instruments and controls. (Reproduced by permission of the Controller, H.M.S.O.) See page 29

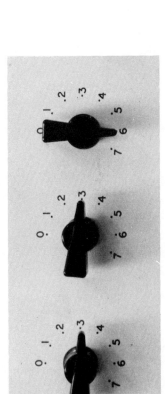

Plate 8 The position of the knob is very much easier to see in the lower example than in the top one. This is partly due to its better shape and partly to its colour contrasting with that of its background. (Reproduced by permission of the Controller, H.M.S.O.) See page 32

Plate 9 Photograph of the winding frames used in the mill experiments. (Reproduced by permission of The Medical Research Council.) See page 215

exposure time for every signal being 14 s in both examples. More channels mean more chances of overlap. When each of these channels is firing at approximately regular intervals, but at a rate different from that of any other channel, action demands are more irregularly spaced along the time scale. This irregularity

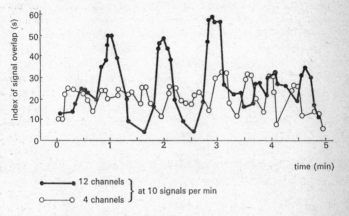

Figure 2 Multichannel display signal and overlap

is shown in terms of time in Figure 2 since the index of overlap for each signal is entered on the scale at the moment of onset of that particular signal. The effect of this same irregularity is more readily seen from Figure 2 in terms of the marked peaks in the overlap readings found with the twelve-channel display but not with the four-channel presentation.

These peaks are usually separated by particularly marked spells of enforced inactivity. The lulls are of no benefit to performance in some forms of task, although they do, of course, keep down the average speed at which work is demanded. It is interesting that these lulls are also misleading in another way because they partially disguise the extent of these vicious upward swings in the readings of overlap. An analysis of this kind seems necessary for a fuller understanding of the situation; for example, the average signal overlap for the twelve-channel display is not very much higher than that for the four-channel – 29·2 s compared with 20·5 s.

Method

An experimental task was devised to test the general hypothesis that peak demands like these were particularly harmful to accuracy. This equipment gave a series of problems in which S had to match two sets of facts directly and immediately available in his environment. Essentially this was a task on the matching of cards; one member of each pair of cards was always the same and remained constantly on view through a window. Other cards were brought one at a time alongside this fixed card by means of a slowly moving belt. This provided a series of comparisons in which S said how many symbols were common to the fixed and moving cards on each occasion. (To make the task more meaningful for S, this was presented as a comparison between two simplified 'flight plans'. Each card had six items of information on a given aircraft and S was therefore supposed to be reporting the extent of the similarity between the information received from two different pilots.)

Apparatus

Figure 3 shows one such window at a stage when a moving card has newly arrived for matching. Here the correct answer would be 'B, Two'.

On different test runs, there were between two and twelve such windows in the display. Although several windows could simultaneously demand attention, all the windows in a display were not necessarily showing pairs of cards at the same moment. The various belts moved at slightly different speeds – the ratio of the fastest to the slowest was never more than $2 : 1$ – hence the pattern of visible cards was continually changing, but S usually had no very great difficulty in deciding the order in which he should take the cards. The complete display covered an area 14×14 in and was set at right-angles to the line of sight. The mid-point of the display was about 36 in from the eyes. It was therefore unnecessary for S to move his head since the display could be read by making eye movements of not more than $\pm 11°$ either laterally or vertically.

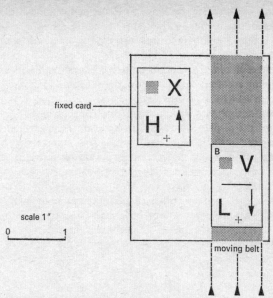

Figure 3 Example of a single-channel display

Procedure

(1) Initial experiment. Eighteen volunteer naval enlisted men between the ages of 18 and 31 yr took part in the first investigation. They were tested singly on a series of twelve runs with this multichannel display. Six runs were given in the morning after a practice run, and six in the afternoon with a further practice run. Each of these runs lasted several minutes and consisted of 100 comparisons between pairs of cards. Two factors were varied; speed and number of channels.

The *speed* was set at one of six levels which determined the average number of seconds allowed S for each comparison. On different runs, speeds were selected which represented for most people the range between a leisurely pace and extremely fast work. These six speeds of 10, 9, 8 7, 6 and 5 s per comparison meant that the whole moving card was visible for about 15, 13·5, 12, 10·5, 9 and 7·5 s respectively.

The *number of channels* was altered by changing the number of windows for different runs of the test. One of six displays was selected to expose 100 moving cards in the given standard time through either 2, 4, 6, 8, 10 or 12 windows.

Each S did each of the six speeds on two occasions and Latin-square planning ensured that the twelve runs for each S included two runs from each of the six displays.

The exposure time was kept constant for a given speed; the actual size of the display windows was reduced whenever there was any increase in the number of channels. The reason for this was that the belt carrying the cards had to move more slowly when there were more windows on the display to ensure that the same number of events occurred in a 5-min run. The implication is that any difficulties in performance found with more display channels could not have been directly due to changes in the exposure times. On the other hand, changes in speed did alter the exposure times and these could have affected performance.

No window ever showed more than one moving card at any stage in the presentation. Another point is that each window became active at approximately regular intervals but the frequency of events was different for the different windows.

(2) *Serial experiment.* Twenty further naval enlisted men aged 18 to 28 yr took part in a more detailed consideration of performance at this task. Particular attention was now paid to a temporal analysis of the effects of presenting the signals through different numbers of channels.

An attempt was made to hold the average speed constant and as close as possible to 6 s per pair of cards, the whole of every moving card being exposed for about 9 s. The effective exposure time was, however, 14 s, from the moment the upper half of the card appeared until the lower half started to disappear. Each run lasted 5 min, during which about fifty events occurred. Five different displays showed these events through either 4, 6, 8, 10 or 12 windows. One important change in the procedure was that the test-material was presented by means of a 35-mm motion picture film to ensure that the immediate time relationships of overlapping signals were held constant. Although the dimensions of the display remained as before, there was inevitably some loss of definition in the projected image.

Every *S* undertook a series of ten runs, all five displays being presented once in the morning and again in the afternoon. The films were given in a Latin square arrangement, varied for each group of five *S*s. The morning and afternoon sessions each took little over an hour and both sessions were preceded by a practice film.

Table 1

Percentage Incidence of Failures

No. channels		Seconds per comparison					
		10	*9*	*8*	*7*	*6*	*5*
Few	2	3·3	4·0	8·7	4·3	10·3	20·7
(2–6)	4	4·3	5·0	7·3	8·3	12·7	30·7
	6	3·7	8·3	8·0	7·7	13·0	19·0
Many	8	10·0	11·6	14·7	18·0	23·3	29·7
(8–12)	10	11·6	10·0	8·3	14·7	23·0	20·3
	12	9·3	9·3	12·7	12·3	22·3	27·7

Results

Initial experiment

The results are given in Table 1 and summarized in Figure 4. The data on the influence of the number of channels have been grouped under the headings of *few channels* and *many channels*, for 2–6 and 8–12 windows respectively. The criterion of performance was the percentage of failures in the comparisons. This measure was the percentage of wrong plus the percentage of missing answers. This was an average for a group of *S*s, since there were six readings for each of the thirty-six experimental conditions.

(*a*) *Average speed stress.* Statistical analysis confirmed the presence of a harmful effect on performance due to the average demanded rate of working. At the speed-stress level of 6 s per

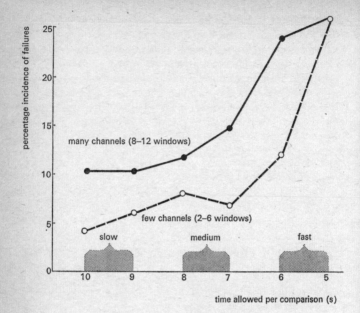

Figure 4 Relationship between failure and speed for multichannel and few channel displays. Multichannel displays give more failures for a given level of speed

comparison there was a statistically reliable increase in failures compared with scores at the 10-s speed. This decrement due to an increase in the average speed stress was found with the few-window and the many-window situation. In the former instance the average percentage of failures rose from 3·8 per cent to 12·0 per cent, in the latter it rose from 10·3 per cent to 22·9 per cent failures. Reliable differences were found on testing the significance of these percentage differences, since the ratios of the mean differences to their standard errors were 5·4 and 8·4 respectively ($p =$ <0·003). See Yule and Kendall (1940, p. 352).

(b) *Number of channels.* The effect of increasing the number of channels is clear from Table 1 and Figure 4. Performance was worse with many windows than with few windows for a given average speed. This decrement due to more channels was considerable; doubling the number of channels usually meant about twice as many failures, even when the average speed was kept constant.

This multichannel effect was present at nearly all levels of speed stress, see Figure 4. At the *slow* working speeds, few windows gave 4·8 per cent failures and many windows 10·3 per cent. Similarly, at the *medium* speeds few windows average 7·4 per cent failures and many windows 13·4 per cent. At the *fast* speeds 19·2 per cent failures occurred with few windows and 24·4 per cent with many. A statistical analysis established the reliability of these differences and the ratios of the mean differences to their standards errors were 9·0, 8·3 and 5·2 respectively, $p = <0·003$. The very highest speed of all was obviously, however, an exception (see Figure 4). Here, in fact, there was a dramatic rise in failures which seemed to be just as marked with few windows as with many. [. . .]

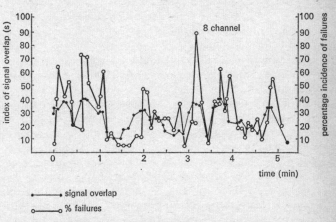

Figure 5 Relationship between index of signal overlap and percentage incidence of failures

Figure 5, for example, illustrates the typical trends for the 5-min run taken from the eight-channel display. [Much further analysis, exploring the relation between omissions and total number of failures, has been omitted – *Ed.*]

Discussion

This paper investigates some of the effects of varying the number of sources of visual information upon performance. It attempts to account for these in terms of the simplest possible expression of the situation – the required rate of work from moment to moment. The underlying assumption is that there must be a fixed maximum to the rate at which a man can think effectively when making comparisons between sets of objects. The idea is that this can matter even when the exposure time is adequate for each separate comparison, i.e. in spite of the objects being on view for a period which would be perfectly ample if this were the only match to be made in that time.

The suggestion is that this upper limit can be exceeded in two quite different ways. The obvious and usual way is when time is short throughout a given task – when the average number of decisions required per minute is in general too high. This form of speed stress is best expressed by the average number of seconds per signal. This index is particularly suitable when the signals are presented through a single-channel display, and are more or less evenly spaced in time.

Displays with more than one source of signal can, however, give trouble even when such average speed stress is low. Difficulties arise with many channels chiefly because the spacing in time of their pooled signals is so irregular that a crisis is created every now and again. Given that each source is firing at a different rate, irregularity will inevitably occur in the pooled series even if each channel is firing quite regularly. This bunching together of signals can also be regarded as a form of speed stress – a transitory burst of activity which leads to a momentary overstepping of the permissible limits for the required rate of decision. Such fluctuating demands call for a new index of speed stress which will measure the demanded rate of decision for each successive signal, i.e. to identify and mark out any treacherous peaks in the stress.

The time between the given signal and the signal nearest to it in the series is an inadequate measure for this purpose, particularly when each signal lasts for a specific period and is not a momentary event. In fact, the index of overlap between signals gives a better understanding of this everchanging speed stress with multichannel displays. This index is the total sum in seconds of the various periods during which the given signal overlaps any of the other signals in the series.

Refinements and modifications are needed to extend the usefulness of this index in analysing behaviour in serial tasks. For example, some adjustment is obviously required to correct for any alteration in average speed stress, when this is also reducing the time during which the signals are exposed.

Already, however, this index of signal overlap is demonstrably of some value in understanding the reasons for faulty serial performance, whether this is in terms of failures or omissions. It can be used within a series of signals of equal length occurring on a given number of channels at a given average number of signals per minute.

Quick bursts of speed stress are the most important effect of adding further sources of signal – provided that there is no general alteration in the average speed at which decisions are demanded. An increase in the number of channels in a display has a further effect on performance, the reasons for which remain as yet obscure. This additional disadvantage of too many channels appears to be directly proportional to the number of channels.

Further experiments are needed to understand this interesting multichannel effect which is *not* due to speed stress as measured by the extent of overlap between signals. Although the present investigations were not designed for this purpose, some speculation is perhaps permissible on the possible causes of these residual effects. It may be that the index could be weighted to correct for this by making some allowance for the *number* of signals involved in a given overlap. This could be tried in practice, but the index would no longer be strictly speaking a straightforward measure of speed stress, intended to elucidate these environmental effects.

Further studies, especially with other related tasks, will determine whether this multichannel effect apart from signal overlap was real or an artifact of the display. The writers believe, however, that several factors could have caused the larger incidence of omissions related to more sources even when there was the same overlap between signals.

In decreasing order of likelihood, the explanations needing experimental investigation are as follows:

(1) More channels in a display led to a greater redundancy in the presentation; each window had its fixed card always on view and obviously not all of these would be relevant at any given moment. This might have given rise to some difficulty because there were more signals to neglect in scanning for new arrivals.

(2) More channels meant that rather more cards arrived nearly simultaneously for comparison during periods of peak stress. This could have increased any difficulty in deciding the most effective order in which to take the various comparisons.

(3) More channels meant higher and longer lasting peaks of stress. Performance might have worsened because there were fewer of those signals previously described which were done better than expected because they came early in a growing peak of stress.

(4) More channels may have caused trouble because the additional irrelevant material required extra eye movements which now began to be a limiting factor.

One line for further work might be studies of the serial matching of objects on similar but more complex material. Achievement at the taking of decisions would be assessed with special regard to the part played by eye movements in selecting a series of essential cues from the mass of detail in the immediate visual world. Analysis of the eye-movement patterns in space and time during such tasks may lead to a better understanding of the relationship between the three main psychological aspects of this kind of work. Verplanck has drawn attention to the presence of two of these functions in problems related to the communication of information: (a) the span of apprehension and (b) the immediate memory-span (Verplanck, 1949, p. 253). It is particularly necessary, however, to add a third function: (c) the shifting of awareness, when continuous work is being considered. Vernon (1954, p. 210) has described this as the 'successive focusing of awareness upon different parts or aspects of the field each of which can be separately and satisfactorily dealt with, assimilated and comprehended.' Grindley (1931, pp. 32–3) found that even with tachistoscopic perception the nature of a peripherally exposed test-object was much less likely to be accurately reported if several other objects were also exposed simultaneously. Often, however, the memory after-image plays an important role in the tachistoscopic work with geometric forms and Ss can report from the memory image rather than the immediate percept. The present studies frequently found Ss using their memory after-images of the upper three symbols on one card to match this with their percepts of the corresponding three symbols on the other card. Then the lower three symbols were compared in the same way. Since Ss tended to take three objects at a time, it is particularly interesting to note that G!anville and Dallenbach objectively determined the span of apprehension for geometric forms at about this number of items. They found that different Ss averaged 3·2, 3·9 and 4·3 objects for their span of apprehension when this was taken at the 50 per cent correct level. These Ss correctly named the forms on most of the cards where only three objects were present, the exposure-time being only 0·08 s (Glanville and Dallenbach, 1929, p. 228).

Consideration of the role of immediate memory in the side-by-side comparison of visual objects could lead to studies of tasks such as the matching of perceived and remembered patterns. Without such a development, these investigations may tend to exaggerate the importance of present perceiving. Alternatively, the experimental situation might be widened to include the coming occasion – the not-quite-yet, to use the term suggested by Bentley (1952, p. 339). For example, the effects of auditory cueing could be considered especially in the structuring of an ambiguous visual scene. Ways may even be found, in time, to study the overlap between signals for action some of which are imminently foreseen rather than physically present in the environment.

Summary

An attempt has been made to understand more fully the problems facing men in situations in which they have to compare quickly many objects presented visually and simultaneously. Current traditions in psychology may well tend to overemphasize the importance of present perceiving, but experimental studies of relatively complex behavior such as human choice in critical and problematical occasions can perhaps at least start by considering activity in relation to the immediate scene. Human limitations were therefore sought in the rate at which each signal in a continuous series could be accurately matched. The physical measure devised was the index of signal overlap which is the total sum in seconds of the various periods during which the given signal is overlapped by any other signal.

A task in which objects had to be matched confirmed the great disadvantages for skilled achievement when further physical sources of demands for action are added to a serial visual presentation. These difficulties are experienced even when there is no change in the average number of signals presented per unit time. The greatest drawback of multichannel displays is believed to be their tendency to give rise to momentary but very damaging peaks of speed stress. These peaks may pass unnoticed unless the physical situation is analysed by some measure such as this index of signal overlap.

There is a definite and rising correlation between this index and faulty performance as the number of channels in the display is increased. A linear relationship has been demonstrated for the regression of missed signals on signal overlap. The greater the peak stress, the higher the proportion of failures due to missed rather than wrong decisions.

Most of the multichannel effect can be traced to peak speed stress. Statistical analysis has, however, also suggested that more display channels may have further effects. Experimental work is in progress to determine whether these are generally found or are artifacts specific to this experimental situation. They could have arisen from a greater redundancy in the immediate display, or from an increased difficulty in choosing the most effective order in which to take up the various comparisons.

References

BENTLEY, M. (1952), 'Forecast, timing, and other primary factors in the government of certain biochemical systems', *Amer. J. Psychol.*, vol. 65.

CONRAD, R. (1951), 'Speed and load stress in a sensori-motor skill', *Brit. J. indust. Med.*, vol. 8.

CONRAD, R. (1954), 'Missed signals in a sensori-motor skill', *J. exp. Psychol.*, vol. 48.

Cox, D. R., and Smith, W. L. (1953), 'The superposition of several strictly periodic sequences of events', *Biometrika*, vol. 40.

Cox, D. R., and Smith, W. L. (1954), 'On the superposition of renewal processes', *Biometrika*, vol. 41.

Glanville, A. D., and Dallenbach, K. M. (1929), 'The range of attention', *Amer. J. Psychol.*, vol. 41.

Grindley, G. C. (1931), *Psychological Factors in Peripheral Vision*.

Vernon, M. D. (1954), *A Further Study of Visual Perception*, Cambridge University Press.

Verplanck, W. S. (1949), 'Visual communication', in *Human Factors in Undersea Warfare*, National Research Council, Washington.

Yule, G. U., and Kendall, M. G. (1940), *Introduction to the Theory of Statistics*, Griffin.

13 L. H. Shaffer

Monitoring Computer Decisions

L. H. Shaffer, 'Problem solving on a stochastic process', *Ergonomics*, vol. 8 (1965), pp. 181–92.

This study is concerned with man–computer co-operation in which the computer initiates decisions and the man monitors and can alter these. The task used involved controlling an information process by making decisions at each of a sequence of points. The problem of control was to find an optimal procedure that jointly minimized two variables.

The solutions of subjects developed over a series of trials were compared with that of an optimal programme under different conditions. Subject performance was nearly always inferior to that of the programme, it was impaired by increasing the rate of the information input and failed to benefit from reduction of uncertainty in the input. Giving trial knowledge of results helped convergence towards an optimal solution.

Subjects who had gained experience in the task were given computer solutions to monitor. They degraded optimal solutions and improved inferior solutions towards their own level of performance and failed to benefit from this experience in subsequent tests.

1. Introduction

This paper is concerned with some aspects of human decision making, in particular decision making that controls and is paced by an information process. A further qualification is that the process presents a continually developing picture rather than a discrete succession of events. Suitable analogies are traffic control at an airport or road junction, rather than, say, the inspection task of accepting or rejecting each of a succession of objects. It is quite proper, of course, to treat the latter type of situation as an extreme simplification of the former.

First a brief point on terminology. Theoretical literature still treats problem solving, concept formation and decision making as distinct topics. In this paper a concept is regarded as a solution to a classification problem; a decision is a solution upon which action is to be taken. It is true that a problem can be solved by logical computation and a decision can be made by arbitrary choice, but these represent extremes of possible methods of solution and when referring to a psychological process it is often presumptive to place a given solution at a point along the spectrum.

The point of departure of the present study is an analysis of man–computer decision systems. The type of system envisaged is that in which a computer is programmed to make decisions based upon a set of rules and a man monitoring these decisions can accept, reject or modify them. The question of the efficacy of such a system can only be explicitly answered by a system analysis that takes into account the actual computer programme, the man acting as monitor and the knowledge available to him. With some sacrifice of explicitness the experiments to be reported examine a class of such systems by using a generalized simulation.

A number of tasks involving sequential decision making can be regarded as problems of serving a queue of customers. Each problem can be specified by the properties of customer arrival, queue behaviour and the service mechanism (Kendall, 1951). The common feature of these problems is that a random input has to be mapped into an output such that the values of certain variables are optimized. Some idea of the scope of this formalism can be obtained from Kendall and from Churchman *et al.* (1957). Such a problem was used in the simulation and will be described later in detail.

Two main experiments were performed. In the first the problem was given to subjects, the rules of play and criteria to be satisfied were stated and it was left to them to develop solutions over a series of trials. It may be noted that since a solution entailed a procedure for mapping input states into output states the task was one of concept formation. Performance was examined under different conditions of time stress and among other things this gave an indication of whether the scoring procedure was sensitive to different levels of performance.

In the second main experiment subjects who had developed

their own solutions were given those of a computer to monitor and were instructed to modify the solutions only if doing so would improve them.

2. Apparatus and Task

The subject sat in front of a sloping panel having an aperture as in Figure 1. A tape moved upwards past the aperture at a fixed speed. Down the centre of the tape was a time track marked in seconds (*modulo* 60). It will be necessary in what follows to distinguish tape time and real time. Numbers were printed at random intervals on the left of the track, indicating customers.

A customer was thus represented by two parameter values, the number mentioned (M) and its corresponding tape time (A). The distribution of customers was a *Poisson* process (Kendall) with mean density 1/5, modified so that the interval between successive customers was never zero or greater than 14 s. The parameter M was determined by $M - A = m = 15$ s. The sequence of customers formed the data input process, which developed as new customers appeared from behind the aperture.

The right of the track was blank and subjects wrote entries on this side, one for each customer. Each entry, against a time S, was a number A and represented the commencement of service of customer A. A transparent shield on the upper right of the aperture restricted the latest point in real time that an entry could be made.

The task can be described abstractly as mapping the sequence of customers at times A on the left of the track into a sequence of entries at times S on the right under two constraints:

(i) $A \leqslant S \leqslant M$;
(ii) the distance between S_i and S_{i+1} should take one of the values $s = 2, 4, 6$ or 8 s, unless no new customer appears within 8 s of the last entry.

The following interpretation is given. Customers (A) arriving at times A could be served only one at a time and each required an amount of time s for service. The customers not yet served joined a queue on arrival, but each was only prepared to wait m sec and was considered lost if his service had not commenced by

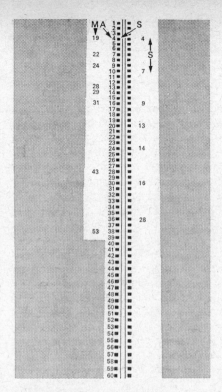

Figure 1 The display. The tape moves upwards past the aperture. The time track appears in the centre. Number pairs (M,A) on the left — (19·4), (22·7), (24·9), etc. — represent customers. The subject writes numbers (A) on the right, assigning a time S at which each customer begins service. Thus customer (31·16) commences service at time S = 30 and is allocated s = 6 s for service. The perspex mask on the upper right restricts the latest time at which subjects can write entries on the tape

a time $S \leqslant M$. The four values of s corresponded to four (hypothetical) service routines that required different times to serve a customer and the server (subject) had a free choice of s for any customer. To serve a customer in $s = 8$, 6, 4 or 2 s entailed a cost to the server of 1, 2, 4 or 8 units. If at any point the

241

queue was empty then the next customer started service at the time he arrived.

The process of queue serving has been described relative to track time. In real time the only constraint on when a subject made his entries was the upper limit imposed by the transparent shield.

The problem for the subject was to find a service procedure, a rule mapping A into S, that jointly minimized the risk of losing customers and the cost score, $\Sigma f(s)$. Note that the cost function $f(s)$ was nonlinear: for every 2 s saved in serving a customer the cost doubled. Hence the minimum cost was obtainable by choosing s close to the average arrival rate (5 s) as often as the variance would permit.

3. Experiment 1

This experiment examined the performance of subjects who were given the queue serving problem and allowed to develop their own solutions over a series of trials. Since this was a simulation study three features that approximate the real situation were included in the design:

(a) subjects were told nothing about the statistical properties of the queue, nor were they advised on service procedures;
(b) they were given no feedback information of the quality of performance following a trial;
(c) no explicit cost was assigned to the loss of a customer, so that there was no unique trading relationship between cost and risk.

Since the queue was statistically stationary over all trials it was still possible under these conditions for subjects to monitor their own performance and so converge upon an optimal service procedure.

Stress in the task can be introduced in three ways; (a) by varying the average rate at which customers arrive and must be served; (b) by varying the latest time at which the subject can make a decision; and (c) by varying the degree of randomness of arrival times. The last two govern the amount of uncertainty of the state of the queue following a decision. If no limiting time is imposed in making decisions this uncertainty can be effectively reduced to zero. In the experiment the first two variables were manipulated, but some information was also obtained on the effects of the third.

Design

Thirty-six servicemen aged 20–30 were used as subjects; six randomly allocated to each of six groups. Each subject was used in only one group and was tested twice a day for four days.

The six conditions examined involved two arrival rates, R, and three levels of queue-state uncertainty, U. At the slow rate R_1, real time = 3 × tape time, and at the fast rate R_2, real time = 1·5 × tape time. These represent average arrival rates in real time of four and eight customers per min respectively. To obtain zero queue-state uncertainty U_0, the transport shield was removed. At low uncertainty U_1, it was adjusted so that the distance of its edge from the point at which customers appeared was 10 s of tape time and at high uncertainty U_2, this distance was 5 s.

A subject received two practice trials, each lasting 20 min, at the U level appropriate to his group and at the rate R_1 except for 5 min at the rate R_2 at the end of the second trial. These trials were not scored. They were followed by six test trials. In each of these there was a different run of sixty customers and the trial lasted 15 or 7·5 min according to R. At the end of a run 'dummy' customers appeared so as to leave the subject uncertain of where the queue ended.

In the first practice trial the task was described as the service of customers with optional service facilities. They were told that each customer was prepared to wait only a limited amount of time as indicated. The importance of not losing customers was stressed. They were also requested to keep down the over-all cost of service as much as possible.

They were not told the parameter values of average arrival rate or of waiting time. The effect of the nonlinear cost function was demonstrated with several numerical examples of service worked out on paper.

After a trial the subject was told how many customers he lost but was never told how costly his service was.

Results

For each test trial three questions were relevant; how many customers were lost, how costly was the trial and how risky was the subject's service procedure? Note that the subject was left to establish his own 'trade off' between service cost and risk and so could legitimately accept a high cost score so as to minimize risk.

If customers were lost then both the cost and time of serving them were saved and in both ways over-all cost was reduced. A fixed procedure was adopted in scoring to modify subjects' data so as to allocate service time to the lost customers. In this way cost was estimated for a no-loss run. In fact it involved little distortion of the data since the number of losses was something less than 1 per cent of all customers. This number was so small that no separate analysis was carried out on loss scores.

Cost and risk scores were obtained by comparing each subject's performance with that of a service model, which will be called OM, that served customers at some acceptably low risk at minimum cost. OM used a simple rule: if two customers or less are waiting give the next one 6 s, if more than two are waiting give the next one 4 s, or if any customer on view will exceed his waiting time use the next shorter service necessary. This rule was applied to the six different runs under uncertainty condition U_2 and all service decisions were made as late as possible. No customers were lost and the third condition of the rule was used only twice.

Although the service costs were 1, 2, 4 and 8 units a slightly different function was used for scoring: 1, 2, 4 and 7. It is easily seen that this does not alter the solution to the problem, but the former emphasizes the effect of the cost differential and so is suitable for demonstrating the problem, while the latter gives the least biased estimate of departures in performance from a minimum cost solution. The cost for a run was obtained by adding the costs for all sixty customers and the final cost score was taken as this total minus the cost obtained by OM on the same run. This final score gives a direct numerical estimate of how often a subject used extreme service times compared with OM, plus his relative efficiency of time utilization. It eliminates as nearly as possible cost fluctuations necessitated by distribution differences on different runs.

A risk score was obtained by subtracting for each customer the entry time, S allocated by OM from that allocated by the subject and adding these signed differences for all sixty customers in a run. In principle, the longer customers were left waiting the greater was the risk that some would be lost and the risk score reflected this.

The product moment correlation between cost and risk over the set of scores for all groups was 0·073, which was not significant, and so it is plausible that the two scores were independent. If they had been more closely related it would have been necessary to make multivariate comparisons, instead of which separate comparisons are presented. Average cost and risk scores per subject-trial for the different groups are shown in Table 1.

Table 1

Average Cost and Risk Scores for Different Conditions of Rate R, and Uncertainty U

		U 0	1	2
1	Cost	6·6	8·1	7·8
	Risk	11·8	40·4	59·1
R				
2	Cost	9·1	10·5	10·9
	Risk	28·0	26·5	15·7

An analysis of variance of cost scores showed that they were significantly higher at the fast rate R_2 than at the slow rate R_1 ($F_{1, 30} = 4·43$, $p < 0·05$). The effect of uncertainty U was not significant. The differences between trials, T, were significant ($F_{5, 150} = 6·84$, $p < 0·001$). There were no significant interactions.

Figure 2 shows the change in cost over trials, with all groups collapsed. This graph indicates that the significant T effect was something other than improvement with practice, that there were differences in trial difficulty encountered with the inferior service procedures used by subjects but not with OM. Inspection of queue runs showed that the more difficult ones included more extreme values of local customer density but attempts to capture this with some statistic failed. Accordingly a model was constructed using an inferior service rule which will be called *IM*.

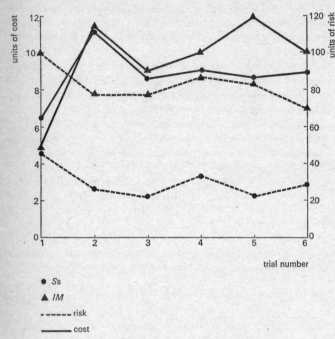

Figure 2 Experiment 1 : cost and risk scores over trials for *IM* and subjects. The latter are averaged across all groups

This rule was: if only one customer is waiting give him 8 s, if more than one is waiting give the next one 6 s or if any customer on view will exceed his waiting time use the next shorter service necessary. It was applied under the same conditions as *OM*. *IM* lost no customers and its cost scores are shown in Figure 2. Except at trial 5 the curve follows closely that of the subjects.

An analysis of variance of risk scores showed no group differences, but there was a significant trial effect $T(F_{5, 150} = 3.68$, $p < 0.01)$. Trial scores are shown in Figure 2 and again, although the values are different, the changes are similar to those of *IM* scores.

Discussion

In assessing the quality of performance on a trial a sufficient criterion of optimality is that, given the cost score, the risk score is the lowest possible and conversely. Of the 216 subject-trials none had a cost score less than *OM*. Only forty-six had negative risk scores and with most of these it could be shown that a lower cost score was possible. Thus subject performance was usually more risky, sometimes more conservative and nearly always more costly than *OM*. It was seldom optimal. Against this it should be noted that the service rule used by *OM* was simple enough to be implemented without difficulty at the input rates used. Since this is not a normative study the main point here is that the problem was not a trivial one for the subjects although it involved fewer variables than in most comparable real situations.

The significant trials effect *T* confounded the effect of practice and the response to chance fluctuations in queue distribution on different runs. As long as local queue density was close to average, choice of service was reasonably constrained since the subject could match output rate against input rate. When local density departed considerably from average, optimal service demanded regulation of a buffer time. In the event subjects were tempted into using 8-s services in low density stretches and were forced to use 2-s services for subsequent arrivals. *IM* scores reflect the average constraint on different runs and Figure 2 shows that except on trial 5 subject performance was dominated by this constraint. The exception is the only evidence that practice led to improvement.

The non-significant effect of queue-state uncertainty *U* shows also that subjects failed to exploit the advance information available to them. While not a recorded aspect of performance it was observed that subjects in all groups tended to make their decisions too early, so throwing away the opportunity to obtain more information. It will be recalled that under condition U_0 the problem could in effect be made determinate. Thus either they were unable to develop fully the implication of the non-linear cost function or under the time stress they were unable to process the available information. Note again that given an accurate appraisal of the queue distribution it is possible to sacrifice much of the advance information and still achieve optimal performance. OM had only to count whether the number of customers waiting exceeded a certain number and note whether any would exceed their waiting times with a given service allocation.

The result that performance at the fast input rate was significantly worse than at the slow rate, while important in itself, leaves unresolved the question of whether time stress affected the ability to form an adequate concept of service or the ability to implement one in local decisions. It would be possible to decide this point by training two large groups of subjects, one at slow, the other at fast rate, and having a single transfer trial in which half of each group transferred to the other rate. A more economical but less direct test is to provide a control group with some feedback information of performance. This was carried out in the second experiment.

4. Experiment 2

A single group of six servicemen, not used before, was given the queue-serving task under the condition R_1, U_2, and after each trial they were told their cost scores, i.e. cost in excess of the minimum possible. Performance was compared with that of the appropriate group in Experiment 1. The conditions of giving or withholding knowledge of results can be labelled K and NK respectively.

An analysis of variance of cost scores showed no difference between K and NK. But the $K \times T$ interaction was significant ($F_{5, 50} = 3 \cdot 58$, $p < 0 \cdot 01$), showing divergent performances on different trials, and the T effect was significant ($F_{5, 50} = 6 \cdot 9$, $p < 0 \cdot 001$). These results are clarified in Figure 3, which shows that K group had a high score on trial 2 but otherwise showed steady improvement over trials, where NK scores showed no consistent trend.

It is inferred that giving trial knowledge of results assisted convergence towards optimal performance. If correct it suggests (but does not demonstrate) that the effect of time stress was not so much to impair decision making as to discourage the search for better solutions in the absence of external guidance or motivation. In fact, and this is of interest in itself, the amount of explicit guidance in the control experiment was small since cost score was a scalar number and had no vector properties and so could not

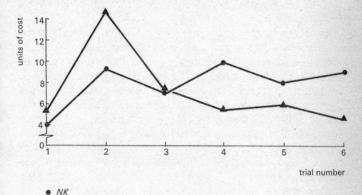

Figure 3 Experiment 2: cost scores over trials for K and NK conditions, averaged within each group

tell the subject why his performance was good or bad. He could only infer over successive trials whether or not changes in tactics were in the right direction: hence the preponderant swing in the wrong direction on trial 2.

Before any strong conclusion can be drawn from this experiment another control should be provided at the fast input rate. More generally it would be interesting to examine the interaction of feedback information K, rate R and uncertainty U. But at this point attention was turned to the main question of the study, the efficacy of a human monitor in a man–computer decision system.

5. Experiment 3

There are often two separable aspects of problem solving, initiating hypotheses and evaluating them. If a division of function based upon these is established in a two person team then the question arises what forms of communication between them are necessary for effective collaboration. More particularly, if a man is to monitor a decision-making computer how much should he know about the information and decision rules available to it? The ramifications of this question are extensive and only a preliminary exploration is attempted here.

Experimenting in the context of the queue-serving problem the first point to decide was whether a computer should offer the monitor a sequence of decisions of service or a decision rule for generating these and at what level the monitor should be allowed to intervene. It was decided that the monitor would receive a sequence of decisions any of which he could modify. In almost any real system a change introduced by the monitor at the output would be fed back to the computer and so affect its subsequent decisions. Such a facility would have been difficult to realize with the apparatus available and instead the computer offered a fixed sequence of decisions.

Subjects were allowed to develop their own solutions over a series of trials. In subsequent trials they were given computer solutions, in the form of recommended service time s for each customer, which they could accept or modify. A transfer design was used to examine how effectively they monitored different levels of solution and how much in turn these affected the subsequent quality of their own.

Design

Thirty servicemen, not previously used, were assigned at random to one of five groups, six in each group.

Four levels of solution were offered to the different groups. They were: I – solutions of OM; II – solutions of IM; III – an alternation of OM and IM solutions on different trials; and IV – solutions of the subject previously obtained on the same runs. In these four groups a subject was not told whether or not he had improved on the offered solution. Group V received solutions of OM and was given this knowledge of results. It should be mentioned that OM solutions cannot be made substantially better but alteration need not degrade them.

All trials were presented under condition R_1, U_2. Each subject received two practice trials followed by three test trials on different runs, in which he gave his own solutions. On each of the next four days he received a run twice. In the morning he gave his own solution and in the afternoon he monitored a given solution, presented as recommended service times, s written next to each customer on the display tape.

Instruction for practice and test trials was the same as previously. Before the monitoring trials the subject was told that recommended service times would be shown for each customer, representing a possible solution of service allocation. He was free to use or alter them, but should make alterations only if he thought they would lead to lower over-all cost.

After each test trial the subject was told his cost score, but only in group V was he told whether he had improved or degraded the monitored solution. He was not told that the run monitored in the afternoon was the same as he had received in the morning and in the event he did not recognize it. Nor was he told in group IV that the solution given him was his own.

Results

Loss scores were again so low they can be ignored. Analysis is confined to cost scores and two questions were asked. Did different types of monitoring trial M have differential transfer effects upon test trials O? Did performance on M trials differ between groups?

Table 2

Average Cost Scores Per Trial for the Early and Late Trials of the Different Groups, Experiment 3

Group	I	II	III	IV	V
O_{1-3}	11·0	13·8	13·1	10·8	12·7
O_{5-7}	8·2	10·1	8·0	7·9	6·6

To answer the first question scores on the first three, O_{1-3}, and last three, O_{5-7}, trials were compared across groups in analyses of variance. Mean scores per trial are shown in Table 2.

Separate analyses were carried out for groups I–IV and groups I and V, the two variables in each being groups, G, and blocks of trials, O. Neither the G nor the $G \times O$ terms were significant in each analysis. Only the O term was significant ($F_{1,\,20} = 12\cdot2$, $p < 0\cdot01$ for I–IV and $F_{1,\,10} = 8\cdot4$, $p < 0\cdot025$ for I and V).

To answer the second question scores on M trials were compared across groups against O trial scores on the corresponding runs in analyses of variance. Mean scores per trial are shown in Table 3.

Table 3

Average Cost Scores Per Trial for O_{4-7} and M Trials of the Different Groups, Experiment 3

Group	I	II	III	IV	V
O_{4-7}	9·0	10·3	7·8	8·8	7·7
M	6·8	10·2	9·0	9·3	5·4

Again there were separate analyses for groups I–IV and I and V, the three variables in each being groups, G, monitoring or test trials, M or O and trials within M or O series, T. In neither analysis was the G term significant. Only for groups I and V was the M or O term significant ($F_{1,\,10} = 8\cdot5$, $p < 0\cdot025$). There were no significant interactions. The T term was significant ($F_{3\cdot60} = 4\cdot9$, $p < 0\cdot01$ for I–IV; $F_{3,\,30} = 5\cdot9$, $p < 0\cdot01$ for I and V) representing improvement with practice over the four days on both O and M trials.

The following picture is obtained by calculating for each subject the distances between his score on an M trial and those of the offered solution and his O trial on the same run. Group I degraded OM scores by 6·8 units ($t = 5\cdot4$, $p < 0\cdot01$) but did better than its O scores by 2·2 units ($t = 1\cdot96$, ns). Group II improved IM scores by 1·3 units ($t = 1\cdot28$, ns) to equal its O scores. Group III degraded OM scores by 9 units ($t = 4\cdot47$, $p < 0\cdot01$) to equal its O scores and improved IM scores by 4 units ($t = 2\cdot16$, ns), leaving them 2·3 units worse than its O scores ($t = 1\cdot23$, ns). Group IV slightly degraded its own O scores ($t = 0\cdot67$, ns). Group V degraded OM scores by 5·4 units ($t = 5\cdot59$, $p < 0\cdot01$) and left them 2·3 units better than its O scores

($t = 2 \cdot 11$, ns). Note that only degradations of OM solutions were significant.

One further question, whose answer involves a new score, is how extensively did subjects alter the offered solutions? A simple estimate was obtained by counting how often in a trial the recommended time s was left unchanged. Table 4 shows the

Table 4

Average Agreement Scores Per Trial for M and Control Trials, Experiment 3

Group	I	II	III	IV	V
M	34·3	33·3	33·0	37·2	40·7
Control	34·8	32·2	33·8	32·1	36·0

average agreement score per trial for each group and controls are included for comparison. For groups I, II, III and V the control was the agreement score between the offered solution and the subject's O solution on the same run. For group IV an M solution was compared with an O solution on that run of someone else in the group, randomly selected.

In no case did the M solution agree with the offered solution significantly more than the control, using 2-tail t-tests. Since the agreement was never high (total agreement was a score of 60) it follows that solutions were extensively modified. However an analysis of variance on agreement scores on M trials between groups showed a significant effect ($F_{4, 25} = 4 \cdot 16$, $p < 0 \cdot 01$) and as Table 4 shows groups IV and V had higher agreement scores than the others.

Discussion

A reasonable summary of results is that given optimal solutions subjects degraded them, given inferior solutions they improved them and given their own solutions they altered them but left the quality unchanged. They revised all solutions towards their own level of performance. The quality of their own solutions improved over trials, but this did not depend upon the solutions monitored and comparison with the results of Experiment 2 suggests that it can be attributed to the knowledge of results on O trials, rather than a transfer effect from M trials.

The simplest hypothesis is that subjects ignored the offered solutions and substituted their own. Counter to this is the evidence that the groups monitoring OM solutions had slightly lower cost scores on M trials than those monitoring other solutions. They were the only groups whose scores on M trials were significantly better than on O trials. In the case of group V, giving knowledge of results on M trials seems to have led to an increased respect for the offered solutions and not only did they alter them less than other groups, they were also constrained (though not significantly) towards adopting them in their own solutions (see Table 2).

Two reasons can be offered for the generally low agreement scores. The first is that despite the instruction, subjects regarded the monitoring task as a challenge to alter the offered solution. The second is that having made an alteration they were often committed to perpetuate it because the given solution ceased to be feasible. Even if they saw that its local performance was then better than their own they could no longer use it and could find no obvious way to return to it. This would probably not arise in real systems in which changes by the monitor become a feedback input to the computer. It might have been avoided in the present task if solutions had been offered as times of entry S rather than service times s. This factor was realized in advance and the main reason for using the latter display is that it was considered easier for the subject to infer the service rule.

The implication of the results is that for effective co-operation in a two-person problem-solving team it is not sufficient for the person initiating solutions to display only their detailed consequences. It may be helpful if he communicates the nature of the solution. It may finally be necessary that the person evaluating the solutions should also be competent to generate them. Although it is still speculative it seems reasonable to suggest that a man can usefully monitor a decision-making computer only if he is competent to write its programme.

In a wider context the paradigm of the two person team includes the pupil–teacher relationship. The teacher has successfully communicated theoretical knowledge not when he has merely conveyed some of its implications but when he has conveyed the basic theory such that the pupil can collaborate in deriving other implications. It is no accident that the recommendations made here are analogous to those made by Gagné and Brown (1961) following their study of the effectiveness of different programmes for teaching number series.

References

CHURCHMAN, C. W., ACKOFF, R. L., and ARNOFF, E. L. (1957), *Introduction to Operations Research*, Wiley.

GAGNÉ, R. M., and BROWN, L. T. (1961), 'Some factors in the programming of conceptual learning', *J. exp. Psychol.*, vol. 62, pp. 313–21.

KENDALL, D. G. (1951), 'Some problems in the theory of queues', *J.Roy. statist. Soc. (B)*, vol. 13, pp. 151–73.

14 R. Conrad

Experimental Psychology in the Field of
Telecommunications

R. Conrad, 'Experimental psychology in the field of telecommunications',
Ergonomics, vol. 3 (1960), pp. 289–95.

Four examples are cited to illustrate the application of the methods and
principles of experimental psychology to practical telecommunications
problems.

(1) The decay theory of immediate memory was used to predict the
relative merits, in terms of error, of the telephone dial and an alternative of a set of ten push buttons. Predictions were also made regarding
the effect of a prefix digit on accuracy of recall. Experiments substantially confirmed the predictions.

(2) Laboratory experiments were used to investigate factors relevant
to the design of long telephone codes for easy remembering. Factors
considered were length, grouping, letters *v*. numbers.

(3) An operational telephone exchange was used for 5 weeks during a
controlled experiment on the effects on operators' performance of
varying the traffic load. Operator time per call was shown to be a
function of traffic per operator.

(4) The frequency distribution of the time to sort letters by key
pressing was recorded in the practical situation. The effect of practice
is shown, and the influence of a machine lag in restraining output is
demonstrated.

1. Introduction

Although ergonomics is an established scientific discipline, there
are very few ergonomists. Contributions to ergonomics research
come therefore from a variety of sources, one of which is experimental psychology. The psychologist in this context is usually
concerned with applying theoretical concepts to practical problems of work. But he is not averse to using those working situations to confirm and expand this theoretical knowledge. The
present paper cites four case histories which illustrate this process.

2. Instrument Design

The decay theory of immediate memory was developed in the earliest days of experimental psychology. No one then imagined that it could have any relevance to telecommunications, in the modern sense of that word. It was argued that seeing or hearing something to be remembered set up some kind of a trace in the mind, which decayed naturally with time – hence forgetting. Few persons today would insist on the exclusiveness of this theory to account for all forgetting, but at the same time there is a good deal of evidence to suggest that some forgetting is due to decay of a not very clearly defined trace of something. As we now know, in effect this means that images perceived or events experienced fade fairly quickly, unless traces initially established are continually strengthened.

Clearly decay theory seems relevant to the problem of remembering a series of digits – say eight or nine – for long enough to dial them by telephone. This is a problem that is becoming increasingly common all over the world as telephone networks grow. The reason why decay theory is interesting in this context is because the telephone dial forces on the person dialling a series of delays between digits – of an average duration of nearly a second. If one wants to use these intervals to rehearse mentally the remainder of the number, one finds that they are just about of borderline value for this purpose. One might be able to use the delay after the nine or zero, but probably not that after one, two or three. So that, according to the theory, during these short delays while waiting for the dial to return, the memory trace established on first reading the number is now decaying, thus increasing the chances of dialling the wrong number (Conrad and Hille, 1958a).

One might think that the solution would be to use a system which minimized inter-digital delays such as, for instance, a set of ten push buttons. It has been possible to test this prediction experimentally, using subjects who were equally experienced at both dialling and keying telephone numbers (Conrad, 1958).

Four experimental conditions were set up, randomized in Latin squares, and each operator took part in all four. These were dialling or keying eight-digit numbers, and dialling or keying eight-digit numbers but always prefixed by the digit 0. This prefix condition simulated the situation in the national trunk dialling system where the digit 0 precedes all trunk numbers and acts as a switch into the trunk network out of the local one. This too, according to decay theory, ought to have led to more recall errors. The results are shown in Table 1.

Table 1

Effect on Recall of Transmitting Procedure

Procedure	Correctly transmitted (per cent)
Keying	56·9
Dialling	50·6
Keying with prefix digit	45·2
Dialling with prefix digit	34·8

3. Dialling Codes

The new national trunk dialling system has just been referred to in connexion with dialling codes. But these codes must first be designed so that a whole nation of people can successfully use them. As an example of the problem which already exists consider the code required to call the meteorological station at Mildenhall from a Cambridge telephone; one dials the following sequence: 96618312274. The initial 9 is remembered as the standard prefix, and the 661831 comes from one directory, the remainder from a second directory. The temptation therefore to try to remember all or part of the number is strong – even for someone well aware of the fragility of immediate memory.

What would help this kind of situation? For brevity three features may be considered. First of all from a psychological point of view, long numbers ought to be short! It is not always realized how few digits or letters can be immediately recalled after hearing or seeing them once. Tests both on naval ratings and on female telephonists, groups which one would expect to be a little better than the average of the country as a whole, show that under ideal conditions an eight-digit number is correctly recalled about six times out of ten. For 100 per cent correct recalls, it is useless with these groups to use numbers longer than five digits. If subjects are distracted for a few seconds between hearing and repeating back a number, then one could not expect 100 per cent success even with a three-digit number.

The second feature is grouping. The optimum size of group proves to be three or four digits (Conrad and Hille, 1957). Too much breakdown is in fact worse than none at all – possibly because when no grouping is suggested in the presentation, subjects create their own.

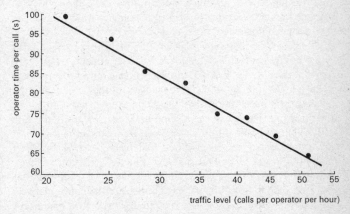

traffic level (calls per operator per hour)

Figure 1 Effect on operator performance of telephone traffic level

Thirdly there is the question of the relative value of digits and letters, and results here are also fairly clear. Letters which appear to be logical in the context, which can be deduced by simple rules, like the first three letters of London telephone exchanges, are always better than the same number of digits. But letters which appear to be drawn at random from the alphabet are much more difficult to remember than digits. All-numeral codes are better than letter-number or number-letter codes. But if random letters have to be used, then they should occur as a group at the beginning rather than at the end. This is because the second half of a sequence of six characters is generally more difficult to remember than the first half (Conrad and Hille, 1957).

4. Staffing a Telephone Exchange

The third example of the use of techniques of experimental psychology in the communications field is drawn from a study made at a telephone exchange. In essence, the problem was to determine the number of operators required to handle the traffic. Correct staffing can be fairly critical. If there is too little traffic per operator, then operators are idle for much of the day. Too much traffic on the other hand will increase subscribers' waiting time in a logarithmic manner, so that, beyond a certain point, this waiting time soars fairly quickly, not only above what is regarded as good service but up to a point at which customers begin to abandon calls.

The Post Office have always dealt with this matter by a modified work study procedure which has enabled them to take into account the different kinds of traffic occurring in varying amounts at each exchange. But underlying the basis of the procedure is the fundamental assumption that the average time required by an operator to set up a call is constant, and independent of the rate at which calls come into the exchange. For some time though in laboratory experiments, evidence had been growing that this assumption was false; that operator time to deal with an item, was a function of the rate at which items had to be dealt with. But since all the laboratory work has been concerned with relatively simple responses, and this was an item of work which might take one or two minutes, the problem was examined experimentally.

Essentially what was necessary was to vary in a systematic manner the amount of telephone traffic entering the exchange. But since one cannot stop subscribers from dialling O, the number of operators available to deal with the traffic was varied. With the help of some records from the previous year, an estimate was made of the number of calls expected hour by hour for the duration of the experiment which was to be five weeks. On this basis the size of staff was varied, also hour by hour so that there was a more or less balanced experimental design which introduced a number of work-loads in a random order (Conrad and Hille, 1958b). The snap-reading method of Tippett (1935) was used to measure the time taken by operators to deal with a call. This gave the average operator time per call for the various traffic loads, a breakdown of the way in which she spent that time, and a measure of the time when she had no work available at all. The results are shown in Figure 1 and it was clear that a substantial decrease in staff could be tolerated, without infringing G.P.O. standard of service.

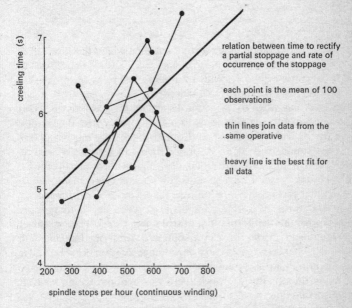

relation between time to rectify a partial stoppage and rate of occurrence of the stoppage

each point is the mean of 100 observations

thin lines join data from the same operative

heavy line is the best fit for all data

spindle stops per hour (continuous winding)

Figure 2 Effect of work-load on performance of textile operatives

To check on the possibility of experimental euphoria, union agreement was obtained to staff the exchange for the whole of the summer of the following year on the basis of the results of the experiment. The experimental results were confirmed and those schedules have continued ever since.

It would be dangerous to dismiss this study merely as yet another example of Parkinson's Law. Figure 2 shows the result of an experiment in a textile mill (Conrad, 1951). In this case, increasing the amount of work *increased* the operator time per item. There is this one general point which may be emerging. If the work is coming in as a single stream, so that only one item at a time need be considered – the case of telephone operators – then increasing the rate of work, may *decrease* operating time per item. But if each item of work involves a choice between alternatives – the textile case – then an increase in the rate of work may lead to an *increase* in the time taken per item.

5. Letter Sorting

The single position letter sorting machine which the Post Office has recently brought into use in field trials, displays envelopes to an operator who, by means of a keyboard, sorts them into 144 boxes. The operation is self-paced; i.e. a new envelope is displayed only when the operator dispatches the previous one. This arrangement inevitably leads to higher sorting rates than would a rhythmically paced system (Conrad, 1955). The machine, however, cannot sort at a rate faster than 110 letters per minute. Although this rate is a good deal higher than the operators' expected average sorting rate, studies are being made to see whether this machine limit affects the operator's performance.

The times to sort each individual letter are automatically recorded in the form of a distribution table. The recording equipment allows for eleven different sizes of time interval. Recording began at a very early stage of practice – but after operators had had training on a simulator – and continued for many months during which there was continued improvement in sorting rate.

Figure 3 shows the performance of three operators. The top set of histograms represents early days in practice – the bottom set the more recent picture. A little care is needed in interpreting these pictures, because an unequal interval scale was used. The first column includes only times between the machine limit of 0·55 s and 0·6 s; there are then steps of a fifth of a second, opening out to half seconds towards the end, and the last column contains all times longer than 3 s.

Even before these operators were fully practised it was obvious that there was something peculiar about these later distributions. Enough is known about the distribution of human response time to know that there are far too many times heaped up at the short end. Operators quickly learn that it doesn't pay to try to sort faster than the machine will permit, but they do want to be ready as soon as the machine is clear. The best indication of this condition to the operator is auditory. It is interesting to see then, that if one adds an auditory reaction time – say 150 ms – to the machine maximum cycle time of 0·55 s one gets 0·7 s which is in fact where most sorting times occur. It seems certain that a machine which permits an operator to sort at his own pace, so long as his pace does not become faster than 0·55 s, is not fast enough – the operators are unavoidably being delayed by the machine.

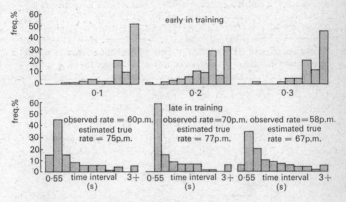

Figure 3 Distribution of the time required to sort a letter by machine

6. Conclusion

As a subject for ergonomics research, the field of telecommunications has the particular interest of its wide-spread ramifications in the life of the nation. Distant communication between people by letter or voice touches everyone. On one hand this means that the communication channel must be a very large industry, with problems affecting many operatives and dealing with 'work units' running into many millions annually, so that a saving of a very small amount of time per unit becomes of importance. On the other hand the input and output ends of the system involved at least every adult in the community. This means that the system must be so designed that everyone understands how to use it, and is able to do so. No selection is possible, and that half of the population which is below average intelligence must also be catered for. This is a challenge to human science which comes but rarely.

References

CONRAD, R. (1951), Preliminary factory studies of the effect of speed and load on cotton winding, *MRC APU Rep.*, no. 147.

CONRAD, R. (1955), 'Setting the pace', *The Manager*, vol. 23, pp. 664–7.

CONRAD, R. (1958), 'Accuracy of recall using keyset and telephone dial, and the effect of a prefix digit', *J. appl. Psychol.*, vol. 42, pp. 285–8.

CONRAD, R., and HILLE, B. A. (1957), 'Memory for long telephone numbers', *Telecommunications*, vol. 10, pp. 37–9.

CONRAD, R., and HILLE, B. A. (1958a), 'Decay theory of immediate memory and paced recall', *Canad. J. Psychol.*, vol. 12, pp. 1–6.

CONRAD, R., and HILLE, B. A. (1958b), 'Telephone operator's adaptation to traffic variations', *J. Inst. elect. Engrs*, vol. 4, pp. 10–14.

TIPPETT, L. H. C. (1935), 'A snap-reading method of making time-studies of machines and operatives in factory surveys', *J. text. Instit.*, vol. 26, p. 51.

Part Five **Training**

It is hardly necessary to insist on the importance of systematic research on training techniques, although the directly industrial contribution of psychologists has formed a relatively small proportion of the available work. Efficient training depends upon the analysis of skill, for which relevant theoretical background is given by Annett and Kay (Reading 15). The survey by Gagné and Bolles (Reading 16) attempts to abstract from the wide literature on human learning the findings of greatest practical value.

A recurrent problem in the transfer of training has been to determine the level of generality at which instruction has most effect. This question is studied by Siegel, Richlin and Federman (Reading 17), the outcome being shown to depend upon job requirements. Appropriate methods may also depend upon the age of the trainees, although the factors studied by Belbin (Reading 18) are of general relevance. Some of her findings have been modified by later experiments, which are listed in the suggestions for Further Reading on page 429.

No attempt has been made to sample the work on programmed learning, which is readily available from other sources.

15 J. Annett and H. Kay

Knowledge of Results and 'Skilled Performance'

J. Annett and H. Kay, 'Knowledge of results and "skilled performance"',
Occupational Psychology, vol. 31 (1957), pp. 69–79.

Introduction

'Knowledge of results is the *sine qua non* of any kind of learning but we cannot say what results are taken note of by the operator learning to track because we do not know of what he supposes them to be the result' (Hick and Bates, 1950). We might say that the present paper accepts the first half of this above statement and attempts to discuss some of the issues raised by the second. Recently (Annett and Kay, 1956) we have outlined an approach to motor skills which emphasizes the significance to the total action of the stream of signals arising both from the external display and from the operator's own responses. Now it is proposed to examine ways in which this approach may be of use in a reassessment of some of the many problems of knowledge of results. After a brief survey of what we will call the perceptual approach to skills we shall attempt to outline some of the different kinds of knowledge of results and discuss some of the problems raised by them.

The Perceptual Approach to Skills

Let us first consider how our present approach to the study of skilled behaviour is connected with the subject of knowledge of results. In skilled performance we have a series of signals arising from two sources; one from the external environment, probably a display in front of the operator, and one from the internal environment, the operator's own musculature and nervous system.

It follows that one of the primary features of skilled performance is the perceptual ability of the operator in receiving incoming signals and an important problem is how we assess this ability. One way is to measure the difficulty of a task by calculating the amount of information carried by its events in terms of their uncertainty. Let us first consider events which are independent of each other. If event x occurs out of a possibility of x and y it carries less information than if the possibility had been x, y and z. Where an event is extremely uncertain or improbable it carries much information, that is its occurrence resolves much uncertainty, and hence a task in which anything might happen is one in which much, perhaps too much information has to be received. In the case of a car driver, whether another vehicle or a pedestrian will be at the cross-roads is an event independent of his own actions. Each is likely and neither carries much information. The motorist is not surprised to find another car at the cross-roads but he is to find an elephant. Some tasks, of which vehicle control – buses, lorries, trains, aeroplanes, etc. – is an outstanding example, may present the most skilled operator with an uneven flow of information, particularly where there is an unexpected situation in which there is nearly too much information to handle. For this reason they are difficult and 'responsible' skills. The operator in the everyday execution of his task may be receiving little information but he must maintain a state of alertness so that he is ready to receive very much more information if necessary. Many industrial tasks try to avoid this state by automatically stopping the machinery if anything untoward occurs. Any skill where this cannot be done and where the operator will have to cope with these high peaks of information will always be responsible tasks.

In those cases where events are not independent the trainee's task is to learn the sequential dependencies and on the face of it this seems easy enough. If a is followed by b then the operator should soon recognize this dependency, but as already noted an operator is receiving messages from two sources, internal and external, and no matter how constant one source may be, say from the display, it may appear very irregular if intermingled with a sequence of random signals arising from the operator's own irregular responses. Several recent experiments have illustrated how confusing this may be, as it was in a study by Von Wright (1955) in which subjects under paced conditions had to learn twelve consecutive responses, each being a movement to either left or right. When subjects attempted to make these responses with a stylus and then observed whether they were correct or not, it took five times as long to learn as when they simply learned the sequence from the display without putting in their own overt and often wrong responses; that is, they learned the constant series of signals from the display so much more quickly when they were not intermingled with other signals from their own responses.

We can say that in those tasks where one event is dependent on a preceding event the trainee is gradually learning to appreciate the redundancy of certain signals. Thus the operator will be able to receive more and more events in any unit time, though receiving the same amount of information, since he has learned to appreciate how certain he can be of so many signals before they occur. As a result in an unpaced task, such as reading English prose, we get an increase in the speed of performance. We have, then, two conditions for this kind of improvement. Firstly that an operator is able to appreciate relative degrees of uncertainty in forthcoming events and secondly that he is able or prepared under some circumstances to 'react' to signals which are less than certain; here he is making predictions and in fact acting on them.

During any training process there may be then a systematic change in the value of particular signals for the operator. Different methods of training may emphasize different signals and of course there is no guarantee that every method will utilize the minimum necessary signals. Touch typing would seem to be an example of one method where this is successfully achieved. Those who use vision for locating the keys are using more cues than necessary so that we have an uneconomical number of signals. It is of note that for most everyday skills which are overlearned an individual receives signals which tend to be redundant. Constant visual control is often unnecessary, as in writing, but the redundancy allows a wide and at times useful margin for the unexpected event and for occasional monitoring, as in the writing example, when crossing *t*s and dotting *i*s.

In more technical skills where the emphasis is upon speed of performance the question of economy through following the best method is all important. To carry out any task an operator will require a certain number of signals but it is important that he should only use the minimum necessary. We might say that any task has for the operator an optimal information content which will be that amount of information which is strictly necessary for carrying out the task, plus that amount of redundant information as will provide the most economical safety margin. An interesting operational example of this point occurred in an investigation by Fritz and Grier (1954) who measured the information transmitted between aircraft pilots and control tower during landing operations. The investigators were surprised by the large amount of redundancy and were forced to the conclusion that some redundancy was necessary in a situation where the loss of even a small amount of information might be disastrous.

Of course, this measure of the amount of information in terms of the number of alternatives is limited, it has nothing to say about the importance of signals, but it does provide us with an elegant means of assessing events which is particularly valuable where we are emphasizing the perceptual aspect of skills and formulating skill problems in terms of the transmission of information rather than in terms of stimulation. Here we can take the analysis a further stage. The operator is not only considered to be receiving signals (information) but he is also, by virtue of his responses, transmitting signals. On the one side we have so much input and on the other so much output and the correspondence between the input and the output messages gives a measure of the capacity of the communication channel, in this instance the skilled performer. Where the operator is given more signals to receive than he can handle he necessarily loses some and the errors in his responses reflect the loss of information. We can infer from this loss that the channel capacity is below this level.

Any training programme aims to teach the operator to handle incoming signals and does so largely by teaching him to recognize the redundancy of others. The problem to be solved by research on knowledge of results is how signals may be optimally presented in order to arrive at this optimal information value for a task in the shortest possible time. If we consider the removal of knowledge of results as a kind of transfer from the training to the operational situation the importance of the way in which extra feedback cues are given will be readily appreciated. Cues, whether 'natural' or 'extra', which carry information essential to the task cannot be removed without a loss of efficiency. However, if the training process is so arranged that extra cues, while helping the operator in the first instance, later become redundant, these cues may then be removed without any serious loss of efficiency. It is therefore necessary to think in terms of the probable optimum cues which will be finally used in the task and then to arrange extra feedback in such a way that the operator will eventually be getting the necessary information from such cues. The following sections develop a few ideas as to how this may be best brought about.

Different Kinds of Knowledge of Results

It is within this context of considering the perceptual discriminations involved in motor skills and the concept of motor performance involving a transmission of information that we wish to examine knowledge of results. The whole task is often a cycle of events in which the operator will not only be receiving a great number of signals, but if the responses are lasting any length of time many of those signals will be the result of his own actions. Hence the receiving of signals from internal and external sources is intrinsic in most skilled performances. Knowledge of results is not then something which a scientist has ingeniously introduced into a training situation – it is something which will be inherent in that situation from the moment when the trainee is given any rudimentary idea as to what he is to try to do. Whether an experimenter does or does not give knowledge of results the adult trainee in nearly all situations will be receiving considerable information about his performance.

This approach then emphasizes two elementary but important points. Firstly there is always some knowledge of results and secondly there are many different kinds. We have commented enough upon the first but the second takes us to the root of the problem. What the trainer aims to achieve by knowledge of results is to add something to those signals which the trainee will normally receive. Knowledge of results will be augmented feedback for the operator. We may now go on to ask in what way this is so, what are the governing conditions which determine when and how knowledge of results should be given, and how this determines the different effects of knowledge of results.

Knowledge of Results as a Directional Indicator

The commonest example of knowledge of results is the end score. Let us say the aim of a task is to perform an operation in a certain time or within a certain degree of accuracy. Here the end score gives the result. As a directional indicator such an end score does not particularize individual responses. Where the task is complicated as in an operation involving a number of responses in quick succession, it is likely that such a score provides little indication to the trainee where and how to amend his performance, though he may be able to guess at the point from a general knowledge of his performance. The same holds for end scores which are given in terms of a mismatch signal of how far a response or responses failed to achieve a criterion. But what both kinds of signals do give the trainee is a much more exact indication of what he has achieved than he is likely to have gained from information received from other sources. Why is this? In the main because such scores will be presented in terms of fairly well-known scales, for it is a feature of such scales that it is generally a simple procedure to translate the terms of one into those of another. For example, an athlete when given his running time for a particular distance can easily determine how far he is above or below his required speed, and this is likely to be more accurate than his subjective impression of how fast he was running. It is one of the trainee's main problems to translate the signals he is receiving into some measurable scale though the skilled man may be able to do this, indeed his ability to do so is often taken as the mark of the expert. In tasks such as that of a wool sorter classifying different bales of wool or a mechanic tracing a fault, it is difficult to identify the precise cues which are being used. But this takes us into the second kind of knowledge of results, as a performance index within the task itself rather than an end score from which the operator has to infer characteristics of his last performance.

Knowledge of Results as Augmented Feedback

As we have noted, in carrying out a skilled task an operator is making a series of responses which in turn give rise to a series of incoming signals. These may be in addition to any signals which the operator is receiving from his external environment and which may be occurring regardless of his own responses. From this series of signals the operator has to learn which are relevant, which can be ignored, which are a guide to events in the future and so on. And to the trainee nearly all these signals will initially be without 'labels', that is they are on no known scale nor tied to known consequences. His task is to learn to identify the signals and to learn their significance. The usual way to meet this kind of difficulty is to provide the operator with some scale indicator which deals with a particular signal and has a clearly defined area signifying one kind of event: for example the car driver finds a thermometer on his dash-board with a marked region near the boiling point mark which tells him if the engine is getting too hot, and similarly with revolution counters and oil pressure gauges. What was vaguely engine noise can then be read off as so many revolutions per minute. But where we have a multiplicity of signals being continuously received as in skilled performance the trainee is faced with several problems. To aid him we have to decide

(i)   which signals are most relevant to the execution of the task;
(ii) which signals are hardest to identify; and
(iii) how far it is possible to provide any further indications for those signals.

(i) In many operations it is by no means an easy problem to decide which are the most relevant signals. The expert exponents have not always agreed on the essentials and theoretical analysis can help here in indicating where the key points are in the operation. For example, as already noted, it would appear that as a trainee learns a skill the functions of some signals change and this is most marked in serial skills where responses and signals are closely linked together. In such tasks many signals become redundant in so far as they could have been predicted from previous signals, and the trainee has to appreciate their unimportance compared with the non-predictable signals carrying most information. Unfortunately signals which become redundant when the skill is properly executed may not be so in the relatively random sequences of a trainee's responses. Hence it is not always possible to get the beginner to train on the same cues as the expert. The final aim is for the operator to receive the maximum of information from the minimum of signals, but the training programme has to recognize that the information value of certain signals may be changing as the skill develops, thereby entailing the use of additional signals in the initial stages of training.

(ii) A signal may be difficult to identify for several reasons. It may occur only briefly, it may be one in a succession of signals, it may involve a comparatively poorly developed discrimination such as a pressure cue as opposed to a spatial movement, or it may be a signal which is only just above the differential or absolute threshold. The trainer having decided upon the key signals has to analyse whether they will be difficult for a trainee and, where this is probable, attempt to provide further means of identifying them.

(iii) How far is it possible to provide any further indications for those signals? It is appreciated that any training procedure, however crude, does attempt to meet this problem. It tells the operator something about what to look for, which indicators are important and which are not. The complexity arises when the signals are not clearcut, when we are not dealing with pointer positions or light indicators but with changes in how a machine 'handles', when a control lever is said to become 'sticky' or has 'too much play'. How is the trainee to recognize these features? The most that can be done is to supplement the existing signals with accompanying signals, probably in another sense modality and generally employing some simple scale. A scale reading has the advantage that the operator can both interpret it immediately and remember it easily. But such additional signals, just because they are so effective, introduce their own problems in so far as the operator can now perform the task observing them alone without attending to the cues which are intrinsic to the task itself. Hence instead of learning the relation between the intrinsic and extrinsic cues, as is intended in such procedures, the operator merely relies on the new signals to aid his performance. While he receives such additional knowledge his performance is satisfactory but once it is taken away and he is left with only the intrinsic signals arising from the operation itself he is lost.

This point brings us to the variety of uses to which the operator may be putting augmented feedback. If the response is of a ballistic kind which cannot be modified during its execution then the feedback is used to amend the response on its subsequent occurrence. But where it is a controlled movement the operator may use the signals to amend the response which he is carrying out. Again, if there are a series of responses then signals about the first response may be used as the basis for modifying the second.

In this context it is worth noting R. B. Miller's distinction between action feedback and learning feedback (Miller, 1953). In our discussion we have thought of signals both as additional cues supplied by the trainer and intrinsic cues which arise from carrying out the task. Such signals may be said to tell the operator what he should do as he continues the response or what he is doing at the moment, while others tell him only what he has just done. This is essentially the difference between action feedback and learning feedback, for action feedback allows the operator to modify his present response, while learning feedback, occurring after the termination of the response, can only indicate how the next response should be modified. This is much more than an academic distinction for experiments have shown that a subject's whole learning of the task is different in these two procedures. Consider a simple example. If one presses on a pair of kitchen scales it is possible by watching the pointer to exert an exact pressure, say 2 lb. It may be possible, and the techniques of some trainers seem to suggest that it is possible, to learn an exact pressure by practising in this way. This would be an instance of the use of action feedback. On the other hand one may press and look at the pointer only when that attempt is completed; then having released that pressure begin again with a further attempt. This alternative technique corresponds to learning feedback.

This theoretical distinction, while illuminating, can be a little blurred in practice. For example, a subject who has used the dial to monitor his response in the previous example is still in a position to regard the dial reading as an indication of what he has just done. Individuals may vary to the extent that they may emphasize the monitoring aspect of the feedback, or perhaps not bother to look until they have completed the response. Similarly in rapid series of responses of the same type an indication of what has just been done will be more closely related to the succeeding response and will serve perhaps as the basis of this response. Hence action and learning feedbacks may in some circumstances tend to adopt the functions of the other and in this case removal of knowledge of results would result in a performance decrement appropriate to each case. It is interesting to note that in Macpherson, Dees and Grindley's work (1949) precisely this seems to have happened. With action feedback we predict quick improvement in performance and a sudden drop on the removal of feedback, and in learning feedback slower improvement and a slower fall off in performance. In the case of the experiment cited, rapidly succeeding trials showed a learning and removal of feedback, a loss more consistent with action feedback. It is particularly interesting in so far as the authors themselves point out the difficulty which any one conventional learning theory has to account for their results.

The distinction between action feedback and learning feedback has brought out that with the human operator, in contrast to the engineer's communication system, the transmission problem is further complicated in so far as his immediate memory allows an overlapping of signals. Thus, though signals may occur in a certain time relationship, some may persist more than others thereby setting up new relationships. This is particularly relevant to knowledge of results which is given in an easily identifiable and retainable form so that the operator can manipulate such signals; that is, he tries to use them both for monitoring present performance and as a criterion for modifying responses in future attempts. Thus we have the paradoxical result that just because this kind of feedback is effective the operator may attempt to do too much with it. His training performance might be improved if he tried to do less and attended more to learning to correct past errors than to modifying present activities.

Though the distinction between action and learning feedback is not always clear-cut it would seem to be of theoretical interest and it certainly has practical importance. For example, on the basis of the above discussion, we would make the unusual prediction that by delaying feedback at certain points we may actually improve learning; that is to say by delaying feedback we ensure that the operator attends to what he has just done and does not attempt to modify his present response – we ensure that the signals operate as learning feedback.

Motivation

It is axiomatic in many studies that knowledge of results will motivate trainees though it is rarely stated why this should be so. It is often implied that there is something intrinsically motivating about knowledge of results and it is discussed as if it were a second order of the law of effect. It is hardly necessary to point out that the giving of scores is likely to stimulate both social and self competition and indeed this competitive element often seems to be what some experimenters have meant by saying knowledge of results will motivate an operator. A point worthy of note is that few experimenters have stated explicitly what the goal of the subject is in any situation. Where improvement is the goal, knowledge of results by giving knowledge of goal achievement may be said to be 'motivating'. However there seems to be nothing contradictory in the notion that it is possible for a subject to have as his goal performance without such knowledge. It does not appear to be necessary to assume an intrinsic motivating factor in knowledge of results but that states of 'motivation' or 'frustration' may be manipulated by presenting goal achievement to the subject via some kind of knowledge of results.

But this is perhaps too much of a negative comment occasioned by a somewhat uncritical assumption on the part of many experimenters. There is the possibility that there is something 'naturally' satisfying about a situation in which the subject has some feedback and something naturally unpleasant about the situation in which the subject is deprived of knowledge of what he is doing. The experiments of Hebb and his associates indicate what happens in the extreme case where a subject is placed in what is very nearly a sensory vacuum. The experience is subjectively most unpleasant and has been likened to that of psychotic illness.

Training

While it would be unwise to generalize from an extreme case it is still a reasonable assumption that deprivation of feedback from a task in hand will tend to be an unsatisfying, if not frustrating, experience. As we have tried to suggest, it is so usual for an operator to receive some knowledge of results and so uncommon to be totally deprived of them.

Summary and Conclusions

We have attempted to outline our approach to skilled performance and its bearing upon how we can examine knowledge of results. It is apparent that knowledge of results may be used in a variety of ways and the trainer will have to be clear about these if he desires to introduce them. Where knowledge of results is introduced it is most likely that the trainee will attempt to use this augmented feedback, but it is certain that how he uses it will vary from one kind of task to another and even within that task from one stage of training to another. We will try to summarize these points in a series of general statements. These are not intended as dogmatic assertions but as postulates which may be verified and accepted or rejected as necessary.

(1) It is convenient to regard an operator performing a task as a communication channel. The operator is receiving signals from his internal and external environment and on the basis of these signals he regulates his responses.

(2) The relative uncertainty of these signals may change during the course of training. In the initial stages there may be many random signals and the second and third members of a series may be as uncertain to the trainee as the first, but when responses tend to become stabilized then the later signals tend to become redundant.

(3) If we assume that the operator can to some extent appreciate the degree of redundancy of parts of the input and is prepared to react to signals which are less than certain, then this forms a sufficient basis for predicting a number of the common phenomena of skilled performance. By appreciating such redundancy the necessary information can be transmitted on the basis of less

input signals so that the operator may improve either in speed of performance, or in anticipation, or, by attending to fewer signals, make the task easier for himself.

(4) An operator is always in receipt of feedback signals, and knowledge of results, augmented feedback as we have called it, is but another kind provided by the trainer. Such feedback is usually presented in some easily identifiable manner.

(5) Knowledge of results may be of different kinds some of which may be extrinsic but some intrinsic to the task.
(a) Results may take the form of an end score. This may serve as a neat summary of performance from which the operator has to draw his own conclusions about any deficiency in the skill. Such an end score may be an exact register of what has been attained but is often a very inexact indicator of what precisely was right or wrong. The end score is of most value to the skilled operator who can interpret it in the light of his knowledge of the task; paradoxically he requires it least because from that same knowledge he can make an accurate assessment of what score he has achieved.
(b) Knowledge of results may take the form of an indicator for a particular signal which is difficult to detect. This can be especially valuable in the early stages of training in delimiting the area of search.
(c) Knowledge of results may be in the form of accompanying signals within the operation. The operator does not always realize that some intrinsic signals occur as a result of his own responses. For example in driving, when starting a car on a hill as the clutch is beginning to make contact the engine note changes although the car is still stationary. The trainee should be made aware of the signals which are intrinsic to the task and be taught how to use them.

(6) In common with other signals knowledge of results may be put to a variety of uses. One distinction lies between those signals which tell the operator what he should have done, learning feedback, and those which tell him what to do next, action feedback. This is R. B. Miller's distinction and whilst it is useful it is not always clear-cut. Characteristic examples of this use are where feedback serves (a) to enable the operator to amend

the same response in a future trial (learning feedback), (b) monitor a present response (action feedback), and (c) adjust subsequent responses in the same series (action feedback).

(7) Such usages are largely determined by the task in hand. Example (a) above is common where the operator is making a single discreet response. Example (b) above is more likely in an extended response involving several adjustments as in a controlled movement when applying a precise pressure. Example (c) is not dissimilar to (b). If we think of the series as involving responses, x, y, z, the operator on observing some inadequacy in x when performing y tries to adjust responses y and z accordingly. This tends to teach him little about x and makes responses y and z more difficult than perhaps they need be.

(8) Since knowledge of results is given in some easily recognizable form it is important to note that where it is being used to identify less distinguishable intrinsic signals the operator does not come to rely on it alone. Where external signals become an end in themselves rather than a means to an end of identification the operator tends to be lost when they are removed. This is particularly the case where a task involves ill-practised responses and the trainee tends to rely on the extra signals where, as in 6(c) above, there is a series of responses and he is attempting to modify one of them because of deficiencies revealed in the last result.

(9) Because of the variety of uses to which knowledge of results is put its removal may have a number of different consequences. (a) In those cases where the operator is carrying out a series of well practised responses removal of knowledge of results will not lead to a sudden fall off in performance. Conversely, where a response is not well known the fall off will be greater.
(b) Where a subject is using knowledge of results as action feedback the fall off will be more dramatic than where he had been using it as learning feedback.

(10) Though it is inevitable that in some cases knowledge of results is used as action feedback in the early stages of training, it is essential that this does not continue if such knowledge will not be given in the operational situation. Probably the surest method

here is to withdraw knowledge of results on some trials during training, say on alternate trials or blocks of trials.

(11) Motivation. Knowledge of results does encourage both self and social competition. In so far as it is normal to receive feedback when making a response, we might expect a situation in which the operator is denied knowledge to be frustrating. There need be nothing intrinsically motivating about knowledge of results but in so far as its removal militates against goal attainment, its removal will be frustrating.

References

ANNETT, J., and KAY, H. (1956), 'Skilled performance', *Occup. Psychol.*, vol. 30, pp. 112–17.

FRITZ, E. L., and GRIER, G. W. (1954), 'Pragmatic communication', in Quastler, *Information Theory in Psychology*, Free Press of Glencoe.

HICK, W. E., and BATES, J. A. V. (1950), *The Human Operator of Control Mechanisms*, Ministry of Supply, H.M.S.O.

MACPHERSON, S. J., DEES, V., and GRINDLEY, G. C. (1949), 'The effect of knowledge of results on learning and performance: III. the influence of the time interval between trials', *Quart. J. exp. Psychol.*, vol. 1, pp. 167–74.

MILLER, R. B. (1953), Handbook on training and training equipment design, *Wright Air Development Center, Technical Report*, no. 53–136.

VON WRIGHT, J. (1955), An experimental study of human serial learning, *D. Phil. Thesis, Oxford University*.

16 R. M. Gagné and R. C. Bolles

A Review of Factors in Learning Efficiency

Excerpt from R. M. Gagné and R. C. Bolles, 'A review of factors in learning efficiency', in E. Galanter (ed.), *Automatic Teaching: The State of the Art*, Wiley, 1959, pp. 21–48.

The Manipulable Conditions of the Learning Situation

Efficiency of learning clearly depends upon the individual who does the learning, the nature of the task to be learned and the conditions under which the particular learning occurs. This report will not deal directly with the first two of these three broad categories, although we may note that work proficiency may be greatly enhanced by properly defining the job and by assigning the proper man to do it. We shall restrict our discussion to the ways in which the learning or training situation itself can be manipulated to produce maximum transfer to the job situation.

In following this aim, we must exclude from consideration in this report the important matter of the trainee's general attitude toward the training program. If the trainee is not willing to submit to the learning situation, then he is not apt to learn much; there can hardly be any effective training possible for him.

Among the conditions of training situations which influence learning and which are accessible, that is, which are manipulable by those in charge of training programs, we may distinguish two classes. First, there are the motivational or preparatory conditions that make the trainee ready for learning. We shall call these *readiness factors*. These include factors ranging from the general level of motivation to very specific sets to associate particular responses with particular stimuli. Second, there are a number of stimulus conditions to determine which specific associations are formed, and how strong these associations are relative to competing associations. These we call *associative factors*. Various degrees of importance are assigned by different writers to motivational and associative factors. But the evidence indicates that both are important, and while they interact in virtually all learning situations, the present analysis is considerably clarified by treating them separately.

Readiness factors

Most theorists seem to agree that in learning to perform some task the individual must actively seek some goal or incentive. The individual must be motivated (that is, he must try) to attain some desirable consequence of his performance. Whether this motivation–goal sequence is a necessary condition for learning itself is a much debated theoretical issue; but there is little doubt regarding the efficacy of motivation in producing overt performance.

Allied with conditions of motivation are the conditions of reinforcement, or, put another way, the conditions which govern how goals are actually attained. The effects of reinforcement or goal attainment are complicated; they serve not only to confirm the subject's preceding behavior but also to maintain the motivational level. Further complications are introduced by the fact that we are interested here primarily in transfer rather than in original learning. Relatively little is known about the role of motivational variables in transfer.

Another important readiness factor in the learning situation is what the learning subject is doing or trying to do. This factor is generally called the subject's *task set*. In general, it can be said that the learner will do better if he knows what he's supposed to do. Task set may be quite general, involving only knowledge of what the completed task is like, or it may be quite specific, as when the person gets ready to press a key at a given signal.

Associative factors

A second broad class of variables comprises associative factors. These are the stimulus conditions that enter into the learning situation because they are the ones with which specific responses are to be associated. According to one somewhat oversimplified picture, the problem of controlling behavior consists simply in strengthening association between some stimulus and the desired response to the point where the response will automatically occur whenever the stimulus is presented. While we recognize the possibility of this simple kind of mediation we believe it is practicable and useful to take advantage of other possible types of mediation. Thus, we want to consider seriously the efficiency of learning situations in which the desired responses are associated with a variety of stimuli, and are also mediated by the verbal or voluntary processes of the trainee. This diversification of mediation would seem to be especially useful in highly conceptual types of tasks, as well as those in which variable rather than fixed behavior is called for. Accordingly, we shall discuss later in the report principles which relate efficiency of learning to the nature of what is learned. It seems likely that, for some kinds of tasks, it is more important that the trainee 'understand the general principles' underlying his work than that he know only something specific about any particular piece of work. Such a training program would call for the acquisition of a mediating process probably not best characterized as a stimulus–response association.

It is well known that if the training task is similar to the job situation then transfer to a final task (of the job) will be directly related to the degree of learning that occurs in the training task. However, to the extent that the training task *differs* from the job situation, initial learning or overlearning will reduce the amount of transfer and thus be inefficient. The precise degree of similarity which determines the transition point, that is, which determines how much learning is most effective, is the crucial parameter here, but one about which we know little. In any particular instance it is an empirical question just how much learning will lead to the most effective transfer. The reason for this practical limitation is that no well-accepted method is available which makes possible the independent measurement of task similarity. In fact, at the present stage of our knowledge we sometimes depend upon the amount of transfer as an index of similarity. None the less, it is generally accepted that in any specific application transfer is improved by increasing similarity.

In the discussion which follows we have distinguished two roles played by both readiness and associative factors. We conceive both to play a part in determining the similarity between training task and job, and both to be involved in determining the extent of initial learning during the training period. Thus, we think of the ideal training schedule as a two-stage affair in which, first, learning of the training task is optimized, and second, transfer is insured by making the training task maximally similar to that of the job situation.

Readiness Factors

Motivation

The place of motivational concepts in behavior theory is ambiguous. Recently some writers have suggested that introducing these concepts into the explanation of behavior contributes little toward its explanation (2, 24). These writers suggest that behavior may best be accounted for in terms of detailed descriptions of the conditions under which it is controlled. On the other hand, we have inherited through the years a good deal of evidence from social mores, from casual observation as well as from psychological laboratories, testifying to the efficacy of controlling behavior by means of controlling what we call motivational variables. Thus, if we seek to produce some particular kind of behavior in a person, we should see to it that the person *wants* to behave in that way.

Such a broad motivational rule would seem to be trivially obvious and beyond question. Probably there is nothing wrong with it as a general principle. Its fault lies in being too non-specific and too general; it tells us nothing about how to proceed in any given instance. Theoretical psychologists as well as those interested in applied problems are concerned with controlling and predicting behavior under specific circumstances. Hence, it is necessary to abandon the general rule and to seek in any given situation those particular conditions that maximize performance. To the extent that it is possible to describe kinds of non-associative conditions that contribute to performance, motivational concepts are useful.

We turn now to the question of how to regulate motivational variables in a training situation so as to maximize performance in that situation. On this question there is a good deal of relevant evidence. The classical finding is that performance improves as motivation increases (30, p. 413 ff.). Thus the most effective training program would be expected to be one for which motivation is maximal. This is probably true provided certain conditions are met. Spence and his co-workers have recently emphasized that before motivation can facilitate performance it is necessary that the correct or otherwise desired behavior be dominant over other possible behavior patterns (40). Thus, if the trainee's strongest or most probable response is not the desired one, increased motivation will lead to interference and to performance decrement. This follows from Spence's assumption that the effect of motivation is to facilitate indiscriminately any and all behavior which may be going on. Thus, for motivation to lead to superior performance, the responses which are required must be the ones which are dominant in a situation. If this view is correct (and it is still open to some question) it would suggest that the most efficient learning procedure would be one in which the level of motivation increases in the course of training so as to parallel the probability of the desired behavior. The efficacy of such a procedure has not yet been tested experimentally, however.

Intrinsic v. extrinsic motivation. Another proviso to the general rule that motivation facilitates performance is that the motivation should be, in some sense, relevant to the task. There are a number of task goals for which humans can be motivated. The task itself often provides some intrinsic motivation; the material to be learned may be interesting in itself. Task completion often serves as a goal; other things being equal, people desire to complete tasks they have started. The value of task completion is further enhanced if the task is one in which the trainee is ego-involved, so that pride in success at the task becomes a goal. Desire to succeed appears, in fact, to be a highly dependable source of motivation for the learning situation.

By contrast with these sorts of goals there are extrinsic goals. Success in the task at hand may serve as a goal if the trainee is motivated to excel his fellows, to compete with them. Another kind of extrinsic motivation which may be applicable in some situations is the desire to please one's superiors. Still another is the fondness for gambling. The tendency of people to like to gamble is as yet a relatively unexploited possibility in the design of teaching machines (39). Some other kinds of extrinsic motivation approach irrelevance. For example, the learner may be motivated by anxiety over possible failure, or over his inability to do as well as his fellow trainees.

During most of the course of learning it is probably important that motivation be relevant, and preferably that it be intrinsic. Once learning has proceeded to a certain level of proficiency, so that the desired behavior is dominant, it may be that the nature of motivation makes little difference; any source of motivation may sustain performance. In any case, the idea that motivation should be intrinsic rests not so much upon the role motivation plays in learning or in performance during learning; rather, it reflects a concern with the transfer criterion. It seems reasonable to suppose that motives and goals intrinsic to the task are more likely to transfer to the job situation. One reason why training performance is frequently an unreliable indication of subsequent job proficiency may be that the trainee's motives so often change between the transfer and the job situation.

It should be emphasized that most of this discussion is necessarily speculative. To our knowledge, nothing has been done experimentally to demonstrate that motivation during the training has *anything* to do with the degree of transfer to subsequent on-the-job performance. Furthermore, it seems likely that, even if a systematic experimental research program should indicate the nature of the relationship between motivation and transfer, it would still be necessary to determine empirically what practical measures are required to maximize transfer in any given application. Motivational variables are perhaps the most exclusive concepts with which psychologists work.

Levels of aspiration. Related to the fact of motivation to succeed is the concept of 'level of aspiration'. The difference between the performance an individual *thinks* he can do, and what he actually accomplishes, has been found to be an important motivational variable (23). Thus, it turns out, that if the person's goal is set too high he may become disappointed at his relative failure to improve subsequently. On the other hand if his goal is set too low that this learnings will not proceed, he will not improve in the task. It is clear that there is an optimum difference between the goal and the trainee's level of aspiration. While this parameter is undoubtedly an important one in learning, or at least in

287

performance during learning, its relationship to subsequent performance in a transfer situation remains an unexplored problem.

Reinforcement

The problem of motivation and the problem of reinforcement are highly interrelated. Generally, when we know what a person's motive is, we also know how we can reinforce his behavior. When motivation is intrinsic, that is, when it depends in some way upon the nature of the task, relevant reinforcement is provided by giving the learner 'knowledge of results'. This is a type of motivation–reinforcement sequence that has been studied experimentally (cf. 17, 30, 58), and several conclusions seem pretty clear. One is that reinforcement should be positive rather than negative, constructive rather than destructive. Reinforcement should be immediate. If it is delayed, the trainee's motivation may lag, and also, the reinforcement fails to provide information which he may need in order to learn anything.

As the effects of delay imply, reinforcement appears to serve two functions. One is to sustain motivation, and the other is to provide information, or feedback. According to some writers this feedback or information value of reinforcement is the only function which the consequences of behavior serve (42). Other theorists ever since Thorndike have contended that the function of reinforcement is in some way to 'stamp in' in some literal sense the stimulus–response association. According to this latter view, reinforcement has little or no effect as far as information is concerned. Whatever the truth of this matter may be, it appears practically reasonable and profitable to administer reinforcement as though its informational value were important. There is ample evidence to show that a trainee's performance may be improved if his scores are reported to him, or if his performance is described and he is encouraged to make improvement (25). It has been found, in fact, that this is one of the most effective ways in which behavior of the trainee can be modified.

A great deal of attention has been paid in recent years notably by Skinner and his students, to the fact that performance is apt to be facilitated if reinforcement is made probabilistic (37). It has been found that under some conditions subjects will work harder if they are reinforced only once in a while rather than upon every occurrence of the desired behavior. It appears, however, that this phenomenon occurs only with respect to performance, and that it is not reflected in superior learning under partial or intermittent reinforcement. It seems doubtful that transfer to a new situation would be improved by this kind of reinforcement schedule. At present, there seems to be no contrary evidence to the general conclusion that learning is facilitated by frequent, immediate and positive reinforcement.

Set

The factors of set and attention are frequently mentioned by writers on the subject of human learning In fact, even the layman would be disinclined to quarrel with such statements as 'the learner must be set for learning', or 'the learner must pay attention'. Yet the scientific literature concerning the effects of these factors on learning is not at all voluminous.

An excellent review of the topic of set was made by Gibson (15) in 1941, in which it was shown that the term has had a variety of meanings in psychological experiments. This is still true today. Nevertheless, a most instructive general meaning has been attributed to the word *set* by Hebb (16), which can be considered as incorporating several of the apparently disparate meanings identified by Gibson. Hebb considers set to be a central neural mechanism comparable to a holding circuit. It is a persisting activity which is set up within the central system, and which has its motor effect only when a second sensory input occurs, with which it acts to produce a response. As a simple example, if we say to an individual 'Add these numbers', and then provide him with various sets of numbers, each of the responses will represent his attempt at adding (not subtracting, multiplying or something else).

In a learning situation, one can think of establishing a task set by such instructions as 'Listen to these pairs of names, and be ready to say the second one of each pair when I give you the first.' Of course, as Gibson points out, a set of this sort might be established in ways other than by instructions, for example. by previous training or sequencing of events. But its importance for learning should not be overlooked or dismissed lightly.

The factor of task set is apparently the same as Thorndike's factor of belonging (41), by which he meant the learner's knowledge of 'what goes with what'. Thorndike performed a series of experiments having the following general pattern. First, he instructed subjects to listen to series of orally presented materials, such as pairs like 'afford 21; equip 34' (in a long list), paying attention as they would if listening to a lecture. After running through the list, in which specific pairs occurred with different frequencies, he then asked the subjects to write the answers to questions like 'What number came after "afford"?' and in contrast, to questions such as 'What word came after 21?' Evidences of considerable learning were obtained in answers to the first type of question, in which the pairs seem to 'belong' together. But almost no learning was found to have occurred *between* the pairs, because, he argued, there was no 'belonging'. Thorndike points out that this evidence demonstrates the inadequacy of sheer contiguity or sheer repetition for learning. Belonging, or what we call a task set, must be present.

In practical training situations, inexperienced teachers may unknowingly violate this principle of task set. In the training of complex tasks, the teacher may state the ultimate goal of learning (for example, to learn to operate a control panel), and then proceed to 'set the student free' to practice. But the principle of task set applies to the *individual items* to be learned, and in such circumstances the student may have to engage in a great deal of needless trial and error behavior before discovering for himself 'what goes with what' (for example, that a particular knob controls the activity of a particular dial). The importance of this principle is, therefore, that to maximize learning efficiency means must be found, usually by instructions, to establish suitable task sets to each of the items of the total task to be learned. Attending to the stimuli which are relevant, as defined by the final task to be performed, is an important condition for the assurance of a high degree of transfer.

Attention

The factor of attention in learning may be conceived in two different ways. The first, which we wish to exclude from consideration in this section, refers to the arousal of a general state of *alertness* (as opposed, perhaps, to drowsiness) in the learner. Although attention in the sense of alertness has been investigated in many ways (e.g. 19, 20), it is of interest to note that none of the references in an extensive bibliography on attention (22) identifies a study which is unequivocally concerned with the relationship of alertness to learning or transfer. It is apparent, therefore, that we simply do not know the significance of this kind of 'attentional' variable; nor do we have any particular theoretical basis on which to make predictions about it.

Intention to learn, on the other hand, has been studied quite extensively. In contrast to the task set described previously, intention to learn is typically induced by instructions that the materials presented are to be committed to memory, as opposed to being simply read, pronounced or attended to in some other manner. The technique of contrasting the performance of one group of individuals who are told to learn, with that of other individuals who act as 'experimenters', and thus repeat the same materials without being told to learn them, is common in modern experiments.

A review of previous studies on intent to learn is given by McGeoch and Irion (26, p. 210 ff.). A recent series of studies has been conducted by Postman and his associates (31–6). These studies have utilized criteria of learning that are relevant to learning efficiency, including measures of retention and retroactive interference, thereby on some occasions obtaining results that contrast sharply with those obtained from simpler situation-bound measures of learning.

Perhaps somewhat surprisingly from the viewpoint of popular belief, the general findings of studies of incidental learning are to the effect that intent to learn is not always, or even usually, an important factor in learning (32, 33, 35). While some particular materials are learned slightly better by those with intent to learn, the incidental learners sometimes perform equally well. Furthermore, associative interference is often reduced under incidental learning conditions, thus actually making the retention of incidentally learned materials superior to intentionally learned ones on some occasions. We are led to the conclusion that intent to learn has not been shown to be a factor worthy of much concern in considering manipulable variables in a training situation. It should, of course, be carefully distinguished from motivation to succeed, the significance of which has been discussed previously.

Associative Factors

When we turn to a consideration of associative factors in learning efficiency, we need to consider the variables affecting the nature of what is to be learned. More specifically, these are the number, order and nature of associative connexions than can be manipulated within the learning situation. As stated previously, we are here considering learning in terms of performance of a final task which is not necessarily the same as the 'materials to be learned'. This means that we must deal with variables that have been investigated in connexion with *transfer of training*, and not simply learning itself.

In all, we shall consider here three classes of factors in relation to learning efficiency. The first is what is to be associated, or the nature of the associations to be established, considered in relation to the task on which performance is desired. The second is *intratrial factors*, or those conditions which may be varied systematically within each trial of learning, applying equally to all trials. The third is *intertrial factors*, which may be manipulated in some orderly way between learning trials, or in stages as learning proceeds.

The nature of associations

The most important characteristics of associations to be learned, if we keep in mind the transfer of learning to a criterion task, pertain to *similarity*. This factor has been subjected to a fair amount of investigation which has been summarized in standard works (cf. 17, 26). Osgood (29) has made an attempt to systematize the empirical data in terms of a 'transfer-retroaction surface', which shows the relationship between similarity of stimuli and similarity of responses to amount of transfer of training.

Stimulus similarity. Concerning the factor of stimulus similarity there has never been any serious disagreement of experimental evidence with the following rule: positive transfer increases with the degree of similarity of the stimuli of the initially learned task to the final task (17, 30). Thus the significance of this principle for learning efficiency is clear; stimuli of the associations to be learned should be made as nearly like the stimuli of the final task as possible. In terms of practical training situations, this principle may well be tempered by feasibility. For example, if an operator must learn to identify the switches, knobs and dials on a panel, can these be represented in photographs (or even drawings) rather than as 3-dimensional objects? The answer appears to be that high amounts of positive transfer may be obtained by representations of stimulus objects (10). This means that the stimuli to be associated in the learning situation can be pictured, rather than 'real', without great losses in transfer; and this finding has considerable practical significance for military training. On the other hand, providing simply conceptual representation for stimuli, as is done when words are used rather than pictures, is another matter entirely; and in such instances the principle of stimulus 'similarity' may in fact be violated. A picture of an amplifier may be highly similar to the amplifier itself, but the word 'amplifier' as a stimulus is by no means similar. In any case, the principle of stimulus similarity is not one on which the books can or should be closed; it will require a great deal more research to provide precise meaning to this phrase.

Response similarity. It would be convenient indeed if we could state that there is a comparable rule about the response members of the associations established by learning, namely, that transfer of training increases with the degree of similarity of responses of the initially learned task and the final task. But although Osgood's treatment (29) of the matter would support this conclusion, we cannot agree that this principle should be considered well-established. There are several reasons for this:

1. Generally speaking, it is known that the mediating responses for motor acts, acquired in initial learning, need not be highly similar to these motor acts in order for high degrees of transfer to occur. If an individual is able to identify the location of objects in a picture by pointing to them, we expect that he can also walk

to them correctly when he is at the actual scene of the picture. Yet the responses in this initial and final task are really quite different (cf. 10). There are not many experiments in this field, probably because the facts have appeared so obvious.

2. Most of the evidence on response similarity has been obtained with the learning of paired associates, and some of the crucial evidence comes from studies employing responses which are similar in meaning (cf. 28). The difficulty may be, that the second member (often called the 'response member') of a pair of associates has a stimulus function, as well as being employed as a response. As a consequence, it interacts with other members which are similar in meaning, and thus has an effect on transfer. But this meaningful similarity is behaving as a *mediating stimulus*, rather than as a response pure and simple. How else, in fact, could *meaningful similarity* of responses be interpreted? That the 'response member' both functions as a response and enters into learning as a stimulus is shown by a study of Feldman and Underwood (9).

3. The results of paired associate learning are strongly influenced by intra-list interference, as has been demonstrated by many studies (13, 14, 43, 44, 47, 48). It seems particularly doubtful that one can draw valid conclusions about 1st task–2nd task similarity unless intra-task similarity has been measured separately or ruled out completely. An analysis by Gagné and Baker (11) points out the importance of intratask similarity to transfer. It is probable, therefore, that the empirical results obtained on response similarity in paired associate learning are quite inadequate for significant conclusions to be drawn concerning the effects of this factor on single associations in learning.

Response similarity has been demonstrated as a factor affecting response strength in studies of generalization (55, 56), as well as in studies of motor skills (1). But this evidence is an inadequate basis for the derivation of principles of learning of verbal and conceptual tasks. In view of this, and the objections raised to existing evidence as listed above, we must conclude that *response similarity* is a factor concerning which we know very little. The question of learning efficiency requires a good deal more systematic knowledge regarding the effects of this variable.

Similarity in serial tasks. Some special mention needs to be made of the effects of similarity of associated items in sequentially learned materials, which are relevant particularly to job tasks of following procedures. In such tasks, each element clearly functions as a response and also as a stimulus to be associated with the next succeeding response in the series. As a number of investigations have shown (cf. 46, 50), the learning of sequential verbal material is influenced both by intratask similarities and by the similarities of the learning task to the final task. In fact, the separation of these two effects has not yet been satisfactorily determined (51).

The learning of sequential verbal tasks increases in rate as the individual members are made less similar to each other. This suggests that when we have a procedural task characterized by associative interference, the mediating task provided for learning may be facilitated by making the associated members less similar to each other than those of the procedural task itself. In other words, it seems possible that the members of the learning task may be made *more distinctive* than the members of the final task, and thus increase learning efficiency. However, it should be remembered that although the effects of such intratask variation are predictable, we do not know what effects this treatment would have on intertask interference; in other words, we do not know its effects on transfer to a job task. It is apparent that, so far as following procedures are concerned, the interplay of similarities among elements and between initial and final tasks is an area in which considerable additional research is needed.

Intratrial factors

In continuing our consideration of associative factors, we next turn to a set of variables that may be manipulated within each and every trial of learning. As we have pointed out previously, these are to be distinguished from variables which are systematically varied from trial to trial, or in stages as learning progresses. There are three primary ways in which such intratrial factors may be manipulated, and we shall discuss them here. For any given response, the stimuli to be associated with it may be varied in number and variety. Second, for any particular stimulus, the individual may be required to learn different numbers of responses. And third, the meaningfulness of the associations may be varied.

Number of stimuli. We can adduce little evidence from the experimental literature concerning this factor and its influence on transfer of training. The experimental question may be described as follows. Suppose we are interested in the performance of an identification task of fifteen components (such as the components of a newly developed weapon). In a standard learning situation we would expose a picture of each item and require the learner to respond with its name. However, being aware of the effects of similarity in producing associative interference, and thus decreasing the rate of learning, we might decide to add additional stimuli to each pictured item, in order to make them more distinctive from each other. Increased distinctiveness, for example, might be added by accompanying each item with a distinctive color, a distinctive symbol, a distinctive border, etc. It is sometimes argued that the effect of this added number and variety of stimuli would be to reduce associative interference and thus speed up the learning. The question as to whether transfer to the final task would be as good or better under these conditions needs to be answered by experimental investigation. The idea of providing extra 'stimulus support' for learning is one of the hypotheses that appears to be involved in the work of Skinner (6, 39) on teaching machines.

Number of responses. This is another factor concerning which no direct experimental evidence exists. Using the fifteen-item identification task as an example again, the standard learning situation in which each stimulus is associated with a single response (e.g. a name) may be contrasted with one in which additional responses are also required to be learned to the same stimulus. For example, we might require the learner to acquire the responses 'square', 'black', 'voltage', as well as 'amplifier' to a picture of an amplifier. Presumably, it would take him longer to learn four responses to each stimulus item than it would for him to learn one. Nevertheless, the experimental question of importance to learning efficiency concerns the matter of the effects of this variable on transfer of training. If the criterion of transfer is employed, it is entirely conceivable that the added effort (and time) required for initial learning might be overbalanced by advantages in transfer of training.

Of some relevance to this question may be the studies which have shown increasing degrees of positive transfer when increasing numbers of verbal lists are learned (cf. 26, p. 306 ff.). Underwood and Richardson's study (52), for example, measured transfer in the learning of a series of paired-adjective lists, in which each successive list required the learning of different responses to the same stimuli. The number of trials required to learn a test list (a measure of transfer) decreased regularly with the number of preceding lists learned Thus transfer was found to be an increasing function of the *number* of previously acquired responses to stimuli.

Also relevant to this question may be the results on meaningfulness, to be discussed below. There can be little doubt about the faster learning of meaningful materials, although an advantage in recall does not appear (53). Noble (27) hypothesizes a direct relationship between meaningfulness and number of associated responses. If one accepts this notion, then the superior efficiency of meaningful learning materials may be attributed to the greater number of previously acquired associations such stimuli have. Another implication is that the meaningfulness of stimuli (and thus their transfer effectiveness) may be manipulated in the learning situation by requiring the learner to acquire a number of responses to the stimulus. Skinner's (6, 39) technique of 'ringing the changes' on a particular principle to be learned may also be basically a matter of increasing the number of responses to single stimuli.

Notwithstanding the existence of this rather indirect experimental evidence, there remains a need for research directly aimed at finding an answer to this question about number of responses and transfer. The possibility exists that requiring the learning of increased numbers of responses to the same stimuli may be a significant factor in learning efficiency, in so far as it can increase positive transfer.

Meaningfulness. As is well known, many investigations of human learning have been concerned with nonsense materials. Frequently, research is conducted with materials for which meaningfulness is held as a constant, preferably low, value. But there is considerable evidence that meaningful materials are learned more rapidly than are nonsense materials. In fact the differences in learning usually found in favor of meaningful materials imply that this is a factor of outstanding importance to learning efficiency (cf. 5, 26). The question of learning efficiency, which has not been directly investigated, may be stated as follows: (a) Given a set of inherently meaningless identifications to be made in a job task, can transfer be most effectively mediated by the acquisition of meaningful associations? (b) Given a more or less meaningless sequence of acts to be performed in following a procedure, can transfer be insured by acquiring a meaningful verbal sequence representing these acts? (c) What effect does degree of meaningfulness of concepts acquired in a learning situation have upon the performance of 'concept using' tasks including problem solving?

The experimental evidence (cf. 17, 26) shows, first of all, that there is a regular increase in rapidity of learning as the material to be learned increases in meaningfulness. This effect is enhanced when the members being associated are connected by some logical sequence. There is a definite relationship between this finding and the long-known effectiveness of mnemonic systems (see references in McGeoch and Irion, 26, p. 478). Cofer's findings (3) on the retention of meaningful materials show that learned concepts may be acquired (as 'ideas') much more rapidly than can exact verbal passages, and that they continue to function as concepts for a long time after exact verbal sequences have been forgotten. This finding is consistent with the suggestion of certain writers (18, 30) that mediation by means of meaningful materials may be most economical of learning time because a small absolute amount of material must be acquired. Putting all these things together, there is some doubt that meaningfulness has ever been accorded quite the importance it serves as a factor in learning within the framework of traditional investigations. Further, the transfer value of meaningful materials has only rarely been emphasized (18).

Intertrial factors

There are two general kinds of factors which may be varied between trials of learning. One of these is the temporal distribution of trials or practice sessions, and the other is change in the learning task.

Massed or distributed practice. The question of whether practice is more efficient if trials are massed or if they are distributed is a classical problem which has been studied extensively (58). Basically, it is clear that if the intertrial interval is too long, everything that has been learned on the preceding trial tends to be forgotten and to have to be relearned on the next trial. Even partial forgetting implies that some relearning could be avoided by reducing the interval between trials. On the other hand, closely massed trials are likely to produce fatigue, boredom and work decrement. In this latter case, however, it is not altogether certain that the decrements so typically displayed actually indicate a retardation of learning. Some studies (7, 21) suggest rather strongly that the decrements apply only to the performance, not to the learning. When rest intervals and a suitable test are introduced following the period of learning, it is found that massed practice groups have actually acquired more than they have demonstrated during learning. Thus massed learning is more efficient than it would appear. Probably the main effect of massed practice is upon motivation rather than on association. Several studies of serial learning (17, 45) have found that performance is facilitated to a greater extent by increasing the time per item during the presentation, than by introducing rest intervals between repetitions of the list. This finding suggests that the most efficient learning program, in terms of total elapsed time, may be one in which material is presented slowly within each trial, but massed in the sense that one trial promptly follows another. Finally, there are studies (4, 8) which have suggested that when the task to be learned is a very difficult one, inhibitory effects of massing trials may be more than offset by the difficulty of remembering procedural details from one trial to the next.

If we conceive of the intratrial interval as being important because it relates to the ease with which the learner can proceed in learning, one obvious solution would be to let the trainee set his own intratrial interval, that is, let him pace himself. Skinner has argued that this is one virtue of his teaching machines (38, 39). It may well be that the learner is the best possible judge of his own level of inhibition and his own best judge of when he is ready to proceed in learning. With such a self-pacing procedure it is usually found that the subject chooses a relatively long intratrial interval early in learning, and decreases this interval as learning proceeds. Again we must note that the temporal sequencing of training which leads to the most efficient transfer to the job situation needs to be determined by experimental study.

Task scheduling. A more complex question concerns how the relevant stimuli should be scheduled. There appear to be two distinct schools of thought on the subject. One of these (18, 54) contends that the underlying principle (or the crucial stimulus element) with which the behavior is to be associated should be emphasized from the first, and should serve as a stable reference point throughout the course of learning. According to such a position, departure from this procedure can only lead to interference and learning decrement. In practice, however, this procedure has the disadvantage of frustrating the learner if he cannot make the correct responses at the outset. On the other hand, Skinner, among others, has maintained that the desired response should be given every possible stimulus support from the outset of learning (6, 39). The purpose of this stimulus support is to insure that the correct response will be made. Once made, it can then be reinforced, and the superfluous stimuli gradually removed. The obvious difficulty with this strategy is that it is quite likely that the reinforcement will strengthen the association of the response to the wrong stimulus. Which procedure leads to the greatest efficiency of learning and the greatest transfer to a new situation, is not presently known.

It seems likely that superiority of one or the other procedure may depend upon many factors. If the correct response is a verbal one, if it can be elicited by instruction or by some other means, and if a suitable task set can draw the trainee's attention to the relevant stimulus, then this would seem to suffice. However, it is clear that there are many learning situations in which all these things cannot be done. This is true, for example, when the correct response and the relevant stimulus cannot be verbally communicated to the trainee. We may note in this connexion Skinner's method of using extra 'stimulus supports' is derived by analogy from his animal studies. While he argues for the efficacy of this method in teaching machines, we do not know that the two procedures have been put to a critical test. One obvious disadvantage of Skinner's procedure is that once the response has been established in the presence of a number of stimuli, it is then necessary to eliminate the irrelevant stimuli from the total stimulus complex, in order that only the relevant one will remain in association with the desired response. This means that learning must proceed as a discrimination problem in which the relevant stimulus must be discriminated from the irrelevant ones, or else the danger is run that the trainee will conclude his training having learned something irrelevant. Thus, there is the possibility that additional training is required, over that which is really necessary for the desired performance, before the trainee is in a position to go into the transfer situation. Those who uphold Skinner's position might well argue at this point that the superfluous stimulus support given the correct response early in learning can be gradually withdrawn so that the over-all learning efficiency is not impaired. This argument fails to recognize, however, that these irrelevant stimuli not only support the correct response but also incorrect and competing responses which may introduce interference. As an example of this problem consider learning of the touch system of typing. The question we are considering may be phrased as follows: Can the touch system of typing be learned better if (a) the names of the keys are present, or (b) if the keys are blank? Most educators seem to agree that while the presence of the letter names on the keys is an aid in early learning, they may actually impede the ultimate level of proficiency desired in touch typing. More research needs to be done before any clearcut answer to this question can be obtained.

Wolfle has pointed out (57) that in any instance of stimulus–response learning, if the contextual stimuli remain constant through the course of learning, they will all tend to become (irrelevantly) associated with the correct response. On the basis of evidence from several studies, he is led to conclude that a desirable condition for efficient learning would involve the use of a variety of contextual stimulus conditions, in which only the relevant stimulus remains invariant. The evidence indicates that learning under these variable conditions is indeed less resistant to extinction than is learning under constant stimulus conditions. Such evidence appears quite inconsistent with what a 'stimulus support' principle would lead us to expect.

Summary and Conclusions

We have attempted in this report to identify the manipulable conditions of learning which may be used to insure maximum transfer from learning to tasks of the job. This is the meaning we have used here for the phrase learning efficiency. In considering this question, we first distinguish three kinds of tasks found in the Air Force for which learning is required. These three are identification, procedure following and concept using. For these kinds of performance, we have described and discussed the evidence regarding training variables which are likely to lead to maximal learning efficiency.

On the whole, our conclusion from this evidence must be that there are few principles which can be directly applied to the problem of making learning efficient. The findings concerning the nature of the learning process in human beings are primarily suggestive for this problem, rather than productive of verified practical rules for the control of conditions of efficient learning. This means that the attempt to manipulate learning conditions, whether carried out by a teacher or by the designer of a teaching machine, must employ a good deal of art and not much science, at the present stage of knowledge.

On the other hand, our review of the factors in efficient learning shows us that there are quite a number of these factors which may, in any given situation, be manipulated to affect learning efficiency. If these could all be systematically controlled by means of a machine, or by an otherwise well-designed learning situation, the possibilities of increasing the efficiency of learning over that which typically results from practical training appear great indeed. A suitably designed machine could, of course, be used to carry out such a program of research. Estimates can be made of the relative importance of these factors we have described to learning efficiency. But to attain the goal of ultimate control over learning, it is even more important to undertake research which will determine how far each of these variables, or combinations of them, can be pushed in making learning efficient. As we have pointed out, such a question is neither asked nor answered by the conventional experimental study of human learning.

References
1. K. E. BAKER, R. C. WYLIE and R. M. GAGNÉ, 'Transfer of training to a motor skill as a function of variation in rate of response', *J. exp. Psychol.*, vol. 40 (1950), pp. 721–32.
2. R. C. BOLLES, 'The usefulness of the drive concept', in M. R. Jones (ed.), *Nebraska Symposium on Motivation*, University of Nebraska Press, 1958.
3. C. N. COFER, 'A comparison of logical and verbatum learning of prose passages of different lengths', *Amer. J. Psychol.*, vol. 54 (1941), pp. 1–20.
4. T. W. COOK, 'Factors in massed and distributed practice', *J. exp. Psychol.*, vol. 34 (1944), pp. 325–34.
5. R. A. DAVIS, *Psychology of Learning*, McGraw-Hill, 1935.
6. W. EDWARDS, 'Skinner's teaching machines', *Laboratory Note ML-LN-56-3, Maintenance Laboratory, Air Force Personnel and Training Research Center*, May 1956 (unpublished communication).
7. B. EPSTEIN, 'Immediate and retention effects of interpolated rest periods on learning performance', *Teach. Coll. Contr. Educ.*, no. 949 (1949).
8. S. C. ERICKSEN, 'Variability of attack in massed and distributed practice', *J. exp. Psychol.*, vol. 31 (1942), pp. 339–45.
9. S. M. FELDMAN and B. J. UNDERWOOD, 'Stimulus recall following paired-associate learning', *J. exp. Psychol.*, vol. 53 (1957), pp. 11–15.
10. R. M. GAGNÉ and H. FOSTER, 'Transfer to a motor skill from practice on a pictured representation', *J. exp. Psychol.*, vol. 39 (1949), pp. 342–55.
11. R. M. GAGNÉ and K. E. BAKER, 'On the relation between similarity and transfer of training in the learning of discriminative motor tasks', *Psychol. Rev.*, vol. 57 (1950), pp. 67–79.
12. E. J. GIBSON, 'A systematic application of the concepts of generalization and differentiation to verbal learning', *Psychol. Rev.*, vol. 47 (1940), pp. 196–229.
13. E. J. GIBSON, 'Retroactive inhibition as a function of degree of generalization between tasks', *J. exp. Psychol.*, vol. 28 (1941), pp. 93–115.
14. E. J. GIBSON, 'Intra-list generalization as a factor in verbal learning', *J. exp. Psychol.*, vol. 30 (1942), pp. 185–200.

15. J. J. GIBSON, 'A critical review of the concept of set in contemporary experimental psychology', *Psychol. Bull.*, vol. 38 (1941), pp. 781–817.

16. D. O. HEBB, *A Textbook of Psychology*, Saunders, 1958.

17. C. I. HOVLAND, 'Human learning and retention', in S. S. Stevens (ed.), *Handbook of Experimental Psychology*, Wiley, 1951.

18. G. KATONA, *Organizing and Memorizing*, Columbia University Press, 1940.

19. J. L. KENNEDY and R. C. TRAVIS, 'Prediction of speed of performance by muscle action potentials', *Science*, vol. 105 (1947), pp. 410–11.

20. J. L. KENNEDY and R. C. TRAVIS, 'Prediction and control of alertness: II. Continuous tracking', *J. comp. physiol. Psychol.*, vol. 41 (1948), pp. 203–10.

21. M. J. KIENTZLE, 'Ability patterns under distributed practice', *J. exp. Psychol.*, vol. 39 (1949), pp. 532–7.

22. G. L. KREEZER, J. H. HILL and W. MANNING, Attention, a bibliography and classification of the psychological literature, *Wright Air Development Center*, *WADC Technical Report* no. 54-455, August, 1954.

23. K. LEWIN, T. DEMBO, L. FESTINGER and P. S. SEARS, 'Level of aspiration', in J. McV. Hunt (ed.), *Personality and the Behaviour Disorders, Vol. I*, Ronald Press, 1944, ch. 10.

24. R. A. LITTMAN, 'Motives, history and causes', in M. R. Jones (ed.), *Nebraska Symposium on Motivation*, University of Nebraska Press, 1958.

25. S. J. MACPHERSON, V. DEES and G. C. GRINDLEY, 'The effect of knowledge of results on learning and performance. II, III', *Quart. J. exp. Psychol.*, vol. 1 (1948, 1949), pp. 68–78, 167–74.

26. J. A. MCGEOCH and A. L. IRION, *The Psychology of Human Learning*, Longmans Green, 2nd edn., 1952.

27. C. E. NOBLE, 'An analysis of meaning', *Psychol. Rev.*, vol. 59 (1952), pp. 421–30.

28. C. E. OSGOOD, 'Meaningful similarity and interference in learning', *J. exp. Psychol.*, vol. 36 (1946), pp. 277–301.

29. C. E. OSGOOD, 'The similarity paradox in human learning: A resolution', *J. exp. Psychol.*, vol. 56 (1949), pp. 132–43.

30. C. E. OSGOOD, *Method and Theory in Experimental Psychology*, Oxford University Press, 1953.

31. L. POSTMAN and L. W. PHILLIPS, 'Studies in incidental learning: I. The effects of crowding and isolation', *J. exp. Psychol.*, vol. 48 (1954), pp. 48–56.

32. L. POSTMAN, P. A. ADAMS and L. W. PHILLIPS, 'Studies in incidental learning: II. The effects of association value and of the method of testing', *J. exp. Psychol.*, vol. 49 (1955), pp. 1–10.

33. L. POSTMAN and P. A. ADAMS, 'Studies in incidental learning, III. Interserial interference', *J. exp. Psychol.*, vol. 51 (1956), pp. 323–8.

34. L. POSTMAN and P. A. ADAMS, 'Studies in incidental learning: IV. The interaction of orienting tasks and stimulus materials', *J. exp. Psychol.*, vol. 51 (1956), pp. 329–42.
35. L. POSTMAN, P. A. ADAMS and A. M. BOHM, 'Studies in incidental learning: V. Recall for order and associative clustering', *J. exp. Psychol.*, vol. 51 (1956), pp. 334–42.
36. L. POSTMAN and P. A. ADAMS, 'Studies in incidental learning: VI. Intraserial interference', *J. exp. Psychol.*, vol. 54 (1956), pp. 153–67.
37. B. F. SKINNER, *Science and Human Behavior*, Macmillan, New York 1953.
38. B. F. SKINNER, 'The science of learning and the art of teaching', *Harv. educ. Rev.*, vol. 24 (1954), pp. 86–97.
39. B. F. SKINNER, 'Teaching machines', *Science*, vol. 128 (1958), pp. 969–77.
40. K. W. SPENCE, *Behavior Theory and Conditioning*, Yale University Press, 1956.
41. E. L. THORNDIKE, *The Fundamentals of Learning*, Teachers College, Columbia University, 1932.
42. E. C. TOLMAN, C. S. HALL and E. P. BRETNALL, 'A disproof of the law of effect and a substitution of the laws of emphasis, motivation, and disruption', *J. exp. Psychol.*, vol. 15 (1932), pp. 601–14.
43. B. J. UNDERWOOD and D. GOAD, 'Studies of distributed practice: I. The influence of intra-list similarity in verbal learning', *J. exp. Psychol.*, vol. 42 (1951), pp. 125–34.
44. B. J. UNDERWOOD, 'Studies of distributed practice: II. Learning and retention of paired-adjective lists with two levels of intra-list similarity', *J. exp. Psychol.*, vol. 42 (1951), pp. 153–61.
45. B. J. UNDERWOOD and R. O. VITERNA, 'Studies of distributed practice: IV. The effect of similarity and rate of presentation in verbal-discrimination learning', *J. exp. Psychol.*, vol. 42 (1951), pp. 296–9.
46. B. J. UNDERWOOD, 'Studies of distributed practice: VII. Learning and retention of serial nonsense lists as a function of intra-list similarity', *J. exp. Psychol.*, vol. 44 (1952), pp. 80–87.
47. B. J. UNDERWOOD, 'Studies of distributed practice: VIII. Learning and retention of paired nonsense syllables as a function of intra-list similarity', *J. exp. Psychol.*, vol. 45 (1953), pp. 133–42.
48. B. J. UNDERWOOD, 'Studies of distributed practice: IX. Learning and retention of paired adjectives as a function of intra-list similarity', *J. exp. Psychol.*, vol. 45 (1953), pp. 143–9.
49. B. J. UNDERWOOD, 'Studies of distributed practice: X. The influence of intra-list similarity on learning and retention of serial adjective lists', *J. exp. Psychol.*, vol. 45 (1953), pp. 253–9.
50. B. J. UNDERWOOD, 'Studies of distributed practice: XI. An attempt to resolve conflicting facts on retention of serial nonsense lists', *J. exp. Psychol.*, vol. 45 (1953), pp. 355–9.
51. B. J. UNDERWOOD, 'Intralist similarity in verbal learning and retention', *Psychol. Rev.*, vol. 61 (1954), pp. 160–66.

52. B. J. UNDERWOOD and J. RICHARDSON, 'Studies of distributed practice: XIII. Inter-list interference and the retention of serial nonsense lists', *J. exp. Psychol.*, vol. 50 (1955), pp. 39–46.

53. B. J. UNDERWOOD and J. RICHARDSON, 'The influence of meaningfulness, intra-list similarity, and serial position on retention', *J. exp. Psychol.*, vol. 52 (1956), pp. 119–26.

54. M. WERTHEIMER, *Productive Thinking*, Harper, 1945.

55. D. D. WICKENS, 'Studies of response generalization in conditioning: I. Stimulus generalization during response generalization', *J. exp. Psychol.*, vol. 33 (1943), pp. 221–7.

56. D. D. WICKENS, 'Studies of response generalization in conditioning: II. The comparative strength of the transferred and non-transferred responses', *J. exp. Psychol.*, vol. 33 (1943), pp. 330–32.

57. D. WOLFLE, 'Training', in S. S. Stevens (ed.), *Handbook of Experimental Psychology*, Wiley, 1951, pp. 1267–86.

58. R. S. WOODWORTH and H. SCHLOSBERG, *Experimental Psychology*, Holt, 1954, rev. edn.

17 A. I. Siegel, M. Richlin and P. Federman

A Comparative Study of 'Transfer Through Generalization' and 'Transfer Through Identical Elements' in Technical Training

A. I. Siegel, M. Richlin and P. Federman, 'A comparative study of "transfer through generalization" and "transfer through identical elements" in technical training', *Journal of Applied Psychology*, vol. 44 (1960), pp. 27–30.

Recently, naval aviation technical training has shifted its focus from a general training program to a training program which introduces trainees directly into specialized instruction. It is the goal of this specialized training to produce men who are immediately useful upon graduation in a short 'pipeline' time.

The newer program may be contrasted with the technical training previously given. This previous training was broader in nature, emphasized more deeply the theoretical aspects of the technical skills involved in maintenance, and relied to a greater extent on in-service training for imparting the specific technical skills needed for specific job performance. The purpose of the present study was to compare in a real situation the technical effectiveness of technicians given specific training (transfer through identical elements) with the efficiency of trainees given a more general background knowledge (transfer through generalization).

Graduates of each training program for three naval ratings were studied: (a) jet aviation machinist's mate, (b) air controlman and (c) parachute rigger. Success as a parachute rigger or a machinist's mate depends upon mechanical ability and perceptual motor skill, while success as an air controlman depends to a considerable degree on verbal behavior and abstract reasoning.

Methods, Subjects and Procedure

For each rating a complete library or listing of the tasks that the technician could be called upon to perform in the fleet was developed and cast in technical behavior check list (T.B.C.L.) form. Each check list contained three parts. Since it was felt that one of the most valid indicators of acceptable performance is the willingness of a man's supervisor to assign him without direct, technical supervision to various technical tasks, Part I determined the amount of time spent by the ratee on each of the tasks within the rating. In Part II, the amount of supervision that the striker required on each of the tasks he performed was requested. Part III acquired an estimation of the criticality, in terms of squadron mission, of each of the tasks listed. In order to study the developmental aspects of the ratees, separate evaluations were obtained in Parts I and II for each of two time periods: the first three months the man being rated was in the fleet (T-1) and the fourth to ninth months he was in the fleet (T-2).

The Ss were graduates of the two naval aviation training programs, the previous general 'A' school program and the more recently established and specialized program. For the air controlmen thirty-nine graduates of the more general training program (henceforth referred to as A.C.G.s) and forty-two graduates of the specialized program (A.C.T.s) were studied on their fleet jobs.

For the parachute riggers, ten graduates of the previous program (P.R.G.s) and twenty-three graduates of the specialized training program (P.R.S.s) were included. In the aviation motor machinist's mate rating, three groups were involved: graduates of the previous general training program (A.D.G.s; $N = 21$); graduates who had received an intermediate type of training which involved specialized training but which did not include training on the specific equipment used in the fleet (A.D.J.I.s; $N = 60$); and graduates of the specialized program who had received specialized training and practice on the specific equipment found in the fleet (A.D.J.S.s; $N = 36$). The subjects were distributed over six naval air stations and thirty-two squadrons.

Derivation of Criterion Instrument

The mean time in hours spent during T-1 and T-2 by each group in each rating on each of the listed tasks was computed. For each task listed in Part II of the T.B.C.L.s, a score ranging from one to five was assigned: a score of five indicated proficient task performance after an initial checkout; a score of one was assigned for tasks on which the striker had received six or more checkouts but on which he was still unable to perform without direct supervision. Scores of four, three or two were respectively assigned as follows: proficient after three to five checkouts, proficient after six or more checkouts, one to five checkouts but not proficient. The mean and variance of the Part II scores for each task on each of the three separate T.B.C.L.s were computed by time period. Additionally, over-all means and over-all variances were computed for each task in each of the three separate T.B.C.L.s. Last, the criticality of each task was derived from the responses in Part III of the T.B.C.L.s.

Three item plots were then made, one for each of the ratings under consideration. The average variance of each task as computed from the T.B.C.L., Part II, data was plotted as the ordinate value, while the abscissa point was determined by multiplying the mean time spent on the task by the criticality of the task as computed from the T.B.C.L., Part III, data. In one sense and in measurement terminology, the ordinate represented the discriminating power of the items (tasks), while the abscissa value represented difficulty level. Inspection suggested fairly clear cutting points on each axis for eliminating items. Essentially, in developing the final criterion T.B.C.L.s, those tasks which were considered 'unimportant' and which are relatively useless in a measurement instrument because of lack of discrimination (variability) between individuals were eliminated.

Thus, three separate final criterion T.B.C.L.s were developed, one for each of the ratings considered. All data henceforth reported are based on these final criterion T.B.C.L.s. The final criterion T.B.C.L. for motor machinists' mates contained thirty-eight tasks; the final criterion T.B.C.L.s for parachute riggers and air controlmen contained forty-three and thirty-four tasks respectively.

Results

Using the same scoring method discussed above, Part II of each T.B.C.L. was rescored with the total score being equal to the sum of the scored tasks divided by the number of tasks attempted. The total scores so derived were then subjected to a variance analysis. The results of these analyses are presented in Tables 1, 2 and 3.

Table 1

Analysis of Variance of Aviation Machinists' Mates Scores

Source of variation	Sum of squares	df	Var. est.	F
Between cells	62,947	5	—	—
Between groups	16,697	2	8,349	1·65
Between time periods	39,737	1	39,737	7·84*
Groups × Times	6,513	2	3,256	$F < 1$
Within cells	905,288	178	5,086	—
Pooled error (4 + 5)	911,801	180	5,066	—
Total	968,234	183	—	—

* Significant at the 0·01 level of confidence.

Table 2

Analysis of Variance of Air Controlmen's Scores

Source of variation	Sum of squares	df	Var. est.	F
Between cells	87,103	3	—	—
Between groups	40,009	1	40,009	12·52*
Between time periods	45,333	1	45,333	14·19*
Groups × Times	1,761	1	1,761	$F < 1$
Within cells	448,751	140	3,205	—
Pooled error (4 + 5)	450,512	141	3,195	—
Total	535,854	143	—	—

* Significant at the 0·01 level of confidence.

Table 3

Analysis of Variance of Parachute Riggers' Scores

Source of variation	Sum of squares	df	Var. est.	F
Between cells	58,874	3	19,625	—
Between groups	7,897	1	7,897	1·91
Between time periods	49,385	1	49,385	11·97*
Groups × Times	1,592	1	1,592	$F < 1$
Within cells	217,021	52	4,173	—
Pooled error (4 + 5)	218,613	53	4,125	—
Total	275,895	55	—	—

* Significant at the 0·01 level of confidence.

These analyses enable a general answer to the question of whether the specialized training had exerted any general effects on fleet technical efficiency. For the aviation machinists' mates and parachute riggers no statistically significant between-groups differences were evidenced. For the air controlmen, the more generally trained group was superior to a statistically significant extent. The between-time period differences noted were to be expected since a trainee would be expected to perform at a superior level during his fourth to ninth months in the service as compared with his first three months.

The next step was to determine where the men in the air controlman's rating were doing well and where they needed improvement. The response score distributions for the five task content clusters included in the final criterion air controlman's T.B.C.L were derived. These distributions are presented as Table 4. The distributions indicated that for each of the five content clusters (using equipment, using publications, testing equipment, receiving and transmitting messages and controlling traffic), the generally trained group had higher means over both time periods. For the first time period both groups were poorest at the tasks involved in receiving and transmitting messages, while in the second time period the generally trained group was, by and large, proficient at these tasks, and the specifically trained group required additional training. Moreover, even in T-2, the specifically trained group remained weakest in receiving and transmitting messages and in controlling traffic. These tasks are believed to involve mostly nonroutine thinking as opposed to the specific information transfer involved in using publications, using equipment and testing equipment.

Similarly, an examination of Table 4 from the point of view of within-group strengths and weaknesses during T-1 suggests that if publication use is ignored, the specifically trained group was best at equipment use and equipment testing, while the generally trained group was best at testing equipment and controlling traffic.

Table 4

Response Score Distribution for Tower Tasks of Air Controlmen

Tasks	T-1								T-2							
	Response %					N	M	σ^2	Response %					N	M	σ^2
	1	2	3	4	5				1	2	3	4	5			
Using equipment																
A.C. (G.)	6	9	22	39	24	67	3·66	1·24	6	8	5	13	68	107	4·30	1·48
A.C.T.	5	29	13	28	25	68	3·40	1·59	15	18	8	9	50	109	3·61	2·48
Using publications																
A.C. (G.)	0	3	5	13	79	67	4·69	0·48	0	0	1	3	96	90	4·94	0·08
A.C.T.	0	11	9	13	68	69	4·39	1·02	7	1	2	2	88	93	4·65	1·11
Testing equipment																
A.C. (G.)	3	8	15	41	33	39	3·95	1·02	6	6	0	7	81	54	4·54	1·25
A.C.T.	3	22	33	17	25	36	3·39	1·35	2	12	4	16	66	56	4·32	1·25
Receiving and transmitting messages																
A.C. (G.)	0	14	18	35	33	88	3·53	1·04	2	10	2	10	76	124	4·50	1·07
A.C.T.	9	39	21	4	27	94	3·01	1·84	15	19	7	10	49	129	3·61	2·48
Controlling traffic																
A.C. (G.)	7	9	26	40	18	124	3·88	1·23	7	13	4	9	67	189	4·15	1·86
A.C.T.	8	17	34	24	17	118	3·25	1·32	17	13	10	10	50	191	3·63	2·54
Totals																
A.C. (G.)	4	8	19	34	35	385	3·88	1·20	4	9	3	9	75	564	4·42	1·35
A.C.T.	5	24	23	17	31	385	3·44	1·66	13	13	7	9	58	578	3·85	2·30
Grand total	4	16	21	26	33	770	3·66	1·48	9	11	5	9	66	1142	4·13	1·92

Discussion

The usefulness of the present findings is dependent to a large extent on the criterion used. A training criterion must possess certain characteristics if it is to be useful. These characteristics include relevance, comprehensiveness, consistency, correctly weighted elements and analysability. Taking these requirements in turn, the T.B.C.L. seems to have met the requisites of relevance and comprehensiveness. All of the included jobs were drawn directly from the training course and/or the actual job. Furthermore, any nontechnical work characteristics were purposefully omitted from the T.B.C.L.s. Consequently, the T.B.C.L.s were relevant by definition. Since space was allowed for addition by the rater of tasks not included in the list and since very few 'write-ins' were made, it can be concluded that the technical jobs were comprehensively covered. Moreover, the fact that the T.B.C.L.s were designed as training criteria rather than as general fleet performance measurements instruments points to the necessity of excluding variance due to performance not associated with what was acquired in training.

The third characteristic, an analysable criterion, has been amply demonstrated in the present study. Total T.B.C.L. scores were computed; the subsections were analysed individually and combined; individual clusters of tasks were analysed in terms of mean performance scores, variance and response distributions. All of these analyses were possible in relation to time and subgroup differences.

The correct weighting of the elements of the criterion received indirect treatment in the present research. The item selection technique emphasized task criticality, frequency of occurrence and variance. High variance tasks are inherently weighted more than low variance tasks. Moreover, the emphasis on criticality tended to eliminate routine jobs from the list. Thus, for instance, the A.D. T.B.C.L. included only twelve tasks involving routine line operations in comparison with twenty-six tasks involving major and intermediate inspections of jet aircraft and jet power plant removal and jet engine build-up.

In order to estimate the reliability of the T.B.C.L.s, product moment correlations were computed. In some cases a given striker was rated independently by two supervisors. In other cases, the same rater was asked to repeat his report. These data were combined in the reliability determination. It can be argued that the combined estimations are perhaps the best indication of total reliability since they consider both inter-rater and intra-rater reliability. The uncorrected reliability for the A.D. T.B.C.L. so determined was 0·84 for T-1 and 0·90 for T-2; for the A.C. and P.R. T.B.C.L.s the uncorrected reliabilities respectively by time period were 0·91, 0·89, 0·76 and 0·81.

In terms of the issue of general versus specific training, it seems that the specialized training for motor machinists and parachute riggers exerted few, if any, debilitating effects on the technical proficiency of the men involved. This contention does not seem to hold for the air controlmen. The differential effects of specialization may be explainable on the basis of the differences in skills involved in the various ratings. For the air controlmen, most of the tasks are of a conceptual nature, while for the parachute riggers and motor machinists mechanical manipulation is largely involved. Moreover, within the air controlman rating those tasks of a conceptual nature seemed to be the most difficult for the specifically trained air controlmen.

Summary and Conclusions

Technical Behavior Check Lists were used for assessing the fleet effectiveness of persons who had received two types of training: (1) specialized task-oriented training and (2) general conceptual training. The effects of rapid, specialized, task-oriented training in the context with which we were concerned varied with the on-the-job performance requisites. For tasks involving mechanical manipulation few debilitating effects were introduced by the specialized training; for abstract conceptual tasks this contention does not seem to hold.

18 E. Belbin

Methods of Training Older Workers

Excerpts from E. Belbin, 'Methods of training older workers', *Ergonomics*, vol. 1 (1958), pp. 207–21.

Three experiments are described which show subjects in middle age to learn more rapidly and thoroughly if they can do so by way of actual performance of the task rather than by memorization of instructions. The first two experiments used laboratory-type card-sorting tasks. The third involved training in the mending of worsted cloth. An experimental training method, which has been described in a previous article (Belbin *et al*., 1957), was compared with the traditional 'exposure' or 'sit-by-me' method. The experimental method aimed at removing the perceptual difficulty which had been found in previous experiments to be a limitation upon success in training young girls to mend. This method was found to yield even better results with middle-aged subjects than it had with school-leavers.

1. Introduction

Most studies of learning in relation to age have shown older subjects to be at a considerable disadvantage (see McGeoch and Irion, 1952). In the majority of these studies literal reproduction has been used as the criterion of learning ability and memorization has assumed a central role. Previous experiments (Belbin, 1956) have indicated, however, that while older people are very much inferior to younger at recalling in words information they have learnt, they may nevertheless be comparatively good at *using* it in a practical task. These experiments, and also those of Speakman (1954), indicate that *some* things can be learned at least as well by older people as by younger, and that the former are better at learning for 'use' – and at learning by 'using' – than at the artificial rote-memorizing tasks of the laboratory.

It is not only in the laboratory that older people are given tasks to memorize. The traditional methods of industrial training often involve learning the job by verbal description, where not only a mass of new terminology has to be memorized but also details from charts and diagrams. In the following experiments, therefore, we have attempted to develop a method of learning which minimizes conscious memorization; to investigate whether such a method is relatively advantageous to the older learner; and to ascertain the extent to which such a method can be applied to the learning of an industrial skill. The first two experiments were conducted with laboratory tasks; in the third we have compared two methods of teaching older people the skill of worsted mending.

2. Experiment I

Subjects were asked to 'post' fifty numbered cards into five slots in the lid of a box. Each slot bore a distinctive colour. There was a systematic relationship between colour and number. For example, all cards in the twenties had to be posted into the pink slot and all those in the thirties into the black slot. The subjects had to learn the relationship between colour and number so that they could 'post' cards as quickly as possible without making errors.

Two methods of training were used:

(a) *Learning by memorizing* The subject was given a chart showing the relationships between colours and numbers and left to memorize these, with the box into which the cards would have to be posted in front of him. When he was satisfied that he had learned the relationship, the chart was removed. His learning was tested by asking him to state the relationships. All subjects were able to do this accurately.

(b) *Learning by 'activity'*. This method involved the subject in finding out for himself the relationship between colour and number. He was given a large pack of coloured cards, each of which bore a number, and told to 'post' these cards into the appropriately coloured slots, noting the numbers as he did so, and gradually to build up the ideas of which numbers were associated with which colour. When he was satisfied that he had achieved this, he was transferred to the main task.

Each subject performed the task twice – once with the first and once with the second method of learning. Half performed first with the first method and then transferred to the second, and half performed the tasks in the opposite order. A different set of numbers and colours was used for each method.

The learning times, the times taken to post the fifty cards, and the number of errors were recorded.

Subjects

Since we were primarily concerned with teaching skills to industrial workers we attempted to use subjects who had an appropriate background. Accordingly forty-four subjects whose ages ranged from 20 to 70, all of whom were drawn from among industrial workers or from rural evening institutes, performed the tasks. All of them had left school at the age of 14 and none of them had had any further academic training. The subjects were divided into four age groups, each with equal numbers of males and females.

Results

The results are shown in Table 1. With the Memorizing method the median times to post the fifty cards rose significantly from the twenties to the thirties and thereafter remained high, while the proportion of subjects with a completely correct performance fell sharply between the twenties and the thirties and fell again between the forties and fifties. With the Activity method the time to perform the task rose gradually from the twenties to the fifties but was never as high as that for the memorization method even among the oldest subjects. The quicker performance by the older subjects following training by this method was not achieved at the expense of accuracy, which tended to be greater with the Activity method in all the age ranges.

These results suggest that it was only when older subjects had learnt to do the task by memorizing the instructions that they were at any considerable disadvantage either as regards time or accuracy. However, it is possible that any or all of the following four factors might have contributed to these results:

(a) The older people took substantially longer than the younger to learn, especially by the Activity method. It may have been that

Table 1

Median Posting Times after Learning by Two Methods

Age range	Number in group	Median posting time in seconds to post 50 cards		Percentage completely correct performances to total		Median learning time in seconds	
		Memorizing method	Activity method	Memorizing method	Activity method	Memorizing method	Activity method
20–29	10	96	96	60·0	70·0	33·5	54·0
30–39	12	152	112·5	33·3	66·7	60·5	115·0
40–49	8	150	122	37·5	50·0	77·5	122·5
Over 50	14	153	131	21·4	50·0	42·5	144·5

These results are tabulated for a point during the progress of performance at which the times taken by the younger subjects after training by both the methods were equal. The posting time of the twenties following training by the Memorizing method was significantly ($P < 0.01$) different from that of the thirties and also from those of the forties and fifties. The posting time of the twenties following the Activity method was not significantly different from that of the thirties or the forties, but was from that of the fifties ($P < 0.01$).

the older people were allowing themselves insufficient time to learn by memorizing. However, the length of time in learning by memorizing bore little relationship to length of performance time. For example, in the over-50 age group, the coefficient of ranked correlation between memorizing time and performance time was +0·61, i.e. those who took least time to learn, tended to be those who performed the task most quickly. In addition, three subjects in the sixties who were unable to do the task at all after memorizing it, although they had repeated and lengthy additional learning periods, were able to perform it reasonably well when learning it by the Activity method.

(b) Learning by memorization involved 'translation' between the chart and box, which may have been relatively difficult for older people. In the Activity method, no such translation was involved, as the numbers to be associated with the colours were always seen going into the appropriate slots.

(c) Memorizing from the chart inevitably involved the learning of colour–number relationships as such, whereas with the Activity method it was possible to ignore the colours and to learn number–spatial relationships, which might conceivably be easier for older people.

(d) Finally, with the Activity method the task during the learning period was closely similar to the main task, and if older subjects, after learning by memorizing, had performed the main task for a longer time, they might conceivably have come substantially closer to the younger subjects and the times achieved by the two methods might have been considerably nearer together.

Experiment II was therefore designed to measure the effects of Activity learning as compared with those of Memorizing at different ages, with these four possibilities either eliminated or controlled.

3. Experiment II

The task was to 'post' cards numbered from 20 to 79 into six different slots in the lid of a box. All the twenties were to go to one slot, all the thirties to another and so on. The subject was required to learn the association between slots and numbers. Again there were two methods of learning.

(a) *Memorizing.* One group learnt to perform the task by memorizing small numbered slips which were attached to the slots in the box. These numbers were removed before the main task was performed. The subjects were asked to state where the numbers should be posted before commencing the experiment.

(b) *Activity.* This group had a pack of cards on which the pattern of the slots was printed. Each card bore one number against its appropriate position among the slots, as shown in Figure 1, and it had to be posted into the slot indicated by that number. The subject was told to notice into which slots the numbers were placed. He was thus discovering the number–position relationship while performing the task. Both groups were told to go on until they were satisfied that they had learnt the positions and were then transferred to the main task. The time taken to learn was measured by a stop-watch as was the time required for posting each six cards of the main task.

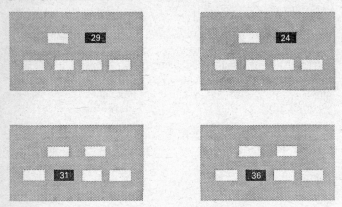

Figure 1 Examples of cards used during the 'activity' method of training in Experiment II

Subjects

For each learning method there were eight subjects between the ages of 18 and 22 and eight between 30 and 49. The younger subjects were naval ratings who had left school at 14, the older ones were trainees from a Government Training Centre, whose previous occupations were in the unskilled or artisan category and included labourers, factory workers, fishermen, lorry drivers, etc.

Results

Table 2 shows the times required by each age group by each learning method to reach an arbitrary criterion performance of 10 seconds to post six cards. With both methods of training the older subjects were slower than the younger to attain this target, but the difference was both absolutely and proportionately very much greater with the Memorizing method than with the Activity method. The younger subjects reached the target time more quickly after learning by Memorizing than after the Activity learning: the older subjects, however, did so more quickly following the Activity learning method. The difference between the age groups in time taken to attain the target time after the Memorizing method is composed of differences both in learning

Table 2

Times Required in Minutes and Seconds to Reach an Arbitrary Criterion Performance of 10 Seconds to Post Six Cards

Method of learning	Age group	Cycle at which the target was attained by the group	i.e. after total learning time of		and after performing the main task for		Total time to reach target by the group	
			min	s	min	s	min	s
Memorizing	young	12th	5	34	18	40	24	14
Memorizing	older	27th	11	15	49	24	60	39
Activity	young	7th	22	10	10	7	32	17
Activity	older	6th	33	47	9	16	43	3

time and in time for performance at the main task. With the Activity method, however, the older subjects were inferior only in length of learning time. The performance time they required to reach the target speed once the task had been learnt was very little different from that of the younger subjects.

The figures may be analysed in a different way to show performances attained after constant time, adding together time taken learning and time taken performing the main task. This has been done in Table 3. Again it is possible to see the same pattern of results: the younger subjects doing better following memorization and the older showing better performance after learning by the Activity method.

Table 3

Average Cycle Time Reached after 2027 Seconds

Method of learning	Age group	Seconds per cycle
Memorizing	Young	9·5
Memorizing	Older	13·4
Activity	Young	10·3
Activity	Older	11·0

As in the previous experiment, both older and younger subjects were slightly more accurate after learning by the Activity method.

The significance of these results for industrial training

The results of both these experiments suggest that the decline in performance with age, which has been so consistently noted in the psychological research on learning, may in part be due to the learning method imposed by the experimenter. It seems that it is not possible to make an over-all comparison between the learning capacities of different age groups of people in the abstract without taking into account the fact that the method of learning a task which is conducive to high performance by one group is not necessarily that which is conducive for the other. The present method of training people for a number of industrial tasks involves conscious memorization by the trainee. With this method of learning older people are likely to be at a disadvantage. This is not to say, however, that they will perform the tasks less well under all conditions: it appears that if an appropriate teaching method can be used they may be able to perform a number of tasks which have hitherto been regarded as outside their range of ability.

One such task is worsted mending in wool textile mills. In this industry it is maintained that all attempts to train older workers have proved unsuccessful. The operation is currently taught by description and demonstration. Our investigations into the difficulties encountered in learning this skill and the methods which we have developed to overcome them have been described previously (Belbin *et al.*, 1956, 1957). In these experiments the performances of three groups of young school leavers were compared during and after 12 weeks of training by three different methods. In the following experiment we have investigated the extent to which it is possible to teach the mending skill to older workers when learning by memorization is minimized.

4. Experiment III

Some idea of the lack of enthusiasm for training older people to mend in the worsted mills may be gained from the results of our appeal to recruit people over 30 for a 12-week training course. An experiment similar to that arranged for younger people was planned, using three groups of subjects. Some 400 firms who were members of the Woollen and Worsted Trades Federation were approached, but only two expressed any interest in the scheme. Accordingly, a modified form of the original experiment was designed and we recruited volunteers from outside the industry.

Experimental procedure

Twelve housewives between the ages of 30 and 50 were recruited. None had any experience of invisible mending. They were divided into two groups of six, and each was trained by one of the two following methods:

(a) *The traditional 'exposure' or 'sit-by-me' method.* This consists of working alongside an experienced mender who describes the weaves and demonstrates the method of mending them. Training periods normally last anything from 6 months to 2 years. The weave most commonly used in a number of mills – and therefore that on which most beginners are taught – is the 2 × 2 twill shown in Figure 2. Trainees are told to 'go over two and under

2   3   4

2 × 2 twill

Figure 2   2 × 2 twill – an example of a weave used in the mending experiment

two', and to 'look for the float' to indicate where to place the needle. The older people who were trained by the exposure method in this experiment were started off on this twill weave, and were trained by two experienced mender-supervisors from a worsted mill.

(b) *A new experimental method.* Training by this method was carried out by the writer. The method is based on a theory that successful performance of a task depends on the initial acquisition not only of the correct method or the required motion pattern but of the correct perceptual 'cues' which make the desired motion pattern possible. The perceptual skill cannot be developed effectively by verbal methods of instruction and training. The essence of the experimental method is rather that the trainee is conditioned to respond appropriately to perceptual cues and this is achieved through successive presentation of tasks in which the key perceptual features are emphasized and the correct responses to these are facilitated. The presentation is controlled by the trainer and varied according to the progress of the individual trainee. In this way the trainee learns the skill through experience and by understanding born of such experience. The experience, however, is gained in a much shorter time than 'on the job'. The method depends from the outset on a fundamental analysis of the skill involved.

In the present experiment the trainees were given practice on specially woven large-scale weaves and were then told to copy them on a small frame, using thick elastic instead of thread. In this way they discerned the details of the weaves for themselves and were enabled to learn without any serious possibility of making errors. They were gradually transferred on to smaller weaves with the aid of industrial magnifiers when they had become accustomed to mending a particular weave structure. Thus at no time was the task too difficult for them.

Each group was given 8 hours of instruction in mending three basic weaves and one smaller weave. This was followed by 12 hours of further practice. Two of the 8 hours of experimental training were spent with the special training devices. The group trained by the exposure method spent the whole 8 hours on actual production work.

Time tests were given at intervals during the 20 hours. Each subject was asked to sew 3-in and 6-in single mends on three of the weaves most commonly used in the industry. This involved replacing a missing warp or weft thread in a plain 1×1 weave, a 2×2 hopsack and a 2×2 twill. Later in the course they were required to sew a double mend, i.e. two missing threads. The material to be mended had been retained from the tests given in the younger trainees' courses so that strict comparison was possible.

The trainees in the two groups were equated as far as possible for age and economic background. The age distribution is shown in Table 4.

Table 4
Numbers of Subjects in Experiment III

Age range	Experimental group	Exposure group
30–35	2	1
35–40	2	3
40–45	–	1
45–50	2	1

Results

Comparison of the two methods for training older subjects. After 2 hours' training in the exposure course one trainee resigned. She had been unable to do the work at all and had no confidence in being able to continue. The times taken by the remaining eleven trainees to complete 6-in mends after 8 hours' training are shown in Figure 3. It can be seen that the experimental group tended to mend much more quickly than the exposure group. This was especially so of the hopsack weave in which the slowest of the six trainees in the experimental group took less time than the fastest of the group trained by the exposure method. Also, three of the latter group mended the 2×2 twill inaccurately, while only one of the former group was unable to complete this mend.

The times taken for the shorter mends are shown in Figure 4. It is again evident that the group trained by the experimental method was considerably faster.

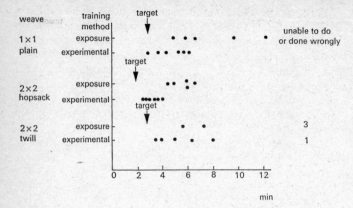

Figure 3 Times taken to mend 6 in of weaves after 8 hours' training. There were significant differences (on t-tests) between the means of the performances of the two groups on the 1×1 plain ($P < 0.05$) and on the 2×2 hopsack ($P < 0.001$). It was not possible to make a similar test of comparison with the twill, since four of the eleven trainees were unable to do the test

Figures 3 and 4 bring out the point, noted in previous experiments, that variation between the performances of different individuals is greater after training by the exposure method than after training by the experimental.

The performance of these older subjects were in many respects remarkably good. For example, in the experimental group, one woman, aged 47, had reached 'target time' on the 1×1 plain weave after 8 hours' training. These targets were assessed by examining the performance of experienced menders in the trade.

Comparison with training schemes for younger people: experimental method. The performance of the experimental group of older trainees may be compared with two groups of younger people from the Training Centre in our previous experiments. Table 5 shows the period after commencement of training when the median performance times after 8 hours' training shown in Figure 3 were attained by the younger groups of subjects. It may be noted that in a matter of hours the older people had learnt to

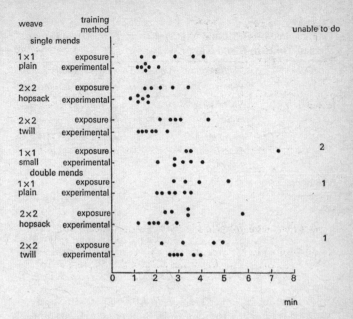

Figure 4 Times taken to mend 3 in of single weaves and 2 in of double. These are the lowest recorded times for each subject during 20 hours of training

mend at a rate which it had taken the younger group several weeks to attain. It must not be assumed, of course, that the older people were able at this stage to maintain their rates of production for any lengthy period. They were not given any tests involving sustained effort.

With the hopsack material every member of the experimental older group was able after 8 hours to mend 6 in in under 4 minutes. It was not until the 12th week of training that every member of the experimental group of school leavers in the Training Centre was able to mend at this rate. At no stage of the 12 weeks' training was every member of the group of school leavers trained by the T.W.I. (training within industry) method able to mend 6 in of hopsack in under 4 minutes: at week 12 three of the total group of ten were still taking considerably longer.

Table 5
Times Taken by Older and Younger Trainees to Attain Equal
Median Times to Mend 6 in of Weave

| | Median times taken to mend 6 in by older people who learnt by the experimental method | Amount of training necessary before these median times were attained by: | | |
| | | Older people | 15-year-old school leavers | |
			experimental method	T.W.I. method
Number of subjects:		6	10	10
Weave				
1 × 1 plain	4·5 min	8 hours	5½ weeks	7 weeks
2 × 2 hopsack	3·1 ,,	8 ,,	10 ,,	not at all
2 × 2 twill	5·5 ,,	8 ,,	3–4 ,,	4 weeks

Table 6
Times Taken by Younger Trainees to Attain Speeds at Short
Test Mends Equal to Those of Older Subjects during 20 Hours of
Training. All Subjects were Trained by the Experimental Method

| | Older Group | Younger Group trained in a Factory |
	Median performance times for mending a weave during the first 20 hours of training	Period of training at which this median speed was attained by the younger people
Number of subjects:	6	4
Weave and mend		
1 × 1 single	1·4 min	week 7 to 8
2 × 2 single	1·23 ,,	week 7 to 8
2 × 2 twill single	1·55 ,,	week 4 to 5
1 × 1 single (smaller weave)	2·95 ,,	week 6 to 7
1 × 1 double	2·6 ,,	week 7
2 × 2 double	2·95 ,,	not at all
2 × 2 twill double	2·9 ,,	week 7

The single mends were 3 in long.   The double mends were 2 in long.

A further comparison may be made with another training course for school-leavers, this time in a factory. Table 6 shows the median performance times for mending 3-in single mends and 2-in double mends by the experimental group of older people during their first 20 hours of training. Column 2 of the table shows the period after commencement of training when the young factory subjects trained by the experimental method achieved similar mending rates. Again it can be seen that the older people attained a performance in a matter of hours which the younger girls had taken several weeks to acquire.

Comparison with training schemes for younger people: exposure method. Although the older people trained by the exposure method had a slower performance than those trained by the experimental, their performance compared reasonably well with that of younger trainees. Table 7 shows the median performance

Table 7

Median Performance Times for Mending 6 in of a Weave. All Subjects Trained by Exposure Method

	Older group median performance times for 6-in mend after 20 hours' training	Younger group number of trainees who were worse at week 12 than the older people's 20 hour median
Number of subjects:	5	8
Weave		
1 × 1 plain	5·6 min	1
2 × 2 hopsack	4·2 ,,	4
2 × 2 twill	5·5 ,,	1
1 × 1 plain double	11·7 ,,	3
2 × 2 plain double	10·5 ,,	3
2 × 2 twill double	13·5 ,,	3

attained by the older people after 20 hours' training by the exposure method, together with the number of younger people trained by the same method who had still not reached these median levels after the 12 weeks of training.

It was difficult to compare the mending performances of different groups on various weaves: some individuals might, for example, have had more practice on some weaves and less on others. It was decided, therefore, to calculate a combined 'mending rate index'. This index was the sum of the target times divided by times actually taken for each of the various weaves. The target times were, as we have already mentioned, based upon the performances of experienced menders studied in the worsted mills. The index was assessed on the tests which were common to all groups, namely, 6-in mends of 1×1 plain, 2×2 hopsack, 2×2 twill, 1×1 plain double, 2×2 hopsack double and 2×2 twill double. The indices for the various groups show relatively good performance by the experimental older group at the end of 20 hours' training as compared with the other groups after approximately 12 weeks' or more training. It may also be noted that in these comparisons the older people were on the whole better than the young after the experimental training, but that after the exposure training the older people were worse than the young. [. . .]

The nature of the difficulty in mending. One factor which might have been an advantage to the older people was that they were all able to sew fairly well. However, this 'motor' aspect of the task could not on its own have been of major importance since firstly, we had already found that among the younger groups there was no correlation between the results of an initial Needlework Selection Test and performance at the end of training; and secondly, although the members of both the older groups were equally efficient needlewomen, the standards of performance they attained differed very significantly between the two training methods.

It was clear from observation and from discussion with the trainees that the main training problem, especially for the older people, was to enable trainees to perceive the weaves. All six trainees in the older experimental group agreed that the most helpful form of instruction was the initial practice on large-scale weave structures. From these large weaves they were well able to understand the visual task of where to insert their needle when either a warp or a weft thread was missing. When they were then given the smaller weaves transfer from one task to another was comparatively easy. On the other hand, the older group trained by the exposure method were quite at a loss to 'understand' where to insert their needles either when commencing the simplest 1×1 or 2×2 plain weaves or at any time during attempts to mend a twill. As one of these trainees expressed it '... the difficulty is in following the trainer's instructions of picking up "one up and one down"', when 'up' and 'down' are indistinguishable and unmeaningful. A correct result is obtained purely by accident, or as a result of a rhythmic movement of the wrist after being started off by the trainer at the correct place. The rhythmic movement would, of course, be useful only as long as the sizes of the threads were of even thickness: which is not often the case. This particular trainee, together with one other, was still unable to commence a twill weave for herself after 20 hours of training and practice.

At no time during the experimental training were the trainees given a task which was perceptually difficult. This ensured two advantages. Firstly, they did not encounter the phenomenon – so apparent from general training experience and from the comments of the older trainees by the exposure method – of stitches 'disappearing as you look at them'. Secondly, the experimental trainee had complete understanding of the mending to be done. The exposure group trainees, however, very soon lost confidence through lack of understanding. Their main concern seemed to be not so much their inability to mend correctly, but their inability to understand why it was incorrect. One trainee by this method at the end of the 20 hours was still unable to discuss whether her mending was correct or not.

It was noted that in the training of the younger menders magnifying lenses were somewhat unpopular, especially after the early stages of learning. The older group, on the contrary, appreciated them highly. It was agreed that they were an essential component of learning the perceptual skill but that after about 20 hours' practice with them on weaves which were fully understood, trainees became able to find the correct place for stitching with the naked eye and to maintain the effort for at least 6 in of a mend without undue strain or confusion of pattern.

The comment of the women conducting the training by the

exposure method about the work of the trainee quoted earlier was '. . . you're learning it by what we call the hard way'. They were unable, however, to overcome the trainee's difficulties of understanding the twill by their continued demonstration and description and used the familiar phrase of encouragement '. . . it will come with experience'. The difficulties of learning to mend by descriptive and verbal methods were very apparent from the comments and performances of all the exposure group trainees. In the face of severe perceptual difficulties, verbal description often served only as a further source of confusion. It was clear that much time was wasted in the use of terminology not understood and not remembered by the trainees. All the six women trained by the exposure method said they found the instructresses difficult to follow: as is so often the case with experienced operatives they were found to be describing something completely familiar to themselves but which was not discernible to the beginner. With the training devices used by the experimental method, this difficulty was overcome: neither description nor technical terms were used.

5. The General Problem of Suitable Training Methods for Older People

The results of our three experiments suggest that older people, if taught by an appropriate method, are able to accomplish a task much more easily that they would otherwise. In each experiment we minimized the need for conscious memorization and, by so doing, several of the difficulties inherent in many of the current methods of training were overcome. A number of these difficulties have been summarized previously (Belbin, 1955); while they may affect all trainees to a certain extent, many of them are proportionately greater for old than for young. Firstly, for example, it has been shown that older people find difficulty in translating data from one medium to another (Szafran, 1953, 1955). The burden of translation from the verbal rules to motor skill was avoided in all our experimental methods of training. Secondly, the older person may be unable to perform a task because he finds proportionately greater difficulty in understanding instructions. Our experimental methods ensured that at all times the task to be performed – and to be learned while being performed – was never difficult enough to prevent comprehension or accurate performance. Thus, thirdly, errors were prevented during the early stages of training and did not have to be 'unlearnt' later, a process which has been shown to be comparatively difficult for the older person (Kay, 1951). In addition, by performing accurately in the early stages, the trainees were prevented from losing confidence in the job, a factor which often prevents successful learning by older people.

Not only were the older people able to learn an industrial task reasonably well by this 'activity' type of method, but their performance compared very favourably with that of younger trainees. The comparison of this method with other methods in our former experiments with young trainees (Belbin *et al.*, 1956, 1957) showed that it yielded somewhat better results than the traditional method, which makes considerable demands on memorization. It seems that the preference for 'activity' learning, while of some importance among younger people, assumes a more enhanced role with increasing age.

This type of learning may, however, not be characteristic of all older people. In our experiments the subjects have been drawn from 'non-academic' groups, school leavers from secondary modern schools and subjects who had ceased all formal learning since leaving school. There is evidence from previous experiments (Belbin, 1956) to suggest that a difference exists between the preferred methods of learning by different people in the same age group: while University students showed preference for, and were superior to, artisan subjects in learning by memorizing, the artisan subjects did comparatively well in learning to *use* information. Further, in some pilot experiments conducted before the design of the present experiments was fully developed, a number of older subjects holding academic posts showed learning responses markedly at variance with those previously encountered in other older persons. They tried to superimpose conscious memorization on the activity method of learning and in consequence found our 'activity' learning task much more difficult than learning by memorizing.

Further work is clearly needed to establish the preferred methods of learning among older people in different walks of life.

We may, however, tentatively advance the theory that learning is best accomplished when the method of teaching is appropriate to the learning activity which the individual has maintained over the years. If this is so, problems of whether training should be in part or in whole, with the aid of written or verbal instructions, with or without incentive, by memorizing or by activity, cannot be answered without reference to the previous experience of the individuals to be trained.

In relation to our present experiments, this type of experiential theory would imply that learning by memorizing is a skill that can itself be learned and maintained by continued exercise, and that the difficulties of memorization by certain older people are due to the skill having fallen into disuse. Where groups, such as older workers, mentally deficient persons or retarded children, have difficulty in learning particular tasks, we may find that it is not that a specific skill cannot be acquired at all, but rather that it could be learnt only if we found methods of teaching based on the previous learning experience of the people concerned. Individual differences in learning ability have not only received very little attention in research on industrial training, but have fallen completely outside the scope of psychological learning theory. It seems likely that while these differences are marked and assume considerable practical importance with regard to the training of older people, they are to be found, at least to some extent, during the years of early maturity. We believe that the evidence gives ground for the belief that this differentiation of preferred learning method should not only assume an important place in the study of ageing, but requires that learning theory and teaching methods should be recast in order to take it into account in the normal teaching of juveniles and adults.

References
BELBIN, E. (1955), 'The problems of industrial training', *Brit. manag. Rev.*, vol. 13, pp. 165–73.
BELBIN, E. (1956), 'The effects of propaganda on recall, recognition and behaviour: II', *Brit. J. Psychol.*, vol. 47, pp. 259–70.
BELBIN, E., BELBIN, R. M., and HILL, F. (1957), 'The comparison between the results of three methods of operator training', *Ergonomics*, vol. 1, pp. 39–50.
BELBIN, E., HILL, F., and BELBIN, R. M. (1956), 'The Bradford training experiment', *Time mot. Study*, vol. 5, pp. 40–45.

KAY, H. (1951), 'Learning of a special task by different age groups', *Quart. J. exp. Psychol.*, vol. 3, pp. 166–83.

MCGEOCH, J. A., and IRION, A. L. (1952), *The Psychology of Human Learning*, Longmans.

SPEAKMAN, D. (1954), 'The effect of age on the incidental learning of stamp values', *J. Geront.*, vol. 9, pp. 162–7.

SZAFRAN, J. (1953), Some experiments on motor performance in relation to ageing, *Unpublished Ph.D. thesis, Cambridge University*.

SZAFRAN, J. (1955), 'Experiments on the greater use of vision by older adults', in *Old Age in the Modern World*, Livingstone.

Part Six **Ageing**

The ages between 40 and 60 are as well represented in the working population as the ages from 20 to 40. It is therefore important to establish what changes in human performance take place as ageing proceeds, what consequent difficulties arise for older workers and what changes in task organization and equipment design become necessary as a result.

The review by Welford (Reading 19) sets out the experimental evidence on the slowing of action and decision, the limitation on short-term memory and the drawbacks and advantages of accumulated experience. The investigations reported by Murrell (Reading 20) confirm that the effects predicted by laboratory experimentation are in fact to be observed in various industrial settings.

19 A. T. Welford

On Changes of Performance with Age

A. T. Welford, 'On changes of performance with age', *Lancet*, part 1 (1962), pp. 335–9.

My purpose here is to outline some of the main behavioural changes that have been shown by research to come with age, to examine such explanations as can be offered for them and to consider their implications for practical situations. It must at once be said that research findings confirm popular beliefs about old age but with important qualifications, so that common knowledge alone is an unreliable guide to practical action.

Speed, Accuracy and Sensitivity

One of the most striking age changes is the slowing of sensori-motor activities. The trend is very clear over a wide range of tasks, although individuals vary greatly and there are some in their 60s and 70s who perform as fast as the average man in his 20s.

In the laboratory this slowing has sometimes been attributed to *unfamiliarity* of experimental tasks placing older people at a disadvantage which could be overcome with practice, or to *unwillingness* on the part of older people to take the tasks seriously. Alternatively it has been attributed to *caution born of experience* leading to emphasis on accuracy rather than speed. The evidence is clear, however, that in some cases, and probably in most, none of these explanations is adequate (Clay, 1957; Welford, 1958).

We seem forced, therefore, to regard slowing with age as due to some loss of *capacity*, and a considerable research effort has gone into the attempt to locate it within the chain of mechanisms leading from sense organs to responding members.

Until about 15 years ago the burden of proof was felt to lie upon those who maintained that the whole of this slowing – and many other age changes besides – could not be accounted for, directly or indirectly, by changes in the structure and function of the sense organs and muscular apparatus. The attitude is understandable in that our peripheral organs seem somehow to be less *ourselves* than the central mechanisms of the brain, and their impairment is less charged with emotion. Peripheral changes certainly limit some performances by older people, and, even if they do not make an activity impossible, they may have subtle indirect effects upon willingness to engage in it.

An elegant demonstration that slowing occurs which is not due to effector factors or to the sensory changes measured by ordinary clinical tests cam from the results of experiments by Weston (1949). These showed a substantial and progressive fall between 20 and 45 in the speed of cancelling, on a sheet of Landolt rings, those having the break in a given direction. The fall occurred even though subjects had been equated for visual acuity by means of Snellen charts and Jaeger test types, and the time required to make the actions of cancelling had been deducted.

Subsequent work analysing performance into reaction times and movement times has shown that the former change more with age than the latter (Szafran, 1951; Singleton, 1954, 1955). The only exceptions seem to be cases in which very simple reactions are made under conditions where a signal 'triggers off' a response which has been prepared beforehand (Miles, 1931; Pierson and Montoye, 1958). Even in these cases the time needed for preparation may rise with age, although this would be very difficult to prove. It seems clear, therefore, that the main changes of speed with age in sensorimotor tasks are in the central processes of perceiving signals and of selecting or 'shaping' actions in response to them. Where action becomes markedly slower with age it does so because of slowing in the central process required for its accurate control. These set limits to speed of performance which are much lower than those set by the muscles (Singleton, 1955).

Researches not connected with ageing have shown that it is fruitful to conceive of the central mechanisms as a communication channel of limited capacity, passing signals from input to output at a speed determined by the amount of information transmitted or degree of uncertainty resolved. Reaction time thus rises with the number of possible actions 'at risk' and with fineness of discrimination, and movement time rises with accuracy in relation to extent (for a review see Welford, 1960). The formulae of this 'information theory' approach fit the experimental results with remarkable precision, but in relation to age they lead to an interesting conflict of evidence. When the subject has to act upon data gathered in a quick glance, the age effect appears as the addition of a *constant* to the times for both easier and more difficult tasks. When he can observe the data for as long as he wishes, reaction times for both young and old are longer and the age effect is a *proportionate* rise of time for all degrees of difficulty. More studies are needed in this area, but the present indications are that much of the slowing with age which occurs when signals can be inspected for a long time is not due to sheer inability to react faster, but to older subjects having difficulty in accumulating data for the achievement of accuracy, or requiring more data than younger in order to attain *confidence* in their judgements (Botwinick *et al.*, 1958; Griew, 1959; Welford, 1961).

Effects of slowing

In all this there are clear indications for the placing of older people at work, and researches in industry confirm the laboratory findings. The advice generally current is that older people should be placed on 'light' work, yet in fact some of the highest proportions of older workers are in moderately heavy jobs. The reason appears to be that many so-called light operations involve pressure for speed or the need for fine visual judgement, and that these are more severe demands than moderately heavy muscular effort for people in later middle age (Barkin, 1933; Belbin, 1953, 1955; Griew and Tucker, 1958; Murrell and Tucker, 1960). This is, perhaps, understandable in view of the fact that while, on average, speed of sensorimotor performance may decline by about 50 per cent or even more from the 20s to the 60s, the corresponding fall of maximum muscular strength, when averaged over various muscle groups, is only about 25 per cent (Fisher and Birren, 1947).

The effects of slowing, whether due to age or to any other factor, are not always straightforward. In some cases they result merely in the same performance taking longer time; but, if there are some explicit or implied time-limits within which action must be completed, slowing may lead to the subject becoming 'overloaded'. In these cases he may attempt to 'shed load' by, for example, ignoring some signals or omitting some actions – he does what he can in the time and abandons what he cannot. Alternatively he may sacrifice accuracy for speed, so that, although he attempts to do everything required, it is hurried and ineffective, while he himself becomes harassed and overactive. Perhaps most interestingly, he may attempt to *simplify* the decisions he has to make by, for example, confining his attention to certain restricted portions of his task. This tendency has been shown to increase with age in some industrial work (Griew and Tucker, 1958), and it is perhaps plausible to suggest that some of the narrowing of interests and restriction of activities seen in old age are due to attempts, either deliberate or more likely unconscious, to shed load in this kind of way.

Causes of slowing

It seems obvious to connect slowing in older people with the loss of active cells and changes in those that remain in the brain, and with other neurophysiological changes such as slowing of electro-encephalogram alpha-rhythm, lower states of arousal and longer synaptic delays (for reviews see Bondareff, 1959; Magladery, 1959). Slowing could derive directly from such changes taken together with the well-known fact that cells integrate impulses impinging on them over a brief period: the combined result would be that the brain was less generally active and so the train of impulses needed to fire any given cell would lengthen.

A different approach, linking age effects to a type of theory popular at present in sensory studies has been suggested by Crossman and Szafran (1956) and by Gregory (1959). The trains of nerve impulses which convey signals occur against a background of random, ambient neural activity ('neural noise') in the nerve pathways and brain. A signal represents a rise of activity above this ambient level. Since, however, the level fluctuates, the signal must be 'sampled' for an appreciable time if it is to be distinguished reliably from the background 'noise', and the length of sample needed will depend on the signal-to-noise ratio, becoming longer as the signal becomes weaker or as the 'noise' increases. This principle would hold not only for the receipt of signals from outside but also for the passing of signals from stage to stage in the brain.

The two types of approach are really complementary. Reduction of brain activity would inevitably lower the signal level, just as would any reduction of sensory sensitivity. Increase in the ambient noise level with age might arise from several causes: a general lowering of activity could go with heightened activity of certain specific kinds such as those which in some patients produce persistent tinnitus; noise could arise in the statistical sense that loss of active cells would mean less smoothing of random activity; Mundy-Castle (1960) has produced evidence that general activation of the brain, once started, tends to subside more slowly in older people, so that after-effects of past stimulation would behave as 'noise' for signals which came later (see also a stimulating paper by Axelrod, 1960). Again, a likely compensatory reaction to lowered responsiveness of the brain would be a rise in the general ambient level of activity: this would restore sensitivity, although at the same time tend to make the brain 'noisy'. It should be noted in passing that such increased ambient activity would reduce the tolerable range of additional stimulation by agents such as amphetamine drugs since these would be liable to drive the system into overactivity.

The fact that some attempts to relate functional losses to neural changes found postmortem have been disappointing is not a crucial argument against a fundamental dependence of the one on the other. If, as we seem to be, we are dealing with a system the operation of which is limited at any time by only one of many sensory, central and motor functions, quite profound changes in parts of the mechanism not normally stressed to their full capacity would have little or no effect on the performance of most tasks. Further it must be remembered that neither clinical psychological tests nor neurology are sufficiently refined at present for any really detailed tie-up to be made between them: indeed such a tie-up might well be impossible to achieve directly because the interference with the organism necessary for making the neurological observations would profoundly affect its performance.

Meanwhile the type of theory which has been outlined here, although neurologically crude, has considerable heuristic value in bringing together a substantial number of facts in the field of ageing and linking them on the one hand to studies in other areas of psychology and on the other to studies of ageing in other disciplines.

Short-Term Retention

Next to slowing, the most widely recognized change of performance with age is probably in short-term memory.

Surprisingly, the test which might be expected to yield the most clear-cut indication of this kind of change – namely, the number of digits which can be repeated back immediately ('digit span') – is little affected (e.g. Gilbert, 1941). The fall with age in the amount recalled is much more severe if some other activity intervenes during the period of retention (Cameron, 1943; Kirchner, 1958). Hebb (1949) and Young (1951) have postulated that short-term memory is carried by self re-exciting neural circuits. These would presumably keep going for a time but would eventually tend to run down or be broken up by 'neural noise'. If so, the age effects are understandable on the theories which have been outlined to account for slowness. Age changes in the brain would mean that the short-term memory traces were weaker in older people. They would still carry data reasonably well so long as they were not interfered with, but would be very vulnerable to effects spreading from other brain activities.

Researches on young subjects have found that overt rehearsal of material to be retained reduces the effect of subsequent interference (Sanders, 1961), and there is some evidence that even a single overt rehearsal is effective in reducing the disadvantage for older people (Speakman, see Welford, 1958): if so, there is an obvious and simple method by which their difficulties can be mitigated.

Effects of short-term memory loss

Short-term memory seems to be a factor in a great many different types of performance, and any impairment of it is therefore likely to have widespread repercussions. It must obviously underlie the piecing together of data arriving at different points of time, and extreme cases of breakdown would lead to the loss of orientation in space and time often observed in senility. Birren and Morrison (1961) have suggested that it is implicated in 'decoding' tasks such as digit-symbol substitution in the Wechsler Adult Intelligence Scale. There is also considerable experimental evidence (Bernardelli, see Welford, 1958; Jerome, 1960; and especially Clay, 1954, 1957) that it is an important factor limiting certain types of problem solving with age: in problem tasks of the type where one part-solution has to be worked out and then 'held' while a second part-solution is found, older subjects tend to forget the first while searching for the second.

It does not seem too far-fetched to regard short-term retention as the key factor limiting certain types of abstraction in older people, especially the 'manipulation of data in the abstract' required for many so-called intelligence tests. In, for example, the type where designs have to be completed by selecting from among a number of possible completing pieces, it is necessary to hold the incomplete design 'in mind' while examining the pieces, and often similarly to hold the pieces in mind while they are 'mentally' turned round or over.

The fragility of short-term retention in both young and old has been recognized as a reason for trying to build memory devices into industrial and other machinery so as to relieve the operator of the need to carry data in his head. Careful attention to routines of work, and indeed to many daily activities, would seem likely to suggest ways in which the need for short-term retention could be reduced by self-reminding devices, systematic writing of notes, and so on. These would be of substantial benefit to people of all ages but especially to the older.

Short-term memory and the programming of action

A further age change which appears to result from loss of short-term retention, although perhaps of a different kind, is connected with complications in the relation between what is perceived and the action taken in response. A simple laboratory example is the difficulty shown by older people when carrying out actions observed in a mirror – the mirror destroys the directness of the relationship between perception and action (Szafran, see Welford, 1958).

It used to be thought that this kind of effect was due to older subjects not being familiar with what one might term the 'rule of translation' from perception to action. Such an explanation seems, however, to be inadequate: older subjects understand the 'rules', but do not apply them quickly and accurately in complex conditions. The errors they make can often be interpreted as attempts, probably unconscious, to reduce the task to one in which relations between perception and action are simpler. Their difficulty seems to be one of storage akin to that of short-term memory, although in this case it is not of detailed data coming from outside but of 'rules' or 'constants' to apply to such data when these have been received.

The basic cause of the difficulty is not known for certain, but it is tempting to note that performance has been shown to fall disproportionately with age as complexity is increased (Kay, 1954, 1955) and that the pattern of results is essentially the same as in Lashley's (1929) classical experiments on the joint effects of complexity of task and brain ablation, with 'age' substituted for 'amount of brain tissue removed'. The temptation is the greater in view of the finding (see Bondareff, 1959) that atrophy of the brain in senile conditions is characteristically greatest in the frontal lobes – that is in an area which seems likely to be specially concerned with the 'programming' of performance. If such a view is correct, these effects of complexity are, perhaps, another facet of the inability to restrain or defer action, which is sometimes marked in old age.

Whatever their cause, the disproportionate effects of complexity suggest a reason why industrial studies have found that older people tend to be doing less skilled production jobs than younger, and are under-represented on jobs demanding high degrees of accuracy or the following of elaborate instructions (Murrell *et al.*, 1957; Murrell and Tucker, 1960). At the same time, the finding that adding two sources of difficulty together has a disproportionately adverse effect on the performance of older people, implies that the removal of one of several sources of difficulty from a task could be disproportionately beneficial.

Perception and the Searching of Memory

Long-term memory seems normally to be well preserved in old age, but there may be difficulty in recovering memories when they are required, and consequent trouble in recognizing objects. Several experiments have shown that, if older people are given pictures to identify under difficult conditions, they tend to confine their identifications to a narrow class until forced to seek more widely (Verville and Cameron, 1946; Wallace, 1956). Older sub-jects seem to find it relatively easy to search within a major class of objects, but difficult to shift from one major class to another (O'Doherty, see Welford, 1958). Similar indications come from non-visual tasks: for example, Birren (1955), who told subjects to write down in two minutes all the words they could think of in a given category, found the number declined less with age in rela-tively narrow categories than in wider ones.

Three other possible effects of difficulty in perceptual search deserve mention:

1. It could in part account for the poorer performance of older subjects at the multiple-classification tasks used in some clinical batteries (Bromley, 1956, 1957), although difficulty in abstracting features of the material as a basis for classification would also play a part.

2. There is a striking increase with age – amounting sometimes to twenty-fold or more – in the time for which unfamiliar objects need to be viewed in order to be identified (Wallace, 1956). Such very large age effects point to an area in which the benefits of careful design of jobs to be done by older people may be especially great.

3. The inability of older people to get away from immediate associa-tions could account for their difficulty, shown by several experiments, in keeping 'wanted' data apart from irrelevant material presented at the same time (e.g. Axelrod and Cohen, 1961; Clay, 1956; Crook *et al.*, 1958). This principle could also account for the over-determination of older people by 'set' in some problem tasks (e.g. Heglin, 1956).

Although perceptual identification has been studied for many years, theory is surprisingly undeveloped and it is thus difficult to discuss causes of this type of age change. A possible lead is con-tained, however, in the lengthening of neural after-effects with age noted by Mundy-Castle (1953, 1960). These would tend to lower thresholds in the areas concerned and so favour the con-tinuation of existing activity. They could thus well make it diffi-cult to switch searching from one area of material stored in memory to another.

The Increase and Ordering of Knowledge

Over against the age changes surveyed so far must be set the effects of experience. The increase of factual knowledge with age

347

is shown in the rise of 'information' scores in such tests as the Wechsler Adult Intelligence Scale and in the tendency for scores on vocabulary tests to improve (e.g. Birren and Morrison, 1961; Foulds and Raven, 1948).

Increased experience may, however, not be an unmixed blessing. Although the probability of knowing how to deal with any situation which may occur will rise with age, the very range of data held in memory may make the finding of an appropriate response more difficult, and the fact that 'new' and challenging situations became rarer may lead to emotional 'flatness'. Also, although the range of things which *can* be done is extended by experience, prejudices due to over-generalization from unpleasant events can greatly reduce the range of things *likely* to be done.

Probably the most important and beneficial effects of experience lie not in the widening of factual knowledge, but in its coordination and ordering and in the building up of manipulative, occupational, mental and social skills. An important part of this process seems to consist of recognizing ways in which groups of objects and sequences of events hang together, and of forming routines of action. Events of both perception and action are thereby 'coded' into larger units, and, by dealing with the codes as unitary wholes instead of with the individual details summed up in them, the 'mental load' upon the subject is lightened.

The effects of such coding upon the performance of older people have not received the research attention they deserve, but it is reasonable to suppose that coding can often largely offset slowing and other factors militating against achievement. It will do so at the risk of some loss of flexibility, since the coded perception and action will not be precisely adapted to the subtleties of a changing environment. Some of the 'rigidity' observed in older people is probably due to the overuse of such standardized patterns of thought and action. The potential net gain is, however, very large, because without coding the amount of data that can be handled in thinking is severely limited and the highest orders of conceptual thought therefore impossible.

Optimum performance will depend on a balance between various types of 'mental agility' on the one hand, and ordered knowledge on the other. Since different tasks vary in their stress upon these two factors, and since the one falls with age while the other rises, it follows that the optimum age for performance must vary from one task to another. It is now well recognized, especially following the work of Lehman (1953), that the age of peak performance does differ in different activities. It follows also that the optimum role for any individual will change as he progresses through the adult years.

Learning

Ability to learn does not appear to decline with age nearly as much as is commonly supposed. Although some laboratory experiments (Kay, 1951; Ruch, 1934) and studies of industrial training (Shooter *et al.*, 1956) indicate that older people have difficulty in learning, other studies show that they learn some things well and quickly and are able to use more of what they have learnt than they can reproduce in words (Belbin, 1956). The main causes of poor performance in industrial training seem to be, firstly, slowness in *comprehension*, which causes essential points to be missed in lectures and demonstrations. Secondly, there may be attempts to teach too much at once and thus overloading of the *short-term memory*, which bridges the few seconds or minutes which must elapse between perception and 'registration' by some kind of submicroscopic change of structure in the brain. Thirdly, wrong impressions once formed seem relatively difficult for older people to modify. Those who set out to master new material for themselves in middle and old age often add the further difficulty that they try to learn too fast – much faster than they would have done when they were young. Belbin (1958) has shown clearly that older people learn much more easily, and may learn as well as or even better than younger, provided their training pays due attention to these points.

All this implies that the development of special training methods for older people is likely to be rewarding, or perhaps, as in industrial work generally, that methods which are optimum are likely to be of greater proportional benefit to older people than to younger.

'Models' of the Ageing Process in Performance

The over-all view that emerges from research on performance in relation to age is of an organism becoming less sensitive and mentally 'agile' but more 'patterned', less active but in some ways more efficient, optimizing the use of its abilities in meeting environmental demands and attempting to manipulate the environment to avoid excessive demands. It works with less margin of reserve as the years pass, but over a wide range of activities it continues to work well.

Research on capacity and performance in relation to age has now attained a considerable sophistication. It has gone beyond the stage of exploratory fact-finding to the building and testing of theories, and current work is attempting to get away from the study of individual tasks to the examination of the inter-relations between changes of performance in a range of tasks. Whether such researches lead to a clearer understanding of the basic functional changes with age or to years of confusion depends very much upon the 'model' of the human organism used to guide and interpret them. The model traditionally used in psychology is of a total capacity made up of many contributory factors which are additive in the sense that any one performance, while it may depend more on one factor than on others, is linearly related to several at once. Some justification for this type of model comes, at first sight, from studies which have correlated performances at different tasks and suggest that certain classes of age change tend to go together (e.g. Birren and Botwinick, 1951; Césa-Bianchi, 1955; Goldfarb, 1941; Pacaud, 1960). On the whole, however, the *absence* of correlation is more striking than its presence: variety seems more prominent than unity in the changes that come with age.

The alternative model postulates that, although several factors operate, only one limits performance at any particular time. The contrast between the two models is well illustrated in their approaches to the assessment of the potentialities of older people. People obviously age at different rates and chronological age is clearly an imperfect indicator of functional capacity. The traditional model attempts to devise a unitary index of functional or psychological 'age' by combining together a number of different criteria, and grades individuals for all purposes in terms of their 'score' on this index.

The alternative model recognizes that different functions 'age' at different rates so that any one individual, although he may be 'old' for one job or activity, may yet be 'young' for another. It leads to attempts to analyse both capacities and the demands of tasks in a set of terms common to both, and to match individuals and tasks together in detail. I venture to suggest that such a procedure, in spite of being somewhat difficult to grasp conceptually and to handle experimentally, not only fits the facts better but is in the long run more likely to appeal to the clinician.

References

AXELROD, S. (1960), *International Research Seminar on Social and Psychological Aspects of Aging*, Berkeley, California.

AXELROD, S., and COHEN, L. D. (1961), *Percept. mot. Skills*, vol. 12, p. 283.

BARKIN, S. (1933), The older worker in industry, *New York Legislative State Document*, no. 60, Albany, N.Y.

BELBIN, E. (1956), *Brit. J. Psychol.*, vol. 47, p. 259.

BELBIN, E. (1958), *Ergonomics*, vol. 1, p. 207.

BELBIN, R. M. (1953), *Occup. Psychol.*, vol. 27, p. 177.

BELBIN, R. M. (1955), *Brit. J. industr. Med.*, vol. 12, p. 309.

BIRREN, J. E. (1955), in *Old Age in the Modern World*, p. 235, Edinburgh.

BIRREN, J. E., and BOTWINICK, J. (1951), *Psychometrika*, vol. 2, p. 219.

BIRREN, J. E., and MORRISON, D. F. (1961), *J. Gerontol.*, vol. 16, p. 363.

BONDAREFF, W. (1959), in J. E. Birren (ed.), *Handbook of Aging and the Individual*, ch. 5, Chicago.

BOTWINICK, J., BRINLEY, J. F., and ROBBIN, J. S. (1958), *Gerontologia*, vol. 2, p. 1.

BROMLEY, D. B. (1956), *J. Gerontol.*, vol. 11, p. 74.

BROMLEY, D. B. (1957), *J. Gerontol.*, vol. 12, p. 318.

CAMERON, D. E. (1943), *Psychiat. Quart.*, vol. 17, p. 395.

CÉSA-BIANCHI, M. (1955), *Publ. dell' Univ. Catholica del Sacro Cuore*, Milan, vol. 49, p. 1.

CLAY, H. M. (1954), *Brit. J. Psychol.*, vol. 45, p. 7.

CLAY, H. M. (1956), *J. Gerontol.*, vol. 11, p. 318.

CLAY, H. M. (1957), *Gerontologia*, vol. 1, p. 41.

CROOK, M. N., ALEXANDER, E. A., ANDERSON, E. M. S., COULES, J., HANSON, J. A., and JEFFRIES, N. T. (1958), *School of Aviation Medicine, Randolph A.F.B. Report*, no. 57-124, Texas.

CROSSMAN, E. R. F. W., and SZAFRAN, J. (1956), *Experientia Supplementum*, vol. 4, 128.

FISHER, M. B., and BIRREN, J. E. (1947), *J. appl. Psychol.*, vol. 31, p. 490.

FOULDS, G. A., and RAVEN, J. C. (1948), *J. ment. Sci.*, vol. 94, p. 133.

GILBERT, J. C. (1941), *J. abnorm. soc. Psychol.*, vol. 36, p. 73.

GOLDFARB, W. (1941), *Teachers' College Contributions to Education*, no. 831, Columbia University.

GREGORY, R. L. (1959), *Proceedings of 4th Congress of International Association of Gerontology*, Merano, 1957, vol. 1, p. 314.

GRIEW, S. (1959), *Gerontologia*, vol. 3, p. 335.

GRIEW, S., and TUCKER, W. A. (1958), *J. appl. Psychol.*, vol. 42, p. 278.

HEBB, D. O. (1949), *The Organization of Behavior*, New York.

HEGLIN, H. J. (1956), *J. Gerontol.*, vol. 11, p. 310.

JEROME, E. A. (1960), *International Research Seminar on Social and Psychological Aspects of Aging*, Berkeley, California.

KAY, H. (1951), *Quart. J. exp. Psychol.*, vol. 3, p. 166.

KAY, H. (1954), *Quart. J. exp. Psychol.*, vol. 6, p. 155.

KAY, H. (1955), in *Old Age in the Modern World*, p. 259, Edinburgh.

KIRCHNER, W. K. (1958), *J. exp. Psychol.*, vol. 55, p. 352.

LASHLEY, K. S. (1929), *Brain Mechanisms and Intelligence*, Chicago.

LEHMAN, H. C. (1953), *Age and Achievement*, Princeton.

MAGLADERY, J. W. (1959), in J. E. Birren (ed.), *Handbook of Aging and the Individual*, ch. 6, Chicago.

MILES, W. R. (1931), *Proc. nat. Acad. Sci.*, vol. 17, p. 627.

MUNDY-CASTLE, A. C. (1953), *EEG clin. Neurophysiol.*, vol. 5, p. 1.

MUNDY-CASTLE, A. C. (1960), *Proceedings of 5th Congress of International Association of Gerontology*, San Francisco.

MURRELL, K. F. H., GRIEW, S., and TUCKER, W. A. (1957), *Occupational Psychol.*, vol. 31, p. 150.

MURRELL, K. F. H., and TUCKER, W. A. (1960), *Ergonomics*, vol. 3, p. 74.

PACAUD, S. (1960), *Proceedings of 5th Congress of International Association of Gerontology*, San Francisco.

PIERSON, W. R., and MONTOYE, H. J. (1958), *J. Gerontol.*, vol. 13, p. 418.

RUCH, F. L. (1934), *J. gen. Psychol.*, vol. 11, p. 261.

SANDERS, A. F. (1961), *Ergonomics*, vol. 4, p. 25.

SHOOTER, A. M. N., SCHONFIELD, A. E. D., KING, H. F., and WELFORD, A. T. (1956), *Occup. Psychol.*, vol. 30, 204.

SINGLETON, W. T. (1954), *Brit. J. Psychol.*, vol. 45, p. 166.

SINGLETON, W. T. (1955), in *Old Age in the Modern World*, p. 221, Edinburgh.

SZAFRAN, J. (1951), *Quart. J. exp. Psychol.*, vol. 3, p. 111.

VERVILLE, E., and CAMERON, N. (1946), *J. genet. Psychol.*, vol. 68, p. 149.

WALLACE, J. G. (1956), *Brit. J. Psychol.*, vol. 47, p. 283.

WELFORD, A. T. (1958), *Ageing and Human Skill*, London.

WELFORD, A. T. (1960), *Ergonomics*, vol. 3, p. 189.

WELFORD, A. T. (1961), *Gerontologia*, vol. 5, p. 129.

WESTON, H. C. (1949), *Trans. illum. Eng. Soc.*, vol. 14, p. 281.

YOUNG, J. Z. (1951), *Proc. Roy. Soc. (B)*, vol. 139, p. 18.

20 K. F. H. Murrell

Industrial Aspects of Ageing

K. F. H. Murrell, 'Industrial aspects of ageing', *Ergonomics*,
vol. 5 (1962), pp. 147–53.

A great deal has been written about the changes which take place
in physical and mental capacity as age advances. That these
changes must influence men in employment might seem to be inevitable, but most industrialists seem to be so little aware of any
effect that they will deny that ageing is of any practical significance
– and it must be admitted that at present there is very little real
evidence to support the contrary view. Murrell (1959) in a paper
dealing with industrial gerontology outlined a number of different areas in which age ought to be considered; these included
job changes, bonus schemes, promotion, training, re-employment
prospects and work design. From this quite large field it would
seem that ergonomists should be mainly, if not entirely, interested
in the last aspect of the subject, that is in the effect of machine
design and work organization on an individual's ability to maintain optimum performance as he gets older. It is quite clear, from
the research which has been done in the laboratory, that there is a
decrement of the faculties with age and if this is to be taken beyond the laboratory stage, it is necessary to understand more
clearly the extent to which these changes may be determining
factors in the different areas which have already been outlined. It
will be agreed that it is not unlikely that the effects of age on a
particular industry will depend to some extent on the nature of
that industry, on the nature of the jobs in that industry and on
whether an industry is expanding or contracting. Thus it seems
likely that there is evidence of different age effects in different
types of industries, such as manufacturing, oil and chemicals,
distribution, agriculture, transport, catering and so on. Of these
only transport seems to have received any very great attention and
that from Ross McFarland (1951, 1954).

To anyone who is interested in industrial gerontology, the natural line of approach would seem to be to start from the admitted decrement in the faculties and to see how this may affect men at their work. Outside the transport industry, there is relatively little which has been done to extend our knowledge of ageing beyond the confines of the laboratory – confirming field work is deplorably absent. It seems that gerontologists are just not interested in the industrial field. In the 900 pages of the recently published *Handbook of Aging and the Individual*, Birren (1959), perhaps rather less than ten pages are devoted to studies of manufacturing industry. It might be thought that this lack of interest is an indication that there is no problem or that, if there is, it is unimportant. This I do not believe and I hope to show industrial gerontology to be a field of valuable and rewarding investigation.

Another difficulty in dealing with the ergonomics of ageing is that, even in the laboratory, most of the studies of an applied experimental nature which form the foundations of ergonomic practice have been carried out on young subjects. A great deal is known therefore about the performance, for instance, of university students, but relatively little is known about the performance and changes in performance of an industrial population.

From the results of laboratory research on ageing, two premises can be developed. First, provided that physical work is not unduly heavy, it can be tolerated up to quite an advanced age. Secondly, heavy perceptual demands, especially when these are accompanied by speed, are not well tolerated by older people. On the basis of these two premises, the industrially oriented research will be reviewed to see whether it supports them or not. First, statistical investigations will be examined and then experimental and field investigations.

Of the nine million or so men between the ages of 20 and 64 who were employed in British manufacturing industry in 1958 (Anon, 1959) some $52\frac{1}{2}$ per cent were over the age of 40. Most industries do not vary by much more than $\pm$ 3 per cent from this figure; on the other hand a few industries do vary by a larger extent from this mean. For instance, of the men engaged in public administration, 64 per cent are over 40 (public administration is not one of the most stressful occupations in which a man can engage); in the textile industry 60·9 per cent are over 40 years of age and in the leather goods industry 60·7 per cent, while at the other extreme we find the building industry with only 43 per cent over 40 years of age. Both the former industries have been contracting in recent years, whereas building has been expanding rapidly; as a result, data from these industries cannot be used for our present purpose but this is not to say that they do not have special problems of their own.

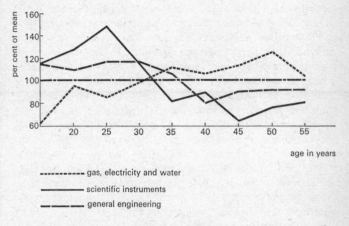

Figure 1 Age distributions of production workers in three British industries expressed as deviations from the mean of all industries

Some other industries, however, have remained relatively static over recent years and three have been selected for examination in which departures from the mean age may perhaps be taken as evidence of effects of age. These are *gas, water and electricity distribution* with 58 per cent of employees over 40 years old, *general engineering* with 48½ per cent and *precision engineering* with 44·2 per cent. The age distribution of parts of three of these industries are illustrated (Figure 1) general (non-electrical) engineering, gas, water and electricity undertakings and scientific instrument manufacture. The curves give the deficiency or excess of employees in different age groups in relation to the number employed in those age groups in manufacturing industry as a whole. It will be noticed in Figure 1 that the gas, water and electricity industry is deficient in men under the age of 40 but at the age of 55 there is a 22 per cent excess. The two engineering industries show an exactly opposite trend. In the scientific instrument industry there is a very large excess of 48 per cent of men in the 30–34 age group, falling to a deficiency of 36 per cent in the 50–54 age group. A similar, but not such a marked trend, is found in general (non-electrical) engineering. Men in the gas, water and electricity undertakings are employed very largely on outside jobs of installation and maintenance of services, jobs which are largely of a physical nature. General engineering makes higher perceptual demands than these undertakings and it would seem that the manufacture of precision scientific instruments would make even greater perceptual demands than would general engineering. On these grounds, then, we would expect to find what we do find, that the industries in which the perceptual demands are believed to be the greatest have the highest proportion of younger men and the greatest deficiency of older men and vice versa.

There are many jobs, of course, comprised in these industries and it is now proposed to have a closer look at one industry, light engineering, which has been studied in detail. It was found (Murrell and Griew, 1958; Murrell, Griew and Tucker, 1957) that purely physical jobs like labourer, packer, store-keeper, lavatory cleaner, have mean ages in the late 50s. On the other hand, the jobs which appear to make the greatest perceptual demands, such as miller, grinder, borer, honer, have mean ages well below that of industry as a whole. Griew (1958) has shown that older men on these 'young' jobs tend to have more accidents than would be predicted and it has also been found that, job for job, men in the tool room tend to be younger than men on production. Further evidence comes from Heron and Chown (1960) who, in their survey of Merseyside industry, found that there were fewer older men 'on jobs making severe demands for attention to fine detail or involving sustained care and concentration'. Belbin (1955) also found that older workers tended to be on physical jobs and so did Richardson (1953), who qualified his findings by pointing out that even while remaining on heavy work, older men tended to move to jobs which were done at a slower pace. The evidence of these statistical studies, therefore, seems to support the notion that jobs which make the greatest perceptual demands are manned by younger people.

Another statistical approach to this problem is the study of output. It is a common industrial belief that the productivity of older people will fall; there is, however, little industrial evidence of this. McFarland and O'Doherty in their chapter in the Hand-

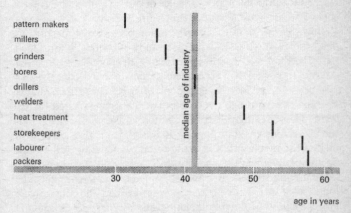

Figure 2 Median ages of representative jobs in light (non-electrical) engineering

book (Birren, 1959) quote only two studies, neither of which shows a decline, whereas Anderson quotes in his chapter another two studies both of which do show a decline. The difficulties of getting evidence from output are rather great and as Clay (1956) points out, men whose output has fallen below an acceptable level, due to age or any other cause, will be separated from their firms either voluntarily or involuntarily. This means that the output of older men who remain cannot, therefore, be much below that of their younger contemporaries. That this may be happening seems to be confirmed by the skilled jobs having been shown to be deficient in older men in the surveys referred to above. Heron and Chown (1960) report an assembly department where the bonus target was set by the informal leaders of the team. 'One or two of these would not "carry" a slowing member' they say, 'and the firm reported having to move several men each year, usually in their low middle

40s and almost always to a lower paid job.' Although highly skilled jobs may be deficient in older men, it is clear that some individuals do survive to continue to do excellent work up to and beyond retiring age. We can therefore perhaps develop our ideas further and suggest that in complex jobs experience can compensate for age up to a point in time, but when this point has been reached then the fall in performance or output will be such that a change of occupation may be deemed necessary.

Now this brings us to a consideration of the experimental and field studies. First we will discuss a study of drilling, a job which has a median age closely approaching that of the engineering industry as a whole; an experimental study of this occupation has just been completed, using groups of experienced men drawn from industry through the courtesy of the Amalgamated Engineering Union, and groups of inexperienced men drawn from university technicians and porters. It was thought that older men might be more uncertain as to the accuracy of aiming at the mark on the plate which they had to drill and might therefore make more aiming strokes. It was also thought that they might take longer to position the plate than younger men and might make longer pauses between completing one aiming movement and commencing the next. When considering the first two measurements, number of aiming strokes and time, it was found that there was little difference between younger and older experienced men, but the performance of the inexperienced older men was substantially inferior to the performance of the young, both experienced and inexperienced. A slightly puzzling finding was that the performance of the inexperienced young was better than the performance of the experienced young. This may perhaps be attributed to two factors. First, the experienced workers had been trained never to make a mistake and therefore may have taken greater care to ensure that the drill was exactly positioned (there was, however, no measurable difference in accuracy between the two groups). Secondly, it is possible that the experienced men had set themselves a norm which accorded with the speed of work acceptable to a particular industrial environment, whereas the younger inexperienced men had no such inhibitions. The time between completing one aiming movement and starting the next showed a difference between the unskilled old and young, the old pausing longer with the drill in contact with the plate. Two main conclusions can be drawn from this work. First, it does appear that the decrement of performance which is found with the inexperienced older men is compensated for by experience. Secondly, the element of the task which involves the driller in having to make up his mind at the completion of an aiming movement sequence what to do next is a perceptual element which is influenced by age, although this too is compensated by experience. Putting this in general terms, it may be said that the effect of age may show itself more clearly in decision-making elements of a task than in the movement elements, a view which is largely confirmed by laboratory studies of reaction time and related cortical functions. There is some additional industrial evidence in support. Murrell and Forsaith (1960), using data from time studies taken in a large engineering firm, found that there was no detectable difference in element times involving movement between young and old workers. Job studies carried out by Griew and Tucker (1958), Murrell and Tucker (1960) have suggested that factors in the job situation which are age-related tend to be those which make the greatest perceptual demand. These include the nature of instructions, the type of measuring instruments used, the degree of tolerance to which the work is to be carried out and the size of the detail. Physical factors such as the amount of physical activity, the load lifted and so on, are not so age-related.

If the concept of capacity, which has been developed by Welford (1958), is used, we can see that a particular job will use up a certain amount of the available capacity of an individual. If an additional stress is imposed the level of demand will be increased; the capacity of an older man may be exceeded and he will then go into a state of overload which, under certain circumstances, may have dramatic and tragic consequences. The job may still be within the capacity of a younger man if he has sufficient experience, but if he is inexperienced he may go into overload before the older man, in spite of his greater capacity. This is illustrated in Figure 3. The purpose of ergonomics in this field then should be to reduce the initial demands of a job to a level at which all foreseeable stresses will be within the capacity of men of all ages. It is quite clear that industry is not thinking in these terms at present. Heron and Chown say: 'When one turns to the idea of modifying jobs in favour of older men, we must report that not one manager in the 116 we interviewed had ever done so.'

In studying the ergonomic approach to ageing, the practice of many writers on the subject will be adopted and discussion will deal first with the task, then its immediate environment, then the general environment and finally problems of organization.

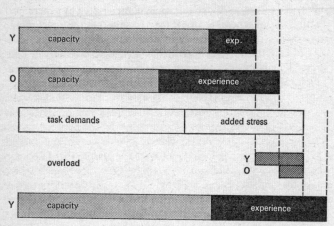

Figure 3 Both capacity and experience are needed to cope with overload on a task with a high initial demand

Almost anything which can be recommended for improving the work situation for older men will also improve the situation for younger men; nevertheless there are some aspects of work design of particular importance to older workers which should receive priority. These will be discussed briefly.

Consider first the elements in the task itself which might well be modified. One of the most important of these is the giving of information. In our job studies we found that the more complex the drawing used, the younger the operator. A study of the comprehension of engineering drawings is now being made which has turned out to be wider in scope than was anticipated. Our first idea was to grade drawings and to get men of various ages to read them, but it became obvious that some understanding of how engineers read their drawings and what conceptual factors are involved had to be reached. A second age-related factor from our job studies was the nature of the measuring instruments used. We found that older men tended to be working on machines with simpler scalar devices and greater degrees of tolerance than young men. For instance, on one type of vernier, on older machines on which older men were working, settings were made on a simple scale. We found that in another (unpublished) study that the older men tended to be left to work on older machines and it seemed likely that difficulty would be experienced with fading vision in reading scales which have become worn. Following the general finding that it is often an advantage to give numerical information in digital form (Grether 1949), an experiment was started in evaluating a micrometer which gives dimensions in this way. For some time experiments have been conducted with the indicator of machine travel designed by Gibbs (1952) which is, in effect, a 'built-in memory'. Preliminary results from this experiment seem to suggest that this device is producing an increase in output which is greater for older men than for younger. This emphasizes a very general principle which is that, wherever possible, equipment should be modified to build memory into it, since, as we have heard, this is a very fallible function in the older man. This means that limits should be marked on our instruments to avoid the necessity of the operator having to memorize values; that dimensions on our drawings should be given directly so that the operator does not have to depend on memorizing one dimension while dealing with another; that the operation of the equipment should be compatible, and so on.

Turning to the immediate environment, that is, the physical arrangement of the equipment around the operator, there is little that can be said which is specific to age. It seems likely that bad posture will affect a man as he gets older but evidence to support this view is as yet non-existent. Older turners with whom this matter has been discussed have, however, expressed themselves very strongly on their dislike of the posture which they are forced to adopt.

In the general environment, the subjects of light, heat, noise, vibration and so on have been considered. Heron and Chown (1960) in their survey found that there were far more semi-skilled men over forty in bad working conditions than young men, and it looks very much as if, when new shops are built, young men get preferential treatment. Impairment of vision, even when corrected by spectacles, may under certain circumstances make it desirable to have special lighting for older workers, e.g. Weston (1949). There is, however, laboratory evidence which suggests that an important factor in lighting is the avoidance of glare: glare which may cause discomfort to the young may cause disability in the old (Bouma 1947). Older men are less well able to work in high temperatures and humidity, and Belding and Hatch (1955) have suggested that a lower heat stress index is required for older people. The adverse effect of heat on older men as demonstrated by accidents was shown by Vernon *et al.* (1931).

It may take a number of years for hearing to be impaired in noisy environments and so obviously more older than younger people will be found to suffer from hearing defects, in addition to presbycusis; individuals with impairment in the region of 4000 c.p.s. may have an improved hearing for speech in a noisy environment. On the whole, there is very little evidence outside the laboratory of the practical effects which these environmental factors have on the older workers. A process of natural selection takes place which will make the collection of evidence very time-consuming and probably unprofitable. It is believed that changes in environment for the benefit of older men should be made as an act of faith, based on our knowledge of the ageing processes.

Finally, some organizational factors must be considered. Since the War there has been a great increase in the introduction of piece-work and bonus schemes, and the effect of these on older men must depend on the extent to which slowing-up occurs. The improbability that this slowing-up will be readily detected by means of a stop-watch has been pointed out by Murrell and Forsaith (1960). Unpublished work carried out in Bristol shows that older men dislike individual bonus and prefer group bonus schemes, whereas younger people have the opposite view. They feel that the older man would slow down and reduce the bonus of the group. Heron and Chown's view on this has already been given. If the best use of older people is to be made organizationally, then they should be put on to jobs where they can work at their own speed, rather than on jobs where they are paced, and competition with younger operators should be avoided. In discussions over productivity in a shoe factory, it was pointed out that while young girls can, at their peak, produce faster than older women, who tend to come back into the industry after they have reared their families, they seem to be more erratic in their work and so do not produce very much greater net output than the older women who work steadily at a lower pace. This is clearly an area in which a great deal more information is required.

Pearson (1957) emphasized that one of the major changes to which older men attach the greatest importance is from shift work to day work. Occupations in which job demands are related to status may cause older men to work closer to the overload limit than is desirable. For instance, on British Railways crack express trains are often driven by men in their late fifties or early sixties, because 'the plum jobs go with seniority'. These express trains are the most demanding and are being driven at an age when it would probably be better for the men to be working slower trains.

There is no doubt that industry should take greater account of the need to fit jobs to older men and women. Older workers have a great many advantages, in quality of performance, in steadiness, in reduced absence, in responsibility, and they are less likely to be involved in costly labour turnover (Heron and Chown, 1960; Murrell, Griew and Tucker, 1957; Smith, 1952). After a period of time, to be sure, the speed with which work is done may diminish, and there is no doubt that this actual physical slowing down in the late 40s and 50s is more likely to be found on jobs with a high demand on perception and transitory memory. What is most needed is a change of view on ageing in industry, and this is not likely to occur to any very great extent until there is a much greater body of field work to support the laboratory findings. When the importance of considering the older worker has been realized, intelligent use of knowledge from ergonomics and intelligent organization for ageing can go a long way towards the maximum utilization of the older part of the working population.

References

ANON (1959), 'Age and regional analysis of employees', *Min. of Lab. Gazette*, vol. 67, pp. 205–10.

BELBIN, R. M. (1955), 'Older people and heavy work', *Brit. J. ind. Med.*, vol. 12, p. 309.

BELDING, H. S., and HATCH, T. F. (1955), 'Index for evaluating heat stress in terms of physiological strains', *Heating, Pip., Air Condit.*, August, pp. 129–36.

BIRREN, J. (ed.) (1959), *Handbook of Aging and the Individual*, University of Chicago Press.

BOUMA, P. J. (1947), 'Perception on the road when visibility is low', *Philips Tech. Rev. Eindhoven*, vol. 9, pp. 149–57.

CLAY, H. M. (1956), 'A study of performance in relation to age in two printing works', *J. Gerontol.*, vol. 11, pp. 417–24.

GIBBS, C. B. (1952), 'A new indicator of Machine Tool Travel', *Occup. Psychol.*, vol. 26, p. 234.

GRETHER, W. F. (1949), 'Instrument reading. I. The design of Long Scale Indicators for speed and accuracy of quantitative readings', *J. appl. Psychol.*, vol. 33, pp. 363–72.

GRIEW, S. (1958), 'A study of accidents in relation to age and occupation', *Ergonomics*, vol. 2, pp. 17–23.

GRIEW, S., and TUCKER, W. A. (1958), 'The identification of job activities associated with age differences in the engineering industry', *J. appl. Psychol.*, vol. 42, pp. 278–82.

HERON, A., and CHOWN, S. (1960), 'Semi-skilled and over forty', *Occup. Psychol.*, vol. 34, pp. 264–74.

MCFARLAND, R. A. (1951), 'Problems relating to aircrews in air transport design', *Ann. N.Y. Acad. Sc.*, vol. 51, pp. 1146–58.

MCFARLAND, R. A. (1954), 'Age and the problems of professional truck drivers in highway transportation', *J. Gerontol.*, vol. 9, pp. 338–48.

MURRELL, K. F. H. (1959), 'Major problems of industrial gerontology', *J. Gerontol.*, vol. 14, pp. 216–21.

MURRELL, K. F. H., and FORSAITH, B. (1960), 'Age and the timing of movement', *Occup. Psychol.*, vol. 34, pp. 275–9.

MURRELL, K. F. H., and GRIEW, S. (1958), 'Age structure in the engineering industry: a study of regional effects', *Occup. Psychol.*, vol. 32, pp. 86–8.

MURRELL, K. F. H., GRIEW, S., and TUCKER, W. A. (1957), 'Age structure in the engineering industry: a preliminary study', *Occup. Psychol.*, vol. 31, pp. 150–68.

MURRELL, K. F. H., and TUCKER, W. A. (1960), 'A pilot job-study of age-related causes of difficulty in light engineering', *Ergonomics*, vol. 3, pp. 74–9.

PEARSON, M. (1957), 'The transition from work to retirement', *Occup. Psychol.*, vol. 31, p. 139.

RICHARDSON, I. M. (1953), 'Age and work: a study of 489 men in heavy industry', *Brit. J. ind. Med.*, vol. 10, pp. 269–84.

SMITH, M. W. (1952), 'Evidence of potentialities of older workers in a manufacturing company', *Personn. Psychol.*, vol. 5, pp. 11–18.

VERNON, H. M., BEDFORD, T., and WARNER, C. G. (1931), Two studies of absenteeism in coal mines, *I.H.R.B. Report 62*, H.M.S.O.

WELFORD, A. T. (1958), *Ageing and Human Skill*, Oxford University Press.

WESTON, H. C. (1949), 'On age and illumination in relation to visual performance', *Trans. III eng. Soc.*, vol. 14, pp. 281–97.

Part Seven Noise

Of all the environmental stresses which accompany industrial processes, noise is probably the most widespread. A great deal of research, not always well-conducted, has been devoted to measuring its effects. These effects, and the frequent absence of anticipated effects, have given rise to a number of theoretical problems. For these reasons and because it is impracticable to assemble a short but representative group of papers on the environmental factors like heat, lighting and anoxia, the topic of noise is chosen to the exclusion of other stresses.

The outlines of the problem are delineated by Jerison's review (Reading 21). In Reading 22 Broadbent examines the evidence in detail, concluding that only certain types of task are likely to be adversely affected by noise. Machine-paced tasks, particularly of the vigilance or monitoring kind, seem the most vulnerable. Broadbent and Little (Reading 23) are able to confirm that adverse effects do occur in an industrial task with these features.

21 H. J. Jerison

Effects of Noise on Human Performance

H. J. Jerison, 'Effects of noise on human performance', *Journal of Applied Psychology*, vol. 43 (1959), pp. 96–101.

Until about 1948, the only proper answer to a question on possible effects of noise on nonauditory performance would have been that none had been demonstrated. Kryter (1950), who reviewed the experimental evidence available then, concluded that nearly all, if not all, studies showing deleterious effects of noise could be criticized severely on the basis of faulty procedures. Since that time, Broadbent (1953, 1954) has demonstrated changes in working efficiency on tasks involving vigilance (alertness) and on a self-paced or externally paced serial reaction task provided the tasks were performed without interruption for relatively long time periods. The experiments to be described confirm Broadbent's results on vigilance and indicate additional measurable performance changes in relatively high energy noise fields.

General Procedure

In the three experiments to be reported here the general procedure was to run Ss individually through three work sessions with one-week intervals between sessions. Subjects were paid volunteer male undergraduates. After all of the Ss for a particular experiment were chosen they were assigned randomly to two subgroups. The subgroups were constituted to counterbalance order effects, and the order of undergoing various procedures is indicated in Table 1. The training session, Session I, was one hour long for Experiment I on vigilance and two hours long for Experiments II and III.

The designation 'quiet' in Table 1 refers to a noise that was used to mask the sounds of equipment. In Experiment I this was about 83 dB re 0·0002 dyne/cm², and in Experiments II and III it

Table 1

General Experimental Design

	Session I	Session II	Session III
Subgroup Q.N.	training (quiet throughout)	control (two hours quiet)	experimental ($\frac{1}{2}$ hour quiet followed by $1\frac{1}{2}$ hours noise)
Subgroup N.Q.	training (quiet throughout)	experimental ($\frac{1}{2}$ hour quiet followed by $1\frac{1}{2}$ hours noise)	control (two hours quiet)

Note.—Sessions were held at 1-week intervals.

was about 77·5 dB. The designation 'noise' refers to the high level noise which was our major concern. In Experiment I it was about 114 dB, and in Experiments II and III it was about 111·5 dB. A spectral analysis of the noise is presented in Figure 1. The noise was generated electronically and broadcast by a loudspeaker mounted in the *S*'s room.

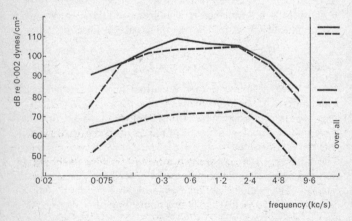

Figure 1 Octave band analyses of noise used in these experiments. Upper curves are of 'noise' in Experiment I (———) and Experiments II and III (– – –). Lower curves are of 'quiet'. Over-all sound pressures (0·02–20 kc) are shown at the right

Method and Results

Experiment I: noise and vigilance

The purpose of this experiment was to check Broadbent's previously reported results that performance on a prolonged vigilance task was poorer in noise than in quiet. The S's task was to monitor a panel of three Mackworth-type clocks (cf. Mackworth, 1950) and to press a response switch under a clock when its hand stepped through twice its usual excursion. The apparatus is illustrated

Figure 2 The display and response panels of Experiment I. Dial pointers normally stepped through 3·5 degree arcs

in Figure 2. Double steps occurred haphazardly at intervals that averaged about once a minute for each clock.

The results of this experiment are summarized in Figure 3 which gives the average percentage correct for the nine Ss of this experiment during their experimental and control sessions. It should be noted that average performance during these two sessions when noise levels were the same, that is, during the first half hour, was about 10 per cent better during the control session. The difference between the sessions during the second and third half hours when the 114 dB noise was present for the experimental session should, therefore, not be attributed to an effect of noise. The parallel orientation of the two curves during the first $1\frac{1}{2}$ hours indicates

371

that noise had essentially no effect on performance at that time. During the fourth half hour the two curves diverge considerably suggesting that noise may depress performance only after a fairly considerable period of time.

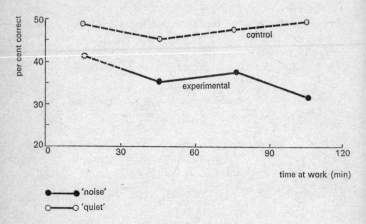

Figure 3 Average performance of the nine Ss in Experiment I during successive half hours of the experimental and control sessions

An analysis of variance of the data of this experiment is presented in Table 2. The difference between average performance during the experimental and control sessions was not statistically significant ($0.20 > P > 0.10$). The difference between rate of change of performance for the two sessions (the sessions by time at work interaction) was significant at the 0.05 level. This supports the impression one gets from viewing Figure 3 that the differentiation of performance in the fourth half hour is a 'true' effect. A more detailed report of this experiment has been prepared for limited circulation (Jerison and Wing, 1957).

Before going on to the next experiments it is of some interest to note that vigilance as measured here did not become less adequate as a result of fatigue alone. This result, the absence of a performance decrement during the 2-hour control session in quiet, is contrary to that reported by Mackworth (1950) for a simpler vigilance task. No explanation for this discrepancy will be

Table 2
Analysis of Variance for Experiment I

Source	df	Mean square	F
Subjects (S)	8	6544·90	
Experimental conditions (E)	1	8490·08	2·93
E × S	8	2900·09	
Clocks (C)	2	489·31	1·24
C × S	16	396·08	
Time at work (T)	3	479·67	6·32**
T × S	24	75·89	
E × C	2	280·52	1·18
E × C × S	16	238·36	
E × T	3	600·47	3·48*
E × T × S	24	172·60	
C × T	6	138·63	1·32
C × T × S	48	105·09	
E × C × T	6	253·10	2·07
E × C × T × S	48	122·13	
Total	215		

* Significant at the 0·05 level.
** Significant at the 0·01 level.

attempted here; it is discussed in greater detail elsewhere (Jerison and Wing, 1957) and has been found again in a subsequent experiment with the same task (Jerison and Wallis, 1957).

Experiment II: noise and complex mental counting

The procedure in this experiment was developed as a result of a suggestion by Miles (1953) that Ss working in high energy noise fields could not keep an accurate count of how far they had gone in a repetitive task. The complex mental counting test is described in detail elsewhere (Jerison, 1955). Briefly, it consists of a display of three periodically flashing lights; the S's task was to count the number of times each light flashed and to maintain separate counts for each light. He responded by pressing a button under a light when that light had flashed N times and began the count for that light again. (For this experiment N was always 10.) The display and response panels used in this experiment are illustrated in

373

Figure 4. Behind the display is the loudspeaker which broadcast the noise. Fourteen Ss were used.

The most relevant results of this experiment are presented in Figure 5 which shows the average percentage of correct responses for the two subgroups separately for the second and third sessions. Subjects in subgroup Q.N. shows no change in per-

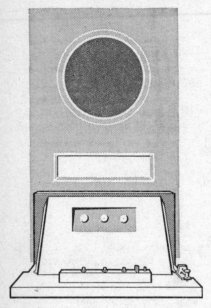

Figure 4 The display and response panels of Experiment II. Behind the display is the loudspeaker cabinet

formance during successive half hours of the second (quiet throughout) session. In the third session, when the noise level was raised to 111·5 dB after the first half hour, a small decrement appeared, though the performance curve is relatively flat. Subjects in subgroup N.Q. showed a steady decrement from their high performance level of the quiet first half hour of their second (experimental) session after the noise level was raised, with a total fall in performance of over 25 per cent. In the third (control) session in quiet this group repeated the pattern showing a drop in performance of about 20 per cent. This general effect (the sessions by experimental conditions by time interaction) was significant at the 0·001 level. A summary of the rather lengthy analysis of variance for this experiment is presented in a more detailed report for limited circulation (Jerison, 1956).

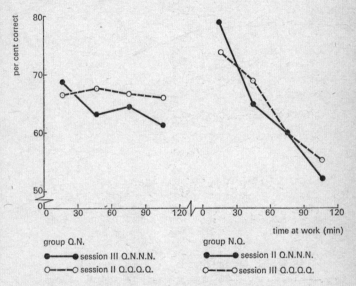

Figure 5 Performance of the fourteen Ss of Experiment II given separately for the seven-subject subgroups 'Q.N.' and 'N.Q.' during successive half hours of the experimental and control sessions

This result suggests that working on this tedious and difficult task for two hours under the Q.N.N.N. regime conditioned Ss to a progressive breakdown of performance, and this conditioning was maintained in the subsequent quiet session. Working in quiet first, on the other hand, appeared to dispose the Ss toward maintaining their original performance level, and this tendency, too, was maintained in the subsequent session despite the presence of noise in that session. Recent experiments by Broadbent (1957, 1958) appear to support this finding.

Noise

Experiment III: noise and time judgement

While performing the counting task the *S*s of Experiment II were also required to press a telegraph key (illustrated in Figure 4, lower right) at what they judged to be 10-minute intervals.

The main results of Experiment III are summarized in Figure 6

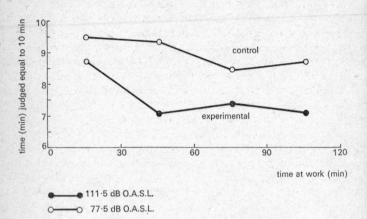

Figure 6 Time judgements for the experimental and control sessions of Experiment III during successive half hours

which shows the average time between *S*'s responses during successive half hours of the experimental and control sessions. (The subgroups were combined, because no order effect appeared here.) The results were analysed with *t*-tests. The differences between half hours within the control session were not statistically significant, nor was the difference between time judgements in the first half hour of the control and experimental session significant. The difference between the first half hour and succeeding half hours of the experimental session were all significant at the 0·05 level or better, and the difference between the averaged judgements of the last one and a half hours of the control and experimental sessions was significant at the 0·02 level. In other words, a significant difference was found between time judgements as measured in this experiment when the comparison was between judgements in noise

376

and judgements in quiet. A more detailed report of this experiment for limited circulation has appeared elsewhere (Jerison and Smith, 1955).

Discussion

It is clear that noise produces readily measureable changes in human performance. The specific changes involved in the three experiments described here are discussed in detail in each of the technical reports devoted to them (Jerison, 1956; Jerison and Smith, 1955; Jerison and Wing, 1957). The purpose of the present discussion is to consider these results in a more general way and to seek some constant features that appear in all of them.

One of the first problems to face is why it has been possible to demonstrate differences between performance in noise and in quiet at all, for, as indicated earlier (cf. Kryter, 1950), most previous work on this problem has given negative results. The main new feature that appears in these experiments is one suggested by Mackworth (1950) and by Broadbent (1953, 1954): performance was measured over long time periods and conditions were arranged to allow effects of boredom and fatigue to interact with possible effects of noise. These conditions were present in all the experiments reported here. The implication is that for short, spurt-like efforts no performance decrements in noise need be expected. When sustained performance is required, however, and the task is not intrinsically challenging, effects of the sort reported here are likely.

These considerations point to an interpretation of the results which de-emphasizes the importance of noise. There is, after all, little reason for regarding noise as a peculiar kind of devil which produces such unusual interactions with fatigue and boredom. It seems reasonable, instead, to regard the more gross effects found as resulting from effects of noise on motivational level or emotional balance, in short, from noise as a source of psychological stress. If this interpretation is correct we should expect similar behavioral effects from other experiments in which other kinds of stress or motivating conditions were investigated. This is, in fact, the case. Mackworth (1950) demonstrated that heat stress resulted in deterioration of performance on a simple vigilance task, and several experiments showing changes in the judgement of time intervals of the order of minutes as a result of different motivating conditions have been reported (Filer and Meals, 1949; Gulliksen, 1927; Rosenzweig and Koht, 1933).

Because stress has been introduced as an explanatory concept a few remarks on its scientific status are in order. The review by Lazarus, Deese and Osler (1952) emphasizes the lack of systematic research on effects of stress on performance, and, although it attempts an analysis of theoretical approaches, this review does not go significantly beyond a statement relating psychological stress to changes in motivation and emotion. There is danger, when using the concept of stress, of believing that an explanation has been achieved. Actually, here, and in most other contemporary usages of the term, we have achieved little more than communication of intuitive judgement about the kind of situation with which we are dealing.

A final point that should be made is related to the kind of noise used. The noise was actually much softer than that found today in many operational situations. Yet even at these levels it was clear that 'higher mental processes' were affected. It is obviously necessary to explore effects of noises of higher intensity on such processes.

Summary

The results of three experiments relating performance changes to noise levels are reported. Noise levels used were about 80 dB representing 'quiet' and 110 dB representing 'noise'. Changes in alertness as determined on a clock-watching task were found after one and a half hours in noise though none were found in quiet. Time judgements – the estimation of the passage of 10-minute intervals – were distorted by noise; Ss responded on the average of every 9 minutes in quiet and every 7 minutes in noise when instructed to respond at what they judged to be 10-minute intervals. A significant but complex effect of noise on a mental counting task was also found. These effects are discussed in terms of noise as a source of psychological stress.

References

BROADBENT, D. E. (1953), 'Noise, paced performance and vigilance tasks', *Brit. J. Psychol.*, vol. 44, pp. 295–303.

BROADBENT, D. E. (1954), 'Some effects of noise on visual performance', *J. exp. Psychol.*, vol. 6, pp. 1–5.

BROADBENT, D. E. (1957), 'Effects of noise of high and low frequency on behavior', *Ergonomics*, vol. 1, pp. 21–9.

BROADBENT, D. E. (1958), 'Effect of noise on an "intellectual" task', *J. acoust Soc. Amer.*, vol. 30, pp. 824–7.

FILER, R. J., and MEALS, D. W. (1949), 'The effect of motivating conditions on the estimation of time', *J. exp. Psychol.*, vol. 39, pp. 327–31.

GULLIKSEN, H. (1927), 'The influence of occupation upon perception of time', *J. exp. Psychol.*, vol. 10, pp. 52–9.

JERISON, H. J. (1955), Combined effects of noise and fatigue on a complex counting task, *USAF WADC Tech. Rep.*, no. 55–360.

JERISON, H. J. (1956), Differential effects of noise and fatigue on a complex counting task, *USAF WADC Tech. Rep.*, no. 55–359.

JERISON, H. J., and SMITH, A. K. (1955), Effect of acoustic noise on time judgment, *USAF WADC Tech. Rep.*, no. 55–358.

JERISON, H. J., and WALLIS, R. A. (1957), Experiments on vigilance. II: One-clock and three-clock monitoring, *USAF WADC Tech. Rep.*, no. 55–206.

JERISON, H. J., and WING, S. (1957), Effects of noise on a complex vigilance task, *USAF WADC Tech. Rep.*, no. 57–14.

KRYTER, K. D. (1950), 'The effects of noise on man. I. Effects of noise on behavior', *J. speech Dis.*, monogr. suppl. 1.

LAZARUS, R. S., DEESE, J., and OSLER, S. F. (1952), 'The effects of psychological stress upon performance', *Psychol. Bull.*, vol. 49, pp. 293–317.

MACKWORTH, N. H. (1950), *Researches on the Measurement of Human Performance*, Medical Research Council, H.M.S.O.

MILES, W. R. (1953), 'Immediate psychological effects', in *BENOX Report, An Exploratory Study of the Biological Effects of Noise*, University of Chicago Press.

ROSENZWEIG, S., and KOHT, A. G. (1933), 'The experience of duration as affected by need tension', *J. exp. Psychol.*, vol. 16, pp. 745–74.

22 D. E. Broadbent

Effects of Noise on Efficiency

Excerpts from D. E. Broadbent, 'Effects of noise on behavior', in C. M. Harris (ed.), *Handbook of Noise Control*, McGraw-Hill, 1957, pp. 10/11–10/34.

Methods of Measuring Efficiency Effects

A great deal of research effort appears to have been wasted in the past through failure to recognize the precautions essential to measurement of human performance. A number, possibly the majority, of studies of effects of noise are scientifically unacceptable. There are two main avenues of investigation, industrial studies on the one hand and laboratory research on the other. Some of the weaknesses in procedure apply to both these avenues; others apply only to industrial investigation, although industrial studies are an essential complement to laboratory ones if we are to ensure that differences found in the laboratory are really important in practice.

The major weakness of industrial studies is lack of control of other conditions besides the noise which is being investigated. Changes in the auditory environment of a worker are commonly linked with a move to a new building, a change in the work which is being done; change in the temperature, lighting and other conditions of work; or similar alterations in the circumstances of the job. Any change in performance may be due to these other changes and not to reduction in noise. This criticism disposes of almost all industrial investigations which have been reported. In addition there are two other dangers to which industrial researches are particularly prone. One of them is the contaminating effect of annoyance. In an earlier section [not included here] it was indicated that a sound might be annoying without necessarily affecting efficiency. But if some feature of the conditions of work is annoying, the worker may stay home unduly long when he is ill, spend longer in the rest room, and similarly reduce his output. In more subtle form this difficulty may appear as that of suggestion. The very fact that an investigator is spending time on noise may cause the workers to believe that they should work better in quiet. This will then have an effect on efficiency, although the effect is not really due to the noise. A second weakness of industrial experiments is that any change in conditions of work may produce a temporary improvement in efficiency. This is particularly true of changes which imply that the management is considering the well-being of the workers. The attitude of the man toward his work becomes more favorable, just as it does if unpleasant conditions are removed; but this does not mean that the noise is truly affecting his efficiency. To put the distinction in monetary terms, it may be very expensive to reduce noise in a workplace, compared with the cost of painting the walls and installing a new canteen. If the effect of reducing the noise is merely to improve the workers' attitude, the latter techniques may be preferable. The final point may be made concerning industrial researches that they have usually measured output, with some attention to absenteeism. Mistakes and accidents are very rarely recorded in investigations of noise, although they have proved good indexes of other environmental conditions; in the section on practical conclusions from the known data, it will be argued that they should be especially useful in studying noise.

Studies in the laboratory, as well as industrial studies, are open to certain other possible weaknesses of technique. First, there is considerable chance fluctuation in the performance of any one person, and there is also chance variation between different individuals. To establish an effect of noise it is necessary, therefore, to report sufficient data for an estimate of this chance variation to be formed, and for the effect which is being claimed to be compared with the chance variation. If a coin is tossed once and comes down heads, we cannot therefore conclude that the coin is biased. Second, performance may vary from one time to another because of other outside causes, in addition to the chance fluctuation. For example, a man may work better because he has become practiced. On the other hand, he may work worse because he has become fatigued. The best way of overcoming this difficulty is to employ two groups of people as subjects for the experiments. One may either give one group noisy conditions throughout and the other group quiet conditions throughout; or else one may start one group under quiet conditions and then change to noisy conditions, while reversing the order of presentation in the second group. A third technique which is rather less satisfactory is to keep one group of subjects but to change them from quiet to noise and then back to quiet again, or vice versa. The weakness of this technique is that a man's performance may first rise and then fall when conditions are kept uniform throughout; we usually say that he has improved with practice and then become fatigued. An industrial experiment, in particular, is likely to have some outside circumstances which may change during the course of an experiment in such a way as to produce first a rise and then a fall in performance. For example, if a group was to work in noise for a year, then in quiet for a year, and then in noise again, it would be quite possible for a change in the general economic situation to produce an atmosphere of prosperity during the second year which was lacking before and after, and which might well be reflected in greater production. Naturally if one changes from quiet to noise and back again repeatedly, the risk of some outside factor of this sort becomes less. If a group works in noise and quiet on alternate days for a year, it would be very bad luck indeed if the economic situation had been particularly bad on alternate days throughout that time. Most of the better investigations of noise effects have therefore used a method of this type, in which noise and quiet are alternated repeatedly. The two-group technique, however desirable, is often impracticable, because it requires the observation of large numbers of people. This is because the difference between different people causes the chance factor in the experiment to be high, and many results must therefore be obtained to ensure a positive conclusion. Even so, there is the danger in the single-group technique that, when two or more conditions of work are rapidly alternated, performance will not adjust itself to each of them in turn but will rather take up an average level.

The last possible snag is that the condition under which a person first meets a task may influence his performance on that task on subsequent occasions even though the conditions are altered. Thus in another field it has been shown that the crew on an aircraft who are given a test after returning from a flight do badly both on that occasion and also later after rest, while those who are first tested after rest do well both on that occasion and also after flying (7). Similar effects have been noticed in some noise experiments. But these difficulties should be detectable by careful consideration of the results, and with modern methods of statistical analysis confident conclusions may be drawn.

The control of noise has been exercised in different ways in different experiments. In the industrial case, the use of sound-absorptive material or of earplugs has been employed. Both these alternatives have their disadvantages, as they introduce extra changes in the situation. A suggestion has recently been made that an industrial experiment utilizing two kinds of earplug of different efficiency would be valuable (4). In laboratory experiments, the quiet condition has normally been the usual circumstances of the laboratory, and the noise has been artificially produced. In the early experiments naturally arising noises such as machinery or recordings of traffic or office noise were used. More recently, laboratory experimenters have tended to use electronically generated noise and to specify it physically with an exactness denied to the earlier workers. Studies giving some indication of the spectrum of the noise, however, as well as the level, are still in the minority, and as yet there is no study of the effect of noise on efficiency which has reported the autocorrelation function or some similar index of the periodicity of the waveform. As is now known, a sound which recurs periodically at some frequency may be heard as having a pitch of that frequency even though the energy in its spectrum is not particularly high at that point. This point is, however, probably an unnecessary refinement; but the different sound levels and spectra employed by different workers may well influence their conflicting results. An additional control which has some merit is the use in recent experiments of an artificially generated steady level of noise at a low intensity as the quiet control. This prevents small incidental sounds from entering the laboratory and disturbing performance.

The tasks used in laboratory studies may be divided into tests of particular functions, such as dark vision or hand-steadiness tests, and tests of complex performances such as decoding, using simulated aircraft controls, or mental arithmetic. It will be found in the appropriate sections that tests of particular functions did not appear to show any effects, while the more complex tasks are divided, some showing effects and some remaining as efficient in noise as in quiet.

Results from Industrial Studies

So far as noise itself is concerned, there appears to be only a single study which cannot be immediately rejected for failures of technique of the type discussed in the previous section. This study is of the efficiency of weavers in Britain (2, 8). In this case ample data are available, including records from some subjects individually week by week for 6 months. There were three experiments, in all of which the noise was that naturally produced by the looms which had a sound level of 96 dB. Comparatively quiet conditions were produced by earplugs which attenuated the noise by 10 to 15 dB. In one experiment 10 weavers were used who wore earplugs on alternate weeks for 6 months. In each of the other experiments two groups were used, one wearing earplugs while the other did not. One of these experiments lasted for 6 months and the other for a year. All three experiments showed a gain in efficiency for the earplugs. The gain was not very sizeable when considered in relation to the amount produced, being only 1 per cent. But in weaving production depends to a great extent upon the loom, and the change in the efficiency of the workers themselves was about 12 per cent.

It is difficult after this interval to assess the value of the latter two experiments. The degree of equality between the two groups was not demonstrated before the earplugs were issued to one of them, in either case. The research belongs to the days when statistical methods of assessing significance were only beginning to be employed, and they were not in this case. Individual data are not available for the workers in the latter two experiments. In the first experiment, however, the data are given for each individual and it appears that every one of the ten workers did better when wearing earplugs. This is undoubtedly statistically significant and in view of the similarity of the results from the three experiments weakens statistical criticism of the second and third. Perhaps more serious is the possibility that the groups wearing earplugs felt additional motivation from being used as subjects for an experiment, and so worked harder. In the third experiment performance of the two groups was less widely different at the end of the year than it was at the beginning; and this might be due to the wearing off of such an increase in motivation. The authors make the point that the two groups separated and came together cyclically throughout the year and that the resemblance between the two levels of output at the end of the year is merely one of these cycles. There is some indication that the two groups were about to diverge again. The records are reproduced as Figure 1. The first

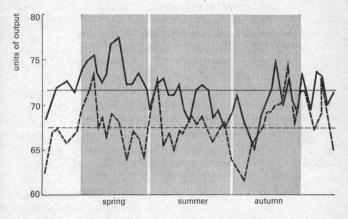

Figure 1 Output of two groups of weavers, both exposed to noise but one group, indicated by the solid line, wearing earplugs. (Weston and Adams, 8)

group again has the advantage where this criticism is concerned, since any general increase in motivation should have affected performance of the group throughout, and not merely on the weeks when they were wearing earplugs. A suggestion effect from current opinion that noise impaired work is not excluded in this group, nor of course in the other two experiments. It should be noted that the opinions of the individual workers on the benefit derived from earplugs are also recorded and that some of them were markedly unfavorable. This agrees with the experience of most people who have tried to make workers defend their ears. Even the unfavorable workers showed an improvement in their performance when wearing earplugs, although there was a statistically insignificant difference between the favorable and unfavorable subgroups. Finally, although the first experiment thus seems to be less open to objection than the other two, the authors of the research were more doubtful of it. This was because of chance differences in temperature and humidity between the weeks on which earplugs were worn and the weeks when the full noise was experienced; in other experiments temperature and humidity have been shown to affect performance. The data on temperature and humidity from the first experiment are given in the report and do not seem in this case to show any connexion with efficiency. It may be that the authors were overcautious in suspecting their results.

The agreement between the three weaving experiments described above is impressive, and there is some answer to each of the possible criticisms that can be leveled against them. But the evidence cannot be said to be overwhelming. The most serious objection is probably the danger of suggestion or other influences upon the workers' attitude. It seems impossible to rule this out in industrial experiments except by the suggestion of using inefficient earplugs for one group. Perhaps it should be added that these criticisms of effects shown in industry do not necessarily mean that the results are false; they merely mean that the effect of noise is not proved to be true. In the light of the discussion under 'An interpretation of the nature of behavior in noise' (page 410) it is reasonable that weaving should show effects. Other industrial processes might not show corresponding effects.

Music in industry

Although not noise by some definitions, music in factories has been the subject of several investigations. Its importance here is that the introduction of music during work is frequently supposed to improve production, rather than impair it. Although levels of intensity are not usually given, it seems likely that such music will reach levels comparable with those of the noises used in some experiments aimed at showing deleterious effects from sound stimulation. The popular opinion that music has a contrary effect thus serves to remind us that we cannot consider effects of noise purely from a physical standpoint. There is little doubt that the presence of music is regarded by the workers as a pleasant feature of the job and that it improves their attitude toward the task and the management. In some studies it has also been shown that production improves when music is present. As usual, there is some doubt as to whether this production improvement is due to the attitude change or to a direct effect of the stimulus provided by the music. The effect on output from one of the earlier experiments is shown in Figure 2. The task concerned in this case was the rolling of paper novelties by hand (9). Three points are worth noting concerning the results. (a) There seems to

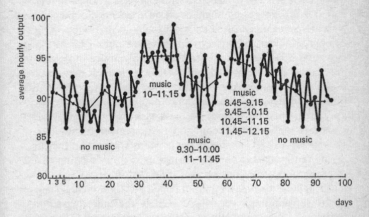

Figure 2 Output in a light manual task under various conditions of noise presentation. (Wyatt and Langdon, 9)

be a difference between the different times of introduction of the music. (b) There appears to be a flywheel effect, such that production takes a little time to settle down to a new level. (c) This effect is merely an average one, an aspect not noted in the figure; some individuals do not benefit from the music. Other studies have also shown improvements in average output, with the same qualifications that individuals may not be affected and that particular schedules of music with particular types of work may fail to show any effect (10, 11, 12). One sizeable study on a skilled task which had remained stable for some time, so that work habits were fairly fixed, did not show any improvement in average output despite an improvement in the workers' attitude as measured by questionnaires (13). This study in fact compared music and quiet conditions on randomly varied days within each of five experimental weeks. This may mean that the workers did not adjust their production to the changed conditions, as they did in the study in Figure 2. On the other hand, production in the weeks before the start of the experiment was no lower than in the experiment itself; so it may be that the other differences between the two tasks were the significant ones. However, there do not appear to be any reports of music causing a deterioration in production, although it may possibly have some slight effect on accidents. Sound as such is clearly not necessarily a cause of low industrial efficiency. In comparing effects of music with effects of noise, the fact that industrial noise levels may rise considerably above those due to music must be remembered; and it is also of interest that music is probably best used for short periods and not continuously throughout the day. The conception that a change in the background stimulation present during a task may improve performance is one which is common to a number of studies of prolonged work. It is noted in the previous section that the effect is sufficiently marked to be a normal hazard in assessing effects of changes in conditions on industrial performance. The use of music appears to be a method of deliberately producing changes in the surroundings. As will be seen in the following section, meaningless noises sometimes produce a corresponding improvement in performance. Music has the advantage that attitudes favorable to the work and to the management are induced, as well as a change in the surroundings which opposes monotony. Both factors therefore operate in the same direction and may produce enhanced performance on suitable tasks.

The Effects of Unfamiliar Noises

It is widely agreed that a novel or unusual noise will produce some decline in the efficiency of work when it is first heard. This effect is considered separately from that of prolonged noise since the latter is more confused and controversial.

In a typical experiment, each subject was presented with a series of letters among which digits were interspersed (14). The task was to add up the series of digits. When a series of such sums had been done, the noise was turned on and continued while another series of sums was done. It was then turned off again and a final series of measurements taken. The noise was provided by an automobile horn mounted 2 ft from the subject. The effect was that the first few sums after the onset of noise were slowed down but that the time per sum then returned to normal. A very important point is that a similar slowing down occurred when the noise was stopped. Once again, performance rapidly returned to normal; but the interest of the finding is that it suggests that the effect of the noise was primarily that of a change in the conditions of work, rather than any effect peculiar to intense sounds. Similar results have also been found using an even more complex task, in which the subject was required to observe a letter through a slot, to encode it into another letter using a code supplied, to take this second letter and encode it into a digit using one of three codes varying according to the color of the original presentation, and finally to press an appropriate key (15). In this case an assortment of bells, buzzers, and other noise makers was used to provide the noise. Individual differences were evident in the results, but on the whole findings appear to be similar to those already given. An initial slowing down was later replaced by unaltered performance, and indeed by improved performance in a majority of the subjects. There were signs of another deterioration when the noise was stopped. Typical results are shown in Figure 3.

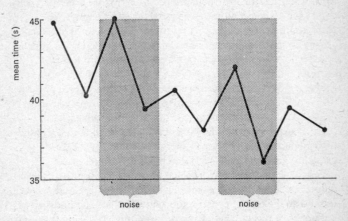

Figure 3 The temporary disturbance caused by turning a noise on and off. (Plotted from the data of Morgan, 15)

Logically, there are two possible aspects of unfamiliarity. There is the unfamiliarity of a noise which has never been heard before, and there is the unfamiliarity of a task which has not been practiced to any great extent. Both are usually regarded as important by investigators in this field, but experiments of the type mentioned earlier probably detect chiefly the effects of familiarity and unfamiliarity of the noise. Performance on the task itself seems to have reached a plateau or constant level of efficiency before the noise is introduced. There remains the possibility that the effect of a given unfamiliar noise may be greater on an unpracticed task than on a practiced one. Oddly enough, no one appears to have done controlled experiments in which noises are repeatedly presented before the task is introduced, or in which the task is given varying degrees of practice before the noise is introduced. However, it seems fair to accept the evidence already given as showing that increasing familiarity with a noise will reduce its effect on a task for a constant level of practice. Perhaps the best evidence that a practiced task is less affected than an unpracticed one comes from an experiment using a fairly complex manual skill in which pegs had to be removed from a moving trolley which approached and receded from the worker at a speed dictated by a machine (3). Some effect was shown on this task from clicking sounds delivered to the subjects through headphones in a rhythm different from that of the machine, although as usual the effect began to die away with continued exposure. When the same subjects were given a different kind of noise, no effect appeared on the task. Unfortunately, no other subjects were tested using this task and the second kind of noise, to show that this noise would have affected the task had it been less well practiced; the point was probably one of minor interest to the particular investigators, as their experimental design was well controlled in most respects.

Other experiments in the same series illustrated both the nature of the effects which may be obtained temporarily when noise is presented, and also the kind of changes which subjects say are taking place in their performance and which cause the noise to reduce its effect. In one experiment two groups of subjects were faced with the task of constructing an unfamiliar apparatus out of a number of pieces. One group received a noise during this task, and more rapid solutions of the problem were obtained in the quiet group. Only three of the noise subjects solved the problem in less than a quarter of an hour, while eight of the quiet subjects succeeded in a similar time, both groups containing twenty-four subjects. Applying modern statistics to the results given in this report, the present writer has confirmed the investigators' tentative conclusion that the results are not due to chance. In another experiment the subjects were asked to solve, not one unfamiliar problem, but a succession of problems of similar type. The problems were to construct certain prescribed digit combinations on an apparatus in which digits could be moved into a register by pressing levers. Only a limited number of moves were allowed. Alternate problems were done in noise and in quiet. This task was at first impaired by noise, but the impairment disappeared until, on the fifth day of work, after the performance of fifty or more problems, the subjects were able to perform as well in noise as in quiet. Similarly, when the subjects were given groups of letters and told to form as many words as possible from these letters, they were at first impaired by noise but later recovered. In both these experiments the subjects reported that as time went on they discovered rules and mechanical techniques of solving the problems, and once this had been done the noise ceased to have any effect. For example, in the word-construction test a useful technique was to take one letter, to take each of the available vowels after this first letter, then to take each next consonant, and so on. This routine performance required little thinking and was undisturbed by noise. A typical comment, from a subject used in the manual-skill experiment, was that once the task was practiced he listened to the noise, but this did not affect the part of his mind which was occupied with doing a task. Noise levels were not stated in these reports (3) but were given elsewhere as being up to 90 dB (16).

Although the evidence for effects of practice on the task itself in reducing interference with the task by noise is not completely satisfactory, the opinion of most of the investigators seems to support it. There is also some evidence from experiments in which one task has to be combined with another task, after varying degrees of practice on the first task. A more practiced task does interfere less with the second occupation, although there is some limit to the extent to which this effect of learning can be used to combine different tasks. If a type of work involves reacting to a succession of different stimuli, and the order of the stimuli is random, there may be little benefit from previous practice in combining this task with another. Yet when the order of stimuli is predictable, practice at the task will mean that another task can be done at the same time more efficiently (17). Practice at one task will also reduce interference with another at times between the occurrence of critical stimuli from the first task (18). In the language of communication theory, interference between two tasks occurs only when a man is required to take in information from both tasks simultaneously. If one task presents a repeating series of stimuli, the information contained in this sequence is low after practice and there is then little interference with another task. In more everyday language, with an unfamiliar task one notices many features of the work which are not essential to its performance, and one cannot at the same time attend to some other work. In a practiced task, one attends only to what is crucial, and if the task is a repetitive one some other work may be done simultaneously. If it is unpredictable, it will be more difficult to combine with other occupations. Most actual tasks will lie between the two extremes, having crucial instants at which information is delivered to the man, and other times at which no such information is arriving. After practice one is aware of this and can alternate attention, dealing with a second task during the intervals in the first. If we take the further step of supposing that there is a tendency for attention to be directed to any change in the surroundings, such as the onset of a noise, it is not surprising that effects on performance due to this mechanism should be less on a practiced task. In other words, the initial response to any situation is diffuse and widespread. This applies whether the situation is a task presented by an experimenter or an interfering noise. It is pointed out in an earlier section that widespread muscle potentials may be detected early in performance but become more concentrated in particular parts of the body at later stages. When both task and irrelevant noise are producing widespread response, there is more likelihood of interference between responses due to the two stimuli. When response to the task has been concentrated in one part of the body and response to a noise has either disappeared or also been concentrated in a different part of the body there will be no interference between the two stimuli. But the worst effects of noise will be produced by a strange and unfamiliar sound on a strange and unfamiliar task, and the least effect of noise will be produced by a familiar sound upon a practiced task. Intermediate cases will be provided by familiar sounds and strange tasks, and by strange sounds with familiar tasks. But if this description is adopted, it is essential to remember that the word 'response' may mean simply some event within the nervous system, not detectable outside. As long as this precaution is observed, it makes little difference whether one speaks of automatizing a task until it requires a low level of awareness, or of reducing the amount of information required to pass through the perceptual mechanism for successful performance, or of eliminating unnecessary responses which interfere and are interfered with when response to a noise is also present.

Although these different ways of describing the process of adapting to a novel noise are probably equivalent, they are not the only possible way in which this process can be regarded. A number of the earlier workers thought rather of a level of efficiency which was lowered by noise and raised again by compensating effort, the effort arriving somewhat late so that an initial drop in measured performance was redeemed only after the noise had been applied for a short time. The reason for viewing the situation in this way was the detectable change in various physiological measures which were referred to in an earlier section. That is, there might be rises in metabolism, in the pressure exerted on reaction keys, and so on. These additional processes seem to die out as the task goes on in noise. Although some reality corresponding to extra effort is undoubtedly present in some cases, it does not seem to be a sufficient explanation for the disappearance of the effect of noise after it has been present for a little while. Nor, if noise automatically lowers the level of efficiency and requires an effort to raise that level once more to the original, is it clear why the sudden cessation of a noise should be disturbing. One would rather expect a sudden spurt in performance followed by a decline to the normal level as effort was reduced. It seems easier to abandon the idea that noise automatically lowers the level of performance and to concentrate rather on the importance of changes in sensory stimulation. The importance of this change in viewpoint is that it means that work in a familiar noise, if efficiency is maintained, is not therefore requiring undue effort from the worker. The effect of an unfamiliar environment seems genuinely to die away, and not to require continued compensation by the worker.

Certain omissions in the literature have already been noticed. Perhaps even more surprising is the lack of any evidence on the kinds of noise which produce this effect most clearly. Since the reality of an initial disturbance in efficiency, lasting perhaps a few seconds with simple tasks and a few minutes with more complex ones, is accepted by most authorities, one might expect that some research would have been done with modern methods to compare the results of, say, bursts of noise, impact sounds or pure tones. Such work would naturally require many experimental subjects since it would be necessary to use people with the same level of practice on the task, and without experience of the particular sound applied. Yet it should be a topic for research well within the resources of modern investigators. All that can be said is that most researches on the subject seem to have adopted noises which might be described as annoying, in view of what is said in the section on that subject. Thus automobile horns, bells, buzzers and similar pulsating sounds figure prominently, while meaningful sounds of fairly low intensity are also particularly likely to cause the effect. Perhaps one reason for this neglect of the subject is that this effect of noise on efficiency is probably of little practical importance. Most industrial and military situations involve tasks which are to some extent practiced and noises which are to a large extent familiar. That an experimental subject faced with a completely new task may show a few seconds' delay when a striking and unusual noise begins is of little bearing for such practical situations; and recent research interests have been much more concerned with effects lasting at least over a matter of minutes. The transient effect of noise may conceivably be important to anybody concerned with the working conditions of men solving extremely new and unfamiliar problems, if the noises to which they are likely to be exposed are also very changeable and unfamiliar. Even then, the effect seems on the existing evidence to be only a question of a few seconds' delay in solution rather than a failure to reach solution; and in such work a delay of seconds is not usually thought important. Furthermore, small numbers of individuals are usually involved in any particular situation of this type, and the individuals may happen to be resistant to noise effects. Another possible field in which the effect may be noticed is in domestic life, since recreations frequently involve new and varying situations. The noises met under such circumstances will also be variable and may consist of a neighbor's radio on one occasion, the sound of a noisy vehicle a little later, an aircraft soon afterwards, and so on. The interference produced on recreational activities may be detectable, and so indirectly contribute to annoyance and complaints. But these situations are somewhat special ones, and their practical importance is very doubtful. If the effects of noises on efficiency consist only of the brief distracting effect at their onset, there is little excuse for large-scale reduction of noise in the hopes of improving efficiency.

Sensory and Motor Functions Known to be Unaffected by Noise

Once the initial effect of the beginning of a noise has worn off, a number of processes are definitely known to show no effect. These processes are specific sensory and motor ones. [. . .]

It can be seen that the sense organs and muscles of a human being are not completely disorganized by the presence of an intense sound field. Any effects which have been found are extremely tentative and may well be due to some unsuspected feature of the experimental conditions. Any decline in the efficiency of more complicated tasks in noise is not due to failure of the simpler links in the nervous system. To recapitulate, most of the tests of sensory function indicated above presented a stimulus at a time when it was clearly expected by the subject or was even under his own control. There were normally intervals between each of the presentations of the stimulus, so that the task was not really continuous. Under such circumstances there is no doubt that the senses may be used as efficiently in noise as in quiet. Equally, tasks in which the movements required are simply repetitive, and no information is transmitted through the man, need show no decrement. A large variety of the tasks performed in noisy places are of this type: thus a man may have to enter a noisy engine shop to take down the readings of gauges or to tighten certain nuts. There is no reason to suppose that his efficiency will be lower in the noise.

Complex Tasks and Familiar Noises

The question to be considered in the present section is the most controversial in the general topic of efficiency in noise. If we take complex tasks rather than simple tests of sensory or motor function, practice them to a level at least sufficient to allow reasonably stable performance and expose the worker to a sound which remains present for some time, shall we get any decline in efficiency? A number of studies have failed to show any effect under such circumstances. Yet they are clearly the conditions of greatest economic importance, as compared with the agreed effect of onset of the noise and lack of effect on simple sensory functions. There is as yet no widespread agreement about the reasons for the positive claims of some researches to show effects of noise, and the failure of others. A possible interpretation of the data does exist but cannot be said to be universally agreed. In consequence the method of presentation which we shall adopt is to outline as far as possible the known results in the present section and to give in the next section an interpretation of these results. This will mean that to some extent the present section will be a catalogue of data but will avoid the danger of too highly selective a presentation of the results in terms of a doubtful theory. Those who prefer to assimilate data to the framework of a general theory may consult the next section before examining the present one.

Intellectual tasks

Classification of the results is not easy. In general, researchers have tended to use the same conditions for their 'noise' and 'quiet' and to vary their tasks. It will be easier to avoid repetition, therefore, if researches are considered in a more or less historical order rather than attempting to classify tasks on which effects have or have not been found. Where convenient, however, results on similar types of tasks will be put side by side. The earlier researchers, for instance, tended to use rather intellectual types of work, in which a succession of problems was to be solved, time taken or errors forming the score used. Two such tasks are described in an earlier section, since they showed effects of the onset of the noise (14, 15). These were a task of adding digits which had to be found among letters, and a task of carrying out two encoding operations on a presented letter. Neither of these studies showed any impairment by noise at the end of the work period, the initial effect having worn off. Another research used arithmetical problems, with records of actual street and office noise as the noise condition rather than the automobile horn of the first experiment and the bells and buzzers of the second. The records of office and street noise were played at sound levels which now seem rather low, the peaks being only 65 dB for office noise and 75 dB for street noise. Once again no detrimental effect was apparent when the sound and the task had become familiar (6). It should be noted that these experiments, although repeated on successive days in some cases, involved work periods of the order of only 10 min. Another rather similar research employed a mechanical noise machine and music as the noisy conditions, with cancellation, addition and transcription tests as the tasks. Once again there was little evidence of any decrement after the noise had become familiar (22). To deviate slightly from a strict chronological order, two recent studies using modern techniques were asked to carry out three clerical tests: one was of addition, each problem requiring the addition of nine five-place numbers (22). The second test was of vocabulary, and required the subject to choose from four words a synonym for the given word. The third test was of number comparison, in which pairs of five-place numbers were given and the subject was required to detect any pairs which were dissimilar. Each test consisted, of course, of a number of problems of similar type, and equivalent sets of problems were prepared for use under the different noise conditions. The sound source used was recorded office-machine noise and was presented at the four 10-dB steps from sound levels of 65 to 95 dB, inclusive, the remaining two conditions employed being no noise and variation in the sound level of machine noise from 65 to 95 dB randomly through the test period. The addition test took 5 min, the vocabulary test $1\frac{1}{2}$ min, and the number-comparison test 3 min. In no case was there any significant difference between the various noise levels in the percentage of error on these tests. Speed and accuracy were not reported separately, probably because they showed nothing of particular interest. The longest test, the addition test, did show a steady trend as the noise intensity was increased. The percentage of correct responses declined with each increase in noise level, the drop becoming greater at the higher levels. But, like other results, this was not significant.

In the other recent research, intermittent bursts of noise from a noise generator were presented at sound levels of 100 dB during the performance of a clerical test and a formboard test (23). The bursts of sound varied from 10 to 50 s in length and were present during half the time that testing was in progress. The clerical test consists of two subtests, each lasting 7 min, one being of the number-comparison type mentioned in the last research and the other being of a similar type but using pairs of names rather than pairs of numbers. The formboard test lasts 14 min and requires the subject to identify the results of assembling a given group of isolated plane figures. Two groups of subjects were employed; so that the same problems were given both in noise and in quiet. In all three tests more items were attempted in noise but less were correct. However, the statistical significance of the results is dubious, since of the twelve differences tested only two were significant. One of these was the percentage of correct responses in name checking, which were of course less frequent in noise, while the other comparison was the number of items attempted on the formboard. The latter score was higher in noise. There is always some doubt concerning the validity of statistical tests on one or two results chosen from a large number of possibilities. The criticism put forward is, in effect, that if we deal ourselves enough hands, sooner or later we shall get a winning one. Yet the significances in this case are fairly high and the results may well be correct; but, as the author says, they are unimportant from a practical point of view.

These studies, and certain others using similar types of problems (24, 25, 26) suggest that paper and pencil work of this sort will not be likely to show effects of noise. If anything, there seems to be a tendency for faster work on the average. There may also be an unimportant increase in errors; both these findings are very slight but appear repeatedly in a number of experiments and may therefore be accepted as possible effects of noise. Similar findings also appear in certain studies using longer work periods and tasks which are somewhat less of the problem-by-problem type. For example, two groups of students were asked to read a chapter from a textbook, while one of the groups was exposed to recorded music (27). This group read slightly more in a half hour than the quiet control group though not significantly so: they did, however, do significantly worse on a test of comprehension. In another research, six subjects performed a number of different tasks under a number of different temperature and noise conditions (28). The tasks included number-comparison tests of the type mentioned several times already, mental multiplication of three-place by two-place numbers, the finding of particular locations in a grid of rows and columns, visual threading of mazes, the tracing of a circular pattern by two controls as in a lathe, and coding using a typewriter which presented the next item to be encoded as soon as one item had been handled. The noise was that of an electric fan and was administered at sound levels of 70, 80 and 90 dB. The work period was of 4 hr, though the same task was not continually performed throughout this period. Yet the tasks were at least half an hour in length each and were therefore somewhat nearer to many practical situations than the short tests cited so far. Once again there was certainly no decline in the speed of work in the higher noise levels: on the multiplication and number-checking tasks the speed was significantly greater at a noise level of 90 dB than at 70 dB. An increase in errors also appears in the mental-multiplication and lathe tasks, being significant in both cases. On the other hand, the locations task showed significantly fewer errors at the highest noise level. It is difficult to decide why one such task should differ from the others, although it might possibly be argued that the locations task comes nearest to the simple sensory-function type of experiment, in which the subject knows exactly when he must look for the particular signal which he is required to distinguish.

Sensorimotor tasks

The lathe task, described above, is a sensorimotor task, rather than an intellectual one. There are some early studies on such tasks, including typing and the striking of small target holes in a moving belt with a stylus, but they are open to objections on the

399

ground of poor experimental technique. Detailed criticism may be found in the review of the literature already cited as including extra papers of insufficient importance to be examined here (1). Among more recent studies, there is an experiment on the accuracy of tracking and of stereoscopic range finding with a gun-control system. In this case the work period was extremely long, by the standard of previous researches, being 4 hr on a single task. Extremely intense noises, having sound levels up to 120 or 130 dB, were inserted for periods of 2 min in some cases and 3 min in others. No consistent deterioration in performance was found in any of the conditions of insertion of the noises. When they were introduced in the middle and end of the prolonged task, there was in fact an improvement (29). This improvement may be compared with the improvement produced by short periods of music in factories during the working day. It seems to have come as a stimulus in the popular sense, relieving monotony and so keeping performance up to a high level.

Other sensorimotor tasks were studied in a research which compared aircraft noise having a sound level of 115 dB with that of 90 dB (19). Besides the tests of visual and motor function which were mentioned above, tasks of translating written material into code and sorting twelve cards into twelve compartments were employed. Neither showed any difference between the two noise levels. Another task giving negative results was that of compensatory tracking using aircraft controls. (Compensatory tracking is the task of keeping an indicator, in this case the spot of a cathode-ray oscillograph and also a galvanometer needle, at a particular mark while outside disturbances attempt to remove it.) A rather similar task from the same research was to use aircraft controls to move a spot of light along a predetermined track. In this case the rate of work was set by the operator himself, and so the time taken to complete a given sequence of operations could be taken as a score, as well as the number of failures in keeping the light on the path. This test did appear to show a difference between the two noise levels, both in speed and in errors. Throughout this experiment the five subjects worked 7-hr days, the noise level being constant throughout each day. They did not, however, work at any one task for a long period. Each task was kept down to 15 min to keep motivation constant. Each subject spent one 15-min session on each of five tasks, then took a short rest and performed all five tasks again. Five such periods occupied the whole day. The sequence of high- and low-noise days was counterbalanced, 16 days in all being used. The subjects were all practiced on the tasks before the main experiment.

The discrepancy between the two tasks involving coordinated use of airplane controls was responsible for the rather skeptical phrasing used above to introduce the effect found on one task. A possible explanation is that this effect was spurious. A test of the speed of accommodation of the eyes was found to show a change with increasing noise level, which was afterwards proved to be partly due to clues given to the subject by relays in the apparatus (19). There were also relays in the apparatus connected to the aircraft-control task. Possibly, therefore, a similar explanation could be advanced, although no similar experiment demonstrating the effect of the relays seems to have been done. In view of the markedly negative results of most other tests used in this research, this explanation (that the results are spurious due to auditory clues) has usually been accepted. There is a slight difficulty, however, that the difference both in time per trial and in errors is much greater for the last period of the day than for the first. Indeed for the first period the quiet days show more errors than the noise ones, although the curves cross soon afterwards. It may be conceivable that very faint audible clues from the apparatus should become helpful only after a relearning period each day, but such an interpretation seems somewhat forced. Another explanation which has been put forward is that the task showing an effect on noise was an unpaced one, in which the subjects worked at the limit of their ability in quiet, and so were impaired in noise. The other task required response only when demanded by the machine and it was recognized as being an easier task. Whatever the explanation, this result is clearly in an ambiguous position; in any case, the changes in speed and accuracy are only 5 per cent, and therefore probably of little practical importance.

A similarly ambiguous result has been obtained on a co-ordination test in which the hand is removed from a button (thus starting a clock), a pencil is removed from one hole and inserted in another, and the button is then pressed again to stop the clock.

On two groups of subjects this task showed a retardation of a little over 5 per cent in jet-engine noise as compared with quiet conditions (20). Unfortunately, while in the first group of three subjects all subjects showed the effect, in the second group of five subjects, two did not show it. The second group were tested under slightly different conditions and had received some jet noise because of accidental circumstances shortly before the instructions and first quiet control period. This result is not therefore statistically valid and is merely suggestive. In any event, as the subjects were not used to jet noise this may belong with the startle response discussed in an earlier section. Most authorities would agree that an unfamiliar noise would impair a delicate task, but this does not mean that a familiar noise would do likewise.

Visual watchkeeping and continuous work

More positive conclusions appear in the next research to be considered, which compared the effects of two noises having sound levels of 70 and 100 dB (30). Three tasks were used, of types found to be particularly sensitive to the effect of other kinds of stress. Two of the tasks required the subject to watch a visual display, of steam gauges in the one case and of indicator lamps in the other, watching for rare signals upon which some action must be taken. The task in each case lasted $1\frac{1}{2}$ hr, and only fifteen signals were delivered during this time. The steam-pressure gauges were considerably harder to read, and a group of ten subjects showed on the average better performance on quiet days than on noise days. The proportion of signals detected in less than 10 s dropped by more than 30 per cent in the higher level of noise. On the easier task, however, a separate group of twenty subjects did not show any effect of noise. There were individual differences apparent in this group. There were also significant changes in the pattern of performance in noise, the center of the display showing a deterioration which was not shared by the ends of the row of lights; and there was a significant tendency for missed signals to be grouped together rather than appear at random throughout the work period. Detailed analysis of the trends in performance with time also showed that in noise performance began worse than in quiet, then become slightly better, and then deteriorated.

The initial stages of this progress are similar to those frequently shown in other experiments described in the last section. But the later deterioration is less common, and suggested to the author that some subjects were making an effort in noise which they could not keep up. The relative decline from the first noise day to the second was statistically significant, although the difference between the second noise day and the second quiet day was not significant. The third task used in this research was a serial reaction task, in which the subject was faced with five lights and five contacts (31). When a particular light was on, a particular contact was to be touched; as soon as a response was made another light lit up, and this continued without interruption. A work period of half an hour was employed on this task, and scores of output of correct responses, number of incorrect responses and number of short intervals of $1\frac{1}{2}$ s (in some experiments 2 s), during which no response whatever was made, were recorded. It has long been known that in tasks of this sort the average rate of producing correct responses does not decline with prolonged performance until very long work periods have been undergone. But at a much earlier stage, after only 10 to 20 min work, the flow of responses begins to show momentary interruptions. In unpracticed subjects these may take the form of 'blocks', that is, intervals without response (32); in more practiced subjects they will rather become errors. (An error is of course not a badly coordinated response, but a response which is incorrectly chosen. That is, one of the contacts is struck, but not the contact corresponding to the signal light.) As the noise experiments involved practiced subjects errors were more important than blocks. A noise having a sound level of 100 dB produced considerably more errors than the quieter condition. The blocks were increased but not significantly so, and the output of correct responses was decreased but very slightly and not significantly; individual variability was much more marked in the latter score than in the others, some subjects getting faster in noise and some slower. The size of the effect on accuracy was substantial, being of the order of 50 per cent. The result has been obtained in three experiments on separate groups of subjects; so that it seems reasonably well established. The first group of eighteen subjects provided a simple comparison between the two conditions; the second group of fourteen subjects were informed in advance, with carefully prepared faked graphs, that noise was expected to improve their performance; and the third group of forty subjects were divided into subgroups and used to compare the effects of different kinds of noise. A result from this latter group will be mentioned again at the end of the section; in this case the worst noise was able to produce 100 per cent more errors than the best noise. To put these rather dramatic sounding figures in perspective, it should be realized that the subjects were, under the worst conditions, producing about 2000 correct responses for every fifty errors. As in the task of watching indicator lamps, it was found that the advantage of quiet conditions increased as the length of the work period increased. The first 5 min of the task would have shown an advantage for noise.

This research obviously gives more positive effects of noise than have been reported in the other experiments. Before considering the reasons for this, we should perhaps note some other experiments from different sources which confirm the general findings. First, it was mentioned in the last section that a research on the visual-contrast threshold had shown that as small a difference in brightness could be seen in a sound level of 90 dB as in 45 dB. The investigators had noted not only the level of brightness of a light which was detected but also the reaction time between the appearance of each light and the subject's response to it. In noise this time was consistently longer, except for the faintest stimulus. The change in reaction time is highly significant. The method of presenting the task in this case was somewhat different from many tests of sensory function. The subject was asked to observe the field of view through a telescope, for $12\frac{1}{2}$ min at a time. The appearance of each test stimulus was signaled by a light to his left eye shortly before the exposure of the stimulus. This light is specified as small and red, and may have been somewhat inconspicuous. Any delay in observing it would naturally be reflected in a long reaction time to the main stimulus. After each work period of $12\frac{1}{2}$ min, a break of $2\frac{1}{2}$ min was taken, and then another period was begun until a total time of 2 hr had been spent in the situation. This is a somewhat prolonged test involving the detection of signals at less definite times than in such a test as the dark vision one, described in the last section, in which the subject presented the stimulus himself. It bears a close relation to the tasks of watching gauges and lights, and the similarity of the findings adds confidence to an acceptance of both sets of results. The only possible point of difference is over the effect of time in the noise. The authors of the contrast-threshold research rightly say that they have no evidence of an increase in the effect of noise with time; although, as is seen in Figure 4, the difference in

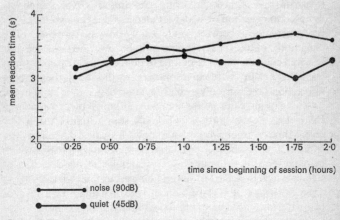

time since beginning of session (hours)

● ————— ● noise (90dB)

● ————— ● quiet (45dB)

Figure 4 Reaction time to an occasional faint visual signal in two levels of noise

reaction times was larger at the end of the work period, the effect was not statistically significant and might have been due to chance. But since this research was done, another computational technique has become available; the data from the contrast-threshold experiment have been recomputed by the present writer and give a highly significant relation with time in the noise. The agreement with the gauge- and light-watching experiment thus remains good.

One last piece of evidence supporting the conclusion that continuous searching for visual stimuli may produce slow reactions in noise comes from an early visual test. This was a test requiring the subject to detect particular patterns among a medley of confusing lines, and required close attention. A series of patterns was presented and the time taken to work through the test was used as the score. A statistically significant deterioration was found when this test was given in noisy surroundings as compared with quiet ones (35). The noise was in this case that naturally arising in a generator room at a factory, as compared with normal quiet conditions. The test itself was done within a booth in controlled illumination so that other conditions beside the noise should have been reasonably constant. Putting these three researches together, it seems that a task involving continuous visual search, as opposed to detection of signals at an occasional known time with rest intervals in between, may show slow performance. The magnitude of the effect should not be overrated; in the last research cited the increase in time to do a test lasting nearly 1 min was only 3 s. In the research on contrast threshold, the increase in reaction time was only a small fraction of a second; and in the watching of indicator lamps and dials, although there was a large change in the proportion of signals seen within 10 s, a less severe time criterion would have shown a smaller difference. The effect is likely to be of practical importance only in cases where extreme speed is necessary, as, for example, in the detection of signals which indicate serious and dangerous faults developing in a machine, or in the inspection of items passing on a conveyor belt which will not be present for unlimited time.

Another research study is similar in the task used to the five-choice serial reaction task which was mentioned earlier. That task did not allow any intervals for rest. Furthermore it showed that when the worker set his own rate of work the rate became more variable towards the end of a session, especially in noise. This means that the effect would be more serious on a task in which the worker could not set his own rate of work but had to keep to that of a machine. Any signal for response arriving at an instant of lowered efficiency would not be dealt with, and at instants of high efficiency the worker could not increase the speed of work to compensate. This more damaging effect on a paced task, as opposed to an unpaced task, was shown for the effect of prolonged work, though not for the effect of noise. The task to be described next resembled the five-choice task in requiring continuous activity but differed in other respects, including the fact that it was paced by a machine. The subject was faced with three lights, each of which was flashing at a particular rhythm. The rates of flash were different and formed a complex pattern such that the order of illumination of the lights did not repeat for a very long time. The slowest light came on nine times in 2 min while the fastest one came on ten times in 1 min. There was a key beneath each light, and the subject was required to press the key beneath a light when that light had flashed a prescribed number of times. The number itself was varied from 4 to 10 but was constant for one testing session. The worker thus had to keep count of three separate series of events at the same time, with no intervals in which he could be sure that nothing would happen. On the average some light or other would come on every 3 s but the unpredictable nature of the pattern would make it difficult to rely on any time in which nothing would happen. This task was continued for 2 hr, two groups being tested, one of which was exposed for 1 hr of their session to a noise having a sound level of 110 dB while the other group received relative quiet. The number of mistakes increased as time went on, was greater in the noise group, and became greater in the noise group relative to the quiet group as the period of exposure to the noise went on. These results are clearly similar to those for errors on the unpaced five-choice reaction task (36). A number of real-life situations somewhat different from those usually studied in the laboratory are clearly parallel to this most ingenious task of counting lights. In many cases a number of different activities must be kept going by alternating between them, without losing the thread of any of them. A simple example is that of cooking in which different items with different cooking times may all be in progress simultaneously. The type of immediate memory involved in such a task may require different functions from the more simply perceptual ones involved in the other tasks mentioned in this section. It was noted that the light flashing at the slowest rate, and the longest number of flashes required before a key pressing, seemed more sensitive than the modification of the task which needed only a shorter span of memory; and this indicated the possible importance of memory functions. The distinction between perception and immediate memory, however, is difficult to make in many practical situations, although its reality or otherwise may be of great theoretical importance. This result, together with those from the serial reaction task, suggest that mistakes may rise rapidly in frequency in a prolonged task of a type which does not allow any relaxation of attention.

To summarize, no clear and obvious distinction appears between tasks which show effects of noise and those which do not. Short paper and pencil tests appear to be quite insensitive to noise, and so are short tests of sensorimotor performance. When the average rate of work over a fair period is taken, there is no consistent decline in performance and there may be an improvement in some special cases. Mistakes are more likely to show effects but will be serious only in tasks in which effects of prolonged work are also serious; these appear on the whole to be tasks requiring completely continuous alertness with no remission even for a matter of seconds. Speed of responding to an occasional visual signal, on the other hand, may be slowed down; provided that the measurement is made under prolonged conditions with, once again, little opportunity for free intervals without any danger of a signal. Prolonged performance as such or prolonged exposure to noise as such did not necessarily involve reductions in efficiency. Further clarification of the difference between tasks which show effects of noise and those which do not is undertaken in the next section.

The kinds of noise showing the most serious effects are not easy to specify since so many investigations have failed to find any effect at all. Some unpublished results are shown in Figure 5, the score used being errors on the five-choice serial reaction task. Machinery noise having a fairly flat octave-band spectrum from 50 to 5000 c.p.s., with no marked periodic character, was recorded on magnetic tape. This recording was then used as a source of two types of noise by filtering above and below 2000 c.p.s. The errors in the high-pitched and low-pitched noises were compared at three sound levels. The effect of noise on errors appears above 90 dB and seems to be more serious for the high-pitched noise. The difference between the effects of the high- and low-pitched noise at lower sound levels is not significant.

The remainder of the literature reveals no statistically satisfactory experiment showing effects of noise at sound levels lower than 90 dB, although some have shown effects at this level. This does not necessarily prove that lower levels will not impair efficiency, but there is no positive evidence that they should do so. One of the experiments, unsatisfactory from a modern point of view, employed subjects for prolonged periods at a dotting task in which they were required to insert a stylus in holes appearing in a moving paper belt (37). This is a task which the most recent results do suggest would show effects of noise, as was claimed, and the early study also found that high-pitched pure tones produced more errors than those lower in frequency.

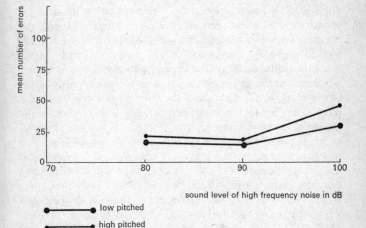

low pitched

high pitched

Figure 5 Some evidence on the errors produced in one particular task by various levels of high- and low-pitched noise. (Broadbent, unpublished data)

This statistically unsatisfactory confirmation of the more damaging effects of high frequencies is all that can be found in the literature. The same study found that a buzz from an audiometer was more effective than any pure tone except the highest frequencies. But the sounds appear to have been compared at equal sensation levels, that is, at equal numbers of decibels above threshold. This may mean that the broader band noise sounded louder than the pure tones to which it was compared. The more recent experiment used equal loudness levels. A rough rule is that the reduction of high frequencies is more important than that of low frequencies; if possible, over-all noise levels should be brought below 90 dB.

An Interpretation of the Nature of Behavior in Noise

The various results given in the previous section are interpreted here to present an over-all picture of human performance in noise. The easiest way to introduce this view of human skill is to consider the familiar phenomenon of blinking. A blink lasts a definite time, and while the rate of blinking may go up and down within wide limits the time for which the eyes are closed for each blink is less variable. During the period for which the eyes are closed there is of course no visual information entering the nervous system; yet performance is only slightly affected, if at all, by this periodic interruption of the intake of information. Reasons for this lack of effect are easily found. If a novel object is presented, blinking may be temporarily suspended while the object is examined. The longer the visual task is continued, the more likely blinks are to appear, but for a short time at the beginning of the task they may be withheld. When a sequence of events has occurred repeatedly, on the other hand, there are two other mechanisms which allow blinking to take place without impairing efficiency. On the one hand, when it is known that incoming information will not be present for a certain specified time, a number of blinks may occur and thus reduce the necessity for blinking at a later time when a crucial signal is expected. On the other hand, if the sequence of events is completely predictable so that all its members after the first are known when the first occurs, then no information is provided by these later events and they need not be observed to be dealt with adequately.

Some concrete examples may make these mechanisms more understandable. A driver in heavy traffic where he is expecting to receive critical signals shows a low blink rate; the same driver in the open country when he knows it is safe to close his eyes occasionally shows a higher blink rate (38). Experimentally, if a man is asked to follow a track appearing from behind a slit, and the track is sometimes straight for a definite period and then oscillates for a period, the blink rate is high before and after the oscillating portion of the track but not during it (38, 39). This shift in the distribution of blinks may allow efficient performance even though the number of blinks over a long period of time remains over the average the same. These examples illustrate the way in which the extent to which time of arrival of information is predictable will influence the occurrence of blinking.

A familiar and domestic example of the second behavioral mechanism which allows us to avoid ill effects from blinking is the ability to follow a familiar route in the dark. In a strange house one needs a light to go upstairs, while in one's own it may not be worth a few extra steps to reach the switch. Performance is determined by stored information, and visual stimuli are unnecessary. Experimentally, one may ask a man to follow an oscillating track with a pointer, and one finds that when he is unpracticed he shows errors either when he blinks naturally or when his vision of the task is interrupted by a shutter (39). With a simple track, such as a sine wave, a practiced subject ceases to show such sizeable errors from blinking or from mechanical interruption of his view. A complex and unpredictable track, of course, still defeats him on such occasions. So long in fact as the world continues to do what it has done in the past, his performance will show no sign of the effect of blinks; it is only when some unpredictable event occurs that we shall see that he is in error. If he is performing some practiced task, he will probably do something completely incorrect at such a time, and if the task is less familiar he will do nothing at all. A motorist on a quiet road would perform quite incorrectly if the gentle curve he saw a moment ago were to straighten itself out during one of his frequent blinks.

The foregoing remarks apply only to blinking, but they have been shown to be true for that case, and they illustrate psychological mechanisms which are important for performance in noise. It is likely that a man working in noise suffers from brief interruptions in the intake of information from a task he is supposed to be carrying out. These interruptions take place internally (Figure 6) and not externally as blinks do. They can be withheld for a brief period so as to allow performance of a novel task, and their distribution in time will vary in such a way as to produce as little disturbance of the work as possible. They will become serious in their effects on efficiency only in tasks in which no momentary relaxation is possible, in particular, in watch-keeping tasks in which stimuli are delivered at unpredictable times

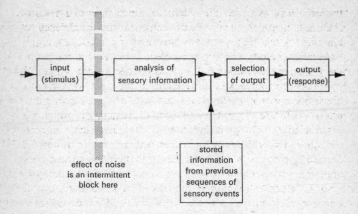

Figure 6 A hypothetical information-flow diagram for the human nervous system, illustrating the interpretation of noise effects given in the text

and in continuous tasks in which successive stimuli follow each other too closely to allow such an interruption in the intake of information. For many purposes blinking provides a useful analogy to illustrate the type of effect which is meant, but there are certain differences between the 'internal blinks' and the external blinks, especially in the time scale of the effect.[1] Thus a man working in noise will as time goes on show intermittent failures in his performance but in between these failures his work

1. An 'internal blink' is suspected to last as long as 1 s, but performance on one task may be maintained for several minutes before 'internal blinking' commences. There is also the point that the cutting off of incoming information does not seem to be absolute, as it is with overt blinking. A stimulus which is easy to discriminate from its background may succeed in entering the nervous system even when one might expect intermittent failures of efficiency to be present. This is shown by the task of watching indicator lamps, described in the last section, and has been shown in a number of different situations for the effects of prolonged performance. A dim brief blip on a radar screen will, after prolonged watch, escape detection; but a bright clear blip may be detected as well at the end of a prolonged session as at the beginning (40). This affords no particular theoretical difficulty to a view which regards the efficiency of the perceptual system as being lowered intermittently but it means that the simple analogy with blinking must be used with some caution.

412

will not necessarily be less efficient. As a background of continually changing stimulation seems to increase the efficiency of behavior (41, 42, 43), the onset of noise and its cessation may produce work which is actually faster than that under normal conditions, during the intervals of time separating internal blinks. It will be remembered that, in the section on industrial experiments, it was noted that short periods of music during the working day improved the rate of work. Similarly, a number of laboratory experiments on noise suggest that performance may become faster in noise. But this effect is independent of the increase in 'internal blinks', so that work may become faster and less accurate or possibly more varied in speed in noise, or alternatively it may show an increase in errors without any increase in speed. Finally, the evidence is not quite conclusive as to the nature of the 'internal blink'; it might be due to a complete, though temporary, block in the analysis of all sensory information, or it might be due to analysis of information from some sense not used in the task. In ordinary terms, a mental blank or a shift of attention are the alternatives. There are reasons for believing the latter. That is, the limited capacity of the human perceptual system makes it necessary for some incoming sensory information to be filtered out before reaching the main analysing centers of the brain. Normally, irrelevant features of the surroundings are ignored and task stimuli control response. But after prolonged work in noise, the auditory stimulation may interfere with the task stimulation and so produce the effect we have called an 'internal blink'. [...]

Practical Conclusions about Noise Reduction and Behavior

When one is considering whether to reduce a particular noise or not, in view of the probable expense of the operation, it may be valuable to bear in mind the various aspects of behavior in noise. Of the three possible measures of behavior, namely verbal complaint, physiological damage, and effects on efficiency, the physiological effects can be neglected except at very high intensities. There is little evidence of any such effect at low intensities with a noise that continues for some time. Annoyance is a different matter; it is distinct from effects on efficiency and may be marked even with sounds that have no other effect on behavior at all. On the whole, noise reduction does reduce annoyance, even though annoyance may be produced by very faint sounds. If one is reducing noise on these grounds, to prevent complaints, high-pitched and intermittent or modulated sounds appear to be the ones worthy of the prime consideration. A good deal of variation in annoyance will occur, however, from one particular case to another. Questions of the history both of the noise and of the persons complaining will produce such variation, and it is to a large extent unpredictable by scientific methods.

The beginning of a noise will produce a startle effect that may interfere with performance on some task, and there may therefore be grounds in some cases for insulating workers from possible sources of variable noise such a roadways. The effect seems to be more marked on more complex and novel tasks, rather than practiced repetitive ones, so that the practical importance of such an effect on efficiency is slight. Once the noise has become familiar most sensory and motor functions will be unimpaired. There is some evidence, however, of an effect which has been described under 'An interpretation of the nature of behavior in noise'. This effect will produce intermittent failures of efficiency interspersed by normal or even faster than normal performance. Because of this, output of work which is carried on at the worker's own speed will probably be unaffected. Mistakes may be increased, because the essence of the effect is that the worker does not notice unexpected features of the surroundings. Accidents also may show an effect of noise for this reason; they have not been investigated as a function of noise, although they are known to be highly sensitive indexes of effects of other stresses such as heat. Output may be affected if the work is paced by a machine, at a speed below the fastest which the human operator can handle. In such a case the intermittent failures of the human operator will cause failure to react, but it will not be possible to make this up by faster response between these intermittent failures. There may thus be a decline in output on paced tasks. The task would need to be one in which each element of the work is present only for a matter of a second or two, and thus this effect is not of general importance. Such conditions may be approximated in a high-speed inspection process, at the end of an assembly line, or similar operations. A good general conclusion, however, is that output will not be affected, but mistakes and accidents may be.

It is interesting to note that reported gains in industry from noise reduction have, in fact, been reported on tasks consistent with the view we have just put forward. The best research on the subject, as reported in the section on 'Results from industrial studies' (page 384), was on weavers. The work of a weaver is of course largely a matter of watching machinery in order to take action if human intervention is needed. It is therefore precisely the sort of work which might be expected to show some effect of noise. Typing also might show an increase in errors in highly noisy conditions. Other industrial processes might not have reported such effects.

It is difficult to say very much about the types of noise producing the greatest effects on efficiency; but there is some evidence that high-pitched noises are once more those producing the worse effects. No effect on efficiency has yet been found with noise levels below 90 dB, although unfortunately annoyance may still arise from such noises, and undoubtedly they will cause some harassing of speech communication. In general, effects on health or efficiency from noise seem to be somewhat slighter than is often thought. It must be borne in mind that unpleasantness is a quality of the environment distinct from effects on health or ability to work. Much of our civilization rests on the assumption that it is worth doing more to the environment than merely securing survival. Reduction of annoyance, or the pursuit of happiness, is not necessarily an ignoble end.

References

1. K. D. KRYTER, *J. speech Disorders Monog.*, suppl. 1 (1950).
2. H. C. WESTON and S. ADAMS, *Industrial Health Research Board Report*, no. 65, H.M.S.O., 1932, part II.
3. K. G. POLLOCK and F. C. BARTLETT, *Industrial Health Research Board Report*, no. 65, H.M.S.O., 1932, part I.
4. W. A. ROSENBLITH, *et al.*, *U.S.A.F.*, *WADC Technical Report*, no. 52-204, 1953, vol. 2.
5. E. CASSEL and K. M. DALLENBACH, *Amer. J. Psychol.*, vol. 29 (1918), p. 129.

6. F. L. HARMON, *Arch. Psychol.*, no. 147. 1933.

7. A. T WELFORD, R. A. BROWN and J. E. GABB, *Brit. J. Psychol.*, vol. 40 (1950), p. 195.

8. H. C. WESTON and S. ADAMS, *Industrial Health Research Board Report*, no. 70. H.M.S.O., 1935.

9. S. WYATT and J. M. LANGDON, *Industrial Health Research Board Report*, no. 77. H.M.S.O., 1937.

10. J. F. HUMES, *J. appl. Psychol.*, vol. 25 (1941), p. 573.

11. W. A. KERR, *Appl. Psychol. Monogr.*, no. 5, 1945.

12. H. C. SMITH, *Appl. Psychol. Monogr.*, no. 14, 1947.

13. W McGEHEE and J. E. GARDNER, *Pers. Psychol.*, vol. 2 (1949).

14. A. FORD, *Amer. J. Psychol.*, vol. 41 (1929), p. 1.

15. J. J. B. MORGAN, *Arch. Psychol.*, no. 35, 1916.

16. F. C. BARTLETT, *The Problem of Noise*, Cambridge University Press, 1934.

17. H. P. BAHRICK, M. NOBLE and P. M. FITTS, *J. exp. Psychol.*, vol. 48 (1954), p. 298.

18. D. E. BROADBENT, *Brit. J. Psychol.*, vol. 47 (1956), p. 51.

19. S. S. STEVENS *et al.*, *OSRD Report* no. 274, Harvard University, 1941, part I.

20. W. R. MILES in *The Benox Report*, Chicago University, 1953.

21. J. OBATA *et al.*, *J. acoust. Soc. Amer.*, vol. 5 (1934), p. 255.

22. T. D. HANLEY and R. J. WILLIAMSON, *U.S.N. Special Devices Center Technical Report*. no. 104-2-2 1, 1950.

23. K. R. SMITH, *Science*, vol. 114 (1951), p. 132.

24. H. M. VERNON and C. G. WARNER, *Personn. J.*, vol. 11 (1932) p. 141.

25. M. A. TINKER, *Amer. J. Psychol.*, vol. 36 (1925), p. 467.

26. H. B. HOVEY, *Amer. J. Psychol.*, vol. 40 (1928), p. 585.

27. F FENDRICK, *J. educ. Research*, vol. 3 (1937), p. 264.

28. M S. VITELES and K. R. SMITH, *Trans. Amer. Soc. Heating Ventilating Engrs.*, vol. 169 (1946).

29. TUFTS COLLEGE, *NDRC Report to the Services*, no. 37, 1942.

30. D. E. BROADBENT, *Quart. J. exp. Psychol.*, vol. 6 (1954), p. 1.

31. D. E. BROADBENT, *Brit. J. Psychol.*, vol. 44 (1953), p. 295.

32. A. G. BILLS, *Amer. J. Psychol.*, vol. 43 (1931), p. 230.

33. S. S. STEVENS, in *Handbook of Experimental Psychology*, Wiley, 1951.

34. A. R. JONCKHEERE, *Biometrika*, vol. 41 (1955), p. 133.

35. M. LUCKIESH, *Elec. World*, vol. 98 (1931), p. 472.

36. H. JERISON *Amer. Psychol.*, vol. 9 (1954), p. 399.

37. D. A. LAIRD, *J. appl. Psychol.*, vol. 17 (1933), 320.

38. G. C. DREW, *Quart. J. exp. Psychol.*, vol. 3 (1950), p. 73.

39. E. C. POULTON and R. L. GREGORY, *Quart. J. exp. Psychol.*, vol. 4 (1952), p. 57.

40. N. H. MACKWORTH, *MRC Special Report*, no. 268, H.M.S.O., 1950.
41. W. H. BEXTON, W. HERON and T. H. SCOTT, *Canad. J. Psychol.*, vol. 8 (1954), p. 70.
42. N. KLEITMAN, *Sleep and Wakefulness*, University of Chicago, 1939.
43. J. C. ECCLES and A. K. MCINTYRE, *J. Physiol.*, vol. 121 (1953), p. 492.

23 D. E. Broadbent and E. A. J. Little

Effects of Noise Reduction in a Work Situation

D. E. Broadbent and E. A. J. Little, 'Effects of noise reduction in a work situation', *Occupational Psychology*, vol. 34 (1960), pp. 133-8.

Introduction

The present state of knowledge concerning effects of noise on man has been reviewed by Broadbent (1957). Roughly speaking, it is that results of laboratory experiments have now established that an effect of high intensity, meaningless and continuous noise may appear on working efficiency in laboratory tasks which are long and require continuous attention. The effect of the noise is to increase the frequency of momentary lapses in efficiency rather than to produce decline in rate of work, gross failures of coordination or similar inefficiency. Effects have never been shown with noises of less than 90 dB (above the usual arbitrary level of 0·0002 dynes/sq. cm). In view of the rather specific nature of the effect found in the laboratory, it remained a doubtful question whether this effect of noise is of any practical importance. Furthermore, no matter how prolonged the laboratory experiments, they cannot hope to involve people who are as accustomed to noise as they would be in a real-life working situation. For these reasons it has become very desirable to check the results of the laboratory experiments in an actual working environment.

There are considerable difficulties in finding a suitable situation for a study of this type. On the one hand, since the effect is expected to be in the incidence of human error rather than in output, the task studied needs to be one which will provide sufficient of such errors for statistical analysis. Furthermore, it is well known that any improvement or even change in working conditions may produce improved working efficiency due to improved morale. Consequently it is necessary to make some attempt at control for this factor, and this means at the very least that one should study one set of people whose noise exposure is reduced, and another set of people whose working conditions remain the same throughout the period investigated. Even this comparison is open to some objection since the group who continue to work in high intensity noise may not feel any improvement in morale due to the experiment, while the group working in reduced noise will naturally show any such improvement. The suggestion has been made by Rosenblith *et al.* (1953), that ear plugs could be issued to workers, some of the plugs being defective so that they would not in fact reduce the noise to which the wearer was exposed. This would in fact be an investigation similar to that of a drug studied with a placebo, but so far no such investigation appears to have been reported. The reason is probably that ear plugs are not usually industrially acceptable when other methods of noise reduction are available.

Failing this type of control of morale factors, it is possible to draw some conclusions from a study in which the same people work both in noisy and in 'quiet' circumstances. The interest taken by the management in their working conditions as shown by expenditure on acoustic treatment, may lead to a rise in morale. This in turn may lead to an improvement of working efficiency which should be shown as much in the noise as in the quiet. The present study concerns such a comparison. A situation was found in which one workplace could be acoustically treated while another, in which the same people sometimes worked, was not. In addition, the type of work was one in which brief failures of perception would produce measurable results, and in which the noise level before sound treatment was above 90 dB, but might be expected to fall below that level after treatment. Thus the situation provided an unusually suitable opportunity of studying the effects of noise reduction, and an investigation was initiated.

Procedure: The Situation Studied

In the production of cine film, the perforations down the sides of the film are inserted at a stage after the film has been coated with emulsion and cut into its final width. The operation is carried out by machines which are loaded rather in a similar way to the loading of a cine projector with film; that is, a reel is placed on the machine and the film threaded through a moderately complex pathway. The machine is then started and proceeds to make the perforations until the whole reel has been finished. While the operation is proceeding, the operator loads other machines. An incentive payment scheme is used, so that he attempts to keep all machines under his charge running as much of the time as possible. For the purposes of payment, the rate of work is recorded. The task is, however, sensitive to any momentary lapses of attention on the operator's part since, if he makes a mistake in threading the film, he is likely to have a breakage of the film, or other breakdown of the machine. These stoppages also are recorded. The operation is carried out in a reduced and controlled illumination, because of the need to protect the film emulsion. The temperature also is controlled.

In the particular plant studied, there were two inter-connected rooms, usually involving about five operators, in which there was a dim safe-light. There were also other rooms involving roughly the same number of people in which there was practically no illumination whatever. Acoustic treatment was carried out in one of the former rooms. Noise in this room was measured in a number of positions before treatment was carried out, using a Dawe sound level meter Type 1400B. When all the machines were operating the level was at least 98 dB in all parts of the room and 99 dB in the middle of the room among the machines. Examination of the noise with a Dawe frequency analyser showed that there were peaks in the spectrum at approximately 80, 175, 250, 500, 700, 1900 and 7000 c.p.s., all reaching approximately the same level $\pm$ 2 dB.

The room was treated by placing absorbent material on the walls and ceiling and by putting absorbent baffles between the rows of machines. As a result of this treatment, the level fell by about 8 to 10 dB in all positions measured, the final level in the position which gave 99 dB originally being 89 dB after the treatment. Unexpectedly, it was also found that a reduction in noise level had occurred in the interconnected but untreated room, the initial and final levels being 98 and 90 dB respectively. This frustrated the original intention of using comparisons of the interconnected rooms as a principal source of data. However, the other rooms operating with in effect no illumination still provided a control in which noise level had remained unchanged.

Types of Measurement Made

1. Communications

While it is generally accepted among students of hearing that noise interferes with the understanding of speech, one occasionally meets people in industry who feel that persons accustomed to a particular job in noise are nevertheless able to understand speech in that noise. Although it is usual to attribute this feeling to the development of lipreading and other non-auditory forms of communication by workers in noise, it is perhaps conceivable that under conditions of prolonged exposure a man might come to understand speech by cues which fall outside the frequency band of the particular noise in which he works. It was therefore thought worthwhile to conduct intelligibility tests in the work-place before and after the acoustic treatment. The technique adopted was to use a tape recording of one of the lists of monosyllabic words, compiled by Hirsh *et al.* (1952) in two different orders. Groups of five or six operators stood against the wall of the perforating room and listened to the tape recorder playing at a level which was kept constant for each group. They attempted to write down the monosyllables as they heard them. Two of these groups carried out these tests on two occasions before the soundproofing as a check on practice effects. They did no better on the second day, and it therefore appeared that with this type of listener under these conditions, practice was unimportant.

Unfortunately, at this stage, because a valve had to be replaced in the tape recorder, it was not possible to make direct comparisons with further tests. However, another two groups carried out the tests once before sound-proofing and their results were compared with another two groups who did the tests after the sound proofing.

2. Measures of working efficiency

The sound treatment began to be installed during the annual holiday of 1957. Various measures of operator efficiency were extracted from the records for a 6-week period following this holiday, and, for comparison, for the 6-week period following the holiday in 1956. The period of 6 weeks was chosen because operators normally shifted from room to room in a systematic cycle of six weeks for reasons quite unconnected with the investigation. Each cycle involved the rooms in which the noise level had remained constant as well as those in which it had declined, so that by taking this period we should eliminate differences in ability between individual workers from any comparisons made between different rooms. Figures were obtained separately for each 'bay' (that is, each group of machines controlled by one operator) for each shift. No very noticeable difference appeared between shifts, and therefore the results for all shifts in each bay were combined.

Succeeding 6-week periods were examined in the same way, except that the periods involving Christmas 1956 and Christmas 1957 were excluded. In all four pairs of 6-week periods were studied, each pair comprising one before noise reduction and one after. We may thus compare performance in 1956/7 and 1957/8 for five bays in which a noise reduction of about 10 dB occurred at a time immediately before the 1957/8 period. A similar comparison can be made for four other bays in which no noise reduction occurred. The measures of working efficiency taken were as follows:

(a) *Point hour*. This is a measure of rate of work during those times in which no stoppage of work has occurred. It is calculated for purposes of the incentive payment scheme. When a stoppage occurs, the operator is paid on time rate.

(b) *Number of broken rolls of film*. These were divided into those attributed to the operator and those due to some other cause such as the machine. Records of both were examined since it is of course possible that some change in classification might have occurred during the period.

(c) *Number of shutdowns of the process other than for broken rolls*. Here again stoppages attributed to the operator were distinguished from those not so attributed.

(d) *Number of calls for maintenance assistance*. It was considered possible that operator error might cause breakdown in the machines, and this index was therefore examined.

(e) *Time occupied by stoppages for maintenance.* If the curing of faults took longer when working in noise this measure might be expected to show some effects.

(f) *Labour turnover.* This is hardly a measure of working efficiency, but was obtained on the same basis as the other measures mentioned since it seemed probable that it might reflect a change in working conditions.

(g) *Absenteeism.* This also was thought to be a possible index of effects of noise, since one frequently encounters the opinion that noise produces minor illnesses and nervous complaints, and the incidence of absenteeism was therefore determined on the same basis as the other measures.

Results

1. Communication

The subjects who listened to the tape recordings after sound treatment correctly identified 69 per cent of the words in the recordings. The separate group of subjects who heard the recordings before treatment identified correctly only 54 per cent of words. The difference is significant at the 0·05 level by a one-tailed test using the tau method (Whitfield, 1947). The difference is also of much the same magnitude as that to be expected from laboratory experiments on intelligibility in noise, so that it suggests that workers used to noise still benefit from the noise reduction.

2. Measures of working efficiency

The more important measures are shown in Table 1.

(a) *Point hour.* It will be noted that the point hour, that is, the rate of work, increased following the acoustic treatment. However, it did so in the untreated bays just as much as in the treated ones. The difference between bays is completely insignificant ($p > 0.5$). Thus it does not seem possible to ascribe the improvement to an effect of noise on working efficiency. On the other hand, all the bays, whether treated or untreated, showed improvement in point hour so that there has undoubtedly been some change in the conditions of work between 1956/7 and 1957/8. This might conceivably be due to general factors such as the economic situation of the country, or the flow of orders through the department of which perforation formed a part. However, as a precaution, the point hour was examined for all other workers in the department, excluding the perforators. There had been a significant fall in point hour among these other workers; which does not suggest that factors of the sort mentioned could be responsible for the improvement of rate of work in the perforators. A plausible explanation is that the reduction of the noise improved the morale and attitude to work of the group studied, and that this effect naturally appeared in whichever bay they were working. The presence of the control, untreated, bays has however saved us from interpreting this morale effect as one due primarily to noise. From the point of view of the practical management of work it may, of course, be quite helpful to have an increase in rate of work from noise reduction even though this is really due to an improvement of morale.

(b) *Broken rolls of film.* It will be seen that the number of film breakages has also declined since the 1957 holiday. However, in this case the decline has been much greater in the acoustically treated bays than in the untreated ones. The statistical significance of this difference is perhaps best assessed by again examining each individual bay, deciding how many of the treated bays showed bigger reductions than the untreated ones, and calculating tau. By this method the difference is significant ($p < 0.05$). It thus seems clear that momentary inefficiencies on the part of the operators have been reduced by the treatment. In view of the main purpose of this investigation, to study long term trends in working efficiency after noise reduction, the individual six-week periods were examined for any sign of a 'wearing off' of the effect of noise reduction as time went on. There was no sign whatever of such a 'wearing-off'; the largest difference between six-week periods was that for the third period, closely followed by the fourth. The second period gave a smaller difference, and the period immediately following the first noise reduction gave the smallest difference of all. (To some extent this tendency for the effect to increase with time may be due to the fact that not all the acoustic treatment was installed during the 1957 shutdown, and some of it was put in after the first six-week period. But this cannot explain the whole trend.)

It will be noted that the entries in Table 1 are only for those broken rolls which were attributed to the operator rather than to factors outside his control. Figures for the other types of breakage were also examined, and showed a slight but insignificant difference in the same direction. It would be surprising if noise reduction had affected breakages due to factors other than human error. A change in the method of attributing broken rolls to operators and to other causes might have occurred after the acoustic treatment to the bays. The slight effect in the number of breakages is important as it means that the main results cannot be explained as due to a change of this nature.

(c) *Other shutdowns.* Other types of shutdown again showed a greater reduction in the acoustically treated bays than in the untreated ones, although the statistical significance of the difference is not quite so satisfactory using the same test as previously ($p < 0.10$ by a two-tailed test). Thus this finding can only be regarded as established if we feel that the laboratory experiments give us sufficient grounds for expecting reduced human error after noise reduction. As before, the effect increased with increasing time since the beginning of the period studied, and it was slightly in the same direction when shutdowns not attributed to human error were examined.

(d) *Calls for maintenance.* Although there was slightly greater reduction in the number of these calls in the acoustically treated bays than in the untreated ones, which again agrees with expectation, the statistical significance of the difference is quite unsatisfactory ($p > 0.5$).

(e) *Time occupied by stoppages for maintenance.* This did not appear to show any effects.

(f) *Labour turnover.* As will be seen, there has been a reduction in the number of staff leaving, but this is too small to be confidently regarded as more than a chance effect. The data have been examined to make sure that the other findings could not be explained on the basis that more highly skilled workers took the place of those who left.

(*g*) *Absenteeism*. There has been a slight reduction in time absent from work, but this appears both in the acoustically treated and in the untreated bays. The difference between bays is actually in a most unlikely direction, the reduction being greater in the un-treated bays, but this difference is, of course, completely insignificant. It may be of possible importance that the remainder of the department, excluding the perforators, showed a slight increase in absenteeism during the same period. The same morale factor may therefore be at work.

Discussion

The results of this investigation completely agree with those of the laboratory experiments mentioned at the beginning of the paper. The rate of work is not improved by noise reduction, except perhaps by a general morale factor; human error is, however, less frequent when the noise level is less. There is no sign that the effects found with these experienced workers are less than those met on the much shorter time scale of the laboratory. Indeed the actual differences shown in Table 1 are larger than those met in the laboratory experiments to such an extent that inquiry was made to see whether any other factor could possibly be intruding and producing a spurious effect. For example, the acoustic treatment might have been introduced at the same time as a change in lighting sufficient to alter the number of errors. However, no change in other working conditions was found which could, by itself, have caused the results obtained; and the most probable explanation for the very substantial effects in Table 1 is that the effect of the noise interacts with some of the other features of this job such as the low illumination. The effect of noise reduction may therefore have been greater than it would have been with a job performed under more normal conditions. Another point which should be borne in mind when observing the reduction of, for example, broken rolls, is that the breakages attributable to the

Table 1

Comparison of Acoustically Treated and Untreated Work Places Before and After Treatment was Carried Out

	Treated bays		Untreated bays	
	1956/7	1957/8	1956/7	1957/8
Broken rolls (attributed to operator)	75	5	25	22
Other shutdowns (attributed to operator)	158	31	75	56
Calls for maintenance (excluding first six week period in each year)	746	597	516	468
Point hour	84·5	89·6	91·2	95·25
Absenteeism (time as % of possible hours worked)	5·18	4·43	2·72	1·556
Labour turnover (mean % per six weeks)	1956/7 = 6·2%		1957/8 = 0	

operator are naturally only a small proportion of the total breakages which occur. Thus one cannot say that noise reduction will produce an economic advantage as great as might appear from this table. Lastly, it must be borne in mind that although we are certain that chance factors are not responsible for producing the reduction in broken rolls, they may have made that reduction appear somewhat larger in these results than it would if another set of observations were to be taken.

While therefore one must not place too much weight on the actual size of the improvement in efficiency achieved by noise reduction, the agreement in the form of improvement found in actual work and in the laboratory experiments is impressive. Noise does produce human error in a real-life situation, even among people who are used to it.

References

BROADBENT, D. E. (1957), 'Effects of noise on behaviour', in C. M. Harris (ed.), *Handbook of Noise Control*, McGraw-Hill.

HIRSH, I. J., DAVIS, H., SILVERMAN, S. R., REYNOLDS, E. G., ELDERT, E., and BENSON, R. W. (1952), 'Development of materials for speech audiometry', *J. speech. Dis.*, vol. 17, pp. 321-37.

ROSENBLITH, W. A. *et al.* (1953), *Vol. II U.S.A.F. WADC Technical Report*, no. 52-204.

WHITFIELD, J. W. (1947), 'Rank correlation between two variables, one of which is ranked, the other dichotomous', *Biometrika*, vol. 34, pp. 292-6.

Further Reading

J. ANNETT, 'Teaching machines in industrial and military training', in K. Austwick (ed.), *Teaching Machines and Programming*, Pergamon, 1964.

W. R. ATCHLEY and D. J. LEHR, 'Troubleshooting performance as a function of presentation techniques and equipment characteristics', *Hum. Fact.*, vol. 6 (1964), pp. 257–63.

E. BELBIN and S. M. DOWNS, 'Activity learning and the older worker', *Ergonomics*, vol. 7 (1964), pp. 429–37.

E. BELBIN and S. M. DOWNS, 'Teaching paired associates: the problem of age', *Occup. Psychol.*, vol. 40 (1966), pp. 67–74.

M. M. BERKUN, 'Performance decrement under psychological stress', *Hum. Fact.*, vol. 6 (1964), pp. 21–30.

J. E. BIRREN (ed.), *Handbook of Aging and the Individual*, University of Chicago Press, Cambridge University Press, and University of Toronto Press, 1959.

M. J. F. BLAKE, 'Time of day effects on performance in a range of tasks', *Psychonom. Sci.*, vol. 9 (1967), pp. 349–50.

D. E. BROADBENT, 'Differences and interactions between stresses', *Quart. J. exp. Psychol.*, vol. 15 (1963), pp. 205–11.

D. N. BUCKNER and J. J. MCGRATH (eds.), *Vigilance: A Symposium*, McGraw-Hill, 1963.

A. CHAPANIS, 'Psychology and the instrument panel', *Scient. Amer.*, vol. 188 (1953), pp. 74–82.

A. CHAPANIS, W. R. GARNER and C. T. MORGAN, *Applied Experimental Psychology*, Wiley and Chapman & Hall, 1949.

D. W. CORCORAN, 'Noise and loss of sleep', *Quart. J. exp. Psychol.*, vol. 14 (1962), pp. 178-82.

E. R. F. W. CROSSMAN, 'Perception study – a complement to motion study', *The Manager*, vol. 24 (1956), pp. 141–5.

P. M. FITTS, 'Perceptual-motor skill learning', in A. W. Melton (ed.), *Categories of Human Learning*, Academic Press, 1964.

D. H. HOLDING, *Principles of Training*, Pergamon, 1965.

D. H. HOLDING, 'Training for skill', in D. Pym (ed.), *Industrial Society: Social Sciences in Management*, Penguin, 1968.

D. LEGGE (ed.), *Skills*, Penguin, 1970.

E. J. MCCORMICK, *Human Factors Engineering*, McGraw-Hill, 1964.

R. M. MCKENZIE, 'On the accuracy of inspectors', *Ergonomics*, vol. 1 (1958), pp. 258–72.

K. F. H. MURRELL, *Ergonomics*, Chapman & Hall, 1965.

Further Reading

R. D. PEPLER, 'Warmth and lack of sleep: accuracy or activity reduced', *J. comp. physiol. Psychol.*, vol. 52 (1959), pp. 446–50.

E. C. POULTON, 'Engineering psychology', *Ann. Rev. Psychol.*, vol. 17 (1966), pp. 177–200.

A. RODGER, *Occupational Psychology*, Penguin, 1968.

J. I. TABER, R. GLASER and H. H. SCHAEFER, *Learning and Programmed Instruction*, Addison-Wesley, 1965.

Acknowledgements

Permission to reproduce the readings published in this volume is acknowledged from the following sources:

Reading 1   Controller of Her Majesty's Stationery Office
Reading 2   American Psychological Association
Reading 3   *Ergonomics* and N. E. Loveless
Reading 4   McGraw-Hill Book Company
Reading 5   *Ergonomics* and H. C. A. Dale
Reading 6   *Educational and Psychological Measurement* and L. Stolurow
Reading 7   *British Medical Bulletin*
Reading 8   Society of Glass Technology and W. P. Colquhoun
Reading 9   *Ergonomics* and L. F. Thomas
Reading 10 American Psychological Association
Reading 11 H. K. Lewis & Co. Ltd and R. Conrad
Reading 12 University of Illinois Press and Jane F. Mackworth
Reading 13 *Ergonomics* and L. H. Shaffer
Reading 14 *Ergonomics* and R. Conrad
Reading 15 *Occupational Psychology*, John Annett and Harry Kay
Reading 16 John Wiley & Sons Inc., Robert C. Bolles and R. M. Gagné
Reading 17 American Psychological Association
Reading 18 *Ergonomics* and E. Belbin
Reading 19 *The Lancet* and A. T. Welford
Reading 20 *Ergonomics* and K. F. H. Murrell
Reading 21 American Psychological Association
Reading 22 McGraw-Hill Book Company
Reading 23 *Occupational Psychology*, D. E. Broadbent and E. A. J. Little

Author Index

Author Index

Author Index

Author Index

Subject Index

Subject Index

Penguin modern psychology readings

Other titles recently published in this series are:

Leadership
edited by C. A. Gibb

The study of leadership constitutes an important meeting point
between psychology and the study of industrial and social relations.
Leadership brings together not only the crucial laboratory
experiments but also investigations in field settings as varied as
Antarctic scientific stations and modern factories. The key variables
in the psychological study of leadership are all reviewed, including
the personality of the leader, his interaction with the organization
of his followers and their satisfaction and efficiency in performing
group tasks. Such studies inevitably raise ethical questions as to how
their findings should be implemented and these, too, receive attention.

Verbal Learning and Memory
edited by Leo Postman and Geoffrey Keppel

This collection of readings reflects both the historical continuity in
research and the innovation and change that has taken place in
psychological study of verbal learning and memory in the last
twenty years. Although traditional distinctions are maintained –
acquisition of verbal material, its recall, the phenomena of
interference and transfer – the common developments in experimental
analysis of these problems are demonstrated. *Verbal Learning and
Memory* provides a representative selection of key papers in this area
from 1939 to the present, with an emphasis on work undertaken in
the last eight years. It is an indispensable aid to any undergraduate
study.

Psychology and the Visual Arts
edited by James Hogg

Our response to the visual arts is not something apart from the rest of our experience. In *Psychology and the Visual Arts* the aesthetic response is examined in the context of contemporary psychology and physiology. Recent American work on the contribution psychologists can make to art education is also included. Non-experimental theories of art are represented – notably those of Sigmund Freud and Anton Ehrenzweig – as well as Rudolph Arnheim's application of Gestalt theory to art. Professor E. H. Gombrich's fascinating considerations of style and art history in the light of psychological findings complete this thorough-going survey.

Cross-Cultural Studies
edited by D. R. Price-Williams

The growing awareness of the need to broaden the basis of psychology is admirably represented in *Cross-Cultural Studies*. Professor Price-Williams has selected papers which deal in depth with the investigation of important psychological variables in African, Latin American and many other societies. The studies range from the nature of perception in non-Western cultures, including pictorial perception and susceptibility to visual illusions, to the significance of psychological symbolism in various societies, taking in dreaming and the linguistic analysis of Freudian symbols. Patterns of child-rearing and defence mechanisms in contrasting cultures are considered in several recent important papers.